TRANSLANGUAGING AND TRANSFORMATIVE TEACHING FOR EMERGENT BILINGUAL STUDENTS

A critical and accessible text, this book provides a foundation for translanguaging theory and practice with educating emergent bilingual students. The product of the internationally renowned and trailblazing City University of New York-New York State Initiative on Emergent Bilinguals (CUNY-NYSIEB), this book draws on a common vision of translanguaging to present different perspectives of its practice and outcomes in real schools. It tells the story of the collaborative project's positive impact on instruction and assessment in different contexts, and explores the potential for transformation in teacher education. Acknowledging oppressive traditions and obstacles facing language minoritized students, this book provides a pathway for combatting racism, monolingualism, classism, and colonialism in the classroom and offers narratives, strategies, and pedagogical practices to liberate and engage emergent bilingual students. This book is an essential text for all teacher educators, researchers, scholars, and students in TESOL and bilingual education, as well as educators working with language minoritized students.

This book is cowritten by the **CUNY-NYSIEB** (CUNY-New York State Initiative on Emergent Bilinguals) team. CUNY-NYSIEB is made up of scholars, researchers, teacher educators, doctoral students, teachers, and school administrators. It draws its work and inspiration from the students, parents, and community members with whom they work.

TRANSLANGUAGING AND TRANSFORMATIVE TEACHING FOR EMERGENT BILINGUAL STUDENTS

Lessons from the
CUNY-NYSIEB Project

*Edited by CUNY-New York State Initiative
on Emergent Bilinguals*

Routledge
Taylor & Francis Group

LONDON AND NEW YORK

First published 2021
by Routledge
52 Vanderbilt Avenue, New York, NY 10017

and by Routledge
2 Park Square, Milton Park, Abingdon, Oxon, OX14 4RN

Routledge is an imprint of the Taylor & Francis Group, an informa business

© 2021 Taylor & Francis

Library of Congress Cataloging-in-Publication Data
A catalog record for this title has been requested

ISBN: 978-0-367-43501-1 (hbk)
ISBN: 978-0-367-43498-4 (pbk)
ISBN: 978-1-003-00367-0 (ebk)

Typeset in Bembo
by KnowledgeWorks Global Ltd.

CONTENTS

List of Figures   *viii*
CUNY-NYSIEB Contributors   *ix*
Teacher/Researchers Participants   *x*
Foreword   *xii*
  Danling Fu
Acknowledgments   *xiv*

Introduction: Overviewing with CUNY-NYSIEB Lentes y
Emergent Pasos   xv
Ofelia García

SECTION I
Foundations: Translanguaging Theory/Practice and a Project   1

1 Conceptualizing Translanguaging Theory/Practice Juntos   3
   Ofelia García and Ricardo Otheguy

2 Constructing Translanguaging School Policies and Practices   25
   Kate Menken and Ofelia García

3 The Backdrop and Roadmap of a Translanguaging Project   41
   Tatyana Kleyn and Maite T. Sánchez

SECTION II
Evolving Juntos Structures   51

4 Different Leaderships: Different Times   53
   Ivana Espinet, Nelson Flores, Maite T. Sánchez, and Kate Seltzer

5 Emergent Bilingual Leadership Teams: Distributed Leadership in
CUNY-NYSIEB Schools 67
Maite T. Sánchez and Kate Menken

6 Working Juntos and Across: Bilingual Education, English as
a Second Language, English Language Arts and Community
Engagement 79
Brian A. Collins, Meral Kaya, Liza N. Pappas, and Karen Zaino

SECTION III
Shifting Educational Spaces **93**

7 Developing Translanguaging Pedagogical Material 95
*Sara Vogel, Kate Seltzer, Kathryn Carpenter, Ann E. Ebe,
Christina Celic, and Kahdeidra Martin*

8 Fostering Bilingual Reading Identities in Dual Language
Bilingual Classrooms 115
Gladys Y. Aponte, Ivana Espinet, and Kate Seltzer

9 Multilingual Ecology in CUNY-NYSIEB Schools 131
Kate Menken, Vanessa Pérez-Rosario, and Luis Guzmán Valerio

SECTION IV
Literacies Juntos: Instruction and Assessment **147**

10 Translanguaging and Emergent Literacy in Early Childhood
Education 149
Zoila Morell and Dina López

11 Translanguaging Literacies: Latinx Children's Literature
and Literacy Instruction 171
Carla España and Luz Yadira Herrera

12 Building on Strengths: Translanguaging and Writing 187
Cecilia M. Espinosa, Laura Ascenzi Moreno, and Sara Vogel

13 Leveraging The "Learning Edge:" Translanguaging,
Teacher Agency, and Assessing Emergent Bilinguals' Reading 207
Laura Ascenzi-Moreno

SECTION V
Inquiry en Comunidad   **217**

14 Interrogating Language Ideologies in the Primary Grades: A
    Community Language Inquiry Unit   219
    *Ivana Espinet, Gladys Y. Aponte, Maite T. Sánchez, Diane Cardenas
    Figueroa, and Ashley Busone-Rodríguez*

15 Hand in Hand: Parent Collaboration in the Classroom Context   239
    Ivana Espinet and Khánh Lê

SECTION VI
Transforming Teacher Education   **255**

16 Transforming Urban Teacher Education: The City University
    of New York   257
    *Cecilia M. Espinosa, Laura Ascenzi-Moreno, Tatyana Kleyn,
    and Maite T. Sánchez*

17 Different Places, Different Issues: Teacher education reimagined
    through the CUNY-NYSIEB Experience   271
    *Heather Woodley, María Cioè-Peña, Sarah Hesson,
    and Cristian R. Solorza*

18 Reimagining Teacher Education for Emergent Bilinguals:
    Going Upstate   285
    Erin Kearney and Kate Mahoney

The CUNY-NYSIEB Team   *301*

Index   *305*

LIST OF FIGURES

7.1	The Structure of CUNY-NYSIEB's First Translanguaging Guide	97
7.2	Episode 3 of "Teaching Bilinguals (Even if You're Not One)" Series	102
7.3	Some of CUNY-NYSIEB's Teacher Ambassadors	103
7.4	Multimodal Topic Brief Dropdown Menu	104
9.1	Mandated NYC Department Of Education Multilingual Welcome Sign	133
9.2	Multilingual Welcome Sign With Frequently Asked Questions	134
9.3	Multilingual Word Wall	135
9.4	Sample Welcome Packet with School Supplies Labeled in English and Polish	136
13.1	Differentiated Miscue Analysis Form	212
14.1	Why Does Language Matter? Classroom Display	224
14.2	Diane's Linguistic Map	225
18.1	Bilingual Families Write their Hopes	293
18.2	Virtual Reality Immersion in Translanguaging-Infused High-School Classroom	294
18.3	Teacher Candidates Immersed in Translanguaging Instructional Segments	295

Teacher/Researcher Boxes

T/R BOX 7.1 FIGURE 7.1	Student #1 Final Paragraph	111
T/R BOX 7.1 FIGURE 7.2	Student #2 Final Paragraph	112
T/R BOX 7.1 FIGURE 7.3	Student #3 Final Paragraph	113
T/R BOX 12.1 FIGURE 12.1	Two-Column notes of a Karen-speaking Burmese Student	203
T/R BOX 12.1 FIGURE 12.2	Frayer model of Karen-speaking Burmese Student	204

CUNY-NYSIEB CONTRIBUTORS

(A full list of CUNY-NYSIEB Team members with their role and affiliation appears in the backmatter)

Gladys Y. Aponte

Laura Ascenzi-Moreno

Kathryn Carpenter

Christina Celic

María Cioè-Peña

Brian Collins

Ann E. Ebe

Carla España

Ivana Espinet

Cecilia M. Espinosa

Nelson Flores

Ofelia García

Luis Guzmán Valerio

Luz Yadira Herrera

Sarah Hesson

Meral Kaya

Erin Kearney

Tatyana Kleyn

Khánh Lê

Dina López

Kate Mahoney

Kahdeidra Martin

Kate Menken

Zoila Morell

Ricardo Otheguy

Liza N. Pappas

Vanessa Pérez-Rosario

Maite T. Sánchez

Kate Seltzer

Cristian R. Solorza

Sara Vogel

Heather Woodley

Karen Zaino

TEACHER/RESEARCHERS PARTICIPANTS

[These teacher/researchers are representative of those who have worked with, and have been inspired by, the work of CUNY-NYSIEB. Except for Busone-Rodríguez and Cardenas Figueroa who are co-authors of Chapter 14, their contributions appear as Teacher/Researcher Boxes]

Lauren Ardizzone
11th grade High School English Language Arts
Bronx NYC [Box #6.1]

Elyn Ballatyne-Berry
4th - 8th grade English as a New Language
Manhattan Chinatown, NYC [Box #7.1]

Tim Becker
4th grade Dual Language Bilingual
Manhattan, NYC [Box #8.1]

Andy Brown
4th grade, Self-contained English as a New Language
Queens, NYC [Box #9.1 and #13.1]

Ashley Busone-Rodríguez
3rd grade Dual Language Bilingual
Manhattan, NYC

Alexandra (Ali) Cabrera-Terry
Kindergarten, Dual Language Bilingual
New Rochelle, NYS [Box #7.2]

Valentina Carbonara
Researcher and Teacher Educator, Università per Stranieri di Siena
Italy [Box#17.1]

Diane Cardenas Figueroa
3th grade, Dual Language Bilingual
Manhattan, NYC

János Imre Heltai
Researcher, Károli Gáspár University of the Reformed Church in Hungary
Hungary [Box #18.1]

Jason Horowitz
4th grade Dual Language Bilingual
Manhattan, NYC [Box #8.1]

Bernadett Jani-Demetriou
Researcher, Eötvös Loránd University
Budapest, Hungary [Box #18.1]

Maeva López-Kaseem
Pre-Kindergarten, Dual Language Bilingual
Buffalo, NYS [Box #10.1]

Rebeca Madrigal
1st grade, Dual Language Bilingual
Manhattan, NYC [Box #14.1]

Annabelle Maroney
1st grade, Dual Language Bilingual
Manhattan, NYC [Box #14.1]

Elizabeth Menéndez
Kindergarten, Dual Language Bilingual
Manhattan, NYC [Box #15.1]

Olivia Mulcahy
Education Specialist, Illinois Resource
  Center
Chicago [Box #16.1]

Nicole Nichter
High School, English as a New Language
Buffalo, NYS [Box #12.1]

Sabrina Poms
Kindergarten, Dual Language Bilingual
Manhattan, NYC [Box #15.1]

Andrea Scibetta
Researcher and Teacher Educator,
  Università per Stranieri di Siena
Italy [Box#17.1]

Hulda Yau
2nd grade, One-way Dual Language
  Bilingual
Rochester, NYS [Box #11.1]

FOREWORD

Danling Fu

This book illustrates how *Translanguaging* as a theory first emerged from practice, then back to practice and finally advanced its conceptualization through practice, recontextualized in different spaces and settings to liberate, empower, and enable minoritized people and students to assert their dignity and voice. Translanguaging theory/practice validates and legitimates bilingual practices. As bilinguals, though we may use the features associated with one named language more than others in a certain situation or context, all of our language stays with us, stored in our hearts, flowing in our blood, vibrating throughout our bodies, and functioning juntos as a unique linguistic repertoire. But this languaging flow has traditionally been described as a language deficiency and was suppressed in the U.S. education of minoritized bilingual students. Here, a team of scholars and educators describe how they have endeavored, as García and Otheguy say in Chapter 1 to "push against boundaries that have outlived their usefulness and have caused so much pain and educational failure."

From chapter to chapter in this book, we see how the CUNY-NYSIEB (City University of New York-New York State Initiative on Emergent Bilinguals) team comprised of scholars, doctoral students, teachers, school administrators, parents and students, and community members worked juntos to implement translanguaging theory/practice in schools heavily populated with emergent bilingual students. In eight years, their implementation was across pre-K-12 levels, across different school programs and disciplines, connecting schools and communities, and impacting teacher education programs across the city and state. Their work has expanded from school to school, college to college, first emerging in New York city, then across the U.S. and now all over the world.

We do not exist in an ideal world. We are bound by the traditions and establishments constructed by ideologies enshrined in scholarship and practice that have compromised and continue to assail the dignity of racialized bilinguals. It has taken the gigantic effort of the entire CUNY-NYSEIB team juntos to break the stubborn walls of racism, linguicism, classism, and colonialism so as to allow minoritized people and students to reach their full potential and gain a dignified existence in society. As the U.S. history shows, it can be extremely hard to break oppressive traditions and allow nondominant groups to share some space and power within established patterns of dominance or to even afford innate human rights to historically mistreated people. Americans shed much blood and sacrificed thousands of lives in a three-year Civil War more than 150 years ago to abolish a slavery system. But slavery's legacy still holds strong in many parts in this society today and continues to insidiously discriminate against and marginalize children of color. In this book, we see how the CUNY-NYSIEB team took on the arduous task of reconciling their theoretical stance with the policies and pedagogical practices that were present in school to liberate emergent bilinguals from the confinement in education.

As García and Otheguy stated in the first chapter, as bilingual language and literacy scholars and educators, many of us had also sensed something missing, and felt an uneasiness about the dominant scholarship that failed to see and recognize bilinguals' being and doing for decades. But we didn't have the words or the theories to name and ground our uneasiness and awkward feelings. Meanwhile, as bilinguals ourselves, we had become victims of colonialist worldviews, trapped in the dominant epistemologies. When translanguaging, we felt guilty as though we were cheating or as handicapped language users. We tried hard to resist, suppress, and refuse to accept our natural instinct and languaging performance. We saw ourselves through the eyes of the dominant caste, tried to sound like others, and confined ourselves to the monolingual trap—a veritable language prison. Worst of all, as ESL/bilingual teachers and educators, we had also victimized our students, indoctrinating them along with us in the dominant monolingual ideologies. Translanguaging theory came as a welcome enlightenment that has legitimated our natural instinct and human right to be what we are, and express how we think, and speak, and write, and has inspired our hearts and minds to run free and teach others not to turn away from their bilingual being. It has liberated us from our language prison and allowed us to be free and proud bilinguals!

The scholars and educators who make up the CUNY-NYSIEB team are pioneers in transforming education for bilinguals. They will continue to influence the bilingual field, and lead us, language scholars and educators, to fight against social injustices and the postcolonial oppressions of Anglo hegemony and English imperialism. Their challenge to us is to continue where and what they have started, and juntos carry on their torch on this long and challenging journey to fight for the legitimacy of being, doing and voicing as bilinguals. We, after all are the majority of the world population!

Danling Fu
Professor, University of Florida, USA

ACKNOWLEDGMENTS

Chapter 9

This is an abbreviated version of Menken, K., Perez-Rosario, V. & Guzmán Valerio, L. (2018). Increasing multilingualism in schoolscapes. New scenery and language education policies, *Linguistic Landscape* 4 (2), 101–127. Used with permission. John Benjamins Publishing Company. https://www.benjamins.com/catalog/ll.

Chapter 13

A portion of the text was reprinted from the New York Association of Bilingual Educator's *Bilingual Times*, Fall 2018. Used with permission. Figure 13.1 was previously published in Ascenzi-Moreno, L. (2018). Translanguaging and responsive assessment adaptations: Emergent bilingual readers through the lens of possibility. *Language Arts*, *95*(6), 355–369. Used with permission. Copyright 2018 by the National Council of Teachers of English.

Chapters 8, 12, 14, and 15

These chapters are drawn from work which we did for CUNY-NYSIEB, aspects of which appeared as *Topic Briefs* (Chapters 8, 14, and 15) and *Teacher Guides* (Chapter 12) on our website, www.cuny-nysieb.org.

Art Work in Cover

This is Samantha Manners' representation of translanguaging. It was submitted as an assignment in a course on Intermediate Spanish taught by Lara Alonso at Hunter College, CUNY.

Other Acknowledgments

The CUNY-NYSIEB team wishes to acknowledge the support of our editor, Karen Adler. Gracias, Karen for being flexible with us and having the courage to take on this project. We also wish to thank Emily Dombrovskaya who as Karen's assistant has kept all the pieces of this project juntos, as well as Sumati Agarwal for putting up with our translanguaging.

INTRODUCTION

Overviewing with CUNY-NYSIEB Lentes y Emergent Pasos

Ofelia García

We finish this book as our heridas hurt. Most of us live in New York City where the sounds of Broadway have been substituted by the sonidos de sirenas, where the streets are desiertas, and the escuelas are closed. Many of us have been ill, although we have fared well as a grupo, surviving Covid-19 up to now.

Although all of us have been impacted by the coronavirus, the virus has had disparate effects on racialized poor comunidades. In April 2020 in New York City, the death rate for Latinx was 22 people per 100,000; for African Americans 20 per 100,000, whereas for whites it was 10 per 100,000 (Mays & Newman, 2020). Seventy-five percent of the workers considered "essential"— mostly grocery clerks, delivery personnel, janitors and nursing assistants—are Latinx or African American (Buchanan et al., 2020), leading to higher rates of infecciones. The poor health care that racialized minorities in the U.S. have received has been also responsible for the higher death rates in these comunidades.

The children about whom this book is about have also been the most affected by the closing of escuelas. Many do not have the tecnología required to do online schooling, and as a *New York Times* article reported (Sharma, 2020), doing online schooling is most difficult for those who do not speak English. At the same time, many of the adults in racialized communities are still working and do not have the luxury of sitting by their children as they do their school tareas. Many emergent bilingual children have been left to school themselves.

The teachers of emergent bilinguals have also been challenged by school closings. They have been taught to listen to and observe children con cuidado, but they cannot do so carefully in an online classroom, even if the children are in virtual attendance. Teachers cannot engage students in meaningful sustained dialogue. They have had to rely more on written textos and mechanical written ejercicios. The rich and significant classroom interactions among the children and their teachers have been tempered. At the same time, teachers have had to make room to escuchar and listen deeply to children's fears, pain, heridas, boredom, and sense of loneliness.

Likewise, all of us as teacher educators and researchers are struggling. How do we ask teachers to teach una lección, to show what they know how to do in real time, with real bodies, in real classrooms? How do we assess teaching when it is all online? How do we make room for easing the fear, el miedo, the heridas and the dolor, as our students deal with the illness and loss of familia and amigos? as they face the threat of job cuts? How do teacher educators help prospective teachers view un futuro en la enseñanza, when the future of education has been shaken? How do we face our own futuros? What is it that is importante to aprender, estudiar, investigar when we have *unlearned* so much as we have had to go into aislamiento? when we have had to pausar?

For a while, this manuscript sat unfinished, as we pondered el futuro de la educación. But as we once again read the manuscrito, we realized that there were also things to *relearn*. The work in this book calls us to question the understandings that we have had about lengua y educación as schools ceased to exist as we knew them. We asked ourselves: What are the lecciones we learned from the CUNY-NYSIEB work that we can still hold onto today? What part of the work helps us navigate the wounds, the heridas that have surfaced in these dark times to reconstruct life anew for all children, and especially for those who are the subject of this book—emergent bilinguals?

We have tried to look through lentes that focus on the emergent bilingual children as we find them in familias, communidades, playgrounds, and not simply through lentes found and imposed by educational systems and traditional scholarship. But as we reread this manuscript, our lentes have once again become fogged through the breath of the masks that we wear in NYC to protect ourselves from the virus. What is it that we can continue to see? How do we carry on cleaning our lentes so that we make visible what had remained invisible about these minoritized bilingual children in many schools and scholarship?

The most important lección that we have relearned as we have reread this manuscript during this time is that of *emergence,* based on what the Chilean biólogo Francisco Varela has called "the loopiness of the thing," the connectedness of cells, of human beings, of life. Rather than understand teaching and learning, and especially language learning, simply as boxes of inputs and outputs, we have focused on visualizing an emergent network that has no beginning and no end. Rather than thinking of languages as home language and school language, we have insisted on the "the loopiness," on the network that cannot separate one part of life from another, one named language from another.

In this volume, we have tried to limit ourselves to a time and place—the work done by one project, the CUNY-NYSIEB project. However, our work around translanguaging also represents an emergent network that has no beginning and no end. The work started long ago with others outside this group and continues under different guises. The banyan tree of translanguaging, an image that I used in my 2009 book on Bilingual Education to capture the rootedness of the work that spreads differently and that is also captured by the Together/Juntos tree of the frontcover, fits well with the emergent network that continues to sprout new branches and spread roots among the team members. For example, Sara Vogel continues to think of translanguaging and computer science with a grant from the National Science Foundation, in which Laura Ascenzi-Moreno and Kate Menken are involved. Tatyana Kleyn has initiated another New York State Education Department Initiative, focused on Immigration and Education, CUNY-IIE, to which Maite Sánchez brings her expertise as Advisor. Maite has provided much of the glue that has kept us rooted in the work throughout the existence of the project. Carla España and Luz Herrera published their book *En Comunidad* recently; Cecilia Espinosa and Laura Ascenzi-Moreno are putting finishing touches on a manuscript on translanguaging and literacy; Maite Sánchez and I are coediting a book focusing on Latinx students and the role of translanguaging. Beyond this, there is much work going on from different members of the team that fill us with expectation and hope for a futuro.

As the chapters here attest, we have grown in all different directions and will continue to do so in the coming years. The different work in which many of us have engaged in the last few years, individually and with others, for example, the conceptualization of raciolinguistics by Nelson Flores with his colleague Jonathan Rosa, continues to shape our understandings of translanguaging. It is indeed an emergent network of scholarship that has grown beyond our specific time and place to other places and times. We hope this greater network of scholars will continue to bear witness to the translanguaging potential of minoritized students. Just as the theory/practice of translanguaging cannot be said to have had a specific beginning, but rests on the lives and scholarship of many throughout the years, its end is not within these pages.

The steps/pasos taken by all of us in the project have been slow, deliberate, at times sideways, sometimes even backward, but always pushing us forward, to act on a vision of what is possible, not in a future, but in the present, to open up a space of potentiality now even during these dark times; to gift the children, their teachers, communities, and families with emergence. They are pasos of emergence.

In this volume, we trace the beginnings of the CUNY-NYSIEB pasos, as the New York State Education Department reached out to the Research Institute for the Study of Language in Urban Society (RISLUS) and the Ph.D. Program in Urban Education at The Graduate Center of the City University of New York. Ricardo Otheguy who was director of RISLUS at the time became principal investigator, with Ofelia García and Kate Menken as co-principal investigators. The work could not have been done without the four project directors that we were fortunate to hire—Nelson Flores who initiated the project with courage and foresight; Maite Sánchez who sustained the project through five years, made us the familia we are today, and continued to offer her leadership and work throughout the life of the project; Kate Seltzer who graced us with her intelligence and organización for one year; and Ivana Espinet who was a formidable closer, always generosa, calm y persistente. As Maite Sánchez has always said, we have become a familia, as we have worked juntos, with some tensions and conflictos, but always with amor for those who have suffered the racismo and discriminación that comes with being a member of a bilingual racialized community, and for their teachers.

The volume starts out with *Section I* in which we lay out the *Foundations* of the project. It starts with the concept that grounds the project—the development of translanguaging theory/practice (García & Otheguy, Chapter 1). This is followed by the role of the process of writing translanguaging school policy visions (Menken & García, Chapter 2), and a roadmap of the proyecto (Kleyn & Sánchez).

Section II, on the *Juntos Structures* of CUNY-NYSIEB, starts out by laying out the different leadership of the project and how it was adjusted to changing times (Espinet, Flores, Sánchez, & Seltzer, Chapter 4). All leadership in CUNY-NYSIEB has been distributed, and this same principio operated in the development of emergent bilingual leadership teams (Sánchez & Menken, Chapter 5). It then incluye un capítulo in which the autores address how they engaged with different stakeholders—teachers in ESL, bilingual education, English Language Arts, as well as community (Collins, Kaya, Pappas, & Zaino, Chapter 6).

Section III addresses the *Shifting Educational Spaces* with which the project worked. We start out with a chapter that describes the material pedagógico that was developed throughout the years (Vogel, Seltzer, Carpenter, Ebe, Celic, & Martin, Chapter 7). One of our concerns was how to work with translanguaging theory/practice in dual language programs. The following chapter shows how this was done in one classroom en particular (Aponte, Espinet, & Seltzer, Chapter 8). We then end la section by considering how we encouraged the development of multilingual ecologías in schools (Menken, Pérez-Rosario, & Guzmán Valerio, Chapter 9).

In *Literacies, Section IV*, we focus on aspects of instruction and assessment. We consider instruction in early childhood classrooms (Morell and López, Chapter 10), followed by two chapters that focus on literacy instruction. Children's literatura takes center stage in Chapter 11 (España & Herrera, Chapter 11), and writing in Chapter 12 (Espinosa, Moreno, & Vogel, Chapter 12). We end *Section IV* with a chapter on assessment (Ascenzi Moreno, Chapter 13).

Because the community was an important part of the project, *Section V* focuses on *Inquiry en Comunidad*. First, there is a chapter which describes a community language inquiry unit (Espinet, Aponte, Sánchez, Cárdenas Figueroa, & Busone-Rodríguez, Chapter 14). This is followed by descriptions of how las familias collaborate in the classroom context (Espinet & Le, Chapter 15).

The last section of the book, *Section VI* is reserved for the *Transformation of Teacher Education*. We first exploramos this topic en el context de City University of New York, CUNY (Espinosa, Ascenzi-Moreno, Kleyn, & Sánchez, Chapter 16), followed by the impact the project had in higher education institutions in which some of us were hired after obtaining our Ph.D. (Woodley, Cioè-Peña, Hesson, & Solorza, Chapter 17). Finally, the section closes with an account of how involvement with CUNY-NYSIEB also transformó the teacher education programs in upstate New York, specifically in the State of New York higher education system, SUNY (Kearney & Mahoney, Chapter 18).

It would be impossible to include all the many teachers, teacher educators, and researchers in New York State, the U.S., and the world, with whom we have interacted and worked throughout these years. But we did not want to exclude their voices, so we decided to include a very small sample. The *Teacher/Researcher Boxes* are only loosely associated with the topics of the chapters, but they give readers an idea of how the particular topic has been taken up differently in various contexts. All the teachers here included have directly worked with CUNY-NYSIEB. The researchers and teacher educators we include in Section VI demonstrate how this work is being taken up in national and international contexts.

We are grateful to Danling Fu who agreed to write a Foreword to the book. Early on, Danling Fu showed us, without naming it, that translanguaging was helpful to develop the writing of bilingual children in New York City's Chinatown. She taught me in particular that with language, the same lesson I had learned from my progressive educational mentors—Lillian Weber and Cecelia Traugh—worked. Start with the children's strength, their own language practices; listen to them, observe them deeply; make them visible in your mind's eye, re-view them; re-listen to them with generosity; and then teach them by building on their strengths. It is all so simple, and yet so difficult. Danling Fu is an important link in the continuous emergent network of scholars who have given us the courage to name and comprehend what has always been here for us to see. 谢谢

References

Buchanan, L., Patel, J.K, Rosenthal, B., & Singhvi, A. (2020). A month of coronavirus in New York City. *The New York Times* (April 1, 2020) https://www.nytimes.com/interactive/2020/04/01/nyregion/nyc-coronavirus-cases-map.html?smtyp=cur&smid=tw-nytimes

Mays, J.C. & Newman, A. (2020). Virus is twice as deadly for Black and Latino people than whites in N.Y.C. *The New York Times* (April 14, 2020) https://www.nytimes.com/2020/04/08/nyregion/coronavirus-race-deaths.html

Sharma Rani, R. (2020). Imagine online school in a language you don't understand. *The New York Times* (April 22, 2020). https://www.nytimes.com/2020/04/22/us/coronavirus-immigrants-school.html

SECTION I

Foundations: Translanguaging Theory/ Practice and a Project

1

CONCEPTUALIZING TRANSLANGUAGING THEORY/ PRACTICE JUNTOS

Ofelia García and Ricardo Otheguy

Introduction

The two of us have spent a lifetime studying language and education. Both of us have lived our lives as bilingual Latinx in New York City, and have brought our experience into our scholarship. Ricardo's doctorate was in theoretical linguistics within the functionalist framework of Columbia School Linguistics under the mentorship of Erica García and William Diver. Ricardo specialized in the Spanish language and started out his academic career teaching linguistics to teachers, and later bilingual teachers as Director of the Bilingual Education program at City College of New York, moving during the second part of his career to teaching doctoral students in linguistics at The Graduate Center of City University of New York (CUNY). Ofelia started out as a teacher who taught bilingually as she pursued graduate work in Spanish and education, and a doctorate in Latin American literature, focusing on semiotics. Ofelia did postdoctoral work on sociology of language under the mentorship of Joshua A. Fishman, and started out teaching in the Bilingual Education program at City College where she met Ricardo.

We start out by telling you something of our personal histories because translanguaging was something that was present from the start in our lives, our homes, and our work, from the time we were children in the United States. And although we experienced it as a linguistic practice of the U.S. Latinx community, we didn't find a theory that reflected it. We were blind to it, as we followed the scholarship about bilingualism that we read in the 1970s and 1980s. Although we learned much from that early scholarship, we often felt it did not represent the ways that the bilingual communities where we lived and worked languaged. We were fortunate to have been taught by critical senior scholars who presented alternative visions of linguistics, and of language and society. But we still felt that the language of the bilingual Latinx community was not being described accurately, theorized correctly, or recognized as valid by much mainstream scholarship of the time, although there were, for sure, plenty of accounts of how it deviated from what was posited as the norm.

As the Portuguese decolonial philosopher Boaventura de Sousa Santos (2007) has said about knowledge in general, understandings about language, bilingualism, and multilingualism have been constructed through the epistemological perspective of those who are only on *one side of the line*, that is, the powerful in command of society. However, the language knowledge of bilingual and multilingual communities on the *other side of the line*, of those who have endured the injustices of colonialism and global capitalism, has most often been rendered invisible in scholarship. Theories about language and language education derived from the understandings and practices of those on the dominant side of the line have been then used to design educational policies, programs, and practices for those who language differently on the other side of the line, producing their educational failure.

For us, translanguaging disrupts the ways in which we were taught to envision language, bilingualism, and education from the powerful side of the line and guides us in trying to construct understandings from both sides of the line. Juntos we started naming what was always there, but had mostly, with very few exceptions, remained hidden in scholarship and especially in theoretical constructs. However, it was not until our work in CUNY-NYSIEB (City University of New York-New York State Initiative on Emergent Bilinguals) that we were able to develop, juntos with the CUNY-NYSIEB team, a theory of translanguaging that engaged with the practice of all and vice versa. Little by little, as the work with translanguaging in the action of CUNY-NYSIEB developed, theory and practice have been adjusted. For us, translanguaging as theory and practice works juntos, as we have worked juntos with each other and with all others.

We do not conceive of translanguaging theory in the abstract as separate from society, but as a theory/practice that can enable or hinder the potential of minoritized bilingual people, and especially of minoritized bilingual students in schools. We have been guided by the question: "What has been *the consequence* of viewing language in education through the lenses traditionally used to observe and theorize about language and bilingualism? Who has it hindered? Who has it helped?" And in conceptualizing translanguaging, we have focused on *its consequences* for minoritized bilinguals, and how it has shaped the dominance of monolinguals.

In what follows, we tell the story of how as more mature scholars we started to listen and view the language of bilingual minoritized communities without some of the theoretical blinders that we had accepted as doctoral students and young scholars. We identify some of the established sociolinguistic and psycholinguistic concepts that translanguaging disrupts. We then describe the role of the CUNY-NYSIEB team in developing a translanguaging theory/practice juntos, as we struggled with reconciling our theoretical stance with the policies and pedagogical practices present in schools. This juntos work with the CUNY-NYSIEB team advanced our understandings of translanguaging, which we attempt to share here. Finally, we end by pointing out some of the challenges of inserting a different vision of language, bilingualism, and language education into a school system that is the product of nation-state ideologies of power and domination over its citizens.

Throughout this chapter, we focus on U.S. Latinx because it is easier to trace the developments of translanguaging theory/practice through our own personal experience with bilingualism as Latinx bilinguals. However, the theory/practice of translanguaging and the work of CUNY-NYSIEB, as we will see in the rest of this volume, encompass *all* minoritized bilingual children and *all* the educational programs in which they're taught.

Removing theoretical lenses to see clearly

Both of us were involved in bilingual education efforts early on. We deeply supported the Latinx community efforts to voice the injustices and colonial oppression to which they had been subjected since the mid-19th century. In so doing, we also defended the Latinx community's right to use the Spanish language to participate in society and in education. This was a right of which the community was gradually deprived when the United States took over territories that were formerly Mexico, after the Guadalupe-Hidalgo Treaty that ended the Mexican American War in 1848 (Hernández-Chávez, 1995), and after the United States took possession of Puerto Rico from Spain at the end of the so-called Spanish-American war in 1898 (Meléndez, 2017). But the Latinx community's conception of their Spanish and their bilingualism, deeply connected to their struggles over discrimination in jobs, housing, and education (Flores & García, 2017), was eventually substituted by a conception of bilingualism that was said to be more objective and scientific, reducing the community's knowledge as something belonging to racialized peasants and indigenous peoples with little or no education. We trace below how these modifications took place, and how these changes transformed our understandings, first of the Spanish language and bilingualism, and then of bilingual education.

Spanish and bilingualism: Early studies and our changing scholarship

As the study of Spanish and bilingualism in the United States moved to high schools and universities in the mid-20th century, the scholarship was built with only one model in mind—that of Anglos becoming bilingual. Spanish had at first been dismissed as not worthy of study, like French and German (Nichols, 1945). And when it did start to be valued, the reference point was the language of Spain, or at best, occasionally, that of some Latin American countries (Espinosa, 1925). The Spanish of the U.S. Latinx community itself was either ignored or seen through linguistic and educational models that tended to devalue it and at times even to denigrate it (García, 1993).

These less than positive approaches provided a good fit with the scholarship on bilingualism being developed at the time. The pioneers of bilingual studies in the United States, Uriel Weinreich (1953) and Einar Haugen (1953), focused on the "interferences" in the languages of bilingual immigrant communities (Yiddish-speaking in Weinreich's case, Norwegian-speaking in Haugen's case), interferences that became noticeable when these U.S. ways of speaking were compared to those of the communities of origin. This work helped to establish the categories used to describe the language of bilinguals: Loan words, calques or loan shifts, and code-switching, which we ourselves have used in our earlier work (Otheguy, García & Fernandez, 1989). Even though we thought that these linguistic descriptions would help normalize U.S. Spanish, showing it to the world as just another local form of language, in reality these features of bilingual speech came to be seen as speaker "mistakes," instances of "random mixing," thus helping to perpetuate negative attitudes about the community's language.

During the 1980s, we followed the work of the Language Policy Task Force of the Centro de Estudios Puertorriqueños under the leadership of Pedro Pedraza. Traditional scholarship on bilingualism claimed that the only way for a community to maintain a minoritized language was through a diglossic arrangement, with one language used in territorial or functional compartmentalization with the other (Fishman, 1966a). However, Pedraza and his team argued that this did not happen in the East Harlem Puerto Rican community that they studied (Pedraza, Attinasi & Hoffman, 1980). We started to question the concepts of language maintenance and shift that were prevalent in the sociolinguistic literature (Fishman, 1966b). In a contribution to a volume edited by Joshua A. Fishman (2001), García, Morín and Rivera (2001) argued that the supposed language shift of the Puerto Rican community was with "vaivén." That is, the community was not simply shifting to English, but staying in place while motioning their language practices back and forth like a cha-cha-chá.

As the scholarship on bilingualism grew, many scholars focused on the orderly or rule-governed character of the language practices of bilinguals. These well-meaning scholars pointed, for example, to the grammatical constraints of what they called code-switching (see, for example, Poplack, 1980). We ourselves used and taught that type of scholarship to teachers, and saw it, as did these scholars, as serving to legitimate the bilingual community and its language practices. We then started to compare the tokens of, for example, orderly code-switching that were being offered in the literature with the ways that language was used in the Latinx community of New York and in our own homes. More and more, we found that the order and constraints, well-meaning as they were, did not correspond to our local observations. This added to our unease with the traditional scholarship on bilingualism generally and on code-switching in particular.

The term "Spanglish" was often used in those days, even by many Latinx bilinguals themselves, to talk about what they considered "incorrect" Spanish. And there were, and are, many bilingual scholars who have claimed the term, in parallel to the claim by the gay community, of "queer" (see, for example, Martínez, 2010; Zentella, 1996, 2016). Ricardo, however, warned that such use is intellectually indefensible because it represents yet another reification of a "dialect" or a "variety", terms that survive in the teeth of widespread and long-standing criticisms that show their invalidity (Otheguy, 2008). Besides being intellectually unsustainable, the notion of Spanglish is dangerous because it confirms for consumers of the term the odd nature of an entity that despite efforts of committed Latinx educators to see it otherwise is stigmatized as mixed and therefore corrupt (Otheguy, 2007, 2009, 2016a; Otheguy & Stern, 2011; see the 2009 debate between Otheguy and Zentella, https://www.youtube.com/watch?v=Nn6P0UdSDYw).

As the number of U.S. Latinx bilinguals increased, second language acquisition scholars turned their attention to the U.S. Latinx children's acquisition of Spanish, but always using as frame of reference the acquisition of Spanish by children in monolingual settings in Latin America or Spain. These comparisons fueled the idea that Latinx children had an incompletely acquired form of Spanish (see, for example, Montrul, 2008). Ricardo pushed back on this concept, pointing out that there is no notion of completeness against which to assess any natively acquired grammar as incomplete. He also noted that the apples-and-oranges comparison of the language of working class Latinx students in the United States with elite college students from Latin America or Spain was a form of prescriptivism passing as science. Language acquisition and socialization among Latinx takes place in local U.S. communities and homes, rendering irrelevant comparison with dominant monolingual communities elsewhere (Otheguy, 2016c).

Bilingual education: Early studies and our changing scholarship

Throughout the mid-1960s and 1970s, and as a consequence of attention to civil rights, the Latinx community managed to establish bilingual education programs that educated Latinx children with histories, stories, poems, songs, and language that reflected their own lives. But as bilingual education became more institutionalized through the Bilingual Education Act (1968) and subsequent reauthorizations (García & Sung, 2018), the practice of bilingual education and the scholarship related to it tended to also adopt the theoretical lens developed for the one model that counted in the United States—that of Anglos endeavoring to become bilingual.

The early scholarship on bilingual education around the world had focused on the education of a few elite students who were taught what was considered a prestigious "foreign language" (FL) that was added to a "first language" (L1). Attention, however, became focused on the new immersion programs in Québec, Canada, as political power there shifted from the Anglophone majority to the Francophone minority (Lambert & Tucker, 1972). These immersion programs were designed as a way for majority Anglophone children to acquire French, it being especially relevant that the social and economic dominance of these children, as well as their identities, language and cultural practices, were in no way threatened by a language of instruction in school that was different from that of home.

In these Canadian immersion programs, each language was considered an autonomous structural entity that corresponded neatly to a different culture. Wallace Lambert (1974) described education programs for dominant majorities that elected to have their children become bilingual as fostering "additive bilingualism." Lambert also posited that, at the same time, the children of nondominant groups were subjected to educational programs that promoted "subtractive bilingualism."

Many bilingual educators in the United States reacted to scholarship like Lambert's by rightly wanting to emulate those powerful groups whose schools had provided their children additive bilingualism in what was described as an enrichment program. In so doing, Latinx bilingual educators started to pay attention to educational models that kept English strictly apart from Spanish. This ideology of language separation, designed for language majority students, started to become prevalent even in the transitional bilingual education programs that the U.S. government was then supporting. Some of us embraced it too; for example, Ricardo's work with Public School 84 in Manhattan advocated language separation.

The strict language separation in bilingual education programs was also based on the concept of diglossia. As we stated before, diglossic arrangements, with each language being used in different domains or for different functions, were considered the only way that minoritized communities could maintain their language (Fishman, 1966a). The Latinx bilingual community was justly concerned with ensuring that they remained Spanish-speaking, something that had been restricted. But although diglossia described well the sociolinguistic situations of bilingual minoritized communities around the world, it did not engage with the political and economic reasons why the minority community's language was restricted to the home and family domains and functions considered "Low" (García, 2009a; Martín-Rojo, 2017). As language-minoritized communities emulated the ways of bilingually educating children of the dominant majority through diglossic arrangements, the analysis of how power impacted language and educational practices was dismissed.

In the late 1970s and 1980s, the United States started receiving many more diverse immigrant students, an outcome of changes in the immigration law of 1965. The Latinx community grew exponentially, with people coming now not just from Mexico, Puerto Rico, Cuba, but increasingly from the Dominican Republic and Central and South America, and often speaking languages other than Spanish. At the same time, immigration increased from countries other than Europe, bringing many more children considered by the federal government "Limited English Proficient" or later "English Language Learners." English as a Second Language (ESL) programs flourished, accommodating the more linguistically heterogeneous students by paying attention only to English. The backlash against bilingual education was promoted by the presidency of Ronald Reagan and the growth of the English Only movement around the same time (Crawford, 2007; García, 2009a; Otheguy, 1982).

As a result of these trends, bilingual education programs, as the Latinx community had originally envisioned them, were wrestled from their hands. By 2000, bilingual education had been declared illegal in California, Massachusetts, and Arizona (for more on this history, see García & Kleifgen, 2018). The wave of restrictions toward bilingual education for the Latinx community only came to an end when it had been redefined as *dual language* education, reinforcing the idea of teaching two *separate* languages, and now again centered on the one model that counted—that of Anglos becoming bilingual.

Many dual language programs are two-way, meaning that half of the children have to be learners of English, and the other half learners of the other language of instruction. These dual language education programs now have little to do with the ways in which bilingualism is actually practiced in the Latinx community. The Latinx community still includes many recent immigrants who could be considered learners of English, although most Latinx children are simultaneous bilinguals, that is, they grow up in homes characterized by bilingual practices. But with its emphasis on teaching *languages*—the language other than English, the English language—the dual language model was never meant to teach *bilingual children*, never meant, in the case under discussion, to educate Latinx children.

Our understanding of the lack of fit between dual language programs and the bilingualism of the community came to a head one day when Ofelia was observing a dual language 1st grade classroom. For a week, she had observed how some, perhaps most, English-speaking six-year-old children remained silent during the Spanish week, and how silence also characterized the Spanish-speaking children during the English week. The idea of these dual language programs was to have the children who were seen as learners of a "second language" have an immersion experience (this is why these programs are also called double immersion). In this classroom, there were also many Latinx children who were bilingual. But their bilingualism remained invisible, since teachers had been instructed to categorize their students as learners of one language or the other, and when these categories did not work, as dominant in one language or the other.

One day Ofelia was visiting another dual language 5th grade classroom. As Ofelia talked to one 10-year-old Puerto Rican child, he said, "Even though Spanish runs through my heart, English rules my veins." As we thought about what the child said, we realized that he was describing a unitary circulation system, where the blood flows uninterrupted from the heart to the veins, even if there are separate organs and one organ rules. We realized that the separate language allocation policies in dual language classrooms stopped the flow from the heart (Spanish) to the veins (English). Rather than helping this bilingual child develop and grow, the separate languages arrangement was stifling his growth and was responsible for much of his academic failure. The seeds of translanguaging as a unitary system that works in concert were firmly planted by this eloquent child's metaphor (see García, 2009a).

From the ground up: Developing a theory/practice

At the same time, some scholars around the world had started to shift their understandings of the bilingualism and the bilingual education of minoritized communities. Colin Baker (2001) first described an instructional approach that Cen Williams (1996) was trying out in Welsh classrooms. Unlike the many other programs where Welsh was used only in Welsh-language spaces, Williams asked students to use one language for input and another for output. He argued that the use of both Welsh and English within the same instructional space provided students with an opportunity to deepen their meaning-making. Williams coined the term *trawsieithu* in Welsh to describe this instructional approach, a term later translated into English by Colin Baker as translanguaging. And Baker and Williams dialogued extensively with Ofelia during this time.

Although this was the first time that the term translanguaging was used, it was not the first time that a bilingual pedagogical approach that did not strictly separate languages was used. We had often witnessed teachers of emergent bilingual students using flexible bilingual pedagogical practices, even if they had been taught to think of them as "wrong." And there had been many scholars who had described these practices in teaching language minoritized communities (see García & Li Wei, 2014, pp. 56–60 for many sources). For example, Fu (2003) used what she called "a bilingual process approach" to teach writing to Chinese emergent bilingual students.

But even though the original use of the term translanguaging, as well as these more flexible bilingual pedagogical practices, referred to an instructional approach that honored students' bilingualism by using it within one space, it still referred to two separate languages. It was the reading around this time of the manuscript of what became Sinfree Makoni's and Alistair Pennycook's book, *Disinventing and Reconstituting Languages* (2007), that allowed us to conceptualize the bilingual practices we had observed our entire lives in a different way.

Of course, this was not the first time that we had read about the invention of languages, implicit in the often-quoted commonplace, attributed to Max Weinreich, that a language is a dialect with a navy. We also knew of Romaine (1994), who had said that "the very concept of discrete languages is probably a European cultural artifact fostered by procedures such as literacy and standardization" (p. 12), and of Khubchandani (1997), who described the essence of Indian plurality in terms of "fuzziness of language boundaries" and "fluidity in language identity" (p. 87). We had also taken note of Bauman and Briggs (2003), who had documented how language was invented by European elites as "reductionist, atomistic, and individualistic" and that this "then became a model not just of communication but of thought, rationality, and sociability" (p. 299). And we knew all along that the same point had been made at the dawn of the study of synchronic linguistics when Saussure (1916) warned that languages were not natural categories (and that neither were dialects). All these authors helped us to see how the concept of the discrete named language has operated as an instrument of colonialism and nation-building to produce and naturalize forms of social inequality in the construction of modernity. But except for Khubchandani (1997), these authors had concerned themselves less with bilingual and multilingual communities.

We started to then understand that the traditional theories of language and bilingualism, and the description of those practices, had not taken into account the knowledge and practices of bilingual communities. Inspired by the work done in Wales, some scholars started to use the term "translanguaging" to try to open up a space in the bilingual literature for these community understandings. For example, Ofelia attempted to tie together the understandings of traditional bilingualism and education with translanguaging when writing about bilingual education (García, 2009a). Creese and Blackledge (2010) wrote about students' translanguaging in the complementary schools they studied in the United Kingdom. And early on, Li Wei (2011) advanced the idea that translanguaging developed the creativity and criticality of bilingual students. Li Wei (2011) described how translanguaging

> creates a social space for the multilingual user by bringing together different dimensions of their personal history, experience and environment, their attitude, belief and ideology, their cognitive and physical capacity into one coordinated and meaningful performance. (p. 1223)

Although this early translanguaging work validated the minoritized communities' bilingual practices, it still fell short of articulating a coherent theory of language, bilingualism, and language education that took these practices into account.

Our readings of decolonial Latin American philosophers had enabled us to understand that what was needed was to decenter our knowledge of bilingualism from what Walter Mignolo (2000, 2002) had called the "colonial matrix of power." We were then guided by what Boaventura de Sousa Santos called the "epistemology of the South" (2009, 2014). Santos clarifies that the epistemological South is not geographical but stands as a metaphor of systemic and unjust human suffering caused by colonialism and global capitalism. If we wanted to bring to the foreground the epistemologies of bilingualism that operated in the minoritized Latinx bilingual community, then translanguaging needed to encompass an ecology of knowledges from, in Santos's terms, both sides of the line. But as Santos had also explained, the delinking from an epistemology of power takes a gigantic decentering effort, and no one can do it individually. We were fortunate that there were scholars around the world that dialogued with us. Among one of the most fruitful early conversations was that which engaged Ofelia and Li Wei and resulted in their 2014 book.

As we were pondering how to think/do translanguaging in ways that had real and just social consequences for minoritized bilingual communities, we came upon the opportunity to engage with schools educating large number of students who were developing English. As the project Ricardo named CUNY-NYSIEB, came into being, we juntos dialogued, discussed, worked, presented, researched, and wrote with different members of the entire team as well as with others, so as to expand our understandings of translanguaging theory/practice. The next section describes the joint effort made with the CUNY-NYSIEB team to clarify how to theorize/do translanguaging in ways that allow bilingual minoritized communities, and especially young people in schools, to re-exist with dignity.

CUNY-NYSIEB beginnings and development of a theory/practice

In 2011, as New York State was confronting what was seen as the failure of many schools with a large number of students they classified as English language learners, Arlen Benjamin-Gómez and Angélica Infante-Greene from the New York State Education Department came to discuss the issue with us. When we agreed to work with New York State to support these schools, we knew we could not continue to act with the same theoretical constructs and pedagogical practices that had resulted in so much academic failure for these children. We also knew that to make an impact, we needed to engage younger scholars who could continue the work for years to come. We reached out to Kate Menken who became the co-principal investigator of the project. The three of us worked on firming up the Vision for CUNY-NYSIEB, articulating translanguaging as a theory based on practices that Ofelia had written about, but that still needed to be formulated in an articulated manner. We were fortunate to then hire Nelson Flores as our first Project Director. We then articulated the two nonnegotiable principles for participating schools (engaging with bilingualism as a resource and with a multilingual school ecology), in this way identifying the commitments that schools needed to make in order to participate in the project.

Ofelia, Ricardo, Kate, and Nelson dialogued frequently about how to implement the vision. One of our first decisions was to engage the CUNY teacher education faculty in ESL and Bilingual Education so that we together could learn more about translanguaging as theory/practice. We knew that changing the teachers' stance toward their bilingual students was most important. And we also knew that for these shifts to occur, we needed time, longer than the year in which we would be engaged with the schools. By engaging teacher education faculty, we hoped not only that we would learn together, but also that they would then carry out the work with future ESL and bilingual teachers (see Chapters 16–18, this volume).

The school teams and school principals of our first cohort of schools had uneven understandings of bilingualism. Our task was then to inform them of traditional bilingual scholarship and to go beyond it. We engaged them in difficult conversations, as we questioned and made visible the practices of racialization, exclusion, and marginalization that were taking place in many schools. The dialogue was not one-way, for we also worked on seeing the realities that teachers and administrators were facing in their schools, and on adjusting translanguaging theory/practice so that it could be implemented.

We started out by proposing to them that what they called English language learners were what we called *emergent bilinguals* (García, 2009b). We impressed upon them the idea that it was impossible to put children into categories, and that we were all emergent bilinguals when confronted with tasks for which we have not used language before. We worked with the idea of *emergence*, that we derived from the work of Chilean biologist Francisco Varela, to ensure that the present possibilities for these children were opened *now* (and not in the future) by having teachers offer them the right type of affordances. We discussed the concept of dynamic bilingualism and how bilingual children used language without regard for the boundaries of what were regarded externally as two languages; and we introduced the term translanguaging.

Because it was important for the CUNY-NYSIEB teams to provide teachers with strategies to implement a translanguaging pedagogical approach, two very seasoned teachers of emergent bilinguals—one in elementary school (Celic), the other in high school (Seltzer)—were contracted to write the first translanguaging guide (Celic & Seltzer, 2012/2013). We wanted the guide to be used by school teams in collaborative ways. The guide was accompanied by a *How to Use* section, as well as *Questions and Answers*, based on our dialogue with schools.

As the project grew under the leadership of its long-standing project director Maite Sánchez, followed by that of project directors Kate Seltzer and Ivana Espinet, different members of the CUNY-NYSIEB team developed material for teachers to use (see Chapter 7, this volume). We as a team also engaged in much collaborative writing (see, for example, García & Kleyn, 2016). And many of us have individually gone beyond the collective understandings that we have held, coming up with positions that have further impacted our collective work on translanguaging. Among this extended scholarship, our collective understandings of translanguaging have benefitted from Nelson Flores' recent work on raciolinguistic ideologies (Flores & Rosa, 2015). Our published scholarship as articles and book chapters has demonstrated how our understanding of translanguaging theory/practice continues to grow and change, as we call attention to different aspects, some represented throughout this volume.

Despite our differences, and our many emphases, we have developed an understanding of translanguaging that attempts to be informed by what Santos (2007) has called *post-abyssal thinking*. That is, we work in schools that are state institutions and that as such tend to reproduce colonial differences by adopting the epistemological perspective of dominant groups. But we work with students who have suffered the systemic and unjust consequences of colonialism and global capitalism. Translanguaging for us, then, situates our epistemological perspective on the social experience of those whose knowledge/practice has been left out. But as we bring forth these other epistemologies to decenter the universal emancipating claims of much educational policies and practices, we also cross the line the other way. We recognize a plurality of heterogeneous knowledges, forever incomplete in different ways. For us, translanguaging theory/practice as defined in the next section is not only a political act, as Nelson Flores said in 2014 (Flores, 2014), as it questions the construction of language and bilingualism that has negatively impacted the Latinx bilingual community. Translanguaging theory/practice is also a way of caring for that community by validating their own knowledge/practice and leveraging it in their education.

Conceptualizing translanguaging theory/practice

Translanguaging is not an easy concept to understand because all of us think we know what language is. Language is English; language is Spanish; language is Arabic; language is Chinese. But when we conceive of language in these terms, we reveal that our understanding of language is the one that nation-states and their institutions have foisted upon us.

Many educators and scholars have simply understood the *trans-* in translanguaging as going *across* from one language to another. In thinking about how to do translanguaging in classrooms, many have gone back to the idea that any use of what is considered a child's home language in instruction (understood as the child's L1) is considered translanguaging. This was an advance back at the time when there were no bilingual programs at all, or in the more recent times when bilingual education programs were closing, and English as a Second Language programs were flourishing.

But the *trans-* in translanguaging is about going *beyond* the traditional understandings of language that have been given to us by countries, schools, and prescriptive grammar books (García & Li Wei, 2014; Li Wei, 2011; Otheguy, García & Reid, 2015, 2019). Translanguaging honors and acknowledges the languaging of people, their language practices (Becker, 1995; Maturana & Varela, 1984). And yet, translanguaging theory does not just accept the languaging of people as practices; it engages with it as the basis for an alternative conception of language. Translanguaging is theory/practice; it does not simply posit that these practices are language because as we have said, our conception of language has been constructed or "invented" as Makoni and Pennycook (2007) have said. It is not simply that all translanguaging is language; it is more that all language is translanguaging.

Otheguy, García and Reid have argued (2015, 2019) that all speakers translanguage, including monolinguals. That is, all speakers select features from their linguistic repertoire that seem to be most appropriate for the communicative task at hand. When monolinguals of the same racial and social class interact with one another, they are free to make use of most of the features in their repertoire, with a few exceptions having to do with the context in which the interaction takes place. For example, in situations considered formal, monolinguals do not usually curse, nor use lexical items that they might use when speaking with children. Likewise, when Latinx bilinguals interact with each other, in homes and communities, they often use more or less their entire linguistic repertoire, without being bound by what society considers English or Spanish. Otheguy,

García and Reid (2015) have defined the translanguaging of bilinguals saying, "Translanguaging is the deployment of a speaker's full linguistic repertoire without regard for watchful adherence to the socially and politically defined boundaries of named languages" (2015, p. 281).

The reason why translanguaging is especially pertinent for bilingual communities is that they are usually expected to behave linguistically as if they were monolinguals. That is, in interacting with monolinguals, bilinguals are often restricted to half or less of their linguistic repertoire. Thus, although all people engage in translanguaging, it is speakers of bilingual minoritized communities for whom the fact of translanguaging has the most relevance and the most tangible consequences. Translanguaging theory/practice makes visible the *injustice* of requiring bilingual people, and especially students, to use less than half of their linguistic repertoire, while comparing them to monolinguals who can use almost their entire repertoire to perform the same task.

When translanguaging theory/practice is brought into schools, as we have done in CUNY-NYSIEB, we are immediately confronted with the reality that for schools, language is considered the so-called standard language found in school texts. It has been important then to simultaneously hold these different knowledges/practices of language—those of school texts, and those of the bilingual students who interact with the texts. Translanguaging, as we have said, refers to the processes and actions whereby bilinguals select and deploy particular features from their *unitary communicative repertoire* that goes beyond the simple addition of two named languages in order to make meaning (Otheguy, García & Reid, 2015, 2019). What is then important is for teachers to simultaneously understand language from both perspectives (Otheguy, 2016b) or as Boaventura de Sousa Santos posits (2007), from both sides of the line—that of the dominant school texts and that of the minoritized bilingual students.

When children, all children, acquire language, they engage in the process of adding features to a unitary linguistic repertoire. Bilingual children acquire language in the same way, whether this is in done simultaneously from infancy at home or sequentially in school. When immigrant children come into schools where the language of instruction is seen as different from the home language, the impression of educators may be that they are acquiring a new language. However, translanguaging theory proposes that what they are acquiring are new linguistic features, to be integrated into their unitary repertoire, one that is unique to them. Only by making the new features part of a valid repertoire that is their own and that includes their own individual and community markings will minoritized children be able to engage in competent performances at schools. Even if the school texts with which Latinx children are expected to interact, orally or in writing, are in the standard language of school, children, if they are to succeed, need to be able to leverage their translanguaging. That is, bilingual children need to utilize all their background knowledge, which includes their own translanguaging. Note well that we haven't said, as we did in years past, knowledge which includes their own language; we've said: Which includes their own translanguaging.

The education of Latinx bilinguals in the United States has focused on literacy because schools' accountability to the government involves reading and writing assessments (see Chapter 13, this volume). But to do school literacy, whether reading or writing, Latinx bilinguals need to enter the text with their full meaning-making repertoire (García, 2020; García & Kleifgen, 2019; see also Chapters 8, 10, 11, and 12, this volume). Many teachers of bilingual students understand this concept, but for them to implement it, they need to develop what García, Johnson and Seltzer (2017) have called a translanguaging stance. To develop such a stance, teachers need to experience translanguaging and how it works in teaching and learning. That is why, very early on, we shared with school principals and teachers Martin Luther King's quote: "You do not have to see the whole staircase, just take the first steps." And to take the first step, our first translanguaging guide (Celic & Seltzer, 2012/2013) includes a section on how a team of teachers can conduct a collaborative descriptive inquiry session using one of the translanguaging pedagogical strategies.

Translanguaging emphasizes the actions of emergent bilinguals as they engage in assemblages of the forms of meaning-making that are available at the moment (Pennycook, 2017). Correctly, Li Wei (2017) and Li Wei and Lin (2019) have emphasized the moment-to-moment nature of translanguaging. Because of the emergent nature of translanguaging, pedagogical translanguaging should respond to these emergent actions, to this process of languaging and learning. Thus, when García, Johnson and Seltzer (2017) laid out the three components of a translanguaging pedagogy, they not only included a translanguaging stance, and a translanguaging design, but they also added translanguaging shifts. These shifts are what teachers need to do to adjust to the moment-to-moment translanguaging of bilingual students in classrooms.

The work of CUNY-NYSIEB has focused on school literacies because it has responded to the priorities of the Education Department of a State. However, by foregrounding the actions of people, translanguaging takes into account participants' simultaneous use of multiple semiotic resources that mutually elaborate each other. Angel Lin (2019) refers to the *trans-semiotizing* aspects of translanguaging, a way to broaden the focus of language as intertwined with many other semiotic resources (for example, visuals, gestures, bodily movement). Translanguaging, Lin (2019) points out, is a whole-body sense-making process. Translanguaging theory/practice includes not only aspects of the spoken and written language but also the sights, the sounds, the objects, and instruments at their disposal, as well as how these are deployed (Hua, Li Wei & Jankowicz-Pytel, 2019; Li Wei, 2017; Lin, 2019; Moore, Bradley & Simpson, 2020).

The potential of leveraging translanguaging to educate bilingual students has been explored by members of the CUNY-NYSIEB group who are represented in this volume, sometimes with others (see the CUNY-NYSIEB website for examples). Our work on translanguaging intersects with the growing scholarship of many others, too numerous to mention, in the United States and in the world (for examples of how translanguaging has been used in the United States, see Teacher/Researcher Box #16.1, and in other parts of the world, see Teacher/Researcher Box #17.1 and #18.1). With regard to translanguaging and Latinx bilingual students, we have benefited especially from the scholarship of many other Latinx scholars (see, for example, among many others, De los Ríos & Seltzer, 2017; García-Mateus & Palmer, 2017; Gort & Sembiante, 2015; Martínez, Hikida & Durán, 2019).

Challenges

It will not have escaped readers of this volume that our biggest challenge has been to ensure that schools that tend to think of language in the ways of the state can imagine their bilingual students and their language differently. In many ways, we have been constrained by many of the mandates from New York State that were in turn the result of federal government mandates. For example, we were restricted originally to work with students who had been classified as English language learners. However, many times these classrooms had other children, sometimes those with disabilities, and many times other racialized students as well (see, for example, the case of Ms. Ardizzone, Teacher/Researcher Box #6.1). We negotiated our work with the State because we were certain that the alternative would have been to leave the children and their teachers behind, when they needed so much help. We were also confident that we could transform the stances of some teachers who would then be able to implement instructional changes, becoming local policy-makers (see Menken & García, 2010).

In order to do this work, we needed, what Walter Mignolo (2002) has called a *language-otherwise*, so as to point to a more inclusive and socially just position. We had to include those who had suffered the injustices caused by what Quijano (2000) has called the *persistent coloniality* of discrimination, racism, linguicism, and classism, reflected in the educational system. At the same time, we had to include the educational reality formulated by the state. We repositioned English language Learners as emergent bilinguals. And we refashioned dual language education programs as dual language *bilingual* education programs, providing translanguaging alternatives to the program's strict language allocation policies (Sánchez, García & Solorza, 2017; Seltzer & García, 2018).

In 2014, New York State changed the student designation from simply "English language learner" to "English Language Learner/Multilingual Learner." We were pleased with the change, although for us the term multilingual learner still contained several problematic features: (1) It continued the silencing of the word *bilingual*, which had signaled so much of the Latinx community struggle for self-determination. (2) It omitted the concept of *emergence* which for us had to do with the shifting nature of bilingual interactions. (3) Although it acknowledged the multilingual nature of New York State's student body, the students' multilingualism was not in any way included in the actual teaching. During the time of our work, New York State also changed the designation of the "English as a Second Language" program to "English as a New language." We understood also the limitation of this new term, since for many of our bilingual students, English was not a new language; in fact, many of them had spoken it from birth. Our formulations in the chapters that follow often demonstrate the ways we negotiated these state terminologies, sometimes adopting them wholesale, other times not, depending on who was our audience.

A lot of our translanguaging work has been used by teachers all over the United States and the world. However, the New York State Education Department has not always been ready to accept it as their own, even after supporting us with generous funding for all these years. A lot of our translanguaging work never made it to their website. For example, at the request of the New York State Education Department, Seltzer and García (2018) authored a Topic Brief about translanguaging and dual language education programs. Although the other Topic Briefs authored that year were uploaded to the NYSED website, that one was excluded. The term "translanguaging" continued to be seen as somewhat threatening, even though we were opening up educational spaces for bilingual students and we remain ardent supporters of bilingual education.

Our relationship with New York State has been cordial and friendly. And we are grateful for their support and their hard work on behalf of emergent bilinguals. Yet, we have not always seen eye to eye on how to publicly address the challenges and opportunities of teaching minoritized bilinguals.

We position our translanguaging CUNY-NYSIEB work within what Gloria Anzaldúa (2015) refers to by the Nahuatl word of Nepantla, the lugar entre medio. We believe that a translanguaging theory/practice provides a liminal space that allows us to look at things from both sides of the line. And yet all of us, members of the CUNY-NYSIEB team and working for the New York State Education Department, often fall prey to the intellectual and emotional allure of a single side of the line, as some of the work in this volume makes evident. Our challenge continues to be to attempt to stay firm within that lugar entre medio that pushes against boundaries that have outlived their usefulness and have caused so much pain and educational failure. Much of our work has been about navigating the cracks between worldviews and epistemologies that have produced the minoritization, racialization, and failure of so many students in New York, the country, and the world.

The translanguaging work of the CUNY-NYSIEB team has taken many forms and will continue to do so in the future. It has been, and remains, a forever challenge, to balance translanguaging theory/practice within a school system that has not always been receptive, but whose mission should always be, and in some fortunate cases indeed is, to provide the best possible education to all children, very much including bilingual children who have been often racialized through their language practices.

References

Anzaldúa, G. (2015). *Light in the dark/Luz en lo oscuro. Rewriting identity, spirituality, reality.* A.L. Keating (ed.). Durham, NC & London: Duke University Press.

Baker, C. (2001). *Foundations of bilingual education and bilingualism* (3rd ed.). Clevedon, UK: Multilingual Matters.

Bauman, R. & Briggs, C.L. (2003). *Voices of modernity: Language ideologies and the politics of inequality.* Cambridge: Cambridge University Press.

Becker, A.L. (1995). *Beyond translation: Essays toward a modern philosophy.* Ann Arbor, MI: University of Michigan Press.

Celic, C. & Seltzer, K. (2012/2013). Translanguaging: A CUNY-NYSIEB Guide for Educators. http://www.cuny-nysieb.org/wp-content/uploads/2016/04/Translanguaging-Guide-March-2013.pdf

Crawford, J. (2007). The decline of bilingual education in the USA: How to reverse a troubling trend? *International Multilingual Research Journal*, 1(1), 33–37. https://doi.org/10.1080/19313150709336863

Creese, A. & Blackledge, A. (2010). Translanguaging in the bilingual classroom: A pedagogy for learning and teaching? *Modern Language Journal*, 94(1), 103–115. https://doi.org/10.1111/j.1540-4781.2009.00986.x

de los Ríos, C. & Seltzer, K. (2017). Translanguaging, coloniality and English classrooms: An exploration of two bicoastal urban classrooms. *Research in the Teaching of English*, 52(1), 55–76.

Espinosa, A. (1925). Where is the best Spanish spoken? *Hispania*, 4, 269–284.

Fishman, J.A. (1966a). Bilingualism with and without diglossia; diglossia with and without bilingualism. *Journal of Social Issues*, 23(2), 29–38. https://doi.org/10.1111/j.1540-4560.1967.tb00573.x

Fishman, J.A. (1966b). Language maintenance and shift. *Sociologus*, 16(1), 19–39. https://www.jstor.org/stable/43644960

Fishman, J.A. (Eds.). (2001). *Can threatened languages be saved?* Clevedon, UK: Multilingual Matters.

Flores, N. (2014). Let's not forget that translanguaging is a political act. [Online] Educational Linguist. Available at: https://educationallinguist.wordpress.com/2014/07/19/lets-not-forget-that-translanguaging-is-a-political-act/ [Accessed 26 Nov. 2018].

Flores, N. & García, O. (2017). A critical review of bilingual education in the United States: From basements and pride to boutiques and profit. *Annual Review of Applied Linguistics*, 37, 14–29. https://doi.org/10.1017/S0267190517000162

Flores, N. & Rosa, J. (2015). Undoing appropriateness: Raciolinguistic ideologies and language diversity in education. *Harvard Educational Review*, 85(2), 149–172.

Fu, D. (2003). *An Island of English: Teaching ESL in Chinatown*. Portsmouth, NH: Heinemann.

García, O. (1993). From Goya portraits to Goya beans: Elite traditions and popular streams in U.S. Spanish language policy. *Southwest Journal of Linguistics*, 12, 69–86.

García, O. (2009a). *Bilingual education in the 21st century: A global perspective*. Malden, MA: Wiley-Blackwell.

García, O. (2009b). Emergent bilinguals and TESOL: What's in a name?. *TESOL Quarterly*, 43 (2), 322–326.

García, O. (2020). Translanguaging and Latinx bilingual readers. *The Reading Teacher*, 73(5), 557–562. https://doi.org/10.1002/trtr.1883

García, O., Johnson, S., & Seltzer, K. (2017). *The Translanguaging classroom. Leveraging student bilingualism for learning*. Philadelphia: Caslon.

García, O. & Kleifgen, J. (2018). *Educating emergent bilinguals: Policies, programs and practices for English Learners* (2nd ed.). New York, NY: Teachers College Press.

García, O. & Kleifgen, J.A. (2019). Translanguaging and literacies. *Reading Research Quarterly*, 55(4). https://doi.org/10.1002/rrq.286

García, O. & Kleyn, T. (Eds.). (2016). *Translanguaging with multilingual students: Learning from classroom moments*. New York and London: Routledge.

García, O. & Li, Wei. (2014). *Translanguaging: Language, bilingualism and education*. London/ New York: Palgrave Macmillan.

García, O., Morín, J.L., & Rivera, K. (2001). How threatened is the Spanish of New York puerto ricans? Language shift with vaivén. In J.A. Fishman (Ed.), *Can threatened languages be saved? Reversing language shift revisited* (pp. 44–73). Clevedon, UK: Multilingual Matters.

García, O. & Sung, K.K-F. (2018). Critically assessing the 1968 Bilingual Education Act at 50 years: Taming tongues and Latinx communities. *The Bilingual Review Journal*, 4(4), 318–333. https://doi.org/10.1080/15235882.2018.1529642

García-Mateus, S. & Palmer, D. (2017). Translanguaging pedagogies for positive identities in two-way dual language bilingual education. *Journal of Language, Identity & Education*, 16(4), 245–255. https://doi.org/10.1080/15348458.2017.1329016

Gort, M. & Sembiante, S. (2015). Navigating hybridized language learning spaces through translanguaging pedagogy: Dual language preschool teachers' languaging practices in support of emergent bilingual children's performance of academic discourse. *International Multilingual Research Journal*, 9(1), 7–25. https://doi.org/10.1080/19313152.2014.9817 75

Haugen, Einar. (1953). *The Norwegian language in America: The bilingual community*. Philadelphia: University of Pennsylvania Press.

Hernández-Chávez, E. (1995). Language policy in the United States. A history of cultural genocide. In T. Skutnabb-Kangas & R. Phillipson (Eds.), *Linguistic human rights. Overcoming linguistic discrimination* (pp. 141–158). New York, NY: Mouton de Gruyter.

Hua, Z., Li, Wei., & Jankowicz-Pytel, D. (2019). Translanguaging and embodied teaching and learning: Lessons from a multilingual karate club in London. *International Journal of Bilingual Education and Bilingualism*, 23(1), 65–80. https://doi.org/10.1080/13670050. 2019.1599811

Khubchandani, L.M. (1997). Language policy and education in the Indian subcontinent. In R. Wodak & D. Corson (Eds.), *Encyclopedia of language and education* (pp. 179–187). Dordrecht: Springer. https://doi.org/10.1007/978-94-011-4538-1_17

Lambert, W.E. (1974). Culture and language as factors in learning and education. In F.E. Aboud & R.D. Meade (Eds.), *Cultural factors in learning and education* (pp. 91–122). Bellingham, Washington: 5th Western Washington Symposium on Learning.

Lambert, W.E. & Tucker, G.R. (1972). *The bilingual education of children.* Rowley, MA: Newbury House.

Li, Wei. (2011). Moment analysis and translanguaging space: Discursive construction of identities by multilingual Chinese youth in Britain. *Journal of Pragmatics*, 43(5), 1222–1235. https://doi.org/10.1016/j.pragma.2010.07.035

Li, Wei. (2017). Translanguaging as a practical theory of language. *Applied Linguistics*, 39(1), 9–30. https://doi.org/10.1093/applin/amx039

Li, Wei. & Lin, A.M.Y. (2019). Translanguaging classroom discourse: Pushing limits, breaking boundaries. *Classroom Discourse*, 10(3–4), 209–215. https://doi.org/10.1080/19463014. 2019.1635032

Lin, A.M.Y. (2019). Theories of trans/languaging and trans-semiotizing: Implications for content-based education classrooms. *International Journal of Bilingual Education and Bilingualism*, 22(1), 5–16. https://doi.org/10.1080/13670050.2018.1515175

Makoni, S. & Pennycook, A. (2007). *Disinventing and reconstituting languages.* Clevedon, UK: Multilingual Matters.

Martín-Rojo, L. (2017). Language and power. In O. García, N. Flores & M. Spotti (Eds.), *The Oxford handbook of language and society* (pp. 77–102). New York and Oxford: Oxford University Press.

Martínez, R., Hikida, M., & Durán, L. (2019). In Pacheco, M., Morales, P.Z. & Hamilton, C. (Eds.). *Transforming schooling for second language learners* (pp. 181–198). Charlotte, North Carolina: Information Age Publishing.

Martínez, R.A. (2010). "Spanglish" as literacy tool: Toward an understanding of the potential role of Spanish-English code-switching in the development of academic literacy. *Research in the Teaching of English*, 45(2), 124–149.

Maturana, H. & Varela, F. (1984). *El Árbol del conocimiento. Las bases biológicas del entendimiento humano.* Santiago de Chile: Lumen, Editorial Universitaria.

Meléndez, E. (2017). *Sponsored migration: The state and Puerto Rican postwar migration to the United States.* Columbus, OH: Ohio State University Press.

Menken, K. & García, O. (Eds.). (2010). *Negotiating language policies in schools: Educators as policymakers.* New York, NY: Routledge.

Mignolo, W. (2000). *Local histories/global designs: Essays on the coloniality of power, subaltern knowledges and border thinking.* Princeton: Princeton University Press.

Mignolo, W. (2002). The geopolitics of knowledge and the colonial difference. *The South Atlantic Quarterly*, 101(1), 57–96.

Montrul, S. (2008). *Incomplete acquisition in bilingualism.* Amsterdam and Philadelphia: John Benjamins.

Moore, E., Bradley, J., & Simpson, J. (Eds.). (2020). *Translanguaging as transformation: The collaborative construction of new linguistic realities.* Bristol, UK: Multilingual Matters.

Nichols, M.W. (1945). The history of Spanish and Portuguese teaching in the United States. In H. Grattan-Doyle (Ed.), *A Handbook in the teaching of Spanish and Portuguese* (pp. 99–146). Boston: D.C. Heath.

Otheguy, R. (1982). Thinking about bilingual education: A critical appraisal. *Harvard Educational Review*, 52(3), 301–314. https://doi.org/10.17763/haer.52.3.g8187157520v0081

Otheguy, R. (2007). La filología y el unicornio: El verdadero referente del vocablo *spanglish* y su función como adjudicador de posiciones de poder en la población de origen hispano en los EEUU. In E.S. Alegre (Ed.), *La incidencia del contexto en los discursos* (*LynX*, Annexa 14) (pp.5–20). València: Universitat de València.

Otheguy, R. (2008). Affirming differences, valuing variation and dismissing dialects in modern linguistics. *Studies in Hispanic and Lusophone Linguistics*, 1(1), 223–234.

Otheguy, R. (2009). El llamado espanglish. In H. López-Morales (Ed.), *Enciclopedia del español en los Estados Unidos* (pp. 222–247). Madrid: Instituto Cervantes & Editorial Santillana.

Otheguy, R. (2016a). Espanglish. In J. Gutiérrez-Rexach (Ed.), *Enciclopedia de lingüística hispánica* (pp. 454–462). London & New York: Routledge.

Otheguy, R. (2016b). Foreword. In O. García & T. Kleyn (Eds.), *Translanguaging with multilingual students. Learning from classroom moments* (pp. ix–xii). New York: Routledge.

Otheguy, R. (2016c). The linguistic competence of second-generation bilinguals: A critique of 'incomplete acquisition.' In C. Tortora, M. den Dikken, I.L. Montoya & T. O'Neill (Eds.), *Romance linguistics 2013. Selected papers from the 43rd linguistic symposium on romance languages (LSRL), New York, 17–19 April, 2013* (pp. 301–320). Amsterdam: John Benjamins.

Otheguy, R., García, O., & Fernandez, M. (1989). Transferring, switching, and modeling in West New York Spanish: An intergenerational study. *International Journal of the Sociology of Language*, 79, 41–52.

Otheguy, R., García, O., & Reid, W. (2015). Clarifying translanguaging and deconstructing named languages: A perspective from linguistics. *Applied Linguistics Review*, 6(3), 281–307. https://doi.org/10.1515/applirev-2015-0014

Otheguy, R., García, O., & Reid, W. (2019). A translanguaging view of the linguistic system of bilinguals. *Applied Linguistics Review*, 10(4), 625–651. https://doi.org/10.1515/applirev-2018-0020

Otheguy, R. & Stern, N. (2013). Scholars and citizens: Judging the unfortunate term "Spanglish." *Anthropology News*, December 2013.

Otheguy, R. & Stern, N. (2011). On so-called Spanglish. *International Journal of Bilingualism*, 15(1), 85–100. https://doi.org/10.1177/1367006910379298

Pedraza, P., Attinasi, J., & Hoffman, G. (1980). *Rethinking diglosia*. New York: Language Policy Task Force, Centro de Estudios Puertorriqueños.

Pennycook, A. (2017). Translanguaging and semiotic assemblages. *International Journal of Multilingualism*, 14(3), 269–282. https://doi.org/10.1080/14790718.2017.1315810

Poplack, S. (1980). Sometimes I'll start a sentence in English y termino en espanol: Toward a typology of code-switching. *Linguistics*, 18(7–8), 581–618.

Quijano, A. (2000). Coloniality of power, ethnocentrism, and Latin America. *Nepantla*, 1(3), 533–580.

Romaine, S. (1994). *Language in society. An Introduction to sociolinguistics*. Oxford and New York: Oxford University Press.

Sánchez, M.T., García, O., & Solorza, C. (2017). Reframing language allocation policy in dual language bilingual education. *Bilingual Research Journal*, 41(1), 37–51. https://doi.org/10.1080/15235882.2017.1405098

Santos, B. de S. (2007). Beyond abyssal thinking: From global lines to ecologies of knowledges. *Review (Fernand Braudel Center)*, 30(1), 45–89.

Santos, B. de S. (2009). *Una epistemología del sur. La reinvención del conocimiento y la emancipación social.* Buenos Aires: Siglo XXI Editores, CLACSO.

Santos, B. de S. (2014). *Epistemologies of the South: Justice against epistemicide.* New York: Rutledge Publishers.

Saussure, Ferdinand. (1916 [1972, 1986]). *Cours de linguistique générale.* Publié par Charles Bally et Albert Séchehaye. Avec la collaboration de Albert Riedlinger. Edition critique préparée par Tullio de Mauro. Paris: Edition Payot. Translated by Roy Harris as *Course in general linguistics.* La Salle, Illinois: Open Court Classics.

Seltzer, K. & García, O. (2018). *Translanguaging and dual language bilingual education classrooms.* http://www.cuny-nysieb.org/wp-content/PDFs/Clarifying-Translanguaging-in-DLE.pdf

Weinreich, Uriel. (1953/1974). *Languages in contact: Findings and problems.* The Hague: Mouton.

Williams, C. (1996). Secondary education: Teaching in the bilingual situation. In C. Williams, G. Lewis & C. Baker (Eds.), *The Language policy: Taking stock* (pp. 39–78). Llangefni, UK: CAI.

Zentella, A.C. (1996). *Growing up bilingual: Puerto rican children in New York.* Malden, MA: Wiley.

Zentella, A.C. (2016). Spanglish. Language politics vs. el habla del pueblo. In R.E. Guzzardo Tamargo, C.M. Mazak & M.C. Parafita Couto (Eds.), *Spanish-English codeswitching in the Caribbean and the U.S.* (pp. 11–35). New York: John Benjamins.

2

CONSTRUCTING TRANSLANGUAGING SCHOOL POLICIES AND PRACTICES

Kate Menken and Ofelia García

Introduction

CUNY-NYSIEB (City University of New York-New York State Initiative on Emergent Bilinguals) offered an opportunity to develop a theory and practice of translanguaging in schools across New York State, as was discussed in Chapter 1 (this book). In this chapter, we describe how our efforts to do so challenged traditional practices and structures in schools for emergent bilingual students in fundamental ways. In accordance with translanguaging theory, we adopted the position that for schools to be successful at meeting the needs of emergent bilingual students, they would need to develop broad ecologies of multilingualism that built on the home language practices of their students. Specifically, schools participating in CUNY-NYSIEB were required to adhere to the two guiding principles of the project: (1) a multilingual ecology for the whole school and (2) bilingualism as a resource in education. Embracing these CUNY-NYSIEB principles required that schools leave behind monolingual and monocultural ideologies that had limited their ability to meet the academic, emotional, and social needs of emergent bilinguals (EBs). Instead, the schools needed to adopt policies and practices that would support the emergence of students' dynamic bilingual development.

Context: Language education policies and practices in New York

Language policies refer to "formal and informal decisions about language use" such as "laws, regulations, and statutes, as well as practice" (de Jong, 2011) and *language education policies* determine how, why, and which language practices are used in instruction (Menken & García, 2017; Tollefson, 2012). Although many countries around the world have language policies that are explicit and codified in national law (e.g., in a country's constitution), the United States does not have an official national language and nor is there an official language education policy that is national in scope, even though English assumes the role of official language in most contexts. As such, U.S. public school's language policies are usually implicit and conveyed through the programming they offer to EBs—where the main options are English-only instruction and/or bilingual education, as detailed below. The educational system of the U.S. is also highly decentralized, and these elements combined offer states, school systems, and the leaders of individual schools great power in determining a school's language policies and making programming choices (Menken, 2013).

The New York State Education Department has an explicit Language Allocation Policy for the education of EBs. The policy mandates that schools serving EBs must offer at least one of the following programs (their terms and constructs):

- Dual language, in which at least 50% of instruction is to be offered in the language other than English;
- Transitional bilingual education, which offers more instruction in English than a dual language program, with the amount of English instruction increasing over time in order to transition students to monolingual English classroom settings; and,
- "Free Standing" English as a new language (ENL), in which instruction is typically monolingual in English (Chancellor's Regulations Part 154, New York State Education Department, 2014; New York State Education Department, 2020).

Most schools in the state offer Free Standing ENL programs, with few offering transitional bilingual education programs, and even fewer dual language programs. Individual schools and local district leaders determine which of these choices will be provided. Yet these choices have a lasting impact on families and communities, as their languaging practices are either strengthened or marginalized by school language policies. When we began our work with CUNY-NYSIEB schools across the State of New York, we found that the schools' language education policies and practices were typically rooted in monolingual and monocultural ideologies, regardless of the type of programming being offered.

The ideological and implementational challenges of translanguaging pedagogy in New York

Bilingual education remains a viable, although rarely available, option for children in New York in spite of the many efforts to dismantle it over the years.

Bilingual education in New York first grew out of the Civil Rights movement and the efforts of Puerto Rican community members in the 1960s and 1970s to improve the educational outcomes of their children. ASPIRA (a Puerto Rican Civil Rights organization) and the New York City Board of Education signed a Consent Decree in 1974, mandating that bilingual education be provided in all schools where there were 20 or more EB students per grade who spoke the same home language (Carrasquillo, Rodríguez, & Kaplan, 2014; García, 2011; Reyes, 2006). This mandate was extended from the city to the entire state and written into the New York State Education Department's education policy guidelines for EBs, which remain in effect until today through the Chancellor's Regulations Part 154 (detailed above). As such, New York is one of just five states in the U.S. where bilingual education is written into state education policy, establishing New York as a state that is supportive of bilingual education (Menken, 2012). Even so, and in spite of the written policy protections it offers, the vast majority of schools in New York provide English-only instruction for EBs. That said, the very existence of Part 154 policy is extremely significant because it disrupts the hegemony of English that characterizes U.S. schooling by allowing for instruction of EBs in languages other than English.

At the same time, we argue that this menu of programming choices, even for the programs that are labeled bilingual, is rooted in monolingual norms, and that this monolingual gaze in implementation closes off spaces to embrace the fluidity of translanguaging. Although bilinguals often language with their entire repertoire, not making distinctions between named languages (Otheguy, García, & Reid, 2015, 2019), "hard boundaries" have been built up between languages of instruction in school contexts. Even within bilingual education programs, languages are strictly separated by class, teacher, period, or day of the week (Cenoz & Gorter, 2011; García, 2009). At the start of the CUNY-NYSIEB project, we found this to be true in: (a) ENL programs, where instruction was typically monolingual in English without building on students' bilingualism; (b) transitional bilingual education programs, where English was overprivileged in instruction; and, (c) dual language bilingual education (DLBE) programs, where language separation was strictly enforced and translanguaging was discouraged. As such, the introduction of translanguaging in schools across New York State disrupted existing language education policies and classroom practices.

When we began the CUNY-NYSIEB project, we found that the greatest resistance to translanguaging came from dual language educators and administrators. DLBE programs in New York and elsewhere are structured to strictly separate the use of the two languages during daily instruction. As the guidelines state, "The two languages are separated by time, space, or teacher and are not used simultaneously ... Translation by the teacher is totally prohibited" (New York City Department of Education, 2015: n.p.). It is important to note that

New York's DLBE guidelines are not extemporaneous, but rather are aligned with other U.S. scholarship encouraging strict language separation and student composition quotas (Howard et al., 2007; Lindholm-Leary & Genesee, 2010; Soltero, 2016). One of the reasons for the language separation is said to be to protect spaces within U.S. schools for minoritized languages.

However, these DLBE structures are increasingly being critiqued as dual language dogma by researchers who argue that such beliefs are rooted in ideologies of linguistic purism that marginalize students' translanguaging practices (García, 2009; García et al., 2018; Gort & Sembiante, 2015; Martínez, Hikida, & Durán, 2015; Menken & Avni, 2017; Palmer et al., 2014) and we have argued elsewhere how translanguaging pedagogy is in fact compatible with DLBE (Sánchez, García, & Solorza, 2018). A translanguaging stance (García, Johnson, & Seltzer, 2017) involves "a necessary mindset or framework for educating bilingual students that informs everything from the way we view students and their dynamic bilingual performances and cultural practices to the way we plan instruction and assessment" (p. 50). For CUNY-NYSIEB, this tension between a translanguaging stance and existing school language policies meant that truly disrupting such established and deeply rooted language ideologies could only occur through intensive work that would be sustained over time.

CUNY-NYSIEB structures

In designing the CUNY-NYSIEB project to support schools in their implementation of the project's vision and principles, we wanted to develop sustained supports for participating educators and administrators, because we knew that we would be asking them to reconsider their ideologies and beliefs about bilingualism and learning. This would be especially challenging for seasoned educators, who had developed their views over many years working in schools. Additionally, schools selected for participation in the CUNY-NYSIEB project served above average numbers of EBs and were all listed as failing schools that New York State referred to as "Schools in Need of Improvement" at the time, due to the performance of their EB students. Because the schools all had been classified in this way by the State's Education Department, they were targeted for many different initiatives aimed at their overhaul; this meant that participating school leaders were also juggling many priorities that competed for their attention. As such, we knew that it would be impossible for the project to be meaningful within the confines of typical professional development opportunities, which consist of just a few workshops. Instead, we designed CUNY-NYSIEB to be intensive, with frequent meetings over a sustained period of time (see also Chapter 3 and 4, this volume).

Specifically, schools formally participated in the CUNY-NYSIEB project for one year, while later cohorts participated for 1.5 years. During their period of involvement, school leaders (including administrators such as school principals and assistant principals, as well as teachers who assumed leadership roles in their buildings) received intensive professional development and technical assistance through seminars they attended at the CUNY Graduate Center. The seminars consisted of a formal lecture on topics relevant to our vision, including dynamic bilingualism and translanguaging, and discussions among school staff about how they might incorporate that vision into their school's programmatic structures and pedagogical practices (for the collaborative descriptive inquiry process followed, see Chapter 4). In addition, schools received monthly on-site visits from project staff. This offered a level of engagement that made it possible for participants to start shifting their beliefs and practices.

School language policies

The two of us were differently concerned with school language policies. Ofelia was more interested in shaping educators' stances and practices, whereas Kate maintained that we also had to engage with policy so that the translanguaging work could connect to the course of action that the New York State was requiring of schools. Ofelia, however, initially wondered how translanguaging and the language allocation policies of the state could work in tandem.

By the second year of CUNY-NYSIEB, Kate had convinced Ofelia that we had to continue to work shifting stances and pedagogical designs in schools, and at the same time engage whole schools in articulating a language education policy that went beyond the language allocation policy schools submitted to the state. We wanted educators to think critically about what they were doing, rather than just select a "model" of instruction that was being handed down to them by the state. We did not want these policy statements to offer rigid inflexible guidelines as to models and strategies. Instead, we wanted the educators to have the possibility of imagining how and why language was to operate throughout the school community. We called these documents "Language Policy Vision Statements."

We were convinced that more important than the statement itself was how engaging in the process of creating a language policy vision could allow for school leaders to reimagine how to educate their EBs and their reasons for doing so (García & Menken, 2015). We wanted the CUNY-NYSIEB teams to be involved in the process, but we also wanted participation of the whole school community. This was part of the juntos collaborative process and philosophy that CUNY-NYSIEB has espoused. We also wanted the process to be long-lasting, as the vision and the document were adapted to the different circumstances that the educators faced.

To carry out this work, each participating school formed an Emergent Bilingual Leadership Team (EBLT) (for more on the composition and work of these teams, see Chapter 5, this volume). Working together with the wider school community and families, each school's EBLT developed a plan for how they would implement the CUNY-NYSIEB vision in their school as part of their Language Policy Vision Statement. As Kate explained to participating school leaders during our seminar on the topic:

> A language policy is derived from the school's language philosophy and is a statement of purpose that outlines a vision for language teaching and learning. It should reflect the needs of the entire school community, with input from everyone affected (e.g., administrators, teachers of different subjects, families, community members, students). CUNY-NYSIEB schools are being asked to consider the current programming and practices that comprise their language policy, and make their policies explicit while ensuring they also carve out spaces for multilingualism.

At the start of their involvement in CUNY-NYSIEB, none of the schools had thought much of why language was used in certain ways throughout the school and in instruction, even though they had to report to the state the program "model" they were following in their official language allocation policy. We asked the schools to consider the programming and practices they offered and that comprised their implicit language policy, and then evaluate it to ensure it supported students' dynamic bilingualism. We then requested that teams use that information to create a language policy vision statement for their school so as to reimagine how to educate their EBs and their reasons for doing so.

Below, we offer examples of Language Policy Vision Statements from three different CUNY-NYSIEB schools across New York State. One is an elementary school, one is a PreK-8 school, and one is a high school. The schools differ by location and the programming they provided for EBs at the start of their involvement in CUNY-NYSIEB. Together, these examples show how CUNY-NYSIEB schools expanded students' bilingualism as a resource in instruction by bringing translanguaging pedagogy into ENL programs where instruction had previously only been in English, by replacing English-only programs with new bilingual education programs, and by replacing transitional bilingual programs with DLBE programs. We found that when schools transformed their vision of multilingualism and changed their language policies because of their participation in CUNY-NYSIEB, they would make choices that increased opportunities for instruction that supported students' own dynamic bilingualism.

These cases also show how translanguaging theory fundamentally challenged existing school structures and was eventually implemented in participating schools. The schools' language policy statements offer insights into the sense-making process of school leaders as they took the ideas introduced by CUNY-NYSIEB and integrated them with the language policies of the state. Through critical questioning of their own practices, educators started noticing why they were making certain decisions about language use in their schools. They then began orchestrating their own stance towards the children's bilingualism and their pedagogical design with the language allocation policy that the school reported to the state.

CUNY-NYSIEB language policy vision Example 1

The first example is from an elementary school in New York City. When they began to work with CUNY-NYSIEB, the school offered ENL, transitional bilingual education, and DLBE to their predominately Latinx population of EB students. The DLBE program at the school was one that had received honors and recognition in the past, and the principal wrote the following about it in her application to participate in CUNY-NYSIEB:

> As the proud principal of a large elementary school in [neighborhood name], I am even prouder of the extensive Dual Language program that exists in grades Kindergarten through 5th...Parents, teachers, administrators and students have adopted this model with a philosophy to promote both Spanish and English as languages of equal value. There are students enrolled in the program that are on their way to becoming tri-lingual! (School Principal, CUNY-NYSIEB Application, 2014)

In this excerpt, the principal makes clear from the outset that she perceives of the school's DLBE program as successful. The school's transitional bilingual education and ENL programs were not mentioned in the application.

When work began with CUNY-NYSIEB, we shared our understandings of bilingualism and translanguaging, but we were careful not to impose our vision. We were confident that our gentle support of the school leadership and teachers would eventually yield changes. The language policy that the school initially drafted was as follows:

- Dual Language Bilingual: Students learn two languages simultaneously through meaningful interactions with a focus on academic achievement and language development.
- English as a Second Language: Students are taught in English only with an emphasis on acquiring English proficiency. Students receive English support from a certified push-in teacher or in an ESL self-contained classroom.
- Transitional Bilingual: Students receive instruction in both English and Spanish until they have successfully acquired the necessary proficiency skills in English to transition to monolingual (English-only) classrooms.

The school did not have a cohesive schoolwide language policy vision. Instead the school adopted different visions for bilingualism and language learning according to each of the program models in place, such that each model had its own language education policy. They incorporated official state descriptions of language education programs as per New York State's Part 154 (described above) into their school language policy. In this way, the language policy vision statement the school leaders wrote at the end of their first semester of involvement in the project exposed their initial resistance to the CUNY-NYSIEB vision, and especially to adopting translanguaging pedagogy.

Over the next year and a half, some changes were made to the school's language policy vision as CUNY-NYSIEB's work began to take root. We had first identified that it would be easier to implement translanguaging pedagogy in the ENL classrooms than in bilingual classrooms. This proved to be the case, as English as a second language teachers experienced how translanguaging pedagogical practices helped their EB students learn.

The emphasis of the CUNY-NYSIEB work on the importance of leveraging the students' bilingualism in instruction also moved the school to start eliminating the transitional bilingual education program and to replace it with a dual language bilingual program. This particular school entered CUNY-NYSIEB the year after a leader within the city's Department of English Language Learners and a bilingual education consultant that the city had contracted to lead professional development had both publicly stated their opposition to translanguaging in bilingual education, and particularly within DLBE programs. So, although the school increased support for students' bilingualism in instruction, educators within the school remained skeptical of translanguaging pedagogy in the dual language program and DLBE teachers resisted leveraging the students' translanguaging in their classrooms.

One DLBE teacher who had become very involved in CUNY-NYSIEB actively tried out translanguaging pedagogy in her classroom. As she recently stated when we asked her to reflect back on that time:

> When [name of CUNY-NYSIEB team member] came in, I remember the DLBE teachers said mostly behind her back that "This is taboo. No, we have to preserve separate languages"… The school had this reputation of an amazing dual language program and they thought that was it, and that's what made the program really strong. When CUNY-NYSIEB came along and introduced all of this it was like, "No, it's going to ruin the program." I began having open conversations about sociolinguistics with my students and talked about how we talk. I remember being observed twice when I taught 3rd grade and I remember deliberately translanguaging in a purposeful way and having a metalinguistic conversation in front of the AP [Assistant Principal] too about how English helps us develop Spanish. I was trying to help students understand the word 'aero.' The AP was blown away. I did presentations with the whole school and definitely did

convince the principal and AP. The point of translanguaging is to lever-age students' bilingualism. (DLBE Teacher Leader, Interview Transcript, 2020)

This DLBE teacher recounted her experiences trying out translanguaging peda-gogy as a way to embrace the actual language practices of her community, and describes how her successes in doing so changed the minds of the school leaders and several other DLBE teachers. This example highlights the initial resistance to translanguaging within DLBE programs, and the ways that translanguag-ing pedagogy disrupts programming rooted in monolingual norms. It also highlights how translanguaging pedagogy within DLBE programs can support these programs to realize their potential to truly serve minoritized communities (García et al., 2018; Sánchez, García, & Solorza, 2018).

CUNY-NYSIEB language policy vision Example 2

A contrasting example is provided by a PreK-8 school in an urban area in Upstate New York. When this school began their participation in CUNY-NYSIEB, they offered an ENL program for EBs across all grades, a transitional bilin-gual program at the elementary grades, and had just started an early childhood DLBE program. Translanguaging and the idea of looking holistically at students' dynamic language practices were new, and they challenged the program models they had in place. But in this case, school leaders did not see translanguaging as incompatible with bilingual education; instead, they saw translanguaging as a means to unify the school's vision.

In their first year of CUNY-NYSIEB, all of the educators on the school's EBLT began trying out translanguaging strategies and then sharing these approaches with other teachers. A main challenge the EBLT had identified was, "One school feels like three schools!" With bilingual education, monolingual education, and elementary and junior high school all within one building, the members of the EBLT wanted the school to feel like one (CUNY-NYSIEB Team, Extended School Profile, Spring 2016). The first approach to address-ing this was setting the following goal in their plans for school improvement: "Increase school cohesion for using bilingualism/multiculturalism as a resource through incorporation of translanguaging as a school-wide instructional prac-tice" (School Improvement Plan, 2015). In other words, although in Language Policy Example 1 described above, bilingual educators were concerned that translanguaging would undermine their program, this school immediately believed that translanguaging pedagogy would strengthen their bilingual edu-cation program as well as their ENL program (a point shared by Sánchez, García, & Solorza, 2018).

When asked to develop a schoolwide language policy, the school's EBLT jumped at the chance to articulate a school-wide vision for EBs. As the CUNY-NYSIEB team working with the school stated in their notes, "EBLT members were 100% in agreement that [school name] needed a school language policy ... After professional development sessions and discussion, [school name] was ready and eager to write a language policy for their school." The Language Policy Vision Statement they wrote was as follows:

> At [School Name], we value biliteracy for all children and promote cultur-ally and linguistically relevant practices in instruction and assessment. This is shown through the current initiative to replace the Transitional Bilingual Education Program with a Dual Immersion Program where all students are Emergent Bilinguals (EB). We value the fluid use of language during inquiry, provocations, projects, and during meaningful activities throughout the day/year and across programs. We believe that students from our school com-munity deserve the same opportunity for high quality language programs as students from more affluent communities. We believe that using the home language and culture in instruction can increase academic achievement, resulting in enduring understanding. This will build bridges to higher stand-ards as well as respect and understanding for all members of the school com-munity. We aspire to create a school ecology that highlights multilingualism, inquiry, learning through art, and student-led projects where parents are cen-tral to the school ecology and are important culture and language brokers.

The policy vision they created and adopted indicates certain policy shifts. It sets their intention to expand the DLBE program such that it would eventu-ally replace the transitional bilingual education program. And it also reflects a renewed understanding of the value of including the children's dynamic bilin-gual practices in instruction.

After developing their language policy vision, school leaders made the deci-sion to expand bilingual education to the higher grades. At first, they began with transitional bilingual education in the upper grades, and planned for it to be replaced by DLBE over time. And, they clarified how translanguaging strat-egies would be used across ENL, transitional bilingual education, and DLBE programs to center students and their languaging practices.

CUNY-NYSIEB language policy vision Example 3

In our experiences, introducing schools across New York State to translanguag-ing theory and pedagogy, we found that schools that offered only ENL programs, in which instruction was monolingual in English, were often open to trying out translanguaging pedagogy from the outset, and many cultivated a translanguaging stance over time. One such example is from a high school located in a large urban school district. During the first year of their involvement in CUNY-NYSIEB, the school developed the following Language Policy Vision Statement:

> At [School Name], we strive to value and support all cultures and the use of all languages present in our learning community. As outlined in our pledge we want our students "to serve our community locally and globally" as they "grow as responsible citizens." We expect all students to work toward bi- or multi-lingualism by working to develop their native and second (or third, or fourth) language literacies. For native English speakers, we offer Spanish and French courses. Native Spanish speakers are also offered classes specifically for their needs. For native speakers of languages other than English, we provide ESL [English as a second language] and ELA [English language arts] classes that develop academic literacy skills in both their home language and English. This connects to our International Baccalaureate mission statement, as well as our overall goals of educating students in the ideals of internationalism.

As stated above, the school established bi/multilingualism as a goal by offering opportunities for all students to learn leveraging all their language practices, including in classes such as English as a second/new language and English language arts where the primary instructional focus was on English learning. In addition, the school offered instruction in Spanish and French for all students, and Spanish as a heritage language classes for Latinx students.

In their first year of involvement in CUNY-NYSIEB, educators at this high school actively incorporated translanguaging pedagogy in all classes:

> In fall 2014, the school formed its Emergent Bilingual Leadership Team (EBLT), bringing together the principal, ENL teachers, Spanish teachers, and students. It was the first time that the school had a team meeting to solely discuss how to support the emergent bilinguals in the school. The Support Team worked with the EBLT members and other teachers during the first year focused on designing and implementing ENL units using translanguaging strategies, and integrating literacy and language strategies in the content area lessons. Members of the EBLT co-taught classes with content area teachers to model those strategies. (CUNY-NYSIEB Team, Extended School Profile, Spring 2016)

The formation of the school's EBLT provided the first time a group of educators at the school had ever been convened to focus on the education of EBs. EBLT team members began piloting translanguaging pedagogy in their classrooms and, as they gained experience, this group expanded the practices schoolwide into all content area subjects.

The principal described their efforts as follows:

> [We try] to understand student learning from the students' point of view and [we are] trying to carve opportunities for them in school that will help them not only to find a safety net but also work on their strengths and work on their weaknesses to convert them to strengths… Looking at the needs of the students, what is it that, as a school community, we need to do to ensure that we are meeting their needs? (Spring 2015 exit interview, May 2015)

In this passage, the principal explains translanguaging pedagogy as privileging students' "point of view" by embracing and extending their language practices. In interviews, teachers and the principal noted how their involvement in CUNY-NYSIEB impacted their thinking about the teaching strategies and programming they provided for EBs in the school.

At the end of their first year participating in CUNY-NYSIEB, the school applied for and received a district grant to start a transitional bilingual education program. Up to then, the school's program for those students classified as "English Language Learners" was designated as "English as a New Language program." In other words, after a year of involvement in CUNY-NYSIEB and after reflecting upon their language policy vision, school leaders decided to further develop their ecology of multilingualism by starting a new transitional bilingual education program in which they would incorporate translanguaging pedagogy. This was a step beyond their use of translanguaging in ESL and ELA classrooms. That year, the school opened the new bilingual program for a cohort of 10th grade students, and since then the program has expanded across the grades. School leaders observed improvement in subject area learning as well as English development of the students participating in the bilingual cohort.

Conclusion

The translanguaging stance that the CUNY-NYSIEB project adopted toward bilingualism sometimes conflicted with some of the language education policies of the state. The state regarded languages as autonomous entities that could be taught and assessed according to understandings about language and bilingualism that had been generated by the monolingual stance of dominant populations. Our translanguaging stance was focused on the languaging of minoritized bilinguals, and had evolved from theorizing those practices (see Chapter 1). The translanguaging pedagogical practices that we designed responded to our committed stance to educate justly those who had suffered the indignities of colonialism and global capitalism. But all of us also wanted the schools, educators, and students to succeed.

We realized that we needed to assist the schools to envision the reasons why they used language, and to reconcile this vision with the language allocation policy that they were reporting to the state. In so doing, we did not impose our own vision of how to do this, although we did make visible what up to then had been rendered invisible—how the theory of language and bilingualism being espoused by the state did not always incorporate the translanguaging of bilinguals, rendering them deficient from the beginning.

Through the Juntos work of the CUNY-NYSIEB teams and the schools' EBLTs, each school developed a language policy vision in which they questioned how bilingualism was being used in the school and imagined other possibilities. At the same time, their renewed understandings of language and bilingualism were brought together with the plan that the schools developed for the state as their Language Allocation Policy. In this process, we juntos learned much. We learned how to find the generative cracks that were made obvious by the lack of fit between a translanguaging vision and the understandings about bilingualism of the state. It was in those gaps that we were able to find space for innovation, resistance, and re-existence of the programs, the schools, the educators, the students, and the family and communities. There were tension and conflicts as we worked through our differences. But we were confident that in cracking the solid traditional understandings of not only monolingualism but also of bilingualism, we would be able to together find the space to create anew. We also hoped that our translanguaging work would help state education departments understand bilingual students differently.

Our work has not been about resistance; it has been about what the contemporary Colombian artist and activist Adolfo Albán Achinte has called re-existence. Achinte's art work makes visible practices of racialization, exclusion, and marginalization. But at the same time, it shows how through aesthetic practices and the senses, it is possible to re-signify life for racialized and minoritized people in conditions of dignity. Translanguaging engages the senses, understandings derived from listening differently, from knowing differently, from touching minoritized people with a different feeling. It is our hope that this enables minoritized bilingual students to re-exist in the mind's eye of educators in their full dignity. It is also our hope that this enables educators to re-exist as dignified policy-makers, negotiating state language education policies for the benefit of the children they teach.

References

Carrasquillo, A.R., Rodríguez, D., & Kaplan, L. (2014). *New York State Education Department policies, mandates, and initiatives on the education of English language learners.* New York, NY: CUNY-NYSIEB.

Cenoz, J. & Gorter, D. (2011). Focus on multilingualism: A study of trilingual writing. *The Modern Language Journal, 95*(3), 356–369.

de Jong, E. (2011). *Foundations for multilingualism in education: From principles to practice.* Philadelphia, PA: Caslon.

García, O. (2009). *Bilingual education in the 21st century: A global perspective.* Malden, MA: Wiley/Blackwell.

García, O. (2011). Educating New York's bilingual children: Constructing a future from the past. *International Journal of Bilingual Education and Bilingualism, 14*(2), 133–153.

García, O. & Menken, K. (2015). Cultivating an ecology of multilingualism in schools: Building interindividuality of voices and ideologies. In B. Spolsky, O. Inbar, & M. Tannenbaum (Eds.), *Challenges for language education and policy: Making space for people* (pp. 95–108). New York, NY: Routledge.

García, O., Johnson, S., & Seltzer, K. (2017). *The Translanguaging classroom: Leveraging student bilingualism for learning.* Philadelphia, PA: Caslon.

García, O., Menken, K., Velasco, P., & Vogel, S. (2018). Dual language bilingual education in New York City: A potential unfulfilled? In B. Arias & M. Fee (Eds.), *Profiles of dual language education in the 21st Century* (pp. 38–55). CAL Series on Language Education. Bristol, UK: Multilingual Matters.

Gort, M. & Sembiante, S. (2015). Navigating hybridized language learning spaces through translanguaging pedagogy: Dual language preschool teachers' languaging practices in support of emergent bilingual children's performance of academic discourse. *International Multilingual Research Journal, 9*(1), 7–25.

Howard, E., Sugarman, J., Christian, D., Lindholm-Leary, K., & Rogers, D. (2007). *Guiding principles for dual language education.* Washington, DC: Center for Applied Linguistics.

Lindholm-Leary, K. & Genesee, F. (2010). Alternative educational programs for English language learners. In California Department of Education (Ed.), *Improving education for English learners: Research-based approaches* (pp. 323–382). Sacramento: CDE Press.

Martínez, R., Hikida, M., & Durán, L. (2015). Unpacking ideologies of linguistic purism: How dual language teachers make sense of everyday translanguaging. *International Multilingual Research Journal, 9*(1), 26–42.

Menken, K. (2012). How have laws regarding English language learners evolved in the United States? In R. Freeman & E. Hamayan (Eds.), *English language learners at school: A guide for administrators* (2nd Edition) (pp. 66–69). Philadelphia, PA: Caslon Publishing.

Menken, K. (2013). Restrictive language education policies and emergent bilingual youth: A perfect storm with imperfect outcomes. *Theory into Practice, 52*(3), 160–168.

Menken, K. & Avni, S. (2017). Challenging linguistic purism in dual language bilingual education: A case study of Hebrew in a New York City public middle school. *Annual Review of Applied Linguistics, 37*, 185–202.

Menken, K. & García, O. (2017). Language policy in classrooms and schools. In T. McCarty & S. May (Eds.), *Language policy and political issues in education* (pp. 1–16). Encyclopedia of language and education (3rd Edition). New York, NY: Springer.

New York City Department of Education. (2015). *Checklist: Primary characteristics of model dual language programs.* New York, NY: Author.

New York State Education Department. (2014). *Chancellor's Regulations Part 154: Services for pupils with limited English proficiency.* Retrieved from http://www.nysed.gov/common/nysed/files/programs/bilingual-ed/terms-154-1-effective-through-2014-15.pdf

New York State Education Department. (2020). *Program options for English language learners/Multilingual learners.* Albany, NY: Author. Retrieved from http://www.nysed.gov/bilingual-ed/program-options-english-language-learnersmultilingual-learners

Otheguy, R., García, O., & Reid, W. (2015). Clarifying translanguaging and deconstructing named languages: A perspective from linguistics. *Applied Linguistics Review*, 6(3), 281–307. https://doi.org/10.1515/applirev-2015-0014

Otheguy, R., García, O., & Reid, W. (2019). A translanguaging view of the linguistic system of bilinguals. *Applied Linguistics Review*, 10(4), 625–651. https://doi.org/10.1515/applirev-2018-0020

Palmer, D., Martínez, R., Mateus, S., & Henderson, K. (2014). Reframing the debate on language separation: Toward a vision for translanguaging pedagogies in the dual language classroom. *The Modern Language Journal*, 98(3), 757–772.

Reyes, L. O. (2006). The aspira consent decree: A thirtieth-anniversary retrospective of bilingual education in New York City. *Harvard Educational Review*, 76(3), 369–400.

Sánchez, M. T., García, O., & Solorza, C. (2018). Reframing language allocation policy in dual language bilingual education. *Bilingual Research Journal*, 41(1), 37–51.

Soltero, S. (2016). *Dual language education: Program design and implementation*. Portsmouth, NH: Heinemann.

Tollefson, J. (Ed.). (2012). *Language policies in education: Critical issues*. New York, NY: Routledge.

3

THE BACKDROP AND ROADMAP OF A TRANSLANGUAGING PROJECT

Tatyana Kleyn and Maite T. Sánchez

Language policies and education in the United States

In order to understand the work of CUNY-NYSIEB (City University of New York-New York State Initiative on Emergent Bilinguals), it is important to contextualize it within the context of language education policies for emergent bilinguals in the United States. Since the late 1800s, community organizations developed bilingual programs in German, French, Spanish, Norwegian, and additional languages. However, the languages of enslaved people and Native Americans were forcefully suppressed (Crawford, 2004; García, 2009). When the United States entered World War I anti-German sentiment and educational policies brought forth Americanization and a hyper focus on the English language. It was not until the end of the 1960s, as part of the struggle for civil rights of racially minoritized groups, that bilingual education became relevant again. But this time, it resulted from the political struggle of Latinx communities against local and state governments that had denied the inclusion of Spanish in education. In 1968, the federal government passed the Bilingual Education Act providing funding to support bilingual programs in schools with large numbers of emergent bilingual students. Bilingual education was also supported in 1974 with the decision of the U.S. Supreme Court in the Lau vs Nichols case, which determined that if a student did not speak English, the mere act of being in a classroom with the same teacher and the same books—all presumably in English—did not constitute an equitable education.

The movement in favor of bilingual education was threatened again in the 1980s, by efforts to make English the official language of the country since the constitution does not designate any language as official. At the beginning of the 21st century, three states passed laws that outlaw bilingual education—California, Arizona, and Massachusetts (California and Massachusetts recently reversed their anti-bilingual education laws). In 2002, the No Child Left Behind Act eliminated the Bilingual Education Act of 1968 to emphasize the acquisition of English, and established standardized achievement tests as the only source of assessment for all students. These exams, which are given primarily in English, have not been designed with bilingual students in mind. In addition, with the increase in immigration, there was a simultaneous rise in conservative, xenophobic, and white supremacy discourse and actions.

The only bilingual programs that have increased in the last decade are the so-called dual language or two-way programs. These bilingual programs generally aim for half of students to be categorized as "English Language Learners (ELLs)" and the other half to be English monolinguals (who are often white and upper middle class). Research warns that these dual language bilingual programs benefit English speakers from the majority more than those who are minoritized (see, for example, Cervantes-Soon, 2014; Valdés, 1997). For the majority students, speaking more than one language is considered a benefit, while for students who already speak a language other than English (LOTE) at home, there are fewer and fewer spaces in bilingual programs (García, 2009).

Language education policies in New York for emergent bilinguals

Educational policies to educate emergent bilinguals in the state of New York are codified in the Commissioner's Regulations (CR Part 154). When a new student enrolls in a New York public school, parents or family members must complete a questionnaire that identifies their home language. If this is not English, they are given an assessment in English to determine their level of proficiency and need for services. When students score below a determined level by the state, they are labeled as an "English Language Learner/Multilingual Learner" (ELL/MLL) instead of "English Proficient" (EP). ELL/MLLs are entitled to two types of programs to support their language development: English as a New Language (ENL) or bilingual education. ENL is the program in which the vast majority of emergent bilinguals participate (83% in 2017 according to the New York City Education Department, 2017) and where English language and content classes are taught primarily through English using specific pedagogy for students who are learning the language. In New York, there are two sanctioned models of bilingual education. The most common is transitional bilingual education (TBE) where the LOTE is used only until the student has learned enough English (measured through another standardized exam). The other program is the so-called dual language (which we have already discussed above). Less than 5% of emergent bilinguals participate in these programs. While New York State is making efforts to increase the number of emergent bilinguals in bilingual programs, just under 20% of students identified as ELL/MLL participate in any type of bilingual education programs. The vast majority of emergent bilinguals in New York receive their education predominantly in English through ENL programs. CUNY-NYSIEB has taken up translanguaging theory and pedagogical practices that respond to this theoretical position to create opportunities that emphasize the dynamic bilingualism of students as beneficial for their learning across programs and content areas. This helps break down the traditional borders that impede language growth and learning for emergent bilingual students.

The CUNY-NYSIEB project

The City Universality of New York (CUNY) is a system of 24 higher education institutions. It consists of two-year community colleges, four-year senior colleges some with graduate programs, a graduate doctoral school (The Graduate Center), and professional schools, such as the Law School and Journalism School. The CUNY colleges are located throughout the five boroughs of New York City. In the following section, we describe the vision of the project, as well as the way in which it operates. We do so to offer a blueprint as to how a state education department, a university system, and K-12 schools can work collaboratively to change practices to educate emergent bilingual students.

Foundations: Vision and principles

The CUNY-NYSIEB vision emanates from students' lives and their linguistic and cultural practices, specifically viewing and referring to them as *emergent bilinguals*. We use this term in place of others that only focus on the learning or absence of English (i.e., ELL or Limited English Proficient/LEP) to emphasize the potential of these students to become bilingual and biliterate, and our vision of how bilingualism emerges. The *vision* of CUNY-NYSIEB is centered on three principles:

1. the creative emergence of individual language practices;
2. the dynamics of bilingualism; and
3. the dynamic processes of teaching and learning of emergent bilinguals (for the entire vision statement, see https://www.cuny-nysieb.org/our-vision/).

The principle of creative emergence of language practices asserts that "bilingual development is not linear, static, or able to reach an ultimate endpoint of completion; rather, it is always emergent, continuous, never-ending, and shaped by relationships with people, texts, and situations" (n.p.). It responds to the contexts in which bilinguals language using their entire repertoire. In this view, a speaker never has a language, but simply uses or performs a language. Through interactions at home, in their community, school and other institutions, bilinguals add linguistic features to their language repertoire, and these features work together in functional interrelationship to shape the bilingual's unitary linguistic system (https://www.cuny-nysieb.org/our-vision/)

The second principle takes the stance that bilingualism is dynamic, and not simply additive (García, 2009). The vision statement continues:

> In our global world, bilingual practices reflect the language user's adaptation to specific communicative situations and to the communicative resources provided by others. Rarely do bilingual individuals learn one language completely and then begin to acquire another. A bilingual speaker is thus never a fully balanced bilingual. Rather, what bilingual speakers do is to language bilingually, or translanguage, in order to make meaning from the complex interactions that are enacted by different human beings and texts (https://www.cuny-nysieb.org/our-vision/)

The final principle—the dynamic processes of teaching and learning—urges educators to encourage and support emergent bilinguals to use their language repertoire in fluid and dynamic ways. When the language practices of bilingual individuals are viewed holistically, rather than as double (or multiple) monolinguals, the pedagogical approach to supporting them also changes. As García and Menken (2015) have said, "bilingual students need to language bilingually, or translanguage, using their entire linguistic repertoire to make meaning and to meet their communicative and academic needs" (p. 99). Educators must provide the affordances and opportunities that are needed for new language practices and understandings to emerge. It is when the right affordances are provided that students can construct new knowledge and understandings of, and with, language. This requires breaking down the rigidity of language separation within classroom so that bilingual individuals can have the affordances and freedom to express themselves fully and to access content completely. In action, teachers honor this tenet when they engage bilingual children with their entire range of language practices, including those associated with English for academic purposes, as their very own. As the vision statement states:

> For bilingual children to successfully perform academically in English, schools support a multilingual context that recognizes the language and cultural practices of bilingual children as an important part of the school's learning community. (https://www.cuny-nysieb.org/our-vision/)

The vision statement has informed the two non-negotiable principles, which all participating CUNY-NYSIEB schools have been required to observe.

Non-negotiable principles

CUNY-NYSIEB worked with schools that vary in myriad ways, and the work that was done with each one was different according to the characteristics of its student body and its local community. However, from the onset, we established two principles that were NOT negotiable for all the schools' participation in CUNY-NYSIEB:

1. That a multilingual ecology be developed in the school, in which all the language practices of the school community were reflected in the visual linguistic landscape and interactions.
2. That the dynamic bilingualism of students, that is their translanguaging, be used in instruction across settings.

Participating schools

For the last seven years, CUNY-NYSIEB has served approximately 70 schools across New York state. To be eligible to participate in the initiative, schools had to apply and meet two criteria: (1) have an above average number of emergent bilingual students and (2) the emergent bilingual students have not met New York State standards in English Language Arts and/or Math. In addition, school principals had to show their commitment to the multifaceted work with the CUNY-NYSIEB team.

Schools admitted to the project have been diverse in many ways. They have been elementary, middle, and high schools. Some of these schools have had only English as a second/new language programs, whereas others have had different types of bilingual programs. In some schools, the majority of students have spoken Spanish, whereas other schools have been very linguistically heterogeneous. In spite of their differences, they all have come together to enact the CUNY-NYSIEB vision in a way that works best for their school-based context, their students, and their communities.

Collaboration and professional development of university faculty

CUNY-NYSIEB has aimed not only to transform practices in schools where there are many emergent bilinguals but also to change the preparation of future bilingual and ENL teachers. For that purpose, we organized a professional team that consisted of bilingual education and ENL professors from five of the CUNY campuses (Brooklyn College, City College of New York, Hunter College, Lehman College, and Queens College) and two professors from the State University of New York (SUNY Buffalo and Fredonia.) Before CUNY-NYSIEB, these professors worked independently, and many did not know each other (see Chapters 16–18, this volume). This professional team was completed with doctoral students in urban education from the CUNY Graduate Center, who were previously bilingual or ENL teachers. The collaboration between professors and doctoral students, who will be the university faculty of the future, resulted in a collective transformation where we worked together with schools to understand the theory of translanguaging and its pedagogical applications.

A multi-level approach

When schools are accepted to CUNY-NYSIEB, their participation is expected on a variety of levels. First, principals and other school leaders must take part in leadership seminars where the vision and non-negotiable principles are presented and deepened. Engaging school principals has been a critical tenet as too many times we have been in schools where we have overheard a Principal tell an Assistant Principal in charge of "ELLs" to do something because "those are not the kids I know about." We wanted to make sure emergent bilinguals were the responsibility of everyone, starting from the school administration. Menken and Solorza (2014) have pointed out that many administrators are not formally prepared with theoretical and practical underpinnings about bilingualism, yet are required to make decisions about programming and practices for emergent bilinguals. We understood the vital role that principals play in schools, and we knew that unless we involved them from the outset, schools and practices cannot be transformed. Because we recognized the importance of distributive leadership (Hunt, 2011), we expected the principals to attend the initial seminars, and then to form an Emergent Bilingual Leadership Team (EBLT) in their schools. The members of these teams were then also invited to participate in the seminars (more on these teams below).

The topics of the Leadership Seminars evolved from the vision and theoretical foundations of dynamic bilingualism and translanguaging and the non-negotiable principles. From there, we moved into translanguaging practices and the strategies that could be used to support translanguaging in different contexts. We discussed current topics including the standards that students were supposed to meet, assessment, immigration, and how translanguaging theory could improve the education of bilingual students.

The all-day seminars were divided into two parts. In the morning, the large group was engaged in lectures that included dialogue and activities. In the afternoon, we broke up into small groups and engaged participants in a process of Collaborative Descriptive Inquiry (CDI). This disciplined process of inquiry derived from the work of Patricia Carini in the Prospect Center for Education and Research (Carini, 2000). The core of the process is, as García and Ascenzi-Moreno (2012) say the "valuing of human capacity to teach and to learn. Through disciplined description of the process of teaching and learning, a group can collaboratively make the complexity of the classroom reality more visible and enlarge understandings that can generate ideas for collective action" (p. 7). Educators came together in small groups by grade levels, geographical area or with their school-based CUNY-NYSIEB teams to reflect and learn from one another. They described their practices and identified areas in which they were grappling related to translanguaging. They were then expected to come up with recommendations for each other, based on their own experiences.

Building off the seminars, work at each school took place in a variety of ways. Each faculty-doctoral student team was responsible to work on-site with three to four schools throughout a year and a half. Each school was required to create an EBLT made up of administrators and teachers from different programs and/ or subject areas. Some schools also included family members and high school students on their EBLT. These teams were then charged with creating a school improvement plan to work with emergent bilinguals (see Chapter 5, this volume). The CUNY-NYSIEB team supported the formation and functioning of the school-based EBLTs.

The faculty member and doctoral student dyad provided support via professional development on translanguaging to teachers and for the EBLT as it implemented the school improvement plan. The teams also worked intensively with a small number of teachers, usually selected or recommended by the principal, to fine-tune their practice and eventually lead the translanguaging work with other teachers in the school. These teachers were selected because they showed interest in translanguaging and demonstrated leadership. The CUNY-NYSIEB teams then coached, modeled, and co-taught with these educators throughout the year.

Following the seminars and school-based visits of the first year, schools in the second year and beyond continued to work with CUNY-NYSIEB in a less intensive manner. They have been invited to attend Circle of Care Seminars that expand on topics addressed in the Leadership Seminars. These sessions have also allowed schools to come together in small groups, deepening the work through CDI in order to consider ways of moving forward. The goal is for schools to take ownership of this work. Some educators and principals from earlier cohorts also return to share their successes and struggles with the newer schools.

Publications and resources

Although the work of CUNY-NYSIEB was initiated in schools across New York, it has been disseminated more broadly through numerous resources that have been produced since its inception. The CUNY-NYSIEB website—www. cuny-nysieb.org—has a range of free resources including guides, videos, web series, webinars, and information about research that has stemmed from the work of CUNY-NYSIEB.

The material developed for the website was initially a response to the needs of CUNY-NYSIEB schools. But over time, the site has become a hub of information for educational scholars and practitioners across the world. The first publication was the *Translanguaging Guide* (Celic & Seltzer, 2012/2013), which has been used in Brazil, Canada, France, Germany, Hong Kong, India, Italy, Spain, South Africa, Sweden, and many other countries. Since then, a number of guides have been published and disseminated through the website. Among them are guides that address the following areas: the 11 most frequently occurring languages of New York State; translanguaging and writing; using translanguaging to adapt prescribed curricula for the needs of emergent bilinguals; teaching different types of emergent bilingual students; using literature where authors translanguage; and many other topics.

The multimodal resources include a web series called "Teaching Bilinguals (Even When You're Not One!)" (www.cuny-nysieb.org/teaching-bilinguals-webseries/). It is made up of five short videos, created by Sara Vogel (2017), to highlight the work of different teacher leaders from a range of programs to show how they learn about their students, approach teaching through a translanguaging lens, and serve as advocates. The website also includes webinars by researchers and educators that lay out their approaches to translanguaging as well as profiles of teacher leaders that demonstrate how they enact a translanguaging pedagogy and stance (see Chapter 7, this volume).

Conclusion

The impact of CUNY-NYSIEB has been far reaching through its multifaceted approach within New York State, where it began, but also globally as its reach has expanded. Our original understandings of translanguaging theory have deepened as the work with schools has expanded and pedagogical practices have been developed (Ascenzi-Moreno & Espinosa, 2017; Espinet, Collins & Ebe, 2018; García, Johnson & Seltzer, 2017; García & Kleyn, 2016; García & Menken, 2015; García & Sánchez, 2015, 2018). We have worked to center bilingual students so that their voices can fully emerge in places where English hegemony has been the norm. CUNY-NYSIEB has worked to challenge power structures while making the teaching and learning process more equitable and inclusive. And this work has been collaborative for those directly involved and accessible for those who seek to learn from this unique initiative.

As we write this, the CUNY-NYSIEB funding cycle has come to an end. It has been eight years of an initiative that has been built with bilingual students and communities at its heart. It has been eight years of an approach that has flourished, not because of, but in spite of long-standing education policies and structures that have not considered emergent bilingual students and their realities. Although the funding has ended the project, the work will continue in different ways.

Translanguaging has been ingrained as a non-negotiable stance for many educators who have been part of CUNY-NYSIEB and for many around the world who have learned with us. Scores of educators have benefitted and continue to do so from the resources and research that has come from this project. The lessons will live on and evolve through the numerous schools, educators, students, families, and scholars who have been a part of the CUNY-NYSIEB familia.

References

Ascenzi-Moreno, L. & Espinosa, C.M. (2017). Opening up spaces for their whole selves: A case study group's exploration of translanguaging practices in writing. *New York State TESOL Journal*, 5(1), 10–29.

Carini, P. (2000). Prospect's descriptive processes. In M. Himley &P. Carini (Eds.), *From another angle: Children's strengths and school standards. The prospect center's descriptive review of the child* (pp. 8–20). New York, NY: Teachers College Press.

Celic, C. & Seltzer, K. (2012/13). *Translanguaging: A CUNY-NYSIEB guide for educators*. New York, NY: CUNY-NYSIEB, The Graduate Center, CUNY, http://www.cuny-nysieb. org

Cervantes-Soon, C. (2014). A critical look at dual language immersion in the new Latin@ diaspora. *Bilingual Research Journal*, 37(1), 64–82.

Crawford, J. (2004). *Educating English learners: Language diversity in the classroom* (5th ed.). Los Angeles, CA: Bilingual Educational Services.

Espinet, I., Collins, B., & Ebe, A. (2018). I'm multilingual: Leveraging students' translanguaging practices to strengthen the school community. In A.M. Lazar &P. Ruggiano Schmidt (Eds.), *Schools of promise for multilingual students: Transforming literacies, learning, and lives* (pp. 118–133). New York, NY: Teachers College Press.

García, O. (2009). *Bilingual education in the 21st century: A global perspective*. Malden, MA: Wiley/Blackwell.

García, O. & Ascenzi-Moreno, L. (2012). How to use this translanguaging guide: The descriptive inquiry process. In C. Celic & K. Seltzer (Eds.), *Translanguaging: A CUNY-NYSIEB guide for educators* (pp. 7–10). New York, NY: CUNY-NYSIEB, The Graduate Center, The City University of New York. http://www.cuny-nysieb.org/wp-content/uploads/2016/04/Translanguaging-Guide-March-2013.pdf

García, O., Johnson, S., & Seltzer, K. (2017). *The translanguaging classroom. Leveraging student bilingualism for learning*. Philadelphia, PA: Caslon.

García, O. & Kleyn, T. (Eds.). (2016). *Translanguaging with multilingual students: Learning from classroom moments*. New York, NY: Routledge.

García, O. & Menken, K. (2015). Cultivating an ecology of multilingualism in schools. In B. Spolsky, O. Inbar-Lourie & M. Tannenbaum (Eds.), *Challenges for language education and policy: Making space for people* (pp. 95–108). New York, NY: Routledge.

García, O. & Sánchez, M. (2015). Transforming schools with emergent bilinguals: The CUNY-NYSIEB project. In I. Dirim, I. Gogolin, D. Knorr, M. Krüger-Potratz, D. Lengyel, H. Reich & W. Weiße (Eds.), *Intercultural education: Festschrift for ulla neumann* (pp. 80–94). Berlin: Waxmann-Verlag.

García, O. & Sánchez, M.T. (2018). Transformando la educación de bilingües emergentes en el estado de Nueva York. *Language, Education, and Multilingualism*, 1(5), 138–156.

Hunt, V. (2011). Learning from success stories: Leadership structures that support dual language programs over time in New York City. *International Journal of Bilingual Education and Bilingualism*, 14(2), 187–206.

Menken, K., & Solorza, C. (2014). No child left bilingual: Accountability and the elimination of bilingual education programs in New York City schools. *Educational Policy, 28*(1), 96–125.

New York City Department of Education (2017). *Division of English Language Learners and Student Support. English Language Learner Demographics Report for the 2016–17 School Year.*

Valdés, G. (1997). Dual-language immersion programs: A cautionary note concerning the education of language-minority students. *Harvard Educational Review*, 67(3), 391–429.

Vogel, S. (Producer). (2017). *Teaching bilinguals: (Even if You're Not One)* [Web series]. CUNY-NYSIEB www.cuny-nysieb.org/teaching-bilinguals-webseries/

SECTION II
Evolving Juntos Structures

4

DIFFERENT LEADERSHIPS: DIFFERENT TIMES

Ivana Espinet, Nelson Flores, Maite T. Sánchez, and Kate Seltzer

Introduction

From the beginning in 2011, CUNY-NYSIEB (City University of New York-New York State Initiative on Emergent Bilinguals) attempted to be collaboratively held and led. Nevertheless, it was the four project directors—Ivana Espinet, Nelson Flores, Maite Sánchez, and Kate Seltzer—who in dialogue with the rest of the team provided the leadership for the project. In this chapter, the four project directors narrate their roles as they took up the leadership of the project over eight years. We start the narrative where it began, with the hiring of Nelson Flores, as interim project director. We continue with the story of the project director who led the project for the longest period of time, five years—Maite Sánchez. We were then fortunate to enjoy the leadership of Kate Seltzer for one year, followed by Ivana Espinet, who was hired to give an end to the funded part of the project, while setting up the structures for the work and the dialogue to continue among team members.

In her book, *Bilingual Education in the 21st Century*, Ofelia García used the banyan tree, common in Southeast Asia, as a metaphor for the interconnectivity and multiplicity of bilingualism and multilingualism. As the four project directors reflected on our practices, we realized that our leadership work was also much like the banyan tree. The ideological foundations of the project, the roots, emerged from Ofelia's work in that book, that moved forward a view that bilingualism is dynamic and an understanding that bilingual speakers engage in translanguaging to make meaning. Throughout the years, the core CUNY-NYSIEB principles guided our work. The banyan tree is grounded vertically and horizontally as it has aerial roots that expand to the sides. As project directors, we built on each other's work, growing our tree vertically at the same time that we spread the roots horizontally, to learn and grow from the work that other members of the team were doing and from the collaboration with educators in a variety of school settings. As a result, while the core values remained the same, our theory and practices around translanguaging grew and evolved.

What is important for the reader to consider as each of us narrates our role is how we were, and continue to be, linked theoretically, ideologically, and practically with each other and with others in the project. Three of us—Flores, Seltzer, and Espinet—received our Ph.D.s from The Graduate Center of the City University of New York, and so we had been close colleagues and had collaborated before. We had been in dialogue with García as our professor and had been exploring concepts such as dynamic bilingualism and translanguaging in our dissertations. Sánchez received her Ph.D. at Boston College and quickly became familiarized with the theoretical grounding of the project, as well as its practical aspects.

As we have stepped away from the project director role and into faculty positions in other institutions, we have carried what we learned in our involvement in CUNY-NYSIEB. While our work has taken us in other directions, we partake of many of the principles that we developed in our role here or have used the lessons learned in these roles to extend understandings. We narrate here how we have been able to hold on to our commitment to improving and changing the education of emergent bilinguals as times have changed, funding priorities shifted, and our experience in schools made us realize what parts of the work were nonnegotiable, and which needed to change. These are our personal leadership stories.

Inception and creation: Flores takes the first steps

In October of 2011, I (Nelson) received a call from Ofelia García. She told me that the New York State Education Department (NYSED) had approached her along with Ricardo Otheguy and Kate Menken to develop a new project that they were calling the CUNY-New York State Initiative on Emergent Bilinguals (CUNY-NYSIEB). They were conceptualizing the project as an effort to apply the theoretical framework of translanguaging to actual classrooms and schools. She asked me if I would be interested in being interim project director for the year while I finished working on my dissertation. I immediately agreed. My immediate goal as interim project director was to recruit CUNY faculty and doctoral students to become members of the CUNY-NYSIEB team. While all of the faculty and doctoral students recruited had relevant expertise in issues related to bilingualism in education, they each brought different disciplinary and classroom perspectives. One of my first jobs was to pair a faculty person with a doctoral student in ways that ensured that their different strengths could complement one another in their work with schools. A second major task was to recruit around 30 schools that were said to be underperforming and that had a very large number of students we call *emergent bilinguals* to become part of the first cohort of CUNY-NYSIEB schools. Yet, I did not want these day-to-day challenges to distract from the long-term goal of supporting the development of an infrastructure for moving translanguaging from theory into practice. Indeed, it was this infrastructure building that would determine the ultimate success and lasting impact of the project.

One of the primary challenges in developing this infrastructure was that some of the theoretical assumptions of a translanguaging stance, such as the idea that named languages are social constructions that have served to marginalize minoritized communities and the rejection of deficit-laden terminology such as "English Language Learner," are fundamentally opposed to the hegemonic theoretical assumptions of mainstream schooling. We found ourselves in somewhat of a dilemma: How do we stay true to a translanguaging stance while being responsive to the day-to-day realities of educators in schools? While I can't say we ever came up with a completely satisfying answer to this question, I do think we worked to develop consensus as to what our tentative answer would be in our work with schools in the first cohort. Our monthly whole team meetings were essential at building this consensus. It was at these meetings where we shared drafts of artifacts such as the "*CUNY-NYSIEB Vision Statement*," and the "*Principles for Principals*," both as a way of building a stronger understanding of how to communicate a translanguaging stance among the team in ways that were responsive to the day-to-day realities of schools. It was also at these meetings where we developed the idea of creating a translanguaging guide that would offer concrete examples of how to implement translanguaging in the classroom. These monthly team meetings also allowed us to incorporate the expertise of the entire team into the final products that were then shared with our partner schools.

We were able to use this emerging consensus of these team meetings as a point of entry ensuring consistent messaging to our partner schools. Our major avenue for this messaging was at the monthly seminars that schools leaderships were expected to attend. We spent the morning at each of these seminars laying the theoretical foundations of translanguaging that we had developed as a team. During the afternoon, we engaged in *collaborative descriptive inquiry* where school leaders had the opportunity to reflect on what they were learning and share the changes that they were planning on making based on what they were learning. In between these monthly seminars, a faculty-student pair would visit each of the schools to provide follow-up support and to guide the school leaders in developing *action plans* that they would implement the following year. By the end of the spring all of the partner schools had developed action plans that they were excited to implement the following year.

While I am proud of all that I accomplished in my year as interim project director at CUNY-NYSIEB, in many ways my most important task was helping to identify a permanent project director. I don't think we could have found a better person than Maite Sánchez who was able to build on and improve the infrastructure that I helped develop in that hectic first year. I left to become an assistant professor at the University of Pennsylvania in Educational Linguistics, where I am now a tenured associate professor.

Developing the work and building collaboration: Sánchez navigates staying on path

I (Maite) took the position of CUNY-NYSIEB project director in July 2012 and stayed until August 2017. When I joined, CUNY-NYSIEB already had strong collaborative processes and structures in place such as bi-weekly meetings between the project director and the co-principal investigators and monthly meetings with all team members. I was impressed by the strong collaborative culture of the CUNY-NYSIEB team, something that I valued and wanted to help sustain and further develop.

During the five years I was the project director, I led the design and implementation of clear processes for ensuring consistency, and easily availability of data collection and sharing among team members. In my first year (the second of CUNY-NYSIEB), I created, with the help of the team, templates for team members' visits reports, and end of the semester and end of the year reflections. For the next four years, these templates were revised to accommodate the needs of the team members and of the work. All these materials helped the team members keep track of the work they did with each of their schools, note observations of what they have seen during their visits, reflect on changes and challenges, and share their ideas on how to address them. For me, the consistency on how this information was collected across teams helped me see how the project was developing across schools. These materials alongside the bi-monthly meetings with each of the teams helped me develop the support systems the team needed.

As we developed our relationship with the first cohort of schools, we realized that a year of support to schools whose students were said to be underperforming was just not enough. Starting with the second cohort, we were able to negotiate with our funding agency, the New York State Education Department. We decreased the number of schools that participated in the project (from 27 the first year, to 16 in year 2, 14 in year 3, and 9 in year 4) so that we could continue supporting them beyond one year.

To ensure the in-school support beyond a year and a half, we organized what we called "*The Circle of Care*" to which all schools were invited to participate. Held once a semester, the Circle of Care seminars included collaborative presentations by members of the CUNY-NYSIEB team and teachers from a CUNY-NYSIEB school. Each meeting featured work related to translanguaging and facilitated activities so that participants reflected on how to implement (or redesign) these activities in their classroom. In this way, we continued to develop relationships with CUNY-NYSIEB schools and to share the important work done by teachers and students.

The decrease in the number of schools beyond the first year also reflected NYSED's interest in expanding our work to schools in upstate and Western New York. This presented a challenge since our team was CUNY-based. To support schools in these new geographical locations (Buffalo, Syracuse, and Rochester), we added to our team faculty affiliated with the State University of New York (SUNY). The schools in Buffalo, Syracuse, and Rochester also had a large number of emergent bilinguals, but many were newly arrived refugees to more rural environments.

During my five years as project director of CUNY-NYSIEB, we witnessed and learned alongside school educators the ways in which they were developing their translanguaging stance and pedagogical practices. As teachers were implementing new strategies in the classroom, many questions arose for which the CUNY-NYSIEB team had no answers. During the monthly team meetings, we also engaged in collaborative descriptive inquiry, grappling with questions that emerged from the experience, and offering each other recommendations for further action. There were two questions to which we returned time and time again. One was: "How can teachers support translanguaging pedagogy if they do not share the languages of the students?" Another was: "How does translanguaging look like in two-way *dual language bilingual programs*?" During those collaborative descriptive sessions, the team brainstormed ideas and identified concrete next steps as well as identified unresolved issues with which we should continue to engage. Many of the issues discussed in the collaborative descriptive inquiry also inspired the team's research agenda. However, we understood that for translanguaging pedagogy to take root in schools, in addition to researching how it worked, we needed to create materials useful for teachers and make them available free of charge. We made sure to redesign materials and resources that team members and teachers developed for their work and made them publicly available on our webpage.

The tension between staying true to developing a translanguaging stance and pedagogy while being responsive to the day-to-day realities of educators in schools was always present over these years. Schools continued to grapple with the hegemony of English evident in federal and state education policies. By 2013, the *Common Core State Standards (CCSS)* were starting to be implemented in New York State. In the years that followed, we witnessed how curricula and materials, and assessments continued to be centered around monolingual English-speaking students; emergent bilinguals were an afterthought, even in bilingual education programs. To address these challenges, we developed a CUNY-NYSIEB guide to show educators how a translanguaging vision and pedagogical practices worked with the standards (Hesson, Seltzer, & Woodley, 2014). To address the question from educators of how translanguaging pedagogical practices could be implemented by teachers who considered themselves monolingual, we developed a series of videos "Teaching Bilinguals [Even if You are Not One]," created by Vogel. We also considered the impact of translanguaging on emergent bilingual students with disabilities. To that end, we developed guidelines, and worked with many bilingual teachers in Integrated Co-Teaching settings (ICT). Many of the contributions in the Teacher/Researcher Boxes address this classroom settings (see, for example, Teacher/Researcher Boxes 8.1, 11.1, and 14.1). We also included on our website classroom videos of teachers who were involved in CUNY-NYSIEB schools. Because we needed to continue to support teachers in thinking about translanguaging and how to implement it in their classrooms, we also created a series of webinars that have been archived on our website. The webinars were open to all participants in CUNY-NYSIEB, as well as teachers of bilingual students throughout New York State.

Research from CUNY-NYSIEB has demonstrated changes in educators' ideologies, leadership practices, and translanguaging pedagogy. However, schools would have benefited from longer in-depth support, as well as wider state and district policies that offset other policies that supported the hegemony of English.

By June 2017, CUNY-NYSIEB had provided direct professional development to 66 schools from different parts of New York State. But it was then that the New York State Education Department changed its funding priorities and requested that the work of CUNY-NYSIEB move away from professional development to solely the development of materials for educators of emergent bilinguals. During my last year, we developed *topic briefs* on how to educate different types of emergent bilingual students accompanied by videos for teachers. We focused on providing instructional ideas and identifying appropriate material. However, we continued supporting, and learning with, a handful of teachers who had participated in our professional development. We also continued to offer the Circle of Care seminars.

The CUNY-NYSIEB team evolved throughout the years. The junior faculty were promoted and received tenure. Doctoral students graduated and became faculty in other institutions (see, Chapter 17, this volume). And yet, everyone continued to be involved in the CUNY-NYSIEB work in one way or another. We have continued holding full-team meetings two to four times a year, in which everyone participates.

I left the project director position when I was hired as assistant professor in the Bilingual Education program at Hunter College, CUNY, in August 2017. I have been fortunate to continue to have an active voice in CUNY-NYSIEB work through my role as advisor to both subsequent project directors, Kate Seltzer and Ivana Espinet.

Bringing back the work with schools: Seltzer reshapes and focuses

When I (Kate) took over the role of project director from Maite in the summer of 2017, I knew there would be challenges as well as exciting possibilities. In addition to braving the steep learning curve of administrating a large research project, my hope was to shift the focus of CUNY-NYSIEB's work—which had centered during the last year on the creation of topic briefs on different sub-populations of students that the state labeled *English Language Learners*—back to what the project always did best: Working directly with classroom teachers on curriculum and instruction.

Though the topic briefs created by the Team were important and informative documents for educators, members of the CUNY-NYSIEB team knew that the greatest impact had always been made through our work in schools. For this reason, in collaboration with the coprincipal investigators and other members of the team, I proposed a scope of work that would enable the team to (a) create a longer-term engagement with teachers who were interested in taking a creative translanguaging approach to their instruction; and (b) work with educational programs where we saw potential for growth in the field—namely early childhood and dual language bilingual education.

For the early childhood work, we proposed collaborations with two schools. In the first school, which had a longstanding commitment to community partnership and the Latinx community, the team would work with teachers in the bilingual prekindergarten and kindergarten classrooms. These teachers had experience with bilingual education but had expressed an interest in growing and extending their practice. In the second school, which was more linguistically and culturally diverse, the team would work with pre-K teachers who had had little experience educating young bilingual children. From both early education programs, the collaborative work resulted in two interrelated resources. The first was a *topic brief on bilingualism and early childhood education* that can serve as a foundational document for teachers' professional development. The second was a framework for educators to create a *Professional Learning Community* (PLC) around early childhood education, play, and bilingualism. (For more on translanguaging in early childhood, see especially Teacher/Researcher Boxes 7.2, 10.1, 11.1, and 15.1).

For the work with dual language bilingual education, we proposed a partnership with a school whose principal, a strong leader who was a consistent advocate for bilingualism and bilingual education, was interested in pushing her program to be more creative and innovative. This leader and the teachers who worked with her were also open to a translanguaging approach to the dual language bilingual model, which traditionally enforces a strict separation of English and the language other than English. At this school, members of the CUNY-NYSIEB team partnered with 4th grade teachers to create a unit that brought together students' language practices in ways that aligned with what Sánchez, García, and Solorza (2017) call *translanguaging transformation*. By organizing this unit around students' bilingualism and bilingual ways of knowing, the team hoped to push the boundaries of dual language bilingual programming and create an exciting learning experience for students. The resources that emerged from this collaboration included a *topic brief on the development of holistic biliteracy in dual language bilingual education programs* and a unit plan that demonstrates how teachers can create transformative spaces for such holistic biliteracy as well as develop students' identities as bilingual readers (for more on this, see Teacher/Researcher Box 12.1).

Lastly, the team also partnered with three teachers at a high school that had been an enthusiastic collaborator with the CUNY-NYSIEB project for several years. Our team worked with three English as a New Language (ENL) teachers to design several instructional units that would enable emergent bilingual students both to add content-specific English practices to their repertoire as well as engage with grade-level content. One unit that was particularly successful with students was centered on preparing them for the high stakes English Language Arts (ELA) Regents Exam (an exam that students in New York State need to pass to graduate from high school) through the use of translanguaging strategies and a multimodal project. The resources that came out of our work with this school became a *topic brief on the development of content-area literacy in secondary classrooms* that serve diverse emergent bilinguals and a resource guide that lays out a genre-based, multilingual approach to preparing diverse students for the ELA Regents Exam (see Teacher/Researcher Boxes 6.1 and 12.1).

Finally, in addition to this school-based work, I endeavored to get the team thinking about CUNY-NYSIEB's legacy after the project officially came to an end the following year. In order to maintain our status as a key resource for educators and researchers interested in classroom translanguaging approaches, we made updates to our website, creating new content as well as an archive of past resources. We also began working on an approach to social media that would keep CUNY-NYSIEB's work visible and accessible. These tactics were all meant to build the project's sustainability so that more and more educators could find practical resources for bringing translanguaging into their practice.

While I was a doctoral student, I had participated in the project as Research Assistant. So when I finished my Ph.D. and became project director, it was not a new beginning, but a continuation of the work I had been doing for five years.

A year later, I was hired as Assistant Professor at Rowan University, where I have continued the work in the TESOL and Bilingual Education programs.

Sunsetting into a new beginning: Espinet rises

I (Ivana) participated in CUNY-NYSIEB as a research assistant for five years, both during the time I was a doctoral student and two years after I received my Ph.D. As with Kate, although my position as project director lasted one year, I felt as if I was now leading a project that had become a part of my intellectual life. I had had a chance to experience different phases of the work and the impact that it had on educators not only in New York State but also all over the world.

As a project director, I wanted to continue to examine, challenge, and grow our understanding of the connections between translanguaging theory and educators' practices, and to set up structures so that the collaboration between the CUNY-NYSIEB team members, some of whom had started as doctoral students and were now faculty, would continue, regardless of CUNY-NYSIEB external funding.

Over the years that I worked with CUNY-NYSIEB, translanguaging theory evolved as we were challenged in our work by policies and practices in schools. In my work as an educator, I found that it was essential to provide space for collaborative reflection and analysis of our practices. One of our challenges was to create spaces in schools for what Sánchez, García, and Solorza (2017) call translanguaging transformation. I, and many of the CUNY-NYSIEB team members, had experience working with educators in inquiry groups modeled after the work of the Prospect Center Descriptive Review (Himley & Carini, 2000), as well as the teacher inquiry groups developed by Fichtman Dana & Yendol-Silva (2003). From this practice, we developed the collaborative descriptive inquiry process in which we had involved the team from the beginning (García & Ascenzi-Moreno, 2012).

During the last year, we engaged with the question of how to provide structures for educators to collaborate on designing translanguaging transformational spaces. We wanted to ensure that they had the space to reflect on their work, share their insights with others beyond their own schools, and write up their experiences. We supported this work in two different settings: (1) working with the entire staff (teachers, service providers, administrators) in one bilingual school and (2) through an inquiry group with a group of teachers of bilingual students in schools in which English was the main language of instruction.

In the dual language bilingual elementary school, we provided professional development for all the teachers and service providers and co-planned a unit with every grade in the school. The goal of the project was for children to become engaged as bilingual ethnographers giving them access to all their meaning-making resources at the same time, something that they were unable to do in a school that separated languages strictly and only made resources available to them in one language or another. Each unit that the grade teams designed was intended to open up a translanguaging space in which the children used their full multimodal repertoires to cocreate knowledge. All the teachers in the school had a chance to share and reflect on their work with their colleagues during professional development sessions. We also set up an inquiry group for teachers who wanted to explore questions about their practices more deeply. During these sessions, the teachers shared student work and their own written reflections and explored their stances as bilingual educators. (See Teacher/Researcher Box 14.1 and Chapter 15, this volume.)

We also started an inquiry group with teachers who worked with emergent bilinguals in settings where English was the medium of instruction. Unlike the teachers in the first project, the students in these teachers' classrooms were very diverse linguistically. Some were high school teachers, others elementary school teachers. When we started the inquiry sessions, everyone had different levels of familiarity with translanguaging. Each teacher created small projects that focused on creating spaces that challenged linguistic boundaries and hierarchies in their classroom so as to challenge the hegemony of English. We met once a month to reflect and think about questions, challenges, and insights that emerged from their work. At the end of the year, they all shared their work in different settings which appears on our website under the teacher leaders' tab. One of the main takeaways from this work was that, in order for our work to continue and evolve, it is essential to cocreate spaces to design and reflect on classroom experiences with educators.

A most important part of the work during the last year was the work we conducted with families. As a parent of bilingual children, I believe that it is essential to reconceptualize the relationships between families and schools (see Chapter 15). While there has been extensive writing about culturally sustainable pedagogies that see families and communities as valuable sources of knowledge, there is still a lot of work to be done to set up spaces to cocreate knowledge and challenge traditional hierarchies. The work with families was twofold:

1. We designed instructional spaces in which families collaborated with educators, both in *dual language bilingual classrooms* and *English as a New Language* classrooms. These spaces focused on bringing and leveraging families' linguistic practices as a source of knowledge.
2. We documented parent advocacy efforts for bilingual education. This portion of the work was inspired by a request from the New York State Education Department, although we extended the scope of our work as we worked with families.

As the project came to an end during this last year, we created resources that can be shared with multiple stakeholders. We shared our work in conferences, academic writing, and on our website as a means to fuel the discussion about how to continue to build translanguaging pedagogical practices. At the end of the year, I was hired as assistant professor at Kingsborough Community College where I work with students who will be teachers.

Reflections

One of the most essential aspects of the work of CUNY-NYSIEB is the intellectual community that we have developed throughout the years. When team members moved on from the CUNY-NYSIEB work because of job- or life-related changes, they continued to be part of the CUNY-NYSIEB Familia. Throughout the years, all team members are invited to participate in advisory meetings. Former members become advisors, providing feedback, helping to develop new materials, and sharing resources.

Many team members have started research projects and professional development projects that have been inspired by their work with CUNY-NYSIEB. The work that was done during many years has inspired the scholarship of many of the CUNY faculty who have continued to develop it. The relationships set up over the course of the project have fostered new collaborations among CUNY faculty and beyond as Familias often do (see Chapters 16, 17, and 18, and Teacher Boxes 12.1, 13.1, and 14.1).

As for the four of us, we have continued to expand the roots of our Banyan tree. The growth in different directions is obvious when we reflect on our work today.

Nelson's roots have expanded both theoretically and practically in his work at the University of Pennsylvania. His work on raciolinguistic ideologies challenges the ways that language and race are co-constructed in ways that frame the language practices of racialized bilingual students as inherently deficient and in need of remediation. This has pushed him to critically interrogate the concept of academic language that is typically used to reinforce deficit perspectives of racialized bilingual students and offer alternative framings that recognize the ways that their language practices are already aligned with state standards. Nelson's work on raciolinguistic ideologies has nourished our critical understandings and furthered our work on translanguaging, deepening our commitment to social justice, and positioning translanguaging as a political act (Flores, 2014).

Maite's roots have taken root in her work with preservice and in-service bilingual education teachers at Hunter College and in her scholarship. Working primarily with bilingual Latinx educators, she creates multiple spaces for them to explore instructional practices in their classrooms that are centered on their students' dynamic bilingualism and community practices. Maite's scholarship not only helps her to extend and deepen the work of CUNY-NYSIEB by focusing on understanding the transformative powers of translanguaging pedagogy, but also in knowing its limits. This work requires a collaborative endeavor with which teachers, students, families, colleagues, and other scholars, something that CUNY-NYSIEB has cultivated and nurtured.

Kate's branches and aerial roots have spread into a new context. At Rowan University, located outside Philadelphia, she works with teachers who teach (or plan to teach) in more suburban areas where there are fewer emergent bilinguals and bilingual programs. In working with these educators, she harkens back to the tenet that always guided the project and her work as Project Director: No matter where we do the work, we must create opportunities for all students to leverage their bilingualism and diverse linguistic resources for their learning. In this way, she will always be a part of the CUNY-NYSIEB project and will continue to root herself—and the educators she works with—in its vision of a more equitable and just education for emergent bilingual students.

Ivana's roots and branches have expanded in her work with students at Kingsborough Community College where many of her students are multilingual and most are students of color. Community colleges are institutions that offer two years of higher education beyond high school and students graduate not with a Bachelor's degree, but with what is called an Associate degree. Many of these students do not go on to four-year colleges, although some transfer to continue their education. Most of Ivana's students have been educated in U.S. schools that did not value their bilingualism. Others are immigrants who were schooled in other countries. To this community college setting, Ivana brings the CUNY-NYSIEB's pedagogical practices to help her students examine their own educational experiences and reflect on how language has been used to stigmatize their language practices. Because Ivana's bilingual students are planning to be paraprofessionals in schools or teachers, she also supports them so that they can leverage their future students' bilingualism, freeing them from the strictures of standard English that schools promote.

While we are all working at different institutions now, we continue to learn from each other. Our different contexts enable us to expand our theoretical and practical understanding of what it means to foster a translanguaging stance and implement pedagogical practices that would leverage bilingual students' translanguaging. We have taken translanguaging into higher education, and especially into teacher education programs. Despite our different contexts—a private elite university, two public universities in two different states, and a public community college context—the students we prepare to teach bilingual students face the same challenges. Our grounding in a translanguaging stance enables us to view our bilingual students' strengths and their translanguaging as an important resource for their education.

References

Fitcham Dana, N. & Yendol-Silva, D. (2003). *The Reflective educator's guide to classroom research: Learning to teach and teaching to learn through practitioner inquiry.* Thousand Oaks, CA: Corwin Press.

Flores, N. (2014). Let's not forget that translanguaging is a political act. Retrieved from https://educationallinguist.wordpress.com/2014/07/19/lets-not-forget-that-translanguaging-is-a-political-act/

García, O. & Ascenzi-Moreno, L. (2012). How to use this translanguaging guide: The descriptive inquiry process. In C. Celic and K. Seltzer, *Translanguaging: A CUNY-NYSIEB guide for educators* (pp. 7–10). New York, NY: CUNY-NYSIEB, The Graduate Center, The City University of New York. http://www.cuny-nysieb.org/wp-content/uploads/2016/04/Translanguaging-Guide-March-2013.pdf

Hesson, S., Seltzer, K., & Woodley, H. H. (2014). Translanguaging in curriculum and instruction: A CUNY-NYSIEB guide for educators. CUNY-NYSIEB. https://www.cuny-nysieb.org/wp-content/uploads/2016/05/Translanguaging-Guide-Curr-Inst-Final-December-2014.pdf

Himley, M. & Carini, P. F. (2000). *From another angle: Children s strengths and school standards.* New York, NY: Teachers College Press.

Sánchez, M. T., García, O., & Solorza, C. (2017). Reframing language allocation policy in dual language bilingual education. *Bilingual Research Journal*, 1–15. https://doi.org/10.1080/15235882.2017.1405098

5

EMERGENT BILINGUAL LEADERSHIP TEAMS

Distributed leadership in CUNY-NYSIEB schools

Maite T. Sánchez and Kate Menken

Introduction

Unlike many countries where there is a central ministry of education that determines educational practices in schools, the educational system of the U.S. is highly decentralized, leaving a wide range of decisions regarding curriculum and instruction in the hands of states and local educational authorities. Although restricted by state and other local regulations, school leaders in the U.S. can be influential in shaping a school's language policy and the overall quality of schooling that emergent bilinguals receive (Ascenzi-Moreno, Hesson & Menken, 2016; DeMatthews & Izquierdo, 2017; García & Menken, 2015; Hunt, 2011; Menken & Solorza, 2014; Reyes, 2006; Rodriguez & Alanís, 2011; Scanlan & López, 2012; Theoharis & O'Toole, 2011; Wiemelt & Welton, 2015). It is for this reason that school leaders are a central focus in the work of CUNY-NYSIEB (City University of New York-New York State Initiative on Emergent Bilinguals).

In this chapter, we describe how distributed leadership structures were put into place in CUNY-NYSIEB schools across New York State through the establishment of what we term "Emergent Bilingual Leadership Teams" (EBLTs). Distributed leadership refers to leadership that is shared among several people who are all involved in decision-making (Leithwood, Mascall & Strauss, 2009; Spillane, 2006). Accordingly, CUNY-NYSIEB adopted this more expansive definition of school leadership to include all members of a school's EBLT. We begin this chapter by locating our efforts within existing research about distributed leadership. We then describe the work of EBLTs in CUNY-NYSIEB schools generally, before offering a detailed example of distributed leadership within one CUNY-NYSIEB high school.

The importance of distributed leadership

U.S. schooling in recent history has been characterized by restrictive language education policies, which limit the use of students' home languages in instruction (Gándara & Hopkins, 2010; McField, 2014; Menken, 2013; Wiley & García, 2016). Federal education policies have emphasized high-stakes testing in English, and this has resulted in a causal link between high-stakes testing and the dismantling of bilingual education programs (García & Kleifgen, 2018; Menken & Solorza, 2014; Palmer et al., 2015). This means that in most U.S. school systems, there will be pressure on school leaders to offer English-only instruction. School leaders interested in offering bilingual approaches must therefore be able to navigate these pressures to preserve and protect spaces within their schools for languages other than English. By making the home language practices of all students central in their education, the CUNY-NYSIEB project demands leadership that is able to go against restrictive policy tides so as to disrupt English-only norms as well as strict language separation in bilingual education programs.

The unfortunate reality, however, is that few school administrators have the preparation they need to do so. Meeting the educational needs of emergent bilinguals necessitates school leaders who are knowledgeable about bilingualism, bilingual education, and about their school's emergent bilingual student population (Brooks, Adams & Morita-Mullaney, 2010; Howard et al., 2018; Hunt, 2011; Menken & Solorza, 2015; Scanlan & López, 2012).

There is a body of research arguing for distributed leadership (also known as collaborative leadership) in the education of emergent bilinguals (Ascenzi-Moreno, Hesson & Menken, 2016; Brooks, Adams & Morita-Mullaney, 2010; DeMatthews & Izquierdo, 2017; Hunt, 2011; Scanlan & López, 2012; Tupa & McFadden, 2009). While taking this approach would not altogether eliminate the need for school administrators to be knowledgeable and prepared, it would share the responsibilities of the school principal with others, and bring educators with expertise in bilingual education and language learning into positions of leadership within a school's leadership structure. Rather than thinking of leadership as concentrated in one individual, distributed leadership considers leadership as interactive and shared among multiple official and unofficial leaders (Leithwood, Mascall & Strauss, 2009). According to Spillane (2006), viewing leadership from a distributed perspective "means that education policymakers must acknowledge that the work of leading schools involves more than the leadership of the school principal" (Spillane, 2006, p. 101).

Thus, leadership according to this perspective is not limited to the principal, allowing for decisions to be determined by teachers with expertise in language learning—such as bilingual and English as a new language (ENL—also known as English as a second language [ESL]) teachers. Brooks, Adams and Morita-Mullaney (2010) examine formal and informal school leaders in schools serving emergent bilinguals, not only noting the important role of teachers as informal leaders but also critiquing traditional school designs where teachers are typically not well-positioned within a school's leadership structures to make schoolwide decisions. The role of teachers as unofficial school leaders is significant, as teachers often act as language policymakers (de Jong, 2011; Menken & García, 2010; Malsbary, 2016; Palmer et al., 2015). Research findings show that when teachers of emergent bilinguals interpret and implement policies in their classrooms, they create new policies in the process, and are thereby language policymakers in their own right (Menken & García, 2010). Recognizing their significant role in language policy making, distributed leadership repositions teachers from being unofficial school leaders to official ones.

Distributed leadership in schools with emergent bilinguals has been found as essential in supporting the needs of these students. In her investigation of successful dual language bilingual programs that have been sustained over time, Hunt (2011) identified collaborative and shared leadership as one of four leadership structures (along with mission, trust, and flexibility). Similarly, in their case study of a bilingual public school, Ascenzi-Moreno and Flores (2012) found that distributed leadership involving shared decision-making among school leaders, teachers, parents, and students allowed for the development of flexible and responsive language education policies that the authors argued reflected the academic and social needs of students. Ascenzi-Moreno, Hesson and Menken (2016) examined the process of school reform in three CUNY-NYSIEB schools engaged in efforts to develop and implement multilingual language education policies that would replace monolingual ones. They found that these efforts were associated with changes in school leadership practices as well. Specifically, they found that distributed leadership replaced hierarchical leadership in schools seeking to support bi/multilingualism and adopt policies promoting multilingualism.

Moreover, the literature is convincing that distributed leadership in schools with emergent bilinguals is key to ensuring student needs are met by bringing bilingual educators and other educators with expertise in language learning and emergent bilingual students into decision-making positions. It is for this reason that CUNY-NYSIEB promoted the adoption of distributed leadership structures in participating schools, as described below.

Distributed leadership in CUNY-NYSIEB: The rationale and design of Emergent Bilingual Leadership Teams

Since its inception, CUNY-NYSIEB envisioned leadership that was distributed in order to improve the learning experiences of emergent bilinguals in participating schools (García & Menken, 2015; Movit, Petrykowska & Woodruff, 2010). Specifically, the project required that schools participating in CUNY-NYSIEB each commit to creating an EBLT comprised of the principal, other key administrators, bilingual teachers, ENL teachers, general education teachers, content specialists, special education teachers, parents/families of emergent bilinguals, and/or students. EBLTs were generally composed of four to six members.

A school's formal participation in CUNY-NYSIEB started with attendance at the first of a series of Leadership Seminars held at the CUNY Graduate Center (see Chapter 3, this volume). The first Seminar meeting included principals of each participating school and two to three other educators per school, and participants were introduced to the CUNY-NYSIEB vision and the nonnegotiable principles for participating schools: (1) developing their school's multilingual ecology and (2) using students' bilingualism as a resource in instruction. They also were guided on how to form an EBLT using the Emergent Bilingual Leadership Team: Planning Resource Packet (CUNY-NYSIEB, 2016). Principals returned to their schools after the first Seminar meeting and, within the next month, established their school's EBLT. EBLTs were to meet bi-weekly, at least in the first few months of initiating the work, and then monthly or bi-monthly.

The responsibilities of CUNY-NYSIEB EBLTs included the following:

- Study the schools' services for emergent bilinguals;
- Create a plan to improve their instruction and programming aligned to CUNY-NYSIEB's nonnegotiable principles;
- Oversee the implementation of the plan; and,
- Develop their school's language policy vision.[1]

CUNY-NYSIEB support teams assigned to each school met with one or more EBLT members during their monthly school visits. They used the different tools available in the CUNY-NYSIEB Emergent Bilingual Leadership Team: Planning Resource Packet (CUNY-NYSIEB, 2016) to support and guide their work. In the next five months, EBLTs created an implementation plan where they detailed changes that they wanted to make in their schools to improve the education of their emergent bilinguals aligned to the two nonnegotiable principles of CUNY-NYSIEB. EBLT members did not have to make all the changes by themselves, but involved other school and community members, as well as the CUNY-NYSIEB support team working with their school.

While all schools that participated in CUNY-NYSIEB created EBLTs as a requirement of their participation in the project, in some schools, the EBLTs changed school leadership practices in ways that went far beyond what was required by CUNY-NYSIEB for the school's formal participation in the project (Ascenzi-Moreno, Hesson & Menken, 2016). In these schools, EBLT members became the leadership body of the school for emergent bilinguals and had collaborative decision-making powers. These EBLT members guided long-term changes in the school. One such example is presented below.

KAPPA's emergent bilingual leadership team and their work

The case narrative presented in this section describes the work of the EBLT at one CUNY-NYSIEB school, Knowledge, and Power Preparatory Academy (KAPPA), which exemplifies how distributed leadership can lead to changes over time to improve and transform the education of emergent bilinguals (for more information about the work of CUNY-NYSIEB at KAPPA, also see Espinet, Collins & Ebe, 2018). KAPPA is a public high school (grades 9–12) located in the Bronx, New York City. The school serves 500 students, 90% of whom are considered economically disadvantaged as measured by the need to receive free or reduced-price school meals. The majority of the population are students of color—Latinx (60%) and Black (33%). Most students in the school speak a language other than English at home, with Spanish being the predominant language other than English, followed by Arabic, Bengali, Urdu, and several African languages. Approximately 15% of students have been formally identified as emergent bilinguals, and almost 10% of these students have been identified as students with interrupted formal education (SIFE) (in New York, this means that students are assessed at least three grades below level).

When KAPPA's principal applied to be part of CUNY-NYSIEB in the 2014–2015 school year, she stated that the school needed to focus on better serving the emergent bilingual student population. While the principal had been a bilingual educator herself at another school, KAPPA only offered emergent bilinguals ENL programming, in which emergent bilinguals received instruction monolingually in English. When the principal convened her EBLT, she started by inviting the three ENL teachers of the school. The ENL teachers were very encouraged by the formation of a team to reflect on how emergent bilinguals could best be supported throughout the school.

In the first month of work, the EBLT met at the Leadership Seminars and in the school with the CUNY-NYSIEB Support Team. While the principal participated in the EBLT meetings on a few occasions, the three teachers quickly took over the EBLT, involving the principal once the group reached consensus on any changes they recommended. Of the three teachers, Ms. Weber (pseudonym) assumed responsibility for convening the meetings and coordinating with the CUNY-NYSIEB support team. During the first few meetings, the EBLT had conversations around their students' needs and decided that the plan for the school was to create spaces for students to use their home languages at school, develop professional development for all teachers in the building to learn about translanguaging pedagogy, and build multilingualism and multiculturalism into the curriculum design. Because students' experiences were so central in the work of the EBLT, the teachers invited two students to join the EBLT. While the students were unable to participate in all of the EBLT meetings, they played a very active role—particularly in identifying students' needs and helping to design experiences to support KAPPA's students.

The EBLT began to reflect on the school's multilingual ecology by doing a walk-through of the school. They noticed that all the signs in the school's entryway and hallways, including the samples of student work that were displayed, were only in English. The EBLT members with support from other teachers enriched their multilingual ecology by visually representing the languages spoken by students at the school. They created new signage around the school and multilingual word walls in classrooms, where vocabulary words were translated into one or more of the students' languages. Student EBLT members, with the help of other students, surveyed their classmates about how their home languages and cultures were represented in the school and what they would like to improve. The EBLT analyzed the results of the student surveys and proposed that the school start organizing an after-school multicultural club that was open to any student who wanted to participate. A few weeks later, students and teachers started running after-school club.

The EBLT also decided to expand their efforts to reach out to bilingual families in the community to recruit new KAPPA students from the community. During the next Open House Night, for the first time, student ambassadors communicated with prospective parents in various home languages. After the success of the Open House Night, students continued to volunteer to be translators for other events with parents, including Parent-Teacher Nights when families had the opportunity to meet with their children's teachers at the school. The EBLT also started a bilingual bulletin board with important information for parents of children enrolled at the school. The principal described the impact of these efforts on families in the following interview excerpt:

> The parents are impressed when they see how the students articulate the vision of the school in their native language and that has given a sense of familiarity and trust, so those parents, and the students as well, are quick to identify our school as a safe environment and a communal environment, and it's because our own students have taken a leadership role and they want to reach out. (Cited in Espinet, Collins & Ebe, 2018, p. 121)

What is more, distributing school leadership to involve students by including them in the EBLT resulted in positive changes in the school's relationship with local families.

The distribution of the school's leadership also resulted in efforts by the EBLT to improve instruction for emergent bilinguals through the implementation of translanguaging pedagogy. The principal and the EBLT had received professional development on translanguaging and, with the support of the CUNY-NYSIEB team, Ms. Weber provided professional development and targeted supports for teachers across the school. These teachers in turn began to incorporate translanguaging pedagogy in their classes. Another ENL teacher described this as follows:

> We did a lot of reading in English, translating it or summarizing it in their home language, and reading the prompt in English, translating [it] to Spanish. Some students were able to read the prompt and answer it in Spanglish right away – English and Spanish mixed in – and I found that to be really positive experience; and some of the students too, they were able to understand the content and move back and forth between the two languages. (ENL Teacher, personal communication, May 2015)

The work of the EBLT at KAPPA resulted in changes to instruction that enabled students to better understand and ultimately master course content, and that increased student participation.

When CUNY-NYSIEB started working with KAPPA, emergent bilinguals were placed into any classroom with students who were not learning English. They received a prescribed number of hours of ENL instruction each day according to their designated English proficiency level, as per the New York State guidelines. The EBLT decided to improve their support for their many Spanish-speaking students, particularly newcomers, in learning English and academic content by creating math and science sections just for them. Two of the teacher leaders on the EBLT spoke Spanish and they worked collaboratively with teachers of social studies, math, and science in a collaborative team-teaching model (Friend & Cook, 2016). Emergent bilingual students in those sections started receiving home language instruction and were encouraged to work together using their entire linguistic repertoire to complete assignments.

This collaborative team-teaching model in which ENL and content area teachers worked together to address the needs of emergent bilinguals, many of whom had interrupted schooling, was very successful. Ms. Weber reflected on the impact of this collaboration as follows: "It's becoming a whole-school topic rather than an ENL and co-teacher conversation, which is tremendously exciting!" (cited in Espinet, Collins & Ebe, 2018, p. 124). In other words, the changes made by the EBLT had schoolwide impact.

For two years, EBLT members and the principal deepened their conversations about the importance of offering a formal bilingual education program so that emergent bilinguals could not only improve their learning of course content but also build bilingualism and biliteracy. In spring 2016, they applied to the New York City Department of Education to open a bilingual program and were approved to start the program in the 2017–2018 school year. KAPPA now offers bilingual education in grades with the largest numbers of newcomers, with plans to expand the program over time to all grades. In the grades where bilingual education is not currently provided through a formal bilingual program, the school continues to offer the collaborative team teaching model with Spanish support. The distribution of leadership at KAPPA has resulted in significant changes to their educational programming for emergent bilinguals and has increased their support for language learning.

Distributed leadership and the EBLT at KAPPA

In support of the findings by Ascenzi-Moreno, Hesson and Menken (2016), this movement from hierarchical to collaborative leadership structures within CUNY-NYSIEB schools through the creation and adoption of EBLTs has improved their programming for emergent bilinguals. This is particularly the case at KAPPA. At the start of the school's participation in the CUNY-NYSIEB project, the principal knew that the school needed to make changes to support their growing population of emergent bilinguals, most of whom spoke Spanish and many of whom had experienced interrupted formal education. She understood that for meaningful changes to occur, she needed to strategically bring the three ENL teachers in the school together into the EBLT to leverage their expertise to design and implement school-wide changes (Brooks, Adams & Morita-Mullaney, 2010; Spillane, 2006). The principal was part of the EBLT at the beginning, and would join it when needed, but it was largely teachers with expertise in the education of emergent bilinguals who were given a formal structure to be language policymakers in the school (de Jong, 2011; Malsbary, 2016; Menken & García, 2010; Palmer et al., 2015).

Leadership at KAPPA has been distributed beyond teachers alone. The teacher leaders involved in the EBLT recognized that if they were to address the needs of students, they needed to distribute school leadership even further by including students in the decision-making process. There is a dearth of research on the role of students in school leadership or as agents of language policy, but the case of KAPPA demonstrates the power of student leadership in decision-making regarding the education of emergent bilinguals. Students know what their needs are and can actively engage fellow students and their families. Many of the changes made at KAPPA were student led.

That said, principals are extremely important in shaping the school's language policy and the overall quality of schooling that emergent bilinguals receive. Simply put, principals can make or a break a program for emergent bilinguals. Unlike the principals of CUNY-NYSIEB schools that Ascenzi-Moreno, Hesson and Menken (2016) studied, who did not have much formal preparation or experience in the education of emergent bilinguals, KAPPA's principal had been a bilingual teacher herself. However, her participation in CUNY-NYSIEB not only deepened her understandings about students' home language practices in their education, it also galvanized the distribution of leadership at her school to allow teachers and students to lead major decision-making. The principal was very supportive of the EBLT and approved all of the requests that they made. When the EBLT needed to bring other teachers to discuss collaborative team teaching, they had the full support of the principal. When they recommended that the school open a Spanish-English bilingual program, the principal worked with the EBLT to complete the NYC Department of Education application.

As the work of the EBLT continued, the principal acknowledged that there needed to be an even more formalized acknowledgment of emergent bilinguals at the center of the school's mission. She created a new position for an Assistant Principal solely responsible for overseeing the needs of emergent bilinguals in the school and promoted Ms. Weber to this position. Ms. Weber has continued being part of the EBLT, which now has greater school-wide formal recognition. This case highlights the important role of school principals in enacting distributed leadership, and how this can impact the education of emergent bilinguals.

Conclusion and action steps

In conclusion, leadership practices in many schools tend to be top-down, with the principal as the primary or sole decision maker. However, the research support for distributed leadership in schools serving emergent bilinguals is an important consideration for school leaders. Especially because principals in most schools do not have as much expertise in the education of emergent bilinguals as specialist teachers, leadership needs to be distributed more widely in schools for emergent bilinguals.

CUNY-NYSIEB Emergent Bilingual Leadership Teams offer a model for doing so. The example of KAPPA shows the changes that the school has been able to make in support of emergent bilinguals by the EBLT with the support of the principal. For other schools serving emergent bilinguals, we recommend that they form EBLTs comprised of the school principal, other key administrators, bilingual and ENL teachers, general education teachers, skill and content specialists, special education teachers, parents/families of emergent bilinguals, and/or students. This collective focus on the education of emergent bilinguals and shared decision-making has proven to be transformative within CUNY-NYSIEB schools and can easily be replicated elsewhere.

To do so, we encourage readers to download the CUNY-NYSIEB Emergent Bilingual Leadership Team: Planning Resource Packet (2016), which includes many activities for EBLTs that were used to guide the work of EBLTs at CUNY-NYSIEB schools (it can be accessed for free online at: https://www.cuny-nysieb. org/wp-content/uploads/2016/05/CUNY-NYSIEB-EBLT-Resource-Package-2015-2016-09-17-15-Final.pdf). We recommend that interested schools begin by completing "Item A: Emergent Bilingual Leadership Team (EBLT)" (pp. 15–17), which offers an activity and considerations to help schools form an EBLT, and then move on to complete other activities in the packet as team members start analyzing the school services to emergent bilinguals and plan changes.

Note

1 School language policies determine which languages will be used in instruction and how those languages will be taught. Individual school language policies in New York are usually implicit rather than explicit, and evident only in a school's language programming choices. Schools participating in CUNY-NYSIEB developed language policy statements to make their broader vision for language teaching, learning, and programming explicit.

References

Ascenzi-Moreno, L. & Flores, N. (2012). A case study of bilingual policy and practices at the Cypress Hills Community School. In O. García, B. Octu, & Z. Zakharia (Eds.), *Bilingual community education and multilingualism: Beyond heritage languages in a global city* (pp. 219–231). Bristol, UK: Multilingual Matters.

Ascenzi-Moreno, L., Hesson, S., & Menken, K. (2016). School leadership along the trajectory from monolingual to multilingual. *Language and Education, 30*(3), 197–218.

Brooks, K., Adams, S., & Morita-Mullaney, T. (2010). Creating inclusive learning communities for ELL students: Transforming school principals' perspectives. *Theory Into Practice, 49*(2), 145–151.

CUNY-NYSIEB (2016). *Emergent bilingual leadership team: Planning resource packet.* New York, NY: Author. Retrieved 4/29/19 from https://www.cuny-nysieb.org/wp-content/uploads/2016/05/CUNY-NYSIEB-EBLT-Resource-Package-2015-2016-09-17-15-Final.pdf

de Jong, E. (2011). *Foundations for multilingualism in education: From principles to practice.* Philadelphia, PA: Caslon.

DeMatthews, D. & Izquierdo, E. (2017). The importance of principals supporting dual language education: A social justice leadership framework. *Journal of Latinos and Education*, published online, 1–18.

Espinet, I., Collins, B., & Ebe, A. (2018). I'm multilingual: Leveraging students' translanguaging practices to strengthen the school community. In A. M. Lazar & P. Ruggiano Schmidt (Eds.), *Schools of promise for multilingual students: Transforming literacies, learning, and lives* (pp. 118–133). New York, NY: Teachers College Press.

Friend, M., & Cook, L. (2016). *Interactions: Collaboration skills for school professionals.* (8th ed.). Pearson. https://www.pearson.com/us/higher-education/product/Friend-Interactions-Collaboration-Skills-for-School-Professionals-Loose-Leaf-Version-8th-Edition/9780134256795.html

Gándara, P. & Hopkins, M. (Eds.). (2010). *Forbidden language: English learners and restrictive language policies.* New York, NY: Teachers College Press.

García, O. & Kleifgen, J. (2018). *Educating emergent bilinguals: Policies, programs and practices for English learners* (2nd ed.). New York, NY: Teachers College Press.

García, O. & Menken, K. (2015). Cultivating an ecology of multilingualism in schools: Building interindividuality of voices and ideologies. In B. Spolsky, O. Inbar, & M. Tannenbaum (Eds.), *Challenges for language education and policy: Making space for people* (pp. 95–108). New York, NY: Routledge.

Howard, E., Lindholm-Leary, K., Rogers, D., Olague, N., Medina, J., Kennedy, B., Sugarman, J., & Christian, D. (2018). *Guiding principles for dual language education* (3rd ed.). Washington, DC: Center for Applied Linguistics.

Hunt, V. (2011). Learning from success stories: leadership structures that support dual language programs over time in New York City. *International Journal of Bilingual Education and Bilingualism, 14*(2), 187–206.

Leithwood, K., Mascall, B., & Strauss, T. (Eds.). (2009). *Distributed leadership according to the evidence.* New York, NY: Routledge.

Malsbary, C. (2016). The refusal: Teachers making policy in NYC. *International Journal of Qualitative Studies in Education, 29*(1), 1326–1338.

McField, G. (Ed.). (2014). *The miseducation of English learners: A tale of three states and lessons to be learned.* Charlotte, NC: Information Age Publishing.

Menken, K. (2013). Restrictive language education policies and emergent bilingual youth: A perfect storm with imperfect outcomes. *Theory into Practice, 52*(3), 160–168. doi: https://doi.org/10.1080/00405841.2013.804307

Menken, K. & García, O. (Eds.). (2010). *Negotiating language policies in schools: Educators as policymakers.* New York, NY: Routledge.

Menken, K. & Solorza, C. (2015). Principals as linchpins in bilingual education: The need for prepared school leaders. *International Journal of Bilingual Education and Bilingualism, 18*(6), 676–697.

Menken, K. & Solorza, C. (2014). No child left bilingual: Accountability and the elimination of bilingual education programs in New York City schools. *Educational Policy, 8*(1), 96–125.

Movit, M., Petrykowska, I., & Woodruff, D. (2010). *Using school leadership teams to meet the needs of English language learners.* Issue Brief. Washington, DC: National Center on Response to Intervention.

Palmer, D., Henderson, K., Wall, D., Zúñiga, C., & Berthelsen, S. (2015). Team teaching among mixed messages: Implementing two-way dual language bilingual education at third grade in Texas. *Language Policy, 15*(4), 393–413.

Reyes, A. (2006). Reculturing principals as leaders for cultural and linguistic diversity. In K. Tellez & H. Waxman (Eds.), *Preparing quality educators for English language learners: Research, policy, and practice* (pp. 145–165). Mahwah, NJ: Lawrence Erlbaum.

Rodriguez, M. & Alanís, I. (2011). Negotiating linguistic and cultural identity: One borderlander's leadership initiative. *International Journal of Leadership in Education, 14*(1), 103–117.

Scanlan, M. & López, F. (2012). ¡Vamos! How school leaders promote equity and excellence for bilingual students. *Educational Administration Quarterly, 48*(4), 583–625.

Spillane, J. (2006). *Distributed leadership.* San Francisco, CA: Jossey-Bass.

Theoharis, G. & O'Toole, J. (2011). Leading inclusive ELL: Social justice leadership for English language learners. *Educational Administration Quarterly, 47*(4), 646–688.

Tupa, M. & McFadden, L. (2009). Excellence is never an accident. *Phi Delta Kappan, 90*, 554–556.

Wiemelt, J. & Welton, A. (2015). Challenging the dominant narrative: Critical bilingual leadership (liderazgo) for emergent bilingual Latin@ students. *International Journal of Multicultural Education, 17*(1), 82–101.

Wiley, T. & García, O. (2016). Language policy and planning in language education: Legacies, consequences, and possibilities. *Modern Language Journal, 100*(S1), 48–63.

6

WORKING JUNTOS AND ACROSS

Bilingual education, English as a
second language, English language
arts and community engagement

*Brian A. Collins, Meral Kaya,
Liza N. Pappas, and Karen Zaino*

Introduction

From the very beginning, the CUNY-NYSIEB (City University of New York-New York State Initiative on Emergent Bilinguals) project had a commitment to work with all schools, programs, and stake-holders in order to support the success of emergent bilingual students. The project carefully sought out the participation of teacher education faculty and researchers, both established and those who were doctoral students and entering the profession, school leaders, and teachers in both bilingual education and ESL programs. This chapter puts alongside the different interests and experiences of the authors and how our work overlapped with common goals. We do this to highlight how our different perspectives added to the implementation of the CUNY-NYSIEB vision, and how we negotiated the differences.

At a time in which the profession is more divided than ever into separate interest groups—those of bilingual educators and those of the TESOL profession—we show here how we were able to negotiate our different interests because our larger purposes were the same. We worked for the benefit of racialized and minoritized bilinguals, their families, and communities. As we worked alongside each other, we learned much about our different perspectives. Here, Collins outlines his role as associate investigator in the project when he was the faculty coordinator of a program to educate teachers of bilingual education. Kaya, however, was educating teachers of English as a second language (ESL), when she joined the project as associate investigator. Pappas became a research assistant as she was completing her doctoral studies in Urban Education policy. Her professional interests had always incorporated family and community engagement, which she brought to the project and writes here about how she extended our work with this interest. Finally, Zaino was just beginning her doctoral studies when we tapped her to colead a translanguaging study group with teachers. A seasoned and committed educator, she brought commitment and developed strategies together with the teachers, as she herself was grounded in translanguaging theory.

Educating teachers for bilingual education classrooms: Collins negotiates bilingual education policies, programs, and translanguaging practices

Bilingual education in New York State is typically offered through either dual language bilingual education or transitional bilingual education programs. In *dual language bilingual programs*, instruction and learning are in both English and a language other than English with a goal of bilingualism and biliteracy. The languages are often strictly isolated and schools vary in how they alternate languages by day, week, or subject. Teachers and students only use the designated language at specific times, classrooms, and subject areas, according to the school or district's language allocation policy. Most dual language programs in New York State are designated as two-way, meaning that there are not only learners of English, but also learners of the other language of instruction (see, for example, Teacher/Researcher Boxes 8.1, 14.1, and 15.1). There are also, however, one-way dual language bilingual programs in which all the children belong to the same language group (see, for example, Teacher/Researcher Box 11.1 for an example of a one-way dual language program). In *transitional bilingual programs*, the focus is often to develop children's' English abilities to succeed in an English-only classroom. These programs provide some initial instruction in the students' home language which is phased out within two to three years. The choice of bilingual education program may reflect community or parental preference or availability of bilingual programs.

When I started working with CUNY-NYSIEB, the question for me was how we were going to be able to negotiate the strict language allocation policies of dual language bilingual education programs and introduce translanguaging theory. We grounded our work on our observations and then met with teachers to develop lessons using translanguaging. I had observed that when languages were strictly separated, students would sometime struggle with their academic work and focus. For example, we visited a school on the lower east side of Manhattan, a school with an established Mandarin and English dual language program and a new principal that was enthusiastic to participate with CUNY-NYSIEB. We observed students from Chinese and English-speaking homes who changed classroom, teacher, and language of instruction (English or Chinese) each week. This strict language allocation plan had been established under the previous leadership, yet the school staff expressed concern that many of these children were not learning during weeks when only one or the other language was being used. Although the teachers recognized the value of integrating both languages into the instruction and materials used every day, they were not sure how to plan and structure instruction for translanguaging. We met with the teachers and co-planned lessons as well as conducted demonstration lessons where teachers from other classrooms were invited to observe. These demonstration lessons utilized and highlighted students' bilingual engagement with instruction and materials that were in English and Mandarin, which was very different from their typical monolingual instruction. After these lessons, we met as a group to discuss teachers' observations and questions and to support them in designing their own lessons using translanguaging.

Teachers began to leverage students' translanguaging to document what their students knew and how they used language for classroom communicative and academic purposes in what Sánchez, García and Solorza (2017) called *translanguaging documentation*. In their lesson planning, teachers also integrated *translanguaging rings* (Sánchez, García & Solorza, 2017). These were meant to expand *individual* students' Zone of Proximal Development by providing them with scaffolding *when appropriate*. This included the use of bilingual instructional materials, technology assistance such as Google Translate, and multimodal provisions including videos to individual students who needed such support. Finally, teachers also planned for more whole-class collective spaces where translanguaging was used, not as scaffold, but for students to experience a transformation. To shape these *translanguaging transformative spaces* collaboration with peers and small group instruction was encouraged, so that students could use all their available multilingual and multimodal resources to make meaning and learn. This gave students possibilities to learn and engage meaningfully and authentically with the lesson. Integrating these linguistic practices validated the translanguaging practices of their communities, developed creative linguistic uses, and disrupted the linguistic hierarchies that are the product of monoglossic ideologies in schools (Sánchez, García & Solorza, 2017).

With all the schools we worked with, we always began with multiple visits. We spent time in the classrooms and meeting with teachers and staff to best understand the schools' structures, histories, policies, and students and communities in order to support them in ways that would be most productive for that specific school. We would then create emergent bilingual leadership teams (EBLT) consisting of teachers, students, and administration to analyze needs and set goals for developing bilingualism in the school (see Chapter 5, this volume). Although each school was unique in many ways, we found that all the schools shared a strong interest in learning more about translanguaging pedagogies and how they could be integrated in their schools.

Since emergent bilingual students' language proficiencies are widely varied and part of a broad bilingual spectrum, a flexible language environment is critical in order to make learning accessible to all students. Furthermore, emergent bilinguals do not necessarily adhere solely to one language when trying to make meaning of a situation, communicating ideas, and formulating questions. We started showing bilingual teachers how students' use of their fluid language practices provided opportunities to speak, read, listen, and write in meaningful ways and contexts.

Because the goal of dual language bilingual classrooms is to educate children who will be bilingual and biliterate, we helped teachers to support their students with strategies to meet the linguistic demands of academic tasks in English, as well as the other language. We introduced translanguaging theory and developed pedagogical practices that leverage bilingual children's full linguistic repertoire to study and learn academic materials. We explored with the teachers how translanguaging is a common discourse practice of bilinguals in many contexts—in families and communities, in the school yard, in the lunchroom, and in unstructured time in the classroom. We analyzed how bilingual children use their language features dynamically in order to interact with others. Our work with schools aimed to extend these practices into academic contexts and create space for language fluidity in the classroom and empower students through translanguaging (García & Leiva, 2014). When bilingual students are encouraged to use their language strengths to discuss and reflect on concepts, they are able to gain a deeper understanding and comprehension of new content.

For many of the school administration and staff we worked with as part of the CUNY-NYSIEB project, the concept of translanguaging was new and at times challenged the existing language structures and practices of the school. However, in most cases after some time working together with demonstration lessons, review of multilingual resources and materials, and lesson planning, school staff became enthusiastic to use more translanguaging in their classrooms. During our seminars, participating schools came together to share their experiences, goals, and challenges as they integrated change in their schools. Teachers found that many of the pedagogical practices could be applied to their classroom regardless if they taught in a dual language bilingual education, mainstream English, or ESL classroom. Teachers shared ways to build on students' background experiences, including their language practices, and encouraged connections between concepts studied in school and those in their own lives, rendering all of it academic and important.

We found overall that schools were most successful when they respect and value their emergent bilinguals, especially their linguistic and cultural diversity. These schools learned to use their students' bilingualism as a resource, regardless of whether the program was officially categorized as dual language bilingual education or transitional bilingual education. Through translanguaging practices, schools were able to bypass program names and structures allowing them to use practices that reflected students' bilingualism and leverage it in the process of acquiring language and new knowledge. Schools created a multilingual ecology in their buildings, proudly displaying their linguistic diversity, and making bilingual resources available for students, teachers, and parents in both English and the language other than English (see Chapter 9, this volume). Students' home language practices were used to teach and learn. At the same time, teachers learned to support the flexible use of their students' entire linguistic repertoire, with translanguaging pedagogies.

A focus on educating teachers for English as a Second Language programs: Kaya opens up space for translanguaging in monoglossic ESL programs

The CUNY-NYSIEB team also worked with teachers and students in ESL programs. One of the biggest challenges facing ESL teachers is to provide comprehensible instruction. In New York State, ESL teachers work in different types of programs. Some are in mainstream classrooms where emergent bilingual students are placed with teachers who may or may not be certified as ESL teachers (see, for example, Teacher/Researcher Box 6.11). Others are pull-out programs in which emergent bilinguals are regularly pulled out of their mainstream classroom for ESL instruction. Yet others are push-in programs in which emergent bilinguals are placed in mainstream classrooms and certified ESL teachers support the instruction for the emergent bilinguals (see Teacher/Researcher Box 12.1). Other times, ESL teachers work in self-contained ESL classrooms (see Teacher/Researcher Boxes 7.1 and 13.1). Whatever the type of program, ESL programs tend to promote a monoglossic English-only ideology. How could CUNY-NYSIEB open up a space for translanguaging, disrupting the ESL monoglossia and favoring a heteroglossia (Bakhtin, 1981) that makes evident the many voices of students in such programs?

When we first introduced translanguaging theory to ESL teachers, and demonstrated translanguaging pedagogical practices, we encountered challenges and resistance from principals and teachers. But the more insight and experience they gained as they implemented translanguaging pedagogical practices, one step at a time, the more they became comfortable utilizing them in the schools and classrooms. It turned out that translanguaging was an important support for comprehensible instruction in a wide range of ESL classrooms. In the beginning, one of the challenges we encountered was teachers' beliefs and attitudes that emergent bilingual students should have constant and ongoing immersion solely in English, since English is considered the target language for students to acquire and accomplish. Some teachers thought that incorporating emergent bilingual students' home language practices would unfairly take time away from their exposure to the target language learning. Therefore, it was challenging for some teachers to envision how to open up translanguaging spaces in their instruction.

The ESL teachers we worked with began to understand that getting to know students meant exploring their prior experiences, and their cultural and linguistic practices both within and beyond school. Over time, the teachers came to reflect on how English monolingual practices were diminishing the value of students' language practices which were not worthy enough to take space in the classroom. Eventually, they saw that translanguaging permeates socially just, inclusive, and equitable teaching that target students' success (García, Johnson & Seltzer, 2017).

Translanguaging highlights students' linguistic and cultural diversity as a strength to be valued and shared. For example, one 3rd grade ESL teacher whom the CUNY-NYSIEB worked with at PS 95Q The Eastwood School located in Queens, New York, incorporated translanguaging practices in her unit "A Poem in the Pocket." Students were exposed to different types of poems and utilized their word knowledge and language style when creating their own poems. Although the teacher did not speak the students' home languages, she was able to use various translanguaging strategies to facilitate their learning of writing their own poem. She brought visuals and key vocabulary in English, Spanish, Bengali, and Haitian Creole her students mostly spoke in their homes. The teacher supported them in writing their poems in their home languages and in English. She asked students to help her pronounce the key words in their home language. When the students finished their poems, they edited them with the help of their parents and read their poems in a poetry night activity with their parents.

Although teachers who were not familiar with the home languages of students were hesitant and uncomfortable at the beginning, they came to understand that their ESL students bring their funds of knowledge through their home language practices to study, learn, and communicate. Viewing their linguistic and cultural diversity as an asset, teachers empowered their students to take charge of their own learning.

The CUNY-NYSIEB team worked specifically with ESL teachers through ongoing discussions and workshops to model pedagogical practices of translanguaging. As a team, we wanted to provide the teachers the opportunities to revisit their beliefs and attitudes as well as to explore practices and resources that would aid in their instructional activities and decisions. For example, as an educator whose home language is different from the teachers, I conducted a lesson in Turkish to put teachers in their students' shoes and allow them to experience learning the content in a language that they don't know. I also modeled translanguaging strategies that would encourage them to dynamically use their own home language (English) as a resource. The team demonstrated how teachers can create a school and classroom ecology that would value and celebrate students' cultural and linguistic diversity. We also supported administrators and ESL teachers to utilize resources in the schools such as special services, parents, parent teacher coordinators, their colleagues, other students, family, and community.

Helping ESL teachers change their mindset about translanguaging also encouraged teachers to present home language practices not as an interference, but as a strength for their children's learning. We supported teachers in creating their units using translanguaging strategies that involved parents in instructional activities. For example, in PS 95Q The Eastwood School, EBLT members created projects that provided space for students' using their home language and invited students and parents to be involved in their own learning through strengthening their home language and nurturing their cultural diversity. Kindergarteners worked on creating family/heritage trees with introductory cards and displayed them in the school. First graders explored the immigrant experience in depth through student-created questionnaires and various activities in English and in their home language with the help of bilingual resources, parents, and staff. In a second-grade unit study, students researched international music and instruments; they then participated in writing activities and music which they performed in the school in both English and their home language. In all the schools where CUNY-NYSIEB was involved, the teams observed how ESL teachers and students created, for example, multilingual books, family and community projects, content-based multilingual word walls, and audio storytelling and art.

Translanguaging in ESL contexts allows teachers to access students' cultural and linguistic repertoires to maximize their meaning-making and learning (García & Li, 2014). Furthermore, it presents teachers with opportunities for multimodal and innovative approaches to accommodate students' needs and to leverage students' success. Therefore, translanguaging can become one of the key objectives of ESL teaching. Teacher education should be geared toward understanding emergent bilingual students' linguistic needs, struggles, as well as cultural and linguistic strengths, and potentials and how translanguaging can play a key role in students' learning and success.

Engaging family and community: Pappas opens spaces for families through translanguaging

CUNY-NYSIEB offered many lessons in working with schools to bolster their programs for emergent bilinguals and strengthen teacher knowledge in guiding the educational success of multilingual children. From the beginning, the CUNY-NYSIEB team knew that we had to extend our work to students' families and communities so that they could understand what translanguaging meant for the education of their children—that it would expand their access to the curriculum, and allow them to contribute their knowledge in ways monolingual classrooms often do not. What we did not immediately recognize is that partnering with families would operationalize a multilingual ecology that our project espoused.

Although the CUNY-NYSIEB was not funded to work with parents, my background in family and community engagement prepared me to encourage the schools that I was working with to involve parents more directly in the project and in its underpinnings. This idea took hold forcefully in one of the schools we worked with because the new administration recognized the importance of engaging parents in discussing the new shifts in programming for emergent bilingual students. In conversations with our team, the principal and assistant principal expressed a desire to build on previous efforts to involve parents. Engaging parents in an academic conversation about translanguaging was both an opportunity to reinforce shared high expectations for students and to tap parents' knowledge and wisdom of their children.

The community of one of the schools I worked in is close to 90% Latinx. Like many schools, the children and their families had a wide variety of language practices. Some of the families speak Spanish only; some English only; others are bilingual in various degrees. Many families we met were immersed in the fluid bilingualism of their neighborhoods in the Bronx and translanguaging was ever present in the community that enveloped the school. Nearby, businesses and restaurants had bilingual advertisements. Education organizing and other community groups promoted campaigns for economic, racial, and educational justice bilingually.

When the new principal came to the school in 2011–2012 (one year before the CUNY-NYSIEB project), disaggregated test scores laid bare that students classified as English Language Learners (ELLs) were struggling most among their peers. On paper the school had a transitional bilingual education program. CUNY-NYSIEB facilitated the administration's deeper dive into practices in its bilingual classrooms revealing that instruction was either in English only or it was in Spanish, usually determined by the comfort level of the teacher. There was little to no use of bilingualism nor of dynamic language practices like translanguaging in the classrooms. Long term bilingual educators had followed an English only mandate set by the previous principal and by district leadership. Like many schools with transitional bilingual classrooms, the unspoken mantra was "more English will amount to more English." The ELA and math test results that year demonstrated the limitation of that mindset. Despite the fact that the share of students classified as ELLs (32%) was more than double the citywide average (13%), the school did not have a focused strategy for attending to their emergent bilingual students' needs and the new administration wanted to change that.

At one of the first meetings we had with the school staff, we invited families of students. I, along with Ofelia García, led the meeting. Ofelia personally demonstrated how to utilize translanguaging as a way to include all of the teachers, some of whom were monolingual English speakers, as well as all the mothers, some of whom were monolingual Spanish speakers. We met with all of them at the same time, both teachers and mothers. We discussed together the role of bilingualism in learning and we introduced the concept of translanguaging using the image of a multi-terrain vehicle (García, 2009; García & Kleifgen, 2018). The community's bilingualism was not simply like a bicycle with two wheels, but its many wheels turned differently depending on the context/surface in which the contact with others was being made.

Even though many think that translanguaging is a difficult concept for educators and researchers, it proved to be a relatable concept for the mothers who attended the meeting. Many spoke freely, sharing stories of their own schooling and language practices. One mother talked about her personal pain in not being able to help her son with homework, since she had not gone to school and could not read or write. In similar instances like this, I remember hearing educators—many well intentioned—describe students and families as having "no language." By contrast, Ofelia recognized this mother's oral language and encouraged her to use it with her child as a support for his learning.

Other mothers in the school's auditorium also offered their experiences in feeling that they lacked knowledge to participate in their children's schooling and feeling shut out of educational decision-making. They also shared personal experiences of how they found ways to participate in their children's education. Translanguaging was a way to acknowledge the many contributions that this one mother, and all parents, bring to the conversation. Ofelia emphasized to parents and caregivers that they do not need to know how to read and write English to participate in their children's education; they can and should use their home language to talk with their children about what they are learning and creating at school.

For those teachers present, who do not often hear about the educational experiences of their students' parents, it was an eye-opener; it was a way to educate teachers that by affirming the language resources of families, they could both depend on their assistance with respect to their individual children, and more formally include them in broader education discussions affecting all students. One teacher expressed feeling the value of translanguaging in this instance, even though she had not fully understood it. Similar to how she interacted with parents, Ofelia encouraged monolingual teachers to participate in the translanguaging event that was taking place by allowing them to draw upon their full communicative repertoire, including gestures and relying on their colleagues to translate for them. While we hoped that bringing teachers and parents together to talk would support the school's new direction for its language programming, we did not fully realize that it would also be a way to integrate their language practices and that this in of itself would help the school community realize the power of translanguaging.

Sharing expertise both-ways: Zaino steps in as expert and learner

When I became a full-time PhD student, I mourned the classrooms, students, and schools I thought I had to leave behind. I had been an English teacher for 12 years. Then I began working for CUNY-NYSIEB as a research assistant, and I realized I wasn't leaving the classroom. Instead, I was gifted with the opportunity to learn from and with far more students, teachers, and schools than I would have otherwise encountered in my previous life. CUNY-NYSIEB introduced me to an ever-growing community of researchers and practitioners united in their efforts to leverage young people's full linguistic repertoires, to "bring the creative and agentive potential of young people to new heights" (García, 2018).

I saw these efforts enacted in multiple classrooms during the year I worked with CUNY-NYSIEB. As the coleader of a translanguaging study group for teachers, I facilitated discussions, visited their classrooms, and ultimately worked with each member individually to help them implement transformative translanguaging pedagogies into their classrooms. Our work was anchored in chapters from *The Translanguaging Classroom* (García, Johnson & Seltzer, 2017). In conjunction with these readings, teachers collectively analyzed their lesson plans, assessments, and student work; they developed curricula and pedagogies that included and developed their students' diverse linguistic practices and identities. In this study group, I learned the power of translanguaging research, research that was inseparable from classrooms, students, and teachers.

All of the teachers in the study group worked in New York City public schools, and their classrooms were as diverse as the city itself. Sunisa (Nisa) Nuonsy taught 12th-grade English Language Arts (ELA) in a high school designed for recent immigrants and refugees. Her students spoke 19 languages and hailed from around the world. Michelle Demeroukas, on the other hand, taught in an English as a New Language (ENL) classroom in an English-dominant school. Her students all spoke Spanish, but the singularity of this named language obscured the diversity of linguistic practices the students brought from their Dominican, Puerto Rican, and Mexican home cultures.

Both teachers were inspired by the work we read in the study group and wanted their students to understand the dynamic power of their multilingual identities. In Nisa's class, she encouraged her students to model themselves as linguistic anthropologists, after Zora Neale Hurston, as they began their unit on *Their Eyes Were Watching God*. Students reflected on their own languaging practices, sharing idioms, folk tales, and figurative language from their home cultures. They laughed when they realized that Puerto Ricans and Dominicans both said *Se está casando una bruja* (The witch is getting married) when the sun shone during a rainstorm. In Colombia, though, an old woman gets married during sun showers. But in Haiti, another student exclaimed, they say the devil is beating his wife. Ultimately, they moved from folk sayings to folktales, sharing their favorites from their home cultures, transcribing the stories into English so that their classmates could learn them. Nisa's work in the study group turned her traditional novel unit into an opportunity for her students to demonstrate their own linguistic and cultural practices, to share their expertise from their classmates as they learned together.

In Michelle's class, meanwhile, she transformed a yearlong unit on reading and writing memoirs into an opportunity for students to refine and demonstrate their dynamic multilingualism. Students began by studying mentor texts in which the authors wrote in English and languages other than English: *When I Was Puerto Rican* by Esmeralda Santiago, *Just Kids from the Bronx* by Arlene Alda, and *Enrique's Journey* by Sonia Nazario. As they read and analyzed these texts, students collectively developed a list of reasons why authors translanguage. Then, after drafting their own stories, they picked moments in their narratives in which they, too, could translanguage, to capture the complexity of their own thinking and speaking. For example, Felicia, a student from the Dominican Republic, wrote a beautiful story about her fear and anxiety on her first day in an American school. At the end of the day, she returns to her apartment, where her mother asks her in Spanish how her day went. It is the only moment in the story when Felicia hears her home language. In the end, she did not include a translation for the reader; she said she wanted monolingual English readers to experience the discomfort of not understanding, as she experienced on her first day of school. This metalinguistic awareness was echoed by her classmates, who shared with each other why they chose the specific moments in their text to translanguage.

These classrooms were just two of the several I visited over the course of the year; more importantly, they are just two of the many classrooms that continue to be impacted by CUNY-NYSIEB's research. During my year with CUNY-NYSIEB, I realized that research at its best does not entail leaving the classroom; instead, it involves *re-entering* the classroom, breaking down the walls between research and practice, with researchers, teachers, and students working to transform education in the only way education *can* be transformed—by working together.

Conclusion

All of our work in CUNY-NYSIEB was united around supporting emergent bilingual students. We recognized that emergent bilingual students often experience different program types and diverse students in their schools. Nevertheless, we saw that translanguaging practices leveraged bilingualism as a resource for learning in school. As we noted in this chapter, many of the practices and experiences the authors encountered were similar regardless of program type and school. First and foremost, there was an appreciation for the backgrounds and knowledge that emergent bilingual students bring to the classroom. By integrating students' home languages and practices, teachers were able to engage students and their families. Minimizing the divide and differences between school and home was central to our work with CUNY-NYSIEB. We all experienced initial resistance as teachers could be reluctant to change previous approaches. Most often though, when teachers were able to become familiar with translanguaging pedagogies and have the opportunity to use them in their classrooms, they were enthusiastic to learn and try more.

In this chapter, we present several examples of our work with CUNY-NYSIEB across distinct contexts. We worked with schools that had established different types of programs based on their student population, community, or in some case simply through legacy. Our work was done closely with school leaders, with teachers and other school staff, and with families. Regardless of where the work was introduced, it almost always was best received by the emergent bilingual students themselves. Based on our observations of classrooms and lessons, we can attest that when new practices were being tried out, there may have been some hesitation from the teachers; however, the students always seemed to take up the practices with zeal and excitement, as though a weight had been lifted. We observed students who previously were silent finding ways to participate that validated their knowledge and abilities. It is reaffirming that our work showed that the different program types and structures may not be as restricting as expected. It is the practices that reach the student that matter most. These are not practices that are ideological; rather, they reflect those of the families and communities of the students. Translanguaging opens up spaces where bilingual students, regardless of program type, can step into, without having to choose practices of either the home or the school. Like Zaino, the acknowledgment and leveraging of students' translanguaging enables them to concurrently become experts and learners, as they share experiences that for them are a simultaneous, although educators have most often interpreted them as an either/or. That is the challenge of translanguaging, to view educators and families, experts and learners, one language or the other in an integrated continuum, rather than separate wholes that function in different planes.

References

Bakhtin, M. (1981). *Dialogic imagination: Four essays.* Austin, TX: University of Texas Press.

García, O. (2009). *Bilingual Education in the 21st Century: A Global Perspective.* Hoboken: John Wiley & Sons.

García, O., Johnson, S. I., & Seltzer, K. (2017). *The translanguaging classroom: Leveraging student bilingualism for learning.* Philadelphia, PA: Caslon.

García, O., & Kleifgen, J. (2018). *Educating Emergent Bilinguals: Policies, programs and practices for English Learners.* (2nd ed.). New York, NY: Teachers College Press.

García, O. & Leiva, C. (2014). Theorizing and enacting translanguaging for social justice. *Heteroglossia as practice and pedagogy* (pp. 199–216). Dordrecht: Springer.

García, O. & Li, W. (2014). *Translanguaging: Language, bilingualism and education.* London: Palgrave Macmillan Pivot.

García, O. (2018). Translanguaging, pedagogy and creativity. In J. Erfurt, E. Carporal & A. Weirich (Eds.), *Éducation plurilingue et pratiques langagières: Hommage à Christine Hélot* (pp. 39–56). Berlin: Peter Lang.

Sánchez, M. T., García, O., & Solorza, C. (2017). Reframing language allocation policy in dual language bilingual education. *Bilingual Research Journal*, 1–15. https://doi.org/10.10 80/15235882.2017.1405098

BOX 6.1 TEACHER/RESEARCHER

Lauren Ardizzone

H.S. English Language Arts

For the past 13 years, I've taught 11th-grade ELA at a traditional public high school in the Bronx. My classes are a blend of general education students, students with disabilities and emergent bilingual students, and with *all* my students I take an approach that builds on their translanguaging.

For example, in an effort to make my curriculum relevant and engaging to students, develop skills essential for success on high-stakes exams, and foster their critical literacies, I designed a project in the style of a multi-genre writing portfolio—a strategy I first learned about through my work with the CUNY-NYSIEB project. As the first part of this portfolio project, students read about and researched a topic related to language (our overall focus for the year), and then wrote a research paper about their findings. As is now common practice in our classroom, students were encouraged to take notes, create outlines, and work through initial drafts in their home language. I stress to all my students, and particularly my emergent bilingual, that when we do "thinking work," we should take notes, annotate, etc. using the kind of language that makes our thinking most clear to us. Our multilingual word wall—cocreated by the students and me—was also available to students at all times to use as a resource when they needed to write their final drafts in English.

Students then engaged with a series of authentic texts to do their own creative writing that aligned with the findings from their research papers. This included a close reading of Amy Tan's essay, "Mother Tongue," watching and reviewing a transcript of the spoken word poem "3 Ways to Speak English" by Jamila Lyiscott, and listening to and annotating another spoken word poem, "My Spanish" by Melissa Lozada-Oliva. I selected texts that modeled the kind of thinking about language and use of a variety of language practices that I was encouraging students to pursue, and I wanted them to see published examples of this kind of writing.

Students were again invited to take notes and annotations in their home language, and a significant amount of time was spent discussing (both in English and in students' home languages) each writer's choices about language. I again wanted to ensure that all students could fully engage with the work, and that all students could bring their expertise and background knowledge about language into their analysis.

When all this work was done, students had the choice of writing poetry, writing an editorial, creating a satirical piece, writing a speech, or creating a dialogue. While the final draft of the research paper had to be written in English, all other multi-genre components could be written using any of the students' multiple language practices.

I would like to think that my work incorporates multiple levels of translanguaging. We engage in a deep study of "language" and start from the idea that having a rich linguistic repertoire is a tremendous asset that the students already possess and are constantly building. I also explicitly incorporate strategies like taking notes, having partner discussions, and annotating texts in their home language, side-by-side translations of directions, prompts, questions or texts, and a multilingual word wall. In response to these shifts in practice, I have found that students are much more likely to engage, participate, challenge themselves, take risks, and recognize the essential role they play in the classroom, as linguistic experts who deftly navigate so many different contexts as they go through their day. I found that students who had previously produced very little written work in English were now eager to turn their notes and annotations into their research papers, and that even though they often chose to write in their home languages, they also pushed themselves to produce writing in English. Students also used the resources available to them, like side-by-side translations and the multilingual word wall, as a springboard to writing in English. I watched time and again as students worked out, in their home language, what they had to do, and then did it—in English.

There are moments when it feels overwhelming to teach students who have just come to the US and need to pass a high-stakes standardized exam in English to graduate. Translanguaging has not only helped me to shift my own thinking from "how much these students need" to "how much these students bring"; it has provided me with concrete ways to put this new mindset to work for my students.

SECTION III
Shifting Educational Spaces

7

DEVELOPING TRANSLANGUAGING PEDAGOGICAL MATERIAL

Sara Vogel, Kate Seltzer, Kathryn Carpenter, Ann E. Ebe, Christina Celic, and Kahdeidra Martin

Introduction

Translanguaging theory refers to the fluid communicative practices of bilingual people (García & Li Wei, 2014). From 2012 to 2019, we, the authors of this chapter, were among a group of researchers with the City University of New York-New York State Initiative on Emergent Bilinguals (CUNY-NYSIEB), working with educators across the state to re-imagine the education of emergent bilinguals—students often marginalized in schools and school systems. Our work was always guided by the question: what could we make happen if we centered students' translanguaging and dynamic bilingualism in classroom practice? Through this work, we saw firsthand just how transformative translanguaging could be as a guiding principle for educators and emergent bilingual students. We also realized that coming to understand and apply a theory as paradigm shifting as translanguaging took time and practice. If we wanted to support teachers on their translanguaging journeys, our team would have to learn to express ideas in multiple formats, media, and for different audiences.

In this chapter, we describe CUNY-NYSIEB's approach to designing pedagogical materials—our dozens of articles, guides, videos, topic briefs, webinars, and professional development activities—all of which currently live at www.cuny-nysieb.org. We share stories from our seven active years: from the birth of our first, and still most popular, print material, *Translanguaging: A CUNY-NYSIEB Guide for Educators* (2012), created for and with partner teachers, to the development of interactive digital topic briefs and video web series viewed by thousands of visitors across the United States and around the world. We aimed for these tools not only to frame translanguaging theory and pedagogy for audiences local and global, but to do so grounded in the realities of public schools. Mirroring the collaborative spirit of our project as a whole, we always sought input from educators on the ground, featured examples of their work prominently, and in many cases, co-authored materials with teachers.

Creating these materials helped CUNY-NYSIEB more clearly articulate examples of translanguaging theory and pedagogy in action for professional development and work with teachers around New York State. CUNY-NYSIEB pedagogical materials brought awareness about translanguaging to partner schools, helped schools develop sustainable practices to support emergent bilingual students and their families, and responded to areas of need identified by teachers at CUNY-NYSIEB schools. In addition to sparking fire locally, they fulfilled a desire of audiences far beyond New York City and State. As the project transitioned away from direct work in schools, our materials creation shifted toward the multimodal and digital to appeal to wider audiences. CUNY-NYSIEB resources are now shared at national and international conferences. Teachers use translanguaging strategies in classrooms across New York State and beyond. Professors use CUNY-NYSIEB resources in their education courses (see Section VI, this book). Our research has influenced countless journal articles and dissertations. Born of our work bridging research and practice, these pedagogical materials will help ensure the longevity of the CUNY-NYSIEB project and our focus on the dynamic translanguaging practices of bilingual people.

A jumping-off point for partner teachers: Our first translanguaging guide

When Ofelia García took up and re-framed Cen Williams' and Colin Baker's concept of "translanguaging" (García, 2009), she was not simply putting forward a theoretical idea about multilingualism or about instruction; she was putting a name to the language use and instructional practices she had observed in actual New York City classrooms and schools. She saw that it was natural for multilingual students to tap into their different language practices as they were learning, and some teachers were taking advantage of this linguistic resource to enhance their students' learning—whether they spoke the students' languages or not.

When CUNY-NYSIEB began working with schools in New York in 2011 to improve the education of emergent bilinguals, translanguaging became a central tenet and a core concept to introduce to educators. Those new to the concept of translanguaging wanted concrete examples of how it could be incorporated in their classrooms. This was the origin of the first guide, *Translanguaging: A CUNY-NYSIEB Guide for Educators* by Christina Celic and Kate Seltzer (2013). The guide was written as a jumping-off point, illustrating specific ways translanguaging could play out in a classroom or school—in the physical learning environment, during collaborative work, as part of literacy and content instruction, and with language development. The guide also contained an introductory section by Ofelia García, "Theorizing Translanguaging for Educators," that described translanguaging (a new concept for most teachers) through a series of practical and straightforward questions and answers about translanguaging and its connection to classroom teaching. This particular section was integral to participating teachers' professional learning within the project and also became a regularly assigned reading in CUNY teacher education classes, demonstrating how eager pre- and in-service educators were for resources that could help them better serve their emergent bilingual students. The guide also contained a protocol for Collaborative Descriptive Inquiry (written by Ofelia García and Laura Ascenzi-Moreno and inspired by Himley & Carini, 2000) designed to support groups of teachers to approach understanding their own pedagogical practices, their students, and student work "from a perspective steeped in openness and curiosity" (in Celic & Seltzer, 2013, p. 7).

The guide was rooted in the authors' experience as classroom teachers, rather than coming from an academic lens. In an effort to examine and name real-world, organic classroom strategies, Christina and Kate described teaching practices they themselves had employed as well as those they had observed in colleagues' classrooms. In fact, many of the vignettes, templates, and examples of student work came from Christina and Kate's actual classrooms. The guide was designed to demonstrate how these translanguaging strategies—from Christina's use of bilingual word walls in her bilingual elementary school classroom to Kate's work with multilingual writing in her English Language Arts class—could be used across different classroom and programmatic settings (see Figure 7.1). The

ELEMENTARY	MIDDLE	SECONDARY
Community Study		

Essential Questions	What is it?
• *How can we create a classroom and school environment that celebrates students' home languages and cultures?* • *How can we raise ALL students' awareness of the different languages and scripts in their communities?* **Alignment with Common Core State Standards:** <u>Language: Knowledge of Language: Standard 3</u> Apply knowledge of language to understand how language functions in different contexts, to make effective choices for meaning or style, and to comprehend more fully when	A community study is a way for *all* students – bilingual and English speakers – to investigate what languages and scripts are visible in their community. Students can do this in a number of ways. They can: • Take pictures of signs in languages other than English • Collect newspapers in languages other than English • Listen for people speaking in languages other than English • See how languages other than English are used in community institutions, such as libraries or schools When students share their findings with the class, you can use this as a springboard to start a grade-appropriate discussion of multilingualism in the community. You can then create a display in the classroom or school of the photographs or realia (newspapers, books, flyers, etc.) students bring in that show multilingualism in their neighborhood. The display should indicate what languages are shown in each image or object. **Translanguaging How-To** 1. Decide how to include a community study in your curriculum • Can you do this at the **beginning of the school year** as part of your "community building" activities?

FIGURE 7.1 The structure of CUNY-NYSIEB's first translanguaging guide

project purposefully chose not to tie the guide to any current mandates such as the Common Core State Standards (CCSS)—which had been adopted for use in New York for the 2012–13 school year—so that the focus would be on enduring ways of teaching and learning with multilingual students. At the same time, the authors of the guide recognized the conditions in which teachers worked. They hoped to demonstrate that translanguaging strategies were not to be used as enrichment activities separate from core subjects but could be used to support students in their learning every day. For this, the team annotated the guide to show alignment between translanguaging strategies, approaches, and the CCSS.

Once the CUNY-NYSIEB team began to use this resource, which came to be referred to as "The Translanguaging Guide," in professional development, we saw exciting results. Teachers and school leaders were able to "see" translanguaging in action and, more importantly, see that their existing practices often aligned with—and were thus supported by—a translanguaging approach. With the guidance of the CUNY-NYSIEB team, participating teachers and administrators were able to read about translanguaging strategies—individually, in small groups or teams, and even in some cases as a whole school community—and then integrate them into their own classroom practice.

One participating teacher, Hulda Yau, who later became an "ambassador" to the project for her longstanding commitment to using translanguaging in her classroom, has told audiences at professional development sessions the story of stumbling across *The Translanguaging Guide* on a table at her school. Though she didn't yet know about translanguaging theory, the ideas appealed to her and she jumped in and started using the "preview-view-review" strategy—in which content is previewed in a home language, read in a new language, and debriefed in the home language—to support her bilingual second graders. In addition to highlighting the passion of educators like Hulda, this anecdote reveals how strongly *The Translanguaging Guide* resonated with teachers of emergent bilingual students and enabled them to act on their desire to find new ways of teaching them (see Teacher/Researcher Box 11.1).

In 2013, *The Translanguaging Guide* was reprinted. This revised edition had an appendix of tools and templates created by Sarah Hesson and new set of Questions and Answers that introduced the guide. The new Questions and Answers, also authored by García, responded to the many questions about translanguaging that we ourselves had, and that teachers asked of us as we worked with them. The shifts in the questions raised, and our understandings, responded to the changing ways in which our theory was shaped by practice, as our practice was shaped by theory. The revisions show how our changing understandings of translanguaging were shaped by the interactions we had with each other, and with others.

Broadening the translanguaging lens:
Guides across curriculum and programs

A tension that surfaced as we put together the first guide was that teachers might come to think of translanguaging as just a set list of strategies. Quite the contrary, CUNY-NYSIEB team members have always viewed translanguaging as a way of thinking, communicating, and learning beyond named languages. Applied to classroom practice, translanguaging theory was meant to help teachers build on and leverage the unique strengths and language practices of students. The first guide was simply an initial attempt to capture some of the ways it might unfold in a classroom or school, and to support teachers who wanted to tap into this resource for learning. But administrators and educators still had questions about how to apply the CUNY-NYSIEB philosophy across content areas, program models, and with different subpopulations and grade levels. We knew we would need to create resources that were based on our work with educators on the ground, and that would demonstrate how translanguaging could be an organizing principle guiding all aspects of teaching and learning with emergent bilinguals.

One key need expressed by educators was that they were often not familiar with their students' languages and countries of origin. For example, in one school, a teacher knew she had some students who spoke Spanish but wasn't sure which countries they were from. In another school, a teacher told us she had students from Africa but admitted she had no idea from which countries specifically or what languages these students spoke. We realized that in order to help teachers draw on students' linguistic and cultural backgrounds as resources, they first needed to understand the importance of getting to know their students. Our answer was the guidebook *The Languages of New York State* (Funk, 2012), which lists and describes linguistic and cultural features of the top ten languages spoken by emergent bilinguals in the State.

Another need centered around ensuring emergent bilinguals would be meaningfully included in New York City and State's rollout of the CCSS. Teachers were expected to align their instruction to these standards and, in many cases, adopt scripted curricula that had been specifically tailored to helping prepare students for assessments that would measure their learning against these standards. As with much scripted curricula, however, there was little thought to the funds of knowledge, language practices, and needs of emergent bilinguals. As such, the CUNY-NYSIEB team formulated a guide that built upon units featured in Expeditionary Learning, a CCSS-aligned curriculum adopted by New York State. This resource, *Translanguaging in Curriculum and Instruction: A CUNY-NYSIEB Guide for Educators* by Sarah Hesson, Kate Seltzer, and Heather Woodley, was published in 2014. This second translanguaging guide showcases how strategies from the original Translanguaging Guide can be seamlessly integrated into units from Expeditionary Learning, allowing teachers to envision how they could make small shifts to an existing curriculum so that it better meets the needs and build on the expertise of emergent bilinguals.

Our team also worked to build practical resources to support teachers' literacy and biliteracy instruction. The *Translanguaging in Latino/a Literature Guide* (Pérez Rosario, 2015) analyzes a series of books for Latinx students in grades PK-12. The featured texts, all written by Latinx authors on themes and topics that are particularly relevant to the Latinx community, provide an analysis of the authors' translanguaging, demonstrating how these books can be used as models for students' own writing. Another guide, *A Translanguaging Pedagogy for Writing* (Espinosa, Ascenzi-Moreno & Vogel, 2016), focuses specifically on writing instruction (see also Chapter 12, this book). It invites teachers to build on their students' rich, complex language practices while practicing writing through strategies such as multilingual dialogue journals, writing from photographs, and composing multimodal and multilingual final products.

Putting the pieces together: A holistic framework for the education of emergent bilinguals

The CUNY-NYSIEB team's work with teachers in New York State classrooms, and authoring the various guides, helped us recognize that teaching emergent bilinguals requires sustained commitment and leadership across a whole school community. Given that individual teachers—even those equipped with our guides—cannot make sustained change on their own, CUNY-NYSIEB created a toolkit for schools to create their own Emergent Bilingual Leadership Teams (EBLT) (also see Chapter 5, this book). Resources in these kits prompted EBLTs—comprised of a core group of passionate educators, administrators, and even parents—to craft a vision statement for the education of emergent bilinguals at their schools, to take an inventory of their school's multilingual ecology, and set goals for improvement.

The most recent CUNY-NYSIEB guide, *CUNY-NYSIEB New York State Multilingual Learner/English Language Learner Guide* (Ebe, 2019) also showcases our holistic approach, bringing together aspects of several of the previous guides and pedagogical materials into one comprehensive resource for teachers. The latest guide discusses how language works from a dynamic bilingual perspective (García & Kleifgen, 2018) provides guidance on ways to get to know and assess students holistically and explores how to create a multilingual ecology and a culturally relevant learning environment. The guide also details how to plan integrated units of study where language and literacy are taught through meaningful content. Finally, the guide provides specific strategies teachers can incorporate into their teaching in order to facilitate the use of students' home languages as resources for learning.

While the *Curriculum and Instruction Guide* of 2014 helped teachers align their instruction to the CCSS which New York State had adopted in 2012–2013, in 2017 New York State adopted a new set of standards for New York State known as the Next Generation Learning Standards. These standards are a slightly revised version of the CCSS. To help facilitate this instructional alignment for teachers on a local level, this latest guide links strategies to relevant Next Generation Learning Standard for English Language Arts or Mathematics.

The variety of guides and pedagogical materials created by CUNY-NYSIEB help demonstrate how translanguaging can be an organizing principle guiding all aspects of teaching and learning with emergent bilinguals although it needs to continuously adapt to the instructional context. While some materials provide helpful links to local curriculum, the principles for working with emergent bilingual students present in all materials are also relevant to a global audience of educators.

Making CUNY-NYSIEB global and multimodal

As CUNY-NYSIEB team members shared our resources at local, national, and international conferences, and in teacher preparation courses in Bilingual Education and Teaching of English to Speakers of Other Languages (TESOL), educators and researchers beyond our partner schools began to take up and use our materials. These members of our extended networks were looking for short, practical excerpts from the guides and examples of classroom practices they could use while running their own classes or professional development sessions. For this, CUNY-NYSIEB began to expand our digital presence.

In mid-2016, Videographer César Rodríguez and Research Assistant Sara Vogel spearheaded a website redesign to transform CUNY-NYSIEB's bare-bones repository of webinar recordings and PDF documents for school partners into an easy-to-navigate, multimodal, colorful resource for local and global audiences. Since the redesign and as of Summer 2019, the site has received over 20,000 visitors from 145 countries. CUNY-NYSIEB leaned into its global appeal by translating an abbreviated version of the translanguaging guide into Spanish. We also experimented with new kinds of digital products. On a tight budget for our materials production, CUNY-NYSIEB could never afford flashy graphics and a state-of-the-art studio. But by simply hanging a black curtain on our office wall—a thrifty setup that co-principal investigator Ofelia García used to call "la bodega"—César transformed CUNY-NYSIEB into a production house which created over a dozen online presentations and webinars with professors, educators, and research assistants, extending our reach beyond the CUNY-Graduate Center's walls. César and videographers like Dani Tenenbaum and Yuval Netter were dispatched with CUNY-NYSIEB team members to record students and teachers living translanguaging theory and learning together, efforts which led to the production of dozens of video clips of classroom practice and interviews, and multimodal topic briefs.

Teaching bilinguals (even if you're not one!)

Our partner schools found our guides most useful when researchers, professors, or coaches curated sections for teachers to read and unpacked content with them in planned activities. But audiences outside of New York could not so easily access our professional development sessions. To demonstrate the basic concepts of translanguaging pedagogy in action, Research Assistant Sara Vogel produced the web series *Teaching Bilinguals (Even if You're Not One!)* in 2017 (Figure 7.2). Modeled after web series like MTV's *Decoded* videos about race, and the popular *PeroLike* YouTube videos about Latinx culture, the five videos in the series are short (between 3 and 6 minutes) and include bouncy music and visually appealing animations. They offer viewers bite-sized peeks into classrooms across New York State where teachers are experimenting with a translanguaging approach.

The series flips the script on traditional narratives that view emergent bilingual students from a deficit perspective, instead framing monolingual and bilingual educators as professionals capable of leveraging the diverse translanguaging gifts that their students bring—even if they do not share their students' language backgrounds. Teachers from real New York State classrooms who have wrestled with the challenges and joys of multilingual classrooms discuss their philosophies, showcase tips, activities, student work, and lesson plans. The series aims to support teachers in making connections between theory and practice in an accessible, conversational way, and can be accessed on-the-go. As one in-service literacy

FIGURE 7.2   Episode 3 of "Teaching bilinguals (even if you're not one)" series

coach completing her master's degree in Bilingual Education at Hunter College, CUNY, put it: "A five minute video taught me more than the couple of hours I spent trying to understand an assigned reading." And she is not the only one engaging with this content: As of Winter 2019, the videos have been watched between 3,600 and 5,400 times each, and they have been included in syllabi for teacher preparation courses taught in person and online around the country.

Teacher ambassador pages

Recognizing the power of classroom examples to innovate translanguaging pedagogy, CUNY-NYSIEB introduced a Teacher Ambassador program to highlight new and promising practices. Teacher ambassadors like Gladys Aponte, a fourth grade teacher working in Jackson Heights, Queens; Andy Brown, a fifth grade teacher in Maspeth, Queens; Charene Chapman-Santiago, an 8th grade teacher in Crown Heights, Brooklyn; and Hulda Yau, a second grade teacher in the Rochester City School District, designed translanguaging forward and often culturally sustaining (Paris & Alim, 2017) activities and units, at times in collaboration with CUNY-NYSIEB researchers (for Brown, see Teacher/Researcher Boxes 9.1 and 13.1; for Yau, see Teacher/Researcher Box 11.1). Teachers shared and solicited feedback from one another during virtual check-ins, and then opened up their classroom doors to our camera crews so that CUNY-NYSIEB could document their implementation. This work resulted in a series of multimedia pages on the CUNY-NYSIEB website featuring videos, lesson plans, interview clips, and curricular resources—for teachers, and by teachers (Figure 7.3).

Multimodal topic briefs

In our work with schools, teachers consistently asked us for resources that would help them connect with certain student populations. These groups included those labeled Long-Term English Language Learners (LTELLs), Students

Our Teacher Ambassadors At Work

Explore videos of translanguaging pedagogy as enacted by CUNY-NYSIEB's most experienced educators!

Andy	Charene	Gladys	Hulda
5th Grade General Education	8th Grade English Language Arts	4th Grade Bilingual Education	2nd Grade Bilingual Education

FIGURE 7.3   Some of CUNY-NYSIEB's teacher ambassadors

with Interrupted Formal Education (SIFE), emergent bilingual students with Individualized Education Plans (EBL-IEPs), Newcomer students, and young emergent bilinguals in grades PK-1. Our team wrote a number of frameworks relating to these student populations, including *A CUNY-NYSIEB Framework For The Education Of Emergent Bilinguals With Low Home Literacy: 4–12 Grades* (2013) and *A CUNY-NYSIEB Framework For The Education Of 'Long-Term English Learners': 6–12 Grades* (2013). We also created "topic briefs" that provided information and offered strategies for teachers relating to these particular subgroups of emergent bilinguals, intended for dissemination during professional development. Public school teachers were an integral part of the review process for these briefs. They provided feedback on each brief to ensure CUNY-NYSIEB recommendations reflected realities on the ground.

However, we realized that in order to reach a broader audience and improve teachers' access to these quality materials, a little reformatting was in order. In 2018, we took elements of these topic briefs and developed them into multimedia pages accessible via our website. Modeled after popular websites for educators like Colorín-Colorado (www.colorincolorado.org), these pages provide background information, principles for student support, and a spotlight on students for each subgroup they outline. Not only that, each resource includes numerous hyperlinks to relevant CUNY-NYSIEB materials such as guides and videos, as well as helpful resources outside the organization. To access the resources, visitors to the website can choose either to scan for the highlights or select information from one of numerous drop-down features on specific topics, as shown in Figure 7.4. Overall, as we have with all of CUNY-NYSIEB's resources, we created these webpages with teachers in mind, featuring highly effective classroom practices we encountered through our school-based work and making them accessible to all educators, even those who had not partnered with the project.

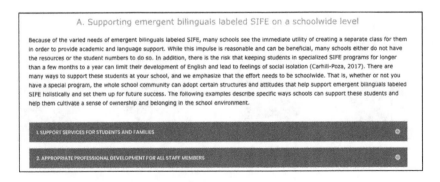

FIGURE 7.4 Multimodal topic brief dropdown menu

Conclusion

This chapter has outlined not only the rich cache of resources created by the CUNY-NYSIEB team but also the approach and thinking that shaped each of these resources and their integral role in the project's work with schools. From the project's first "Translanguaging Guide," written for and by classroom teachers of emergent bilinguals, to its more recent digital content centered around what our innovative participating teachers and administrators have done and continue to do with translanguaging in public schools, CUNY-NYSIEB's pedagogical resources have reached educators and researchers from New York State and well beyond. It is our hope that these resources continue to find an audience, particularly among classroom teachers and those working on the ground with emergent bilinguals, so that students' translanguaging and dynamic bilingualism are centered in classroom pedagogy that highlights their linguistic gifts.

References

Celic, C. & Seltzer, K. (2013). *Translanguaging: A CUNY-NYSIEB guide for educators*. CUNY-New York State Initiative on Emergent Bilinguals. http://www.nysieb.ws.gc.cuny.edu/files/2013/03/Translanguaging-Guide-March-2013.pdf

Ebe, A. (2019). *Working with multilingual learners (MLLs)/English Language Learners (ELLs) resource guide*. New York, NY: New York State Education Department Office of Bilingual Education and World Languages. Available from: http://www.nysed.gov/common/nysed/files/programs/bilingual-ed/resource-guide-working-with-mlls_ells-obewl-2-a_1.pdf

Espinosa, C., Ascenzi-Moreno, L., & Vogel, S. (2016). *A Translanguaging pedagogy for writing: A CUNY-NYSIEB guide for educators*. CUNY- New York State Initiative on Emergent Bilinguals. http://www.cuny-nysieb.org/wp-content/uploads/2016/05/TLG-Pedagogy-Writing-04-15-16.pdf

Funk, A. (2012). *The Languages of New York State: A CUNY-NYSIEB guide for educators*. City University of New York-New York State Initiative on Emergent Bilinguals. https://www.cuny-nysieb.org/wp-content/uploads/2016/05/NYSLanguageProfiles.pdf

García, O. & Kleifgen, J. A. (2018). *Educating emergent bilinguals: Policies, programs, and practices for English Language Learners* (2nd Edition). New York: Teachers College Press.

García, O. & Li, Wei. (2014). *Translanguaging: Language, bilingualism and education*. London, United Kingdom: Palgrave Macmillan Pivot.

García, O. (2009). *Bilingual education in the 21st century: A Global perspective*. Malden, MA and Oxford, United Kingdom: Wiley/Blackwell.

Hesson, S., Seltzer, K., & Woodley, H. (2014). *Translanguaging in curriculum and instruction: A CUNY-NYSIEB guide for educators*. New York: CUNY-NYSIEB, The Graduate Center, The City University of New York. Available from: https://www.cuny-nysieb.org/wp-content/uploads/2016/04/Translanguaging-Guide-March-2013.pdf

Himley, M., & Carini, P. F. (2000). *From Another angle: Children's strengths and school standards : The Prospect Center's Descriptive Review of the Child*. New York: Teachers College Press.

Mahoney, D. K. (2017). *The Assessment of emergent bilinguals: Supporting English Language Learners*. Bristol, UK: Multilingual Matters.

NYSED (2017a) *Next Generation English Language Arts Learning Standards*. Available from: http://www.nysed.gov/common/nysed/files/programs/curriculum-instruction/nys-next-generation-ela-standards.pdf

NYSED (2017b) *Next Generation Mathematics Learning Standards*. Available from: http://www.nysed.gov/common/nysed/files/programs/curriculum-instruction/nys-next-generation-mathematics-p-12-standards.pdf

Paris, D. & Alim, H. S. (2017). *Culturally sustaining pedagogies: Teaching and learning for justice in a changing world*. New York: Teachers College Press.

Pérez Rosario, V., & Cao, V. (2015). *Translanguaging in Latino/a literature: A CUNY-NYSIEB guide for educators*. CUNY-NYSIEB, The Graduate Center, the City University of New York. https://www.cuny-nysieb.org/wp-content/uploads/2016/05/CUNY-NYSIEB-Latino-Literature-Guide-Final-January-2015.pdf

Sánchez, M. T. (Maite), García, O., & Solorza, C. (2017). Reframing language allocation policy in dual language bilingual education. *Bilingual Research Journal*, 41(1), 37–51. https://doi.org/10.1080/15235882.2017.1405098

Appendix

Below, find a list of guides, videos, multimedia pages, and other pedagogical materials created by CUNY-NYSIEB researchers and educators over the years, current to Winter 2020. These can all be found on our website, www.cuny-nysieb.org

CUNY-NYSIEB Guides:

- *Translanguaging: A CUNY-NYSIEB Guide for Educators* by Christina Celic and Kate Seltzer (2012, 2013)
- *The Languages of New York State: A CUNY-NYSIEB Guide for Educators* by Alexander Funk (2012)
- *Translanguaging in Curriculum and Instruction: A CUNY-NYSIEB Guide for Educators* by Sarah Hesson, Kate Seltzer, and Heather Woodley (2014)
- *Translanguaging in Latino/a Literature Guide: A CUNY-NYSIEB Guide for Educators* by Vanessa Pérez Rosario with Vivien Cao (2014)
- *El Translenguar: Una Guía de CUNY-NYSIEB Para Educadores – Versión Abreviada en Español* by Christina Celic and Kate Seltzer, translated by Diego Vargas Barona, Luis Guzmán Valerio y Maite (María Teresa) Sánchez (2016)
- *A Translanguaging Pedagogy for Writing: A CUNY-NYSIEB Guide for Educators* by Cecilia Espinosa, Laura Ascenzi-Moreno, and Sara Vogel (2016)
- *Translanguaging in Dual Language Bilingual Education: A Blueprint for Planning Units of Study* by Cristian R. Solorza, Gladys Y. Aponte, Tess Leverenz, Timothy Becker, Bianca Frias with special contributions by Ofelia García and María Teresa Sánchez (2019).

Resource compilations:

- *Relevant Literature on Latino/a Culture and Language* guides for all students; Middle and High School; Elementary School. Contributors: Laura Ascenzi-Moreno, Gladys Aponte, Andy Brown, Kathryn Carpenter, Ann Ebe, Cecilia Espinosa, Sarah Hesson, Leo Smith, Cristian Solorza, Heather Woodley, and Hulda Yau (2019)
- *Relevant Culturally Relevant Literature (Non-Latino/a Culture).* Contributors: Laura Ascenzi-Moreno, Gladys Aponte, Andy Brown,
- Kathryn Carpenter, Ann Ebe, Cecilia, Espinosa, Sarah Hesson, Leo Smith, Cristian Solorza, Heather Woodley, and Hulda Yau. (2019)
- Social Issues Book Club List (2018)
- Recommended Children's Books and Music for Early Childhood by Cecilia M. Espinosa & Alison Lehner-Quam (n.d.)

Teacher training materials:

- *School Leaders and Bilingualism: A CUNY-NYSIEB Guide to Professional Development* by Daria Witt and Megan Mehr (2012)
- *CUNY-NYSIEB Emergent Bilinguals Leadership Team: Planning Resource Packet* (CUNY-NYSIEB, 2016).
- *Presentations for Professional Development*: *Building a Strong Emergent Bilingual Resource Team* by Kate Menken (2015) and *Building, Deepening and/or Extending the Multilingual Ecology in your School* by Brian Collins and Luis Guzmán Valerio (2015)
- *Online Presentations*: 6-video Training series for the CUNY-NYSIEB resources *Translanguaging: A CUNY-NYSIEB Guide for Educators* (2015) and *Translanguaging in Curriculum and Instruction: A CUNY-NYSIEB Guide for Educators* (2016)

Web-based resources and videos:

- Interactive web resources:

    - *Supporting Emergent Bilinguals with Individualized Education Plans: Tips from CUNY-NYSIEB* by Kathryn Carpenter, Kahdeidra Martin, and Louis Olander
    - *Supporting Newcomer Emergent Bilinguals: Tips from CUNY-NYSIEB* by Kathryn Carpenter, Sara Vogel, and Tom Snell
    - *Supporting Emergent Bilingual Learners Labeled Long-Term English Language Learners (LTELL): Tips from CUNY-NYSIEB* by Kathryn Carpenter, Ivana Espinet, and Elizabeth Pratt
    - *Supporting Emergent Bilinguals Labeled SIFE: Tips from CUNY-NYSIEB* by Kathryn Carpenter, Ivana Espinet, and Lisa Auslander

- *Supporting Young Emergent Bilinguals: Tips from CUNY-NYSIEB* by Gladys Aponte and Laura Ascenzi Moreno
- *Developing Students' Identities as Bilingual Readers and Writers* by Gladys Aponte and Laura Ascenzi-Moreno
- *Fostering Bilingual Reading Identities in Early Childhood Programs: Storybook Extensions* by Gladys Aponte and Laura Ascenzi-Moreno

- *Webseries: Teaching Bilinguals (Even if You're Not One)* by Sara Vogel (2017)
- *CUNY-NYSIEB Ambassadors*: Videos and examples from the classrooms of teachers who have had success with translanguaging. Featuring Gladys Aponte, Andrew Brown, Charene Chapman-Santiago, Michelle Demeroukas, Sunisa Nuonsy, and Hulda Yau.
- *Reports/Topic Briefs*:

  - *Supporting Emergent Bilinguals in New York: Understanding Successful School Practices* by María Teresa Sánchez, Ivana Espinet, and Kate Seltzer
  - *New York State Education Department Policies, Mandates and Initiatives on the Education of English Language Learners* by Angela Carrasquillo, Diane Rodriguez and Laura Kaplan
  - *Translanguaging and Dual Language Bilingual Education Classrooms* (2018) by Kate Seltzer and Ofelia García

- *Webinars*:

  - *A Presentation on Principles and Practices of Bilingual Programs for Secondary Schools – Manhattan Bridges High School* featuring Mirza Sanchez Medina, Principal, and Izagma Alonso, Susan Lally, and Michelle Leonor, teachers, from Manhattan Bridges High School in New York City (2015)
  - *A Presentation on Principles and Practices of a Bilingual Program for Elementary and Middle Schools – PS/IS 210, Twenty-First Century Academy for Community Leadership* featuring Evelyn Linares, Principal, and Christina Cepero, Elizabeth Silva, and Isabel Lobelo, teachers, from PS/IS 210 in New York City (2015)
  - *Teaching Practices and Translanguaging Pedagogy in Elementary Transitional and One-Way Dual Language Bilingual Programs* featuring Hulda Yau, teacher at School #28, Rochester, New York (2016)
  - *Starting a Dual Language Bilingual Education Program for Young Bilinguals* featuring Tori Hunt and Alcira Jaar from Dos Puentes Elementary School, New York City (2016)
  - *Developing and Sustaining a High School for Newcomers: Bilingual Approaches* featuring Lindsey Maehlum, assistant principal at High School of World Cultures, New York City (2016)

- *A Blueprint to Incorporate Translanguaging in Dual Language Bilingual Education* featuring Cristian Solórza, director of Bilingual/Dual Language Programs at Bank Street College of Education with Gladys Aponte and Timothy Becker, bilingual teachers in New York City (2016)

CUNY-NYSIEB has also produced the following materials for the New York State Education Department Website: http://www.nysed.gov/bilingual-ed/bilingual-education-resources-supporting-and-sustaining-initiative

- Resource Guide

  - *Working with Multilingual Learners (MLLs)/English Language Learners (ELLs) Resource Guide* by Ann Ebe (2019) http://www.nysed.gov/common/nysed/files/programs/bilingual-ed/resource-guide-working-with-mlls_ells-obewl-2-a_1.pdf [nysed.gov]
  - Topic briefs

    - *Building on Emergent Multilingual Learners' Language Practices in Pre-School and Kindergarten Programs* (2019) by Gladys Aponte
    - *Supporting Developing Multilingual Learners/English Language Learners in New York State* (2019) by Kahdeidra Monét Martin, Heather H. Woodley, Sara Vogel, and Ann Ebe
    - *Supporting Former Multilingual Learners/English Language Learners in New York State* (2019) by Ivana Espinet, Heather Homonoff Woodley, and Ann Ebe
    - *Supporting Long-Term Multilingual Learners/English Language Learners in New York State* (2019) by Ann Ebe and Sara Vogel
    - *Supporting Students with Interrupted/Inconsistent Formal Education in New York State* (2019) by Ivana Espinet, Lisa Auslander and Elizabeth Pratt

  - Other Guides

    - *A Professional Learning Community – Understanding, Validating, and Building on the Language Practices of Emergent Multilingual Learners (EMLLs) in Prekindergarten* (2019) by Gladys Aponte and Laura Ascenzi-Moreno
    - *Developing Biliteracy in Dual Language Classrooms through Culturally and Linguistically Sustaining Literature* (2019) by Ivana Espinet and Gladys Aponte
    - *Using a Genre-based, Multilingual Approach to Prepare for the English Language Arts Regents Exam* (2019) by Kate Seltzer and Ivana Espinet with contributions from Lauren Ardizzone.

BOX 7.1 TEACHER/RESEARCHER

Elyn Ballantyne-Berry

4th to 8th grade, English as a New Language (ENL)

Currently, I am an ENL teacher in Chinatown Manhattan, NYC. The school I work in is a K-8 school with the elementary school and middle school functioning as two separate schools. I primarily work with emergent bilinguals in 4th to 8th grades. The vast majority of my students identify as Chinese, both born in the USA and China. Their home languages vary from Cantonese, Mandarin, Fujianese, Fukanese, to Toisanese. I also have a few Spanish speakers that are from countries all over the Caribbean and the Americas. The emergent bilinguals that I work with range from newcomers to those who have advanced English proficiency.

One assignment I worked on with my newcomers in fifth and sixth grades was to write a persuasive paragraph about their favorite season. I used translanguaging strategies throughout the lessons. I created lessons about weather, temperature, and clothing. Throughout these lessons, students were able to turn and talk with partners that spoke the same language, create multilingual word wall with illustrations, write independently, and practice speaking what they wrote. Through these partnerships, they practiced new vocabulary with someone that could help them navigate new words.

For the final paragraph, students were to write about what they thought was the best season. All of the vocabulary that was learned and discussed in previous lessons was written in English. The last sentence of their paragraph was up to them; they were to share a favorite thing to do during that season. As this was not taught in class, students had the option to write it in English or their home language. Some students wrote it in their home language in their notebooks but on the final copy decided to write in English. The important part was that they were able to share something that was important to them using all the features of their repertoire. The students were happy to share their ideas in different languages both with each other and in writing. Since they took the time and effort with this mini project, they were also able to share them with each other verbally. First, they practiced it with their partners and then shared with the whole group.

In the final copy, they were also asked to draw a picture to go along with their paragraph. I used the picture as a way to gain a deeper understanding of what some of them wrote in a language other than English. The final products were posted in the classroom and students excitedly showed their work

Summer is the best season.
You can wear t-shirts and shorts.
The days are hot. My favorite
thing is Jugar con mis hermanos
en el parque.

T/R BOX 7.1 FIGURE 7.1   Student #1 final paragraph

to their parents during the next parent-teacher conference. Teacher/Research Box Figures 7.1, 7.2, and 7.3 are examples of students' final paragraphs.

Providing the steps necessary for students to be successful and allowing them to show me some of who they are through their language choice has given me the chance to both get to know them as learners and how they choose to represent themselves as individuals. For me, translanguaging provides flexibility in my lessons so that students have more time to discuss topics

Winter is the best season. You can wear sweater and boot. The days are cold or freezing. The nights are freezing. My favorite part of winter is 和朋友一起在外面玩.

T/R BOX 7.1 FIGURE 7.2 Student #2 final paragraph

in which they already have background information while developing practices in English. It allows reprieve in their school day to be more than just an English Language Learner and be a child that knows a language, or two, and is developing new features to use.

T/R BOX 7.1 FIGURE 7.3 Student #3 final paragraph

BOX 7.2 TEACHER/RESEARCHER

Alexandra (Ali) Cabrera-Terry

Kindergarten, dual language bilingual

¿Qué es translanguaging in the clase? Often, my thinking isn't fully Spanish or fully English. If this is how I formulate thoughts, why would I not allow my kindergarten students to express themselves in the same way?

For 20 years, I've taught emergent bilingual children. Although these students' academic performance has often been perceived as substandard, the true issue is that we have not allowed them to use their full linguistic repertoire to demonstrate their ability.

Most of us, as bilingual literate adults, are able to make an educated decision as to when and how to use language based on social situations. However, many classroom settings oblige students to express the depth of their knowledge using only one form of language.

Through my work with CUNY-NYSIEB, I discovered that translanguaging could be a valuable strategy to help our especially our very young bilingual students achieve success. My classroom is a fluid language space where the language spoken by the young kindergarten children is the language that the students own—the language that they use without inhibitions. When they speak, read, or write, they know there are no linguistically incorrect answers. The empowerment granted to the students yields much better academic result.

Throughout the year, I now include a study of cognates. This fascinates little children, as they discover the vast knowledge they have. All of my students come from homes in which Spanish is spoken. Most aren't aware of the relationship between Spanish and English. In my classroom now what is important is that my five- and six-year-olds speak and speak cogently and freely. On day, Jesús said: "I like to eat frutas." In the past, I would have corrected him and would have said to him, you mean "fruits." But now I responded: "Fantástico, me too; I love to eat fruits." I validated Jesús translanguaging by using mine, and then introduced the English cognate, a way of ensuring that Jesús adds this new word to his repertoire without being chastised.

Students in an art class are not limited to just use charcoal or pencil to create their art—they are given the different mediums to express their ideas and feelings; likewise, the linguistic tableau through which students express themselves is enhanced and enriched by translanguaging.

8

FOSTERING BILINGUAL READING IDENTITIES IN DUAL LANGUAGE BILINGUAL CLASSROOMS

Gladys Y. Aponte, Ivana Espinet, and Kate Seltzer

A vignette as introduction

GAUDY: I get it, how she was calling her *Mary López*, pero no estaba su nombre. So, I mean… no importa que [habían] muchas … Marías. No importa cuanto … tú tienes que llamar alguien su nombre de verdad.

KARINA: Yo pienso que la maestra no estaba respecting el nombre de María Isabel. Como ella, I think she felt like she's a child, so she wouldn't know the difference … Y una cosa que yo like I noticed es que cuando Marta was with her in the library, she didn't call her Mary, she called her María.

GAUDY: She respects her!

KARINA: Exactly!

CATHERINE: Everybody should respect María Isabel's name!

GAUDY: Ok, so, I don't think that the teacher was disrespecting her … Ella estaba como, como, she was like complicated. She didn't really want to call somebody that …

CATHERINE: … Maybe she was afraid that if she said *María*, then all the other Marías would be like 'What?', and then …

KARINA: That's why she has the *Isabel* part. That's why she has the *Isabel* part.

CATHERINE: Exactly.

GAUDY: Yeah.

In the vignette presented above from a dual language bilingual New York City public school classroom, three fourth-grade students critique the actions of the teacher in the novel *My Name is María Isabel/Me llamo María Isabel* by Alma Flor Ada. Rather than call the main character by her name, *María Isabel*—namesake of her two grandmothers—the teacher refers to her as *Mary López* because there are two other *Marías* in the class. Gaudy, Karina, and Catherine engaged in this discussion as part of their social justice literary unit, which their teachers, Mr. Jay and Ms. Rubio, redesigned using a translanguaging perspective that welcomed critical, bilingual conversations like this one.

Ms. Rubio and Mr. Jay are the co-teachers of this self-contained English/Spanish dual language bilingual classroom. This classroom is what is called in New York City a "Classroom with Integrated Co-Teaching" (ICT). This means that it includes students who have been identified as having a disability and have an Individualized Education Program (IEP). No more than 40% of the students can have an IEP in these classrooms. According to the New York City Department of Education (2019), "there are two teachers—a general education teacher and a special education teacher. They work together to adapt materials and modify instruction to make sure the entire class can participate." (For teachers in other ICT classrooms, see Teacher/Researcher Boxes 11.1 and 15.1). The teachers began the unit by inviting the class to generate a list of social issues they cared about, based on their personal experiences and texts that they had previously read. With the language of instruction alternating daily, students were grouped according to their reading level in each language to read books featuring a variety of social issues. Although the texts were primarily written in English or Spanish, the teachers made sure to also incorporate books in which authors translanguage across other languages, such as *Drita, My Homegirl* (English and Albanian) *and The Keeping Quilt* (English and Yiddish).

In our experiences working with bilingual students and classroom teachers around issues of biliteracy, several practices have stood out as particularly promising. In this chapter, we will share several examples from classroom teachers who have collaborated with The City University of New York-New York State Initiative on Emergent Bilinguals (CUNY-NYSIEB) to design pedagogy that develops students' bilingual reading identities, which includes the application of students' lived experiences as bilingual, bicultural people to their understandings and readings of texts. While we believe that biliteracy development should be approached holistically with the understanding that literacy instruction is a system that includes four instructional elements: Oracy, reading, writing, and metalanguage (Escamilla et al., 2014) which are intrinsically connected to one another during instruction, in this chapter we focus on reading. Based on our work with these bilingual teachers and students, we have identified five central principles for fostering students' bilingual reading identities: (1) begin from students' bilingual readings and language practices, (2) choose texts thoughtfully, (3) leverage students' metalinguistic and bilingual awareness, (4) go beyond the text through linguistic and cultural extensions, and (5) foster bilingual orgullo.

Teaching two languages or teaching students bilingually?

In recent years, school districts have begun creating and expanding dual language bilingual education (DLBE) programs across the United States. Contrary to transitional bilingual education programs, which temporarily use students' home languages while they develop English, the goal of DLBE programs is to develop bilingualism and biliteracy. Language and content are taught simultaneously, and students are expected to perform academically across the content areas in both English and the other language of instruction. However, DLBE programs are often structured based on policies that rigidly separate the languages of instruction and allocate specific times or spaces for each language (Sánchez, García & Solorza, 2017). This strict separation of languages—informed by a monoglossic view of bilingualism rather than dynamic language practices of bilingual communities— creates a linguistic hierarchy that positions standardized versions of each language as more valuable than students' home language practices. Students learn to undo their bilingualism, and bilingual identities are prevented from flourishing in bilingual classrooms (García & Kleifgen, 2018; García & Otheguy, 2017; García & Tupas, 2019; Palmer & Martínez, 2016).

As Sánchez, García and Solorza (2017) discuss, we must ask ourselves if these programs are merely *teaching two languages* or *teaching students bilingually*? In order to foster bilingual reading identities (García, 2020), educators must embrace a dynamic understanding of bilingualism and make space for translanguaging activities. Translanguaging recognizes that bilinguals have one complex, unitary linguistic system from which they agentively use features to communicate and make meaning (García, 2009; García & Li Wei, 2014; Otheguy, García & Reid, 2015, 2018). Teachers who take a translanguaging approach understand that reading is also a unified process, in which students fluidly use features from their full linguistic repertoires to make meaning of texts, regardless of the language of those texts (Ascenzi-Moreno, 2018; García & Kleifgen, 2019). Rather than view bilingual children as two monolinguals in one and teach literacy in each language separately, educators must "support emergent bilinguals' reading development by acknowledging and encouraging them to use their entire linguistic repertoire as they read" (Ascenzi-Moreno, 2018, p. 357). Since linguistic features are tied to cultural backgrounds, it is essential that teachers design flexible bilingual spaces for students to critically reflect on their unique bilingual, multicultural perspectives (Lee, Hill-Bonnet & Gillespie, 2008).

Fostering bilingual reading identities: Five key principles

While it is important that DLBE classrooms preserve spaces for each language of instruction, it is also necessary for students to have access to and reflect on their full linguistic repertoires when engaging in literacy activities. The act of reading involves a critical dialogue between students' analysis of the meaning of a text and their understanding of the world in which it is produced and shared. To help students understand their developing bilingual worldviews and their identities as bilingual readers educators must think beyond the monolingual perspectives (España & Herrera, 2020; García, 2020; García & Kleifgen, 2019). In the following sections we discuss five principles that can guide teachers in fostering an environment that supports the development of students' bilingual reading identities.

Begin from students' bilingual readings and language practices

Bilinguals perceive the world differently than monolinguals. This means that when bilinguals read, write, learn, and communicate, they draw from repertoires that are rich in a variety of cultural and linguistic features. Fostering bilingual reading identities entails welcoming, celebrating, and then leveraging the unique bilingual worldviews and language practices that individual students bring into the classroom.

García, Johnson and Seltzer (2017), conceptualize the *translanguaging corriente* as "the current or flow of students' dynamic bilingualism that runs through our classrooms and schools" (p. 21). Since schools regularly teach students to suppress their dynamic bilingualism and see the world from monolingual perspectives, teachers must leverage this translanguaging corriente by bringing students' bilingual reading practices to the surface (García, 2020; García & Kleifgen, 2019). This can be done, in part, by drawing on what bilingual readers already do as they read bilingually. For example, prior to the conversation in the opening vignette, Mr. Jay and Ms. Rubio modeled how they use their bilingual repertoires during reading. Both teachers were explicit about their ideological perspectives in support of translanguaging, or their *translanguaging stance*, which informed their pedagogical framework (García, Johnson & Seltzer, 2017). They organized collaborative student-led reading experiences where students were encouraged to use Spanish and English flexibly and to share the bilingual reading strategies they used. Moreover, while everyone read books in the language of instruction, they provided emergent bilingual students with the text in both languages allowing all students to make meaningful connections and participate in group discussions. As a result, Gaudy, Karina, and Catherine felt comfortable interacting bilingually, and confidently applied their bilingual perspectives to analyze the injustices of being called Mary versus María Isabel.

It is important to emphasize the sociocultural nature of learning by designing grouping structures that foster collaborative work (Cappellini, 2005). Literature circles, also called book clubs, can provide a platform to leverage collaborative learning to teach biliteracy if they are grounded in students' dynamic bilingualism. This means that their traditional structure must be adapted in order to leverage and extend students' linguistic practices. For example, in traditional literature circles, students take turns in specific roles such as "discussion director," "word wizard," or "connector" (Cappellini, 2005). In working with bilingual students, DLBE teachers must be explicit about how they can bring their bilingualism to each role. A "word wizard" finds new vocabulary in a text and shares the definition of a word with the group. In a bilingual setting, the "word wizard" could make connections between the two languages of instruction, while also finding new or important words in the text. The "connector" might try to make connections between books that they read in both languages, or ask questions about how the author uses language in different parts of the book. In addition, while it is important to provide some language supports for interactions in the language of instruction, such as sentence starters for the group discussion, it is also essential that students be able to use their full linguistic repertoire, moving fluidly between the two languages to make sense of the text.

Choose texts thoughtfully

To foster students' bilingual reading identities, it is essential that they engage with culturally and linguistically sustaining (Paris & Alim, 2017) texts (CUNY-NYSIEB, 2018; España & Herrera, 2020; see also Chapter 11, this volume). These include texts originally written in the language of instruction, books that have been translated, and books in which authors translanguage. Children also benefit from texts that explore and represent a variety of cultural and linguistic experiences. It is important to select some texts that include bilingual/biliterate characters so children have access to stories set in a world where bilingualism is the norm (García & Li Wei, 2014). Reading starts with the background the readers bring to text. Children come from diverse backgrounds with different ideas about the world, previous experiences and knowledge that they use to make sense of texts. Having culturally and linguistically sustaining books in the classroom enhances reading comprehension (Alanís, 2007; Ebe, 2010; Freeman, Freeman & Freeman, 2003) and gives students the opportunity to engage their bilingual imaginations and relate their bilingual and multicultural lives (Callow, 2017).

In Ms. Rubio's and Mr. Jay's class, *My Name is María Isabel/Me llamo María Isabel* was thoughtfully selected for being culturally and linguistically relevant to their students. The book speaks to the experience of many (im)migrant children, with the main character, María Isabel, starting school in a new place after moving from Puerto Rico. As she adjusts to various changes, the story addresses themes such as personal identity, prejudice, responsibilities, and power differences that the fourth-graders could relate to. Since the book is available both in English and Spanish, the teachers used it during the program's "Spanish days" and "English days." Students were then able to refer to both books to compare the author's use of language, including how Alma Flor Ada, the author, uses translanguaging as a literary device. For example, early in the book, when she describes María Isabel's first time in her class, she writes that the teacher asked her name and she responded: "María Isabel Salazar López." The author continues: "In Spanish, she would have added 'para servirle.'" Some of the questions that the children discussed are: Why did the author write the last phrase in Spanish? How does using Spanish help the author convey María Isabel's feelings upon entering a new school where they don't speak Spanish? When do people use "para servirle"?

Analyzing books from bilingual authors that portray bilingual characters in situations and contexts that are recognizable to bilingual students can help them understand the power of using translanguaging as a literary device. Students come to see that, just like in their own lives, authors use language in myriad ways to connect with bilingual/bicultural readers and to convey the bilingual/bicultural lives of characters in texts. The use of culturally and linguistically relevant books provides authentic opportunities for students to use their bilingualism to make sense of texts and to develop better understandings of their bilingual identities.

Leverage students' metalinguistic and bilingual awareness

Developing students' bilingual reading identities also means fostering students' understandings of how language is used in their families, communities, school, and in society at large, as well as why it is used in these ways. In bilingual classrooms, there are many possibilities for engaging students in metalanguage—thinking and talking about language and the relationships between languages (Escamilla et al., 2014). This entails helping students engage in critical analyses of how others may judge and interpret language practices in different contexts (Alim, 2005; Emdin, 2016; García & Kleifgen, 2018; Paris & Alim, 2017), as well as explicitly teaching them how to utilize their full linguistic repertoires to comprehend texts and to understand how the skills and knowledge that they learn in one language help them build on what they know and can do in an additional language (Escamilla et al., 2014).

Prior to the conversation that opened this chapter, the students in the fourth-grade classroom had engaged in various classroom activities that enhanced their bilingual awareness. In particular, Ms. Rubio and Mr. Jay made an effort to highlight how their own bilingualism allowed them to enjoy and make sense of texts in ways that monolinguals cannot. One way they did this was by modeling how they ask themselves questions and make interpretations in one language even when the text is written in another language. Students were guided in analyzing their own bilingual reading practices as well. The teachers also encouraged students to take up their bilingual lenses in order to make inferences and enhance their reading comprehension. For example, they created an activity that reminded students how their bilingual perspectives could help them deduce the meaning of unknown cognates. Presented with unfamiliar words such as *remedy, edifice,* and *matrimony* on an English day, students were able to determine their meaning by relating to words that they use frequently in conversational Spanish—*remedio, edificio,* and *matrimonio.* Moreover, Ms. Rubio and Mr. Jay often placed texts side-by side for students to analyze how idioms, expressions, and punctuation are used differently across languages. Strategic activities like these activate students' bilingual lenses and remind them to employ/engage their entire linguistic repertoire as they read.

Creativity and criticality (Li Wei, 2011) are central to honing bilingual students' metalinguistic awareness. Since many bilingual authors move between languages flexibly as a narrative technique, teachers should engage students in a variety of critical metalinguistic analyses of how authors use translanguaging as a literacy device. For example, when reading the English version of *My Name is María Isabel,* Ms. Rubio asked questions such as: Why did Alma Flor Ada maintain Spanish terms like "Papá" and "para servile" in María Isabel's dialogue and internal thoughts?

To further build students' metalinguistic awareness, the teachers used read alouds to foster whole class discussions about authors' uses of translanguaging. For example, Mr. Jay engaged the class in a read aloud of the book *Eagle Song,* by Joseph Bruchac, about an Iroquois boy who moves to Brooklyn, New York. Throughout the book, the author teaches about Native American culture and he does it often through the use of language. At one point in the book author used the term "heh," which in Mohawk means: "Yes, I want to hear a story." Mr. Jay paused while reading so the students would turn to a partner and discuss the possible reasons for the author's use of the term. Many of the children were able to explain that this is very particular cultural expression that wouldn't have the same effect in English. Later, Mr. Jay realized that after the discussion students began to look for similar patterns in their books during independent reading.

During this process, the class kept a growing anchor chart where they continued to add reasons authors might translanguage in a text. Some of the reasons that the children observed and recorded included: To illustrate the character's cultural and linguistic background, convey a character's personality, to add humor, and because their word cannot be translated. As they analyzed the many reasons authors choose to translanguage, students became empowered to use language in ways that transcended boundaries in their own writing.

Overall, modeling metalinguistic analysis and teaching strategies for students to use their bilingualism to make sense of texts enriches students' understandings of language and provides them with tools to build their reading identities as bilinguals. By drawing students' attention to the myriad ways they can use their bilingualism to engage with texts on a deeper level—namely by drawing on the metalinguistic awareness fostered in their own bilingual homes and communities—teachers can enrich students' understandings of those texts and the linguistic choices of authors. By modeling metalinguistic analysis and providing students with new ways of explicitly bringing their bilingualism into their reading, teachers can help students build and expand their own "toolkits" with which they can build their reading identities as bilinguals.

Go beyond texts through linguistic and cultural extensions

While centering culturally and linguistically sustaining literature is fundamental, it is also important for educators to support students in going beyond texts through linguistic and cultural extensions. This requires flexibility, creativity, and an in-depth understanding of students' backgrounds and their communities.

Early childhood teachers play a key role in fostering bilingual readers, since it is critical that children begin to recognize their developing bilingual reading identities from an early age. As children engage in emergent literacy activities, teachers should leverage their natural bilingual interpretations and multimodal ways of languaging. Singing, drawing, and book-related pretend play (Welsch, 2008) are powerful methods of encouraging young emergent bilinguals to play *beyond* the text in inventive ways that expand the story's elements and reflect their dynamic bilingual worlds (also see Chapter 10 and Teacher/Researcher Box 10.1, this volume).

One way we have seen educators extend students' bilingual interpretation of texts is by providing opportunities for students to re-present them (Walqui, 2006) in ways that align with their bilingual and bicultural realities. For example, in one English/Spanish bilingual kindergarten classroom, children were encouraged to use their bilingual imaginations to re-envision traditional tales like *The Little Red Hen.* The teacher asked students to imagine the story taking place in their hometowns, or to imagine characters that shared their cultural and linguistic backgrounds. Moreover, since play is central to early childhood learning, the teacher elicited bilingual ways of playing by added culturally relevant playthings to the play centers.

The kindergarteners' bilingual interpretations of the story took various forms through their play. In the kitchen area, children created bilingual menus and pretended to make and sell dishes like flan, arepas, empanadas, and quipes. In the puppet show center, one group reenacted the story in a campo of the Dominican

Republic, where many of the students' families were from. The hen grew her crops in the conuco and prepared her goods in the outdoor kitchen's fogón. The children decided that the characters spoke English, Spanish, Haitian Creole, and Papiamento—languages that reflected the classroom language practices. By setting up activities that encouraged students to use all of their communicative resources in the play centers, this teacher helped her students bring their bilingual imaginations and diverse language practices into their play. Students' reimagining of *The Little Red Hen* clearly demonstrates their understandings of their own bilingual, bicultural communities and their pride in those cultural elements represented in their play.

Partnerships with families are essential in going beyond texts through linguistic and cultural extensions. Family members bring a broad range of understandings, language, culture, histories, and funds of knowledge (Moll, Amanti, Neff & Gonzalez, 1992) which should become part of the classroom's literacy (García, Herrera, Hesson & Kleyn, 2013; García & Kleifgen, 2018). In the kindergarten classroom, for example, families helped select pretend foods, dress-up clothing, and playthings that encourage students' cultural and linguistic diversity to shine as they engage in reenactments, portray characters, and even refer to bilingual books during their play. Adding such culturally relevant and book-related props (Welsch, 2008) to play areas promoted students' bilingual interpretations of texts.

Going beyond texts also means expanding conventional notions of "texts" and taking flexible and creative approaches toward achieving reading standards (García, Johnson & Seltzer, 2017). During the process of re-presenting a text, for example, it is fundamental to encourage students to flexibly use various modes of expression so that they can enrich their re-presentation by using images, sounds, music, and any other semiotic devices that are part of their everyday lives. Digital storytelling, intergenerational interviews, artistic displays, music, film, websites, memes, podcasts, dance, and drama are other ways students can engage with multimodal literacies (García, Herrera, Hesson & Kleyn, 2013). Family members can bring bilingual oral storytelling to the classroom, or if they are not available to be present in person they can share audio and video recordings that can serve as supplemental texts (see Chapters 11 and 15, and Teacher/Researcher Box 15.1, this volume). These diverse literacies help narrow the linguistic and cultural gap that exists between many schools and bilingual communities and help students see themselves as bilingual readers of multimodal texts.

Foster bilingual orgullo

At the heart of each of the principles presented above is the importance of maintaining a strong culture of bilingual orgullo. Bilingual students must come to understand and constantly reflect on the virtues of their bilingual identities—within and beyond the school setting. As illustrated throughout this chapter, there are numerous ways educators can highlight the advantages bilingual perspectives give students in their literacy practices. But educators should also build opportunities to cultivate bilingual pride through their curricula.

Mr. Jay and Ms. Rubio regularly find ways to authentically and creatively celebrate their students' bilingualism throughout the school day. One way they have done this is by allowing students the space to write and share songs and poems about their bilingualism. Another way they foster bilingual pride is by enthusiastically making an effort to learn language with and from students and their families. The fourth graders begin and end the day by greeting each other in all of the languages of the classroom, including Arabic, Hebrew, and Urdu, even though Spanish and English are the languages of instruction in their bilingual classroom.

In addition to these creative approaches, Ms. Rubio and Mr. Jay embed opportunities to highlight the beauty of being bilingual in everyday lessons. For example, when teaching the structure of an essay, the teachers' model, reading an essay about the social benefits of being bilingual. During math class, students practice interpreting and creating bar graphs by representing the languages spoken in their families. When writing narratives, Mr. Jay and Ms. Rubio encourage students to develop bilingual characters who speak more than one language in their story. And for their biographical unit, students are encouraged to choose from a range of bilingual role models, including authors, mathematicians, celebrities, and scientists. Learning about bilingual individuals and their journeys can set the stage for students to explore their bilingual and bicultural identities in a way that leads to a deeper understanding of and pride in their own bilingualism. Moreover, organizing instruction in this transformative way invites translanguaging transformation spaces (Sánchez, García & Solorza, 2017) that are necessary for students to challenge existing linguistic hierarchies in school and society overall.

Conclusion

Learning in two languages alone does not foster children's identities as bilingual learners. Developing bilingual reading identities is a fundamental practice for all educators of bilingual students. Regardless of the classroom structure and the content area being taught, teachers must recognize that bilinguals view the world differently than monolinguals. The five principles discussed in this chapter—beginning from students' bilingual readings and language practices, choosing texts thoughtfully, leveraging students' metalinguistic and bilingual awareness, going beyond texts through linguistic and cultural extensions, and fostering students' bilingual orgullo—can guide teachers as they work to develop students' bilingual reading identities and challenge the monoglossic ideologies that inform literacy curricula. Students' dynamic bilingual practices are always present in the classroom, either overtly or covertly. Teachers have the power to design instructional spaces that leverage those practices and bring them to the surface. In doing so, they increase student engagement in literacy practices. By creating opportunities for students across programs to develop identities as bilingual readers, educators can take a powerful step toward disrupting the hierarchies of language practices that often exist in schools, including in dual language bilingual programs.

References

Alanís, I. (2007). Developing literacy through culturally relevant texts. *Social Studies and the Young Learner, 20*(1), 20–32.

Alim, H.S. (2005). Critical language awareness in the United States: Revisiting issues and revising pedagogies in a resegregated society. *Educational Researcher, 34*(7), 24–31.

Ascenzi-Moreno, L. (2018). Translanguaging and responsive assessment adaptations: Emergent bilingual readers through the lens of possibility. *Language Arts, 95*(6), 355–369.

Callow, J. (2017). "Nobody spoke like I did": Picture books, critical literacy, and global contexts. *The Reading Teacher, 71*(2), 231–237. https://doi.org/10.1002/trtr.1626

Cappellini, M. (2005). *Balancing reading & language learning: A resource for teaching English language learners, K-5*. Stenhouse Publishers.

CUNY-NYSIEB. (2019). *Culturally relevant books and resources*. Retrieved from https://www.cuny-nysieb.org/translanguaging-resources/culturally-relevant-books-and-resources/

Ebe, A.E. (2010). Culturally relevant texts and reading assessment for English language learners. *Reading Horizons, 50*(3). Retrieved from https://scholarworks.wmich.edu/reading_horizons/vol50/iss3/5

Emdin, C. (2016). *For white folks who teach in the hood, and the rest of y'all too: Reality pedagogy and urban education*. Boston, MA: Beacon Press.

Escamilla, K., Hopewell, S., Butvilofsky, S., Sparrow, W., Soltero-González, L., Ruiz-Figueroa, O., & Escamilla, M. (2014). *Biliteracy from the start: Literacy squared in action* (pp. 25–26). Philadelphia, PA: Caslon Publishing.

España, C. & Herrera, L. (2020). *En Comunidad: Lessons for centering the voices and experiences of bilingual Latinx students*. Portsmouth, NH: Heinemann.

Freeman, Y.S., Freeman, A., & Freeman, D. (2003). Home run books: Connecting students to culturally relevant texts. *NABE News, 26*(3), 5–12.

García, O. (2009). *Bilingual education in the 21st century: A global perspective*. Malden, MA: Wiley/Blackwell.

García, O. (2020). Translanguaging and Latinx bilingual readers. *The Reading Teacher, 73*(5), 557–562. https://doi.org/10.1002/trtr.1883

García, O., Herrera, L., Hesson, S., & Kleyn, T. (2013). *A CUNY-NYSIEB framework for the education of emergent bilinguals with low home literacy: 4–12 grades*. New York, NY: CUNY-NYSIEB, The Graduate Center, The City University of New York. Retrieved on April 28, 2019, from: https://www.cuny-nysieb.org/wp-content/uploads/2016/05/CUNY-NYSIEB-Framework-for-EB-with-Low-Home-Literacy-Spring-2013-Final-Version-05-08-13.pdf

García, O., Johnson, S., & Seltzer, K. (2017). *The translanguaging classroom. Leveraging student bilingualism for learning.* Philadelphia, PA: Caslon.

García, O. & Kleifgen, J. (2018). *Educating emergent bilinguals: Policies, programs and practices for English learners* (2nd ed.). New York, NY: Teachers College Press.

García, O. & Kleifgen, J.A. (2019). Translanguaging and literacies. *Reading Research Quarterly, 55*(4). https://doi.org/10.1002/rrq.286

García, O., & Otheguy, R. (2017). Interrogating the language gap of young bilingual and bidialectal students. *International Multilingual Research Journal, 11*(1), 52–65. https://doi.org/10.1080/19313152.2016.1258190

García, O., & Tupas, R. (2019). Doing and undoing bilingualism in education. In A. De Houwer & L. Ortega (Eds.), *The Cambridge handbook of bilingualism* (pp. 390–407). Cambridge, UK: Cambridge University Press.

García, O. & Li, W. (2014). Translanguaging and education. In *Translanguaging: Language, bilingualism and education* (pp. 63–77). London: Palgrave Macmillan.

Lee, J., Hill-Bonnet L. & Gillespie J., (2008) Learning in two languages: Interactional space for becoming bilingual speakers. *The International Journal of Bilingual Education and Bilingualism, 11*(1), 75–94. https://doi.org/10.2167/beb412.0 [doi.org]

Li, Wei. (2011). Moment Analysis and translanguaging space: Discursive construction of identities by multilingual Chinese youth in Britain. *Journal of Pragmatics, 43*, 1222–1235. https://doi.org/10.1016/j.pragma.2010.07.035

Moll, L.C., Amanti, C., Neff, D., & Gonzalez, N. (1992). Funds of knowledge for teaching: Using a qualitative approach to connect homes and classrooms. *Theory into Practice, 31*(2), 132–141. https://doi.org/10.1080/00405849209543534

New York City Department of Education. (2019). *District Schools: Integrated Co-Teaching Services (full or part-time).* Retrieved from https://www.schools.nyc.gov/special-education/school-settings/district-schools

Otheguy, R., García, O., & Reid, W. (2015). Clarifying translanguaging and deconstructing named languages: A perspective from linguistics. *Applied Linguistics Review, 6*(3), 281–307. https://doi.org/10.1515/applirev-2015-0014

Otheguy, R., García, O., & Reid, W. (2018). A translanguaging view of the linguistic system of bilinguals. *Applied Linguistics Review, 10*(4). https://doi.org/10.1515/applirev-2018-0020

Paris, D.H., & Alim, S. (Eds.). (2017). *Culturally sustaining pedagogies: Teaching and learning for justice in a changing world.* New York, NY: Teachers College Press.

Palmer, D. & Martínez, R. (2016). Developing biliteracy: What do teachers really need to know about language? *Language Arts, 93*, 379–385.

Sánchez, M.T., García, O., & Solorza, C. (2017). Reframing language allocation policy in dual language bilingual education. *Bilingual Research Journal*, 1–15. https://doi.org/10.1080/15235882.2017.1405098

Walqui, A. (2006). Scaffolding instruction for English language learners: A conceptual framework. *International Journal of Bilingual Education and Bilingualism, 9*(2), 159–180. https://doi.org/10.1080/13670050608668639

Welsch, J.G. (2008). Playing within and beyond the story: Encouraging book-related pretend play. *The Reading Teacher, 62*(2), 138–148. https://doi.org/10.1598/RT.62.2.5

BOX 8.1 TEACHER/RESEARCHER

Jason Horowitz & Tim Becker

4th grade dual language bilingual

We teach 4th grade at a dual-language bilingual school in New York City that serves a population of students who are linguistically, ethnically and socio-economically very diverse. Most of our students speak both English and Spanish at home, some speak only English at home, some speak only Spanish at home, and some also speak other languages as well, such as Mixteco or French. Many of our students are immigrants or children of immigrants coming especially from the Dominican Republic, Mexico and Central America.

At our school, there are three classes per grade. In the fourth grade, where both of us teach, two of the classes follow a side-by-side model, meaning that students switch daily between and an English classroom and a Spanish classroom. Jason is the "English side" of one of those classrooms. The third classroom is what in New York State is called an integrated co-teaching (ICT) classroom where a special education teacher and general education teacher work together and where approximately 40% of students have been classified as "students with disabilities." In this classroom both teachers teach in both languages. Tim is the general education teacher in this classroom. As with the other two classrooms, the instructional time is divided into an English day and a Spanish day.

As a dual language bilingual school, we have explicit times and spaces designated as English or Spanish, as described above. However, as bilingual educators, we have come to understand that bilingual and multilingual children naturally translanguage all the time to make sense of the world around them. As such, throughout the day we are exploring how we can incorporate translanguaging as both a scaffold for language learning and also as a critical lens. With this work, we have decided to set aside certain times dedicated to translanguaging, when children are encouraged to use their whole linguistic repertoire to critically study language in our community and our broader society. We describe here the social issues book club unit in which we initiated our translanguaging work.

Our fourth graders are a curious and critical bunch. They are very tuned into fairness. They naturally raise questions about why one group of people or one language is treated differently from another. In our social issues book club unit, students work together to uncover social issues, such as racism, unemployment or immigration, in their books. When we began thinking about where to incorporate translanguaging into our curriculum, our social issues book club unit was a natural fit.

One way that we incorporated translanguaging into the unit, was through the purposeful selection of mentor texts. We wanted texts that showed interesting examples of how authors use translanguaging. For the book clubs, we included books where translanguaging was used by the authors, like *My Name is María Isabel* by Alma Flor Ada or *La Mariposa* by Franciso Jiménez. We also brought in books where authors other than Latinx ones used translanguaging, such as *Drita My Homegirl* by Jenny Lombard or *The Keeping Quilt* by Patricia Polaco. By carefully connecting children with the right books, we set them up to discover how and why authors use translanguaging.

We also used translanguaging strategies to support students' access to the books. For example, some of the students have a much lower reading level in one language. We wanted to make sure all students could think critically about social issues in both languages. To do this, we found some books that were available in both Spanish and English, and we allowed some students to preview the book in their stronger language. As a result, they could read the book again in their developing language with their book club and access those rich discussions in their developing language.

Once students were paired with the right books, we wanted to give them the tools to identify and analyze examples of translanguaging. We chose *My Name is Jorge*, a book of bilingual poems by Jane Medina, to read aloud as a class to introduce the idea of translanguaging. When we first introduced the idea of translanguaging, many students assumed that the author translanguaged because she did not know a certain word. Studying the poems together carefully, the students came to see there were many reasons to translanguage. For example, after reading the poem "Chocolate Icing," one student partnership identified multiple reasons that the author might have translanguaged when using the word "la chula" in a poem that was otherwise written in English. Alemmy noted that the word, "*... esa palabra no existe en inglés.*" Her partner, Alexa observed that "*... lo dijo en español para ser chistoso,*" alleging that the author uses Spanish as a mechanism to be funny. Students were quickly able to identify reasons for the author's linguistic practices, as they realized they already had experience using language this way. It felt powerful to have a name to give recognition to students' translanguaging moves.

We also wanted students to examine how the power differential between languages can be a social issue itself. Sometimes, students discovered this through the eyes of the character. For example, in *My Name is María Isabel*, the teacher tells María Isabel that she should use the name Mary at school. Our students could see that the teacher was not treating María Isabel fairly because she had a Spanish name. The students also saw this issue outside of the books when we began discussing translation. Students noticed some of our books had been translated and began asking questions. Why is it that many of our books were originally written in English and then translated to Spanish, but not the other way around? Why our some of our books translated into a variety of Spanish from Spain instead of a variety of Spanish from the Americas?

Throughout the translanguaging social issues book club unit, there were several notable outcomes that teachers experienced and observed. For our multilingual teaching team, bringing translanguaging into our classrooms shifted our understanding of language use in academic communities. Considering the fact our dual-language program separates language, this work helped recognize the coexistence of students' diverse language knowledge and practices and build a space for it in our classrooms. Before implementation, we considered several possible implications and outcomes of translanguaging: Would one language be more dominant? Would Spanish or English language development falter? We also hoped that unifying language spaces would foster increased empathy for the multilingual and multicultural differences that existed in our community. As a multilingual community, this became an entry point to collectively analyze, recognize, and celebrate the intentional linguistic choices that both student and professional authors make on a daily basis.

Teachers observed an increase in student interest as they began to analyze and consider their diverse language practices. The social issues mentor texts provided authentic examples of professional authors translanguaging, which in turn validated the students' own writing practices. Importantly, the authors and characters in our books became relatable role-models with whom many students were able to identify. Finally, students demonstrated more confidence and autonomy when making linguistic choices in their speech and writing, while teachers became more aware of the intention of such choices.

The reactions from students continued to manifest themselves in the coming months, especially during our writing units. One student, Welicer, wanted to write his personal essay in English class about a drink from the Dominican Republic, *Morir Soñando*. While brainstorming ideas, he asked for permission to write about this topic, because he didn't think that he was "allowed" to use Spanish words in his English writing. The lack of confidence and need for "permission" exhibited by Welicer, turned into pride and validation, as he wrote, *"Have you heard about the juice of morisoñando? Many people don't know but the juice of morir soñando is special. Many people like the juice of morir soñando because its special to the Dominican culture."* In this case, Welicer was under the impression that in school, Spanish and English knowledge existed in two separate spaces, but he came to see that he had the agency to translanguage in academic writing.

Months after our social issues book club unit, we noticed that translanguaging became a regular term in our classroom vernacular, as more students began to actively incorporate diverse language practices into their written work. During a Historical Fiction writing unit, a student named Brooke Lynn wrote a story set in Cuba. She free-flowingly made purposeful language choices; *"...I work with my papá Elario. Vivo sola en Cienfuegos. Me and my father work in the plátano fields. Me and him work very hard."* Some examples included culturally specific terms, while others aimed to convey emotions. *"...Living sola is very lonely, every night I wonder what living with people is like. I ask Papá Dios for guidance..."* The culmination of this work resulted in a collective shift in the teachers' perceptions of language knowledge and use in a bilingual classroom, while concurrently observing a profound change in the linguistic behavior of students. Overall, this process was transformative to our teaching practices and classroom environments.

In conclusion, we observed a gradual sequence of effects on students after the implementation of our translanguaging work. First, students gained *awareness* of the choices made by authors, and began to identify and analyze these choices intentionally. This eventually leads to a sense of *empowerment*, as students understood that they can also make choices about their own language practices across settings. Next, they gained *consciousness* about the language choices that were being made in their classroom and their community. They demonstrated excitement to openly discuss and contemplate the social and academic value of multilingualism, which we celebrated at a year-end assembly. Our students chose to adapt a poem to show what they learned about translanguaging. In, "Ode to Dos Puentes/Oda a Dos Puentes," they acknowledged their bilingual use and their translanguaging: *"Tanto como en inglés, como en español, y usamos translanguage."* This process was extremely impactful to our academic community, as students began to demonstrate a deeply rooted sense of *orgullo bilingüe*, or bilingual pride. We hope that continued inquiry and discussion about translanguaging will empower students to make personally relevant linguistic choices in the classroom and view their multilingualism and multiculturalism as a source of academic and social pride.

9

MULTILINGUAL ECOLOGY IN CUNY-NYSIEB SCHOOLS

*Kate Menken, Vanessa Pérez-Rosario,
and Luis Guzmán Valerio*

Introduction

In order to participate in CUNY-NYSIEB (City University of New York-New York State Initiative on Emergent Bilinguals), schools committed to the project's two principles: (1) developing a multilingual ecology for the whole school and (2) using bilingualism as a resource in education. This chapter focuses on the efforts made at CUNY-NYSIEB schools regarding the first principle—developing a multilingual ecology. Multilingual ecology as defined by CUNY-NYSIEB means that the entire range of language practices of all children and families are made evident in a school's linguistic landscape, as well as in the interactions of all members of a school community. That is, in addition to English, the languages of all students within a school are visible, represented in signs throughout the school, in texts in the library and classrooms, and heard throughout the school in conversations. Furthermore, the students' languaging practices and cultural understandings are engaged as resources for learning. Doing this involves major disruptions to the hegemony of English typically found within U.S. schools, and of corresponding monoglossic educational approaches (García, 2009).

In spite of rapid immigration growth rates and great student diversity, the linguistic landscape of New York City schools has largely remained monolingual in English. This is often in marked contrast to the linguistic landscape of the streets surrounding school buildings, where many community languages are visible, particularly in commercial signage (Shohamy, Ben-Rafael, & Berni, 2010). In this chapter, we examine changes made to the linguistic landscape of 23 CUNY-NYSIEB schools during the first two years of our work with them, and show how these physical changes were tied to pedagogical changes whereby students' languaging practices began to be incorporated in instruction. And, we report the impact that changing linguistic landscape and instructional practices had on students, their families, and the school community as a whole. Our findings show how changes to a school's visual linguistic landscape often served as a pathway from monolingual to multilingual language education policies.

Linguistic landscape in schools

Research to date about linguistic landscape in schools includes studies of the visual linguistic landscape in school buildings (Brown, 2012; Garvin & Eisenhower, 2016; Gorter & Cenoz, 2014; Landry & Bourhis, 1997; Pakarinen & Björklund, 2018) and studies that consider linguistic landscape for pedagogical purposes (Cenoz & Gorter, 2008; Clemente, Andrade, & Martins, 2012; Dagenais, Moore, Sabatier, Lamarre, & Armand, 2009; Jakonen, 2018; Malinowski, 2015; Sayer, 2010). Scholars of linguistic landscape have in recent years challenged and extended the boundaries of the field well beyond signage. For instance, Shohamy and Gorter's (2009) definition included "language in the environment, words and images displayed and exposed in public spaces" (p. 1). More recently, linguistic landscape researchers have moved beyond what is seen in public spaces to also consider "smellscapes" (Pennycook & Otsuji, 2015), "semiotic landscapes" (Jaworski & Thurlow, 2010), "multimodalities" (Shohamy, 2015), as well as "linguistic soundscaping" (Scarvaglieri, Redder, Pappenhagen, & Brehmer, 2012). For the purposes of this chapter, which focuses on linguistic landscape in schools—or, what Brown (2012) calls "schoolscapes"—we adopt here a broadened definition of linguistic landscape that moves beyond discussion of the many physical representations of languages within school buildings to also consider the languages heard and spoken. This includes seeing and hearing students' languages in classrooms, particularly in instruction; these components together comprise CUNY-NYSIEB's "multilingual ecology."

Methods

A total of 27 schools across New York State participated in CUNY-NYSIEB from 2012 to 2013, of which 23 schools were located in New York City. Our research centers on the work of these 23 New York City schools during the 1.5 years of their official involvement in CUNY-NYSIEB (January 2012 to June 2013) and for several years afterwards (from 2013 to 2016). We wanted to better understand how CUNY-NYSIEB schools changed their multilingual ecology, and the impact of those changes on students and their families.

The main data sources for this research study are interviews and photographs taken in the schools. We also included school profiles and notes taken by CUNY-NYSIEB teams, as well as publicly available data about the schools. A total of 37 interviews were gathered and analyzed. The interviews asked school leaders (including administrators and teacher leaders) a broad range of questions about their experiences in CUNY-NYSIEB and perceptions of its impact. Photographs of the schools' linguistic landscape were taken by team members during their visits to the schools involved in the project, and each school was visited three to four times per semester from Spring 2012 through Spring 2013. Photographs focused on classrooms, hallways, and the school entrance.

Changes to the visual linguistic landscape in schools

When schools began working with CUNY-NYSIEB, typically the only languages other than English in their visual linguistic landscape were those in the multilingual welcome poster that the New York City Department of Education (NYCDOE) mandates be displayed in all school entranceways. A photograph of the required multilingual poster hanging in the entrance of one of the schools can be seen in Figure 9.1.

In order to move beyond the poster and increase the multilingualism of their linguistic landscape, participating schools typically needed to create their own materials with help from staff members, teachers, parents, students, and other members of the school community. This section documents some of their efforts.

Almost all of the participating schools created their own multilingual welcome sign that displayed the languages present in their school community. One

FIGURE 9.1 Mandated NYC department of education multilingual welcome sign

assistant principal, for example, described how her school had a welcome sign in English with blank stars in the school entrance, and changed the sign such that each star said "welcome" in a different language spoken by students at the school. As she explained:

> It was just a welcome board, "Welcome to [elementary school]". After we came back from one of the CUNY-NYSIEB meetings, … we suggested that we should put "Welcome" not just in English, but in all the languages we have in the building. (Ms. T, elementary school assistant principal, exit interview)

Students and families from the community entering saw their languages for the first time in their school, due to this homemade display.

One school developed a welcome sign to greet families in their languages and provide important information. The school posted "Frequently Asked Questions" posed by parents, guardians, or community members, and translated these into the six languages other than English most widely spoken in their school community. When entering the school building, families could then simply indicate to school staff the question(s) they wanted answered. This display can be seen in Figure 9.2.

In another example, an assistant principal remarked on how school staff, students, and families helped create multilingual word walls for their classroom,

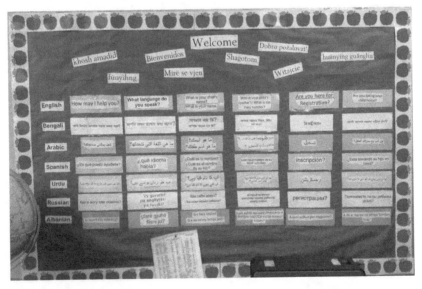

FIGURE 9.2 Multilingual welcome sign with frequently asked questions

where vocabulary words are translated into one or more of the students' languages (Ms. V, elementary school assistant principal, exit interview). Figure 9.3 shows a photograph of a multilingual word wall that was created by a teacher at one of the schools in our sample, in which key vocabulary words were translated into three languages other than English spoken in her classroom.

CUNY-NYSIEB schools were encouraged to increase the multilingualism of their visual linguistic landscape in ways that responded to their own situated realities by recognizing all of the languages of their students (García & Menken, 2015). One school created a labeling team "to put labels around the school, so that our school building is more accessible" (Ms. K, elementary school lead teacher, exit interview).

Some schools created multilingual welcome packets or other informational resources for families enrolling in U.S. schools for the first time. In one school's welcome packet, they included "pictures of places around the school" for new students (Ms. S, elementary school assistant principal, exit interview). This packet was translated into Spanish and Chinese and included an audio-recorded welcome message from the principal, a map of the school that was explained by a partner student during a building tour, and materials for the students to familiarize themselves with basic classroom vocabulary and routines. Another

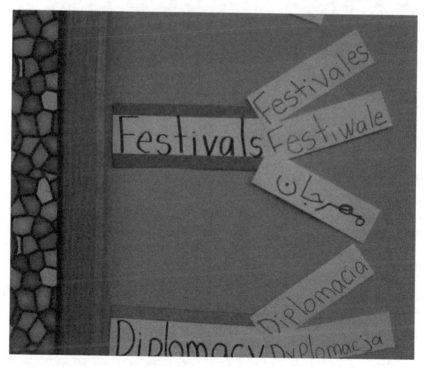

FIGURE 9.3 Multilingual word wall

FIGURE 9.4 Sample welcome packet with school supplies labeled in English and Polish

elementary school prepared information about the school that included pictures of school supplies labeled in English and Polish, as shown in Figure 9.4.

Many participants made efforts to change their multilingual ecology by adding home language resources to school libraries and classrooms, such as books in students' home languages or those with translanguaging in the text. One school acquired such books for the school library, and the principal describes their rationale for doing so in the following interview excerpt:

> When they go to the library, we want them to feel part of it, by having the languages available for them. (Ms. T, elementary school principal, initial interview)

These efforts extended beyond schoolwide libraries and into classrooms too. For instance, one classroom library provided books in five languages (English, Polish, Arabic, Ukrainian, and Spanish), including monolingual and translanguaging texts.

In some schools, particularly those where instruction was monolingual in English at the outset of their participation in the CUNY-NYSIEB project, the home languages of students had never been displayed, read, or spoken during instruction before. In other schools, such as those with bilingual programs, two languages were spoken but were not supposed to be used at the same time; instead, hard boundaries were in place such that the languages were strictly separated by time and/or space, and rarely if ever appeared simultaneously. As such, simply the presence of multilingual word walls such as those displayed above or texts demonstrating translanguaging as a literary device disrupted monolingual and monoglossic settings. In a later section of this paper, we describe how multilingual materials such as these were used in teaching and learning in CUNY-NYSIEB classrooms, and how these opened up translanguaging spaces in participating classrooms.

Changes to instructional practices: Toward multilingual schoolscapes and soundscapes

All of the CUNY-NYSIEB schools we studied increased their recognition of home language practices, which were leveraged in instruction and sustained. Thus, students' home languages were used orally in teaching and learning, and translanguaging practices were engaged in instruction, with students' languages and languaging visible in student work, libraries, instructional materials, word walls and other displays in classrooms. Teachers and administrators noted how these efforts had a positive effect on student participation and learning in general:

> When you go in the classrooms, you'll see artifacts, and artifacts are even done in Hindi and Bengali...They understand that it's okay for children to talk in their own language and converse in their own language in order to learn the English language... So you see that, where children are actually writing in their own language because they cannot, when they get stuck writing [in English]...they'll write it in their own language. (Ms. T, middle school principal, exit interview)

In this passage, a principal reflects on how a multilingual linguistic landscape offered a way for students to participate who would otherwise have been silenced.

While teachers varied in the extent to which they took up the project's invitation to develop their school's multilingual ecology, the teacher quoted in the following passage radically changed the visual linguistic landscape of his classroom, and describes here the impact of doing so (note PD refers to professional development and Mr. A is the pseudonym we use to refer to the elementary school teacher interviewed):

> After having a few PD sessions, I really just got obsessed with making sure anything I had in the room was written in the languages that kids would understand, whether it's Polish, Arabic, Spanish, Ukrainian… and then some students would correct me. And then after a while a couple of kids actually gave me a blank notebook and said, "If you ever have a word you want written in Polish or Arabic, write in this book and I'll translate it for you." So that got them more involved in the process as well … They can help me out that way and then they feel part of the classroom, it's more of a student-run classroom. (Mr. A, elementary school teacher, follow-up interview)

Mr. A often relied on electronic translations of his classroom materials (e.g., Google translate). As such, occasionally he made errors, which students would correct. Mr. A explains how engaging with his classroom's linguistic landscape collectively with his students meant that the students were able to assume more power in the classroom. What is more, the display of students' languages and subsequent discussions about them opened up spaces for discussions about translanguaging. These discussions fostered a dynamic multilingual use that went beyond the official English language instruction of the classroom, but also beyond the other languages that students were said to speak. Doing so allowed students to access and engage with course content, encouraged students' multilingual awareness, and also recognized and extended students' translanguaging.

Language education policy shifts

In addition to infusing students' home languages in instruction in the ways outlined above, several schools made significant changes to their language education programming and policies for emergent bilinguals. For example, some schools began to offer a formal class during the school day taught through the medium of the students' home language in a course entitled "native language arts" or NLA (note that ESL in this quotation refers to English as a second language):

> We have native language arts now, which we didn't have before. [D]epending on their level, they all get ESL, and then they either get NLA or the Great Books program in English. (Ms. C, middle school assistant principal, exit interview)

This is reiterated in a CUNY-NYSIEB middle school where, as the principal describes, the school "made a drastic move to make sure our newcomers are getting native language arts... a massive change that just took effect today" (Ms. O, middle school principal, exit interview). Instruction in these courses uses home language practices and the curriculum typically mirrors that of English language arts courses.

In New York, policy dictates that schools may elect to provide transitional bilingual education and/or dual language bilingual education in lieu of English as a new language (ENL, also known as ESL), which is typically in English only. Both forms of bilingual education provide home language instruction for emergent bilinguals, albeit to varying degrees. Transitional bilingual education offers home language instruction for a shorter period of time with the aim of rapidly moving students into English-only instruction, while dual language bilingual education programs are developmental, and typically provide at least 50% of instruction in the home language for an indefinite period of time. While the schools in our sample offering ENL instruction all brought students' home languages into instruction through translanguaging strategies, some schools increased home language instruction by converting their transitional bilingual education programs to dual language bilingual education programs.

> I know [Ms. B (principal)] was able to do away with one of our first grade transitional bilingual classrooms...So that has been one of, one of the changes, ...trying to do it as a whole. (Ms. A, elementary school bilingual education coordinator, exit interview)

In this passage, Ms. A describes how the school's leaders made the decision to replace their transitional bilingual program with a dual language bilingual program, which offers more home language instruction.

Other schools made an even more extreme move from monolingual to bilingual instruction by replacing ENL programs with a bilingual education program.

> So we decided we needed to create a new class so they opened a newcomer class... [Students] are in a transitional bilingual education program now... We had never had bilingual support like that before – they were just in the monolingual classes. (Ms. C, middle school principal, follow-up interview)

In this quotation, Ms. C describes her school's decision to implement a bilingual education program two years after their participation in CUNY-NYSIEB.

Another middle school replaced their ENL program with dual language bilingual education during their involvement in the project. The principal said:

> That is the most dramatic change we have made, opening up that particular program ... It seemed it was the only logical place to go as opposed to doing another transitional bilingual class where we would do Spanish

and reduce it, reduce it, reduce it. Why do you want to do that when the research shows that it is not what you should do? (Mr. K, middle school principal, exit interview)

The preceding quotation explains this school's decision to begin offering dual language bilingual instruction (which included translanguaging spaces as described in Sánchez, García, & Solorza, 2018), replacing the English-only program that was in place beforehand. Here Mr. K references research arguing that dual language bilingual education achieves better educational outcomes than other approaches for emergent bilinguals (e.g., Steele et al., 2017; Umansky & Reardon, 2014).

Reported impact: "Even simple things would have a big impact"

While changing school language policies will have a lasting impact on students, families, and entire communities for years to come, we also found that changing a school's visual linguistic landscape had an immediate impact on these groups. Even changes to a school's linguistic landscape that were easy for schools to do (e.g., multilingual signage) were found to be significant for students and their families.

In the following example Ms. V, the assistant principal, is talking to Ms. B, the principal, about the impact of simple additions, like multilingual signage and increased use of languages other than English not only on students, but also on families:

> Ms. V: On the front door it says "general office" and then it says "office" in Polish and Spanish. And a Polish family came in, and the husband, the father came in and said, "Oh my goodness what a nice surprise to see my language on the door!" And he made a big deal about it, and he was very impressed, and so I felt good about that, you know. We did that!
>
> Ms. B: Like putting up the signs, putting up the flags...just including different languages in the announcements in the morning. I think just, I don't know, put a different value on it, and made it more valuable to us, and even parents noticed...
>
> Ms. V: So even simple things would have a big impact. (Ms. B and Ms. V, elementary school principal and assistant principal, exit interview)

In the preceding passage, the school principal and assistant principal mention a number of their efforts to recognize the languages of their students in their multilingual ecology, such as multilingual signage, hanging flags of students' countries of origin, and making morning announcements including the Pledge of Allegiance to the U.S. flag in different languages. In the preceding excerpt, a student's parent who is bilingual in English and Polish was greatly impacted by the visibility of his home language in signs in the school hallway, even though the translation was not actually necessary for him for comprehension purposes.

In this case, the visible presence of a language other than English was symbolic, yet still clearly important to the parent.

We also heard examples reported in interviews of multilingual linguistic landscape enabling participation by families and students who do not speak English, particularly in the schools in our sample where all instruction is in English only. For instance, one school had a parent center and hired a parent coordinator in an effort to improve the relationship between schools and families, but they found that parents who did not speak English would stay away. Once they began to translate the materials sent home and bring in volunteer translators (such as school staff who speak languages other than English and parents who are bilingual), they found that parental involvement increased (Ms. S, elementary school assistant principal, exit interview).

One school leader noted that seeing signs in multiple languages helped students make connections between languages. As she said, "they see their languages up and posted, they know and they can make that connection, 'Oh! This means that, okay'" (Mr. S, elementary school principal, exit interview). It also offers affordances in literacy, as a student described as being on a beginning reading level in English surprised school staff by demonstrating advanced literacy skills when given the chance to read in his home language (Ms. B, elementary school principal, exit interview).

Making students' languages visible in the multilingual ecology was also found to be significant as a means to recognize and support student identity. The following is an example of student responses to receiving classroom materials in their home languages and being asked to speak their language in school for the first time:

> Ms. V: There was one girl, it was Delila, and she knew a word in Spanish, and I said, "Oh, wow, oh, Delila, you know Spanish?" She said, "Yeah." I said, "How do you know Spanish?" "Oh, I know it from home." I said, "That is so special that you know another language." And she just kind of sat there. She was like, wow…It was really special to see like that look on her face…
>
> Ms. B: Students are not shying away from saying this is my language, this is my culture because it's being valued in the building.
>
> (Ms. B, elementary school principal, and Ms. V, elementary school teacher, exit interview transcript)

Bringing students' languages into the classroom through the schoolscape was significant for recognizing students and their translanguaging practices.

A challenge of taking up a heteroglossic translanguaging stance in the linguistic landscape is that signs and materials were typically monolingual in one language or another—for instance signs in English appeared beside a translation of that sign into other languages. However, the presence of multilingual signs or texts opens up a channel of understanding in the bilingual person who interacts with them as they translanguage, as they bring all their resources to make meaning. When the linguistic landscape is only in English, it is as if a channel of understanding is closed to emergent bilinguals. Moreover, this section has detailed how the visual and oral presence of students' language practices in schools had a positive effect on the students and their families in the CUNY-NYSIEB schools we studied, and were found to be extremely significant to them, either when these efforts were functional (as in the case for non-English speaking students and family members) or symbolic.

Discussion and conclusion

In this chapter, we detailed ways that schools participating in the CUNY-NYSIEB project transformed their ecology of multilingualism, and how doing so was in many schools tied to the adoption of a heteroglossic view of bilingualism in education, marking a significant ideological shift. We presented the changes that school leaders described having made to the linguistic landscapes of their school buildings. We documented many of the ways educators in our sample incorporated their students' home languages visually and orally in their schoolscapes, and supported students' translanguaging. And we documented how some schools went further, codifying these ideological and pedagogical changes in new programmatic structures and language education policies that are multilingual rather than monolingual while taking up a translanguaging stance.

We found in our study that transforming the physical linguistic landscape of CUNY-NYSIEB schools by making students' languages visible served as a steppingstone for many schools to make further changes. This finding is captured well in an interview with a principal who refers to changing their language displays as the "early win" or the "easy win," for instance by creating and hanging a multilingual welcome sign:

> I think we also went for the early win… Some of the early easy wins were the visuals, so we prioritized that. The next big thing we prioritized were the instructional shifts, so now we're focusing on language objectives, and resources and materials. (Ms. C, middle school assistant principal, exit interview)

As this principal explained in her interview, the school began by focusing on the school's signage and displays as their starting point, which then paved the way to making instructional shifts. Later, the school turned their attention toward changing classroom practices, and eventually their language education policy, as theirs was one of the schools that went on to start a formal bilingual education program.

Most of the schools began to address the challenge of increasing the multilingualism of their schoolscapes by changing the physical linguistic landscape as a first step. For instance, multilingual welcome signs in the front hallways were quickly developed and displayed in almost every school, and hallway information likewise was presented in many languages. This transformation alone was extremely significant to students and their families, as described in our findings, and served as an open contestation of the English-only policies and practices that are commonplace in U.S. schooling. At the same time, it was relatively easy for CUNY-NYSIEB schools to develop multilingual signs and displays—hence the principal quoted above describes doing so as an "easy win," and identifies the work of transforming instruction as more challenging.

It is important to note that for the purposes of this chapter, we focused on ways CUNY-NYSIEB schools developed their multilingual ecology, but this is not to imply that all schools were equally engaged or active in the project. Our findings in fact suggest there was a trajectory of change in the sample of participating schools, starting with the visual linguistic landscape, moving on to pedagogy and language ideologies, and then making structural changes such as starting a formal bilingual education program in which they infused a heteroglossic translanguaging stance. A few schools in our sample just changed their displayed linguistic landscape in a limited way, and stopped there. Most schools changed both the visual linguistic landscape and their instructional practices, albeit to varying degrees. Some took this even further to codify new ideologies about language in official language education policies.

On one hand, our findings offer further support for the pedagogical value of multilingual schoolscapes (Cenoz & Gorter, 2008; Malinowski, 2015; Sayer, 2010). For instance, we showed how the presence of multilingual word walls, books, and other materials offered students the possibility to access course content and participate in classrooms where previously they had been silenced, and to do so by engaging their entire linguistic repertoire rather than strictly separating their languages. A multilingual linguistic landscape thereby served both functional and symbolic purposes in schools. On the other hand, our research differs from past linguistic landscape research in schools, which has typically focused on the dominance of certain languages at the expense of others, and exposed how the linguistic landscape perpetuates language ideologies and (re)asserts the status of dominant languages. By contrast, our research offers a counter narrative whereby minoritized languages are brought into schoolscapes with the aim of disrupting existing language hierarchies. Specifically, the hegemony of English was challenged when bilingual students' home languages were brought into the linguistic landscapes of CUNY-NYSIEB schools, which led to new multilingual language education policies in some schools. In this way, our findings suggest that the relationship between linguistic landscape and language policy may be bidirectional; a school's linguistic landscape can simply reflect its language education policies or it can influence them. This is a powerful finding, as it suggests that changing a school's multilingual ecology—even in more simple ways that may at first seem superficial or symbolic—can lead to broader and deeper disruptions of monolingual norms over time.

References

Brown, K.D. (2012). The linguistic landscape of educational spaces: Language revitalization and schools in southeastern Estonia. In D. Gorter, H.F. Marten, & L. Van Mensel (Eds.), *Minority Languages in the linguistic landscape* (pp. 281–298). Basingstoke: Palgrave Macmillan.

Cenoz, J. & Gorter, D. (2008). The linguistic landscape as an additional source of input in second language acquisition. *Iral, 46*, 267–287.

Clemente, M., Andrade, A.I., & Martins, F. (2012). Learning to read the world, learning to look at the linguistic landscape: A primary school study. In C. Hélot, M. Barni, R. Janssens, & C. Bagna (Eds.), *Linguistic landscapes, multilingualism, and social change* (pp. 267–285). Frankfurt, Germany: Peter Lang.

Dagenais, D., Moore, D., Sabatier, C., Lamarre, P., & Armand, F. (2009). Linguistic landscape and language awareness. In E. Shohamy & D. Gorter (Eds.), *Linguistic landscape: Expanding the scenery* (pp. 253–270). New York, NY: Routledge.

García, O. (2009). *Bilingual education in the 21st century: A global perspective*. Malden, MA: Wiley/Blackwell.

García, O. & Menken, K. (2015). Cultivating an ecology of multilingualism in schools: Building interindividuality of voices and ideologies. In. B. Spolsky, O. Inbar, & M. Tannenbaum (Eds.), *Challenges for language education and policy: Making space for people* (pp. 95–108). New York, NY: Routledge.

Garvin, R. & Eisenhower, K. (2016). A comparative study of linguistic landscapes in middle schools in Korea and Texas: Contrasting signs of learning and identity construction. In R. Blackwood, E. Lanza, & H. Woldemariam (Eds.), *Negotiating and contesting identities in linguistic landscapes* (pp. 215–231). New York, NY: Bloomsbury.

Gorter, D. & Cenoz, J. (2014). Linguistic landscapes inside multilingual schools. In B. Spolsky, M. Tannenbaum, & O. Inbar (Eds.), *Challenges for language education and policy: Making space for people* (pp. 151–169). New York, NY: Routledge Publishers.

Jakonen, T. (2018). The environment of a bilingual classroom as an interactional resource. *Linguistics and Education, 44*(2018), 20–30.

Jaworski, A. & Thurlow, C. (Eds.). (2010). *Semiotic landscapes: Language, image, space*. London, UK: Bloomsbury.

Landry, R. & Bourhis, R.Y. (1997). Linguistic landscape and ethnolinguistic vitality: An empirical study. *Journal of Language and Social Psychology, 16*(1), 23–49.

Malinowski, D. (2015). Opening spaces of learning in the linguistic landscape. *Linguistic Landscape, 1*(1/2), 95–113.

Pakarinen, S. & Björklund, S. (2018). Multiple language signage in linguistic landscapes and students' language practices: A case study from a language immersion setting. *Linguistics and Education, 44*(2018), 4–11.

Pennycook, A. & Otsuji, E. (2015). Making scents of the landscape. *Linguistic Landscape, 1*(3), 191–212.

Sánchez, M.T., García, O., & Solorza, C. (2018). Reframing language allocation policy in dual language bilingual education. *Bilingual Research Journal, 41*(1), 37–51.

Sayer, P. (2010). Using the linguistic landscape as a pedagogical resource. *ELT Journal, 64*(2), 143–154.

Scarvaglieri, C., Redder, A., Pappenhagen, R., & Brehmer, B. (2012). Capturing diversity: Linguistic land- and soundscaping. In I. Gogolin & J. Duarte (Eds.), *Linguistic superdiversity in urban areas: Research approaches* (pp. 45–74). Amsterdam: John Benjamins.

Shohamy, E. (2015). LL research as expanding language and language policy. *Linguistic Landscape*, *1*(1/2), 152–171.

Shohamy, E., Ben-Rafael, E., & Berni, M. (Eds.). (2010). *Linguistic landscape in the city*. Bristol, UK: Multilingual Matters.

Shohamy, E., & Gorter, D. (Eds.). (2009). *Linguistic landscape: Expanding the scenery*. New York, NY: Routledge.

Steele, J., Slater, R., Zamarro, G., Miller, T., Li, J., Burkhauser, S., & Bacon, M. (2017). Effects of dual-language immersion programs on student achievement: Evidence from lottery data. *American Educational Research Journal*, *54*(1S), 282S–306S.

Umansky, I. & Reardon, S.F. (2014). Reclassification patterns among Latino English learner students in bilingual, dual immersion, and English immersion classrooms. *American Educational Research Journal*, 51, 879–912.

BOX 9.1 TEACHER/RESEARCHER

Andy Brown

4th grade, self-contained English as a new language

Before the school year begins, I make sure the visual landscape of my class-room shows the multilingualism of my students with labels in English, Span-ish, Polish, Arabic, Chinese, Romanian, Greek, and any other languages my students speak. For students in the early stages of English language develop-ment I make sure to have charts, posters, teaching points, essential ques-tions, language objectives, Promethean Slides, etc. in various color-coded languages. Usually English is blue, Spanish is red, Polish is green, Arabic is purple, and other languages are in black. It is a lot of work, but in my expe-rience, it makes all the students feel welcome, especially those who speak languages other than English at home.

Imagine being from Greece and entering school speaking very little Eng-lish and coming into your brand-new school in your brand-new country and seeing:

Καλώς ήρθατε στην τάξη μας
[Kalós írthate stin táxi mas]
Welcome to Our Class

as you step into my fourth-grade classroom. I write signs with the appropri-ate alphabet as in the sign above written in the Greek alphabet. I include a transliteration into the Roman alphabet so that students would have an idea of how it sounds, and then a translation into English. This helps all students understand that languages have different scripts, and that written language is different from oral language. In addition, this creates a sense of commu-nity and helps a student who may feel like an "outsider," feel as if he or she belongs. For example, one of my Spanish-speaking students wrote: "The Goliath bird eating spider is the largest spider in el mundo." By accepting the students' own words and writing I am learning from my students, and they are learning from each other. This has a huge impact on student learning, engagement, and class participation, which leads to an increase in student confidence. And it's not only emergent bilinguals who are learning "English," everyone is adding different language features to their repertoire.

SECTION IV

Literacies Juntos:
Instruction and Assessment

10

TRANSLANGUAGING AND EMERGENT LITERACY IN EARLY CHILDHOOD EDUCATION

Zoila Morell and Dina López

Introduction

Young children learn to read and write within the context of their own families, cultures, and languages (Goodman, 1992). Their first exposures to written symbols in books, handwriting, cereal boxes, environmental print, etc., occur in the deeply familiar settings of their homes and in the languages spoken there. Experiencing the interconnectedness between spoken and written language enables children to grasp the concept of symbolic representation. Even very young children understand how drawings and paintings are representations of objects, not the objects themselves (DeLoache, 2004). This understanding deepens as text accompanies drawings, as in storybooks or recorded narrations, and gives rise to foundational emergent literacy skills (Sulzby, 1992), the precursors to conventional reading and writing. The field of early childhood education (ECE) widely recognizes the role of parents, teachers, and other adults, in supporting a child's emergent literacy skills; we know a lot about the age-appropriate activities and experiences that constitute literacy instruction in the early childhood classroom (NAEYC, 2009).

Promoting emergent literacy in ECE calls for a careful consideration of the multimodal ways in which children use language and symbols to learn, make meaning, and express their ideas. Empowered to manipulate materials and resources in their environment, children are active constructors of their own language competencies (Clay, 2015). The young emergent bilingual child draws from experiences in the home language(s) as well as the language of the early childhood classroom, extending the concept of multimodal learning to include the spontaneous, dynamic use of any and all languages present in the child's world. Translanguaging theory and pedagogy undergird the development of emergent literacy skills for the emergent bilingual child in ECE.

Evolving multilingual practices in ECE

After decades working in the field, we want to first acknowledge what we have observed in ECE and the transformation in emergent literacy instruction brought about by the work of CUNY-NYSIEB (City University of New York-New York State Initiative on Emergent Bilinguals). As bilingual educators in New York, we have always been expected to use our multiple languages as a condition of employment. However, the ability to speak more than one language was always tightly controlled by the school environment. We may have been interpreters or translators as called upon, but the expectation was that we would model for children and families, an inexorable shift toward English. We actually praised emergent bilinguals if they could "say it in English."

Even in bilingual classrooms, we may have been recognized as bilingual teachers, but our natural, intuitive language practices were controlled by the curriculum that scripted teacher talk, or by coaches and administrators observing our lessons. Other common practices in ECE, such as highlighting student work on bulletin boards, was expected to demonstrate English if it was to be viewed as an exemplar. Our classrooms and hallways may have housed bilingual children, but English was the language of the print in the environment. Personally, we can recall a time when words in any language other than English were strictly forbidden for the Word Wall.

These rules and prohibitions disadvantaged young emergent bilinguals as they disabled the ability to connect spoken and printed language. Making this connection is the very beginning of emergent literacy skills. They also compromised the effectiveness of bilingual educators who may have made those connections for children but were forbidden by the prevailing ideology about language in ECE.

As CUNY-NYSIEB articulated translanguaging practices and translanguaging pedagogy, through the work of Ofelia García, we are living an evolution toward multilingual practices in ECE. This represents a powerful boost to emergent literacy instruction for bilingual children that is in keeping with research identifying gains in literacy where children's home language practices have been integrated and promoted in instruction (Farver, Lonigan, & Eppe, 2009; Lindholm-Leary, 2014; Méndez, Crais, Castro, & Kainz, 2015; Roberts, 2008).

In light of this history and evolution, this chapter focuses on how emergent literacy is promoted in the prekindergarten classroom with three and four-year old bilingual children. In addition, because the preschool population is more culturally and linguistically diverse than any other age group (Frey, 2011), we consider how translanguaging pedagogy is embedded into the emergent literacy work that preschoolers are asked to do.

Using the state of New York as the example, we begin by describing the preschool population and we continue with a discussion of translanguaging and emergent literacy in the early childhood classroom. We then discuss how translanguaging theory can transform our understandings of language and literacy, and the implications it has for play-based instruction, pedagogical practices, and family engagement.

Serving New York's preschool population

Despite the importance of understanding and responding to the needs of three and four-year old preschoolers, there is still very limited demographic information about these young bilingual children. In their national report on bilingual children, the National Academies of Sciences, Engineering, and Medicine (2017) indicate that there are more children in early care and education programs recognized as "English Language Learners" than there are in kindergarten. With shifting demographics and increasing linguistic diversity across the United States, more children are growing up in homes where they are developing a bilingual repertoire—one that includes both language practices associated with English, as well as with one or more other languages.

In 2016, New York's Universal Prekindergarten (UPK)[1] served 120,000 three and four-year-olds. This constitutes only 63% of the children actually eligible for these services (New York State Education Department, 2017a). But data on the home language practices represented in this group is nonexistent (Morell, 2017). In order to better plan for instruction and programming, New York State, with the assistance of Zoila Morell, developed a protocol to identify the bi/multilingual preschool population upon entry into UPK programs, adopting the term "Emergent Multilingual Learner" (EMLL) to refer to any child who speaks a language other than English at home (New York State Education Department, 2017b). Slated for full implementation in 2020, the protocol will provide invaluable information about New York's preschoolers.

Guiding instruction in prekindergarten, the *New York State Prekindergarten Early Learning Standards* (New York State Education Department, 2019) articulate the competencies children should develop, across developmental domains, as part of their learning. Within the play-based environment we describe below, learning standards serve as the "guardrails" that organize instructional planning. In this case, the prekindergarten standards, by design, describe many of the competencies associated with emergent literacy in early childhood (see http://www.p12. nysed.gov/earlylearning/standards/documents/PKStandards2019accessability. pdf). For example, indicators for the domain of *Communication, Language, and Literacy* (PK.AC.6), lists the following skills for children to develop (p. 16):

PK.AC.6. Demonstrates their ability to represent ideas using a variety of methods Indicators:

a. Uses facial expressions, body language, gestures, or sign language to express ideas
b. Uses existing objects to represent desired or imagined objects in play or other purposeful way
c. Uses visual media to represent an actual experience
d. Reviews and reflects on their own representations
e. Writes and/or draws to communicate meaning with peers and adults during play

The linguistic diversity of the population in prekindergarten classrooms calls for a specialized understanding of the ways in which a child's language(s) interacts with the development of emergent skills.

Bilingualism, translanguaging, and emergent literacy in early childhood

Language learning is dependent on social interaction. Research with infants and young children indicates that exposure to language through media (for example, video, music, television) does not produce growth in vocabulary, even when the material is age-appropriate and child-friendly. In order to develop language, children are reliant on human *interaction* to make the crucial connections between a spoken (or signed) word and what it represents (DeLoache et al., 2010). The very nascence of emergent literacy for children then, is the language learning that takes place in an exchange with a more knowledgeable interlocutor.

Consider how a typical prekindergarten student uses emergent literacy abilities. Within a few days into the academic year, she is expected to navigate complex social situations with peers and adults where she must effectively negotiate her preferences for toys, turn-taking, games, following rules, maintaining routines, cooperating with her teachers, expressing her needs, etc., all the while separated from family members and familiar situations. She is further challenged to demonstrate very explicit ways of languaging, such as inventing or narrating a story, retelling a common storybook narrative, responding to direct questions about text or other occurrences, and deciphering the multiple messages presented to her in the environment in the form of pictures, charts, color-coded signs, graphic organizers, and symbols such as letters or numbers. What she has brought with her to this enterprise is her cumulative knowledge of family, culture, and concrete experiences, *conveyed through her language.*

For the young child, the meaning-making inherent in emergent literacy skills begins with (spoken or signed) language (DeLoache, 2004). When the prekindergarten emergent bilingual child cannot use her home language practices in the classroom, her primary tool for developing emergent literacy skills is essentially disabled. Additionally, many young children growing up in bilingual homes do not simply have *one* home language, but various home language practices and they engage in translanguaging. This is important to note as most emergent bilinguals in daycares and preschools across the country are *simultaneous* bilinguals, who are learning and developing two or more languages at the same time, rather than *sequential* bilinguals who are exposed to one named language first and then another (de Houwer, 2009). This is a strong imperative for her teachers to implement strategies and instructional approaches that maximize the use of home language practices.

Integrating multiple home language practices in the prekindergarten classroom may challenge the monolingual teacher who may have been very well trained for instruction in English only. However, there are increasingly more creative strategies and approaches available to early childhood professionals (we include recommendations below) to inform the teacher's work. In order to understand how and why these language strategies work, we first briefly discuss the nature of bilingual children's language use.

Research with very young children highlights their impressive ability to recognize different languages and to quickly "assess" whether an individual is speaking a new or familiar language (Bialystok, 2007). In fact, young bilinguals demonstrate considerable knowledge *about* language—its features, its uses, its practices, etc. It is said that their exposure to different language practices provides them with greater metalinguistic awareness (Bialystok & Barac, 2012; García, 2009). But the child herself uses all the linguistic and semiotic features with which she is familiar to make meaning or to make herself understood. Sometimes they use gestures, sounds, words, and they draw on their full semiotic repertoire to communicate, demonstrating sophisticated command of language. That is, at home, young bilingual children engage in translanguaging, as they communicate with different members of the household at different times. Yet, the ability to use language features beyond the boundaries that have been drawn around named languages, including multimodal features other than linguistic ones, has traditionally been stigmatized as evidence of having inadequate language development. When young bilingual children use linguistic features that are socially associated with different "named" languages, they are said to be "code-switching." What is then seen as going from one language to another is discouraged in classrooms. As educators, it is important to expand our understanding about bi/multilingualism as not just simply the addition of two named languages that happen sequentially or that people go "across." Rather, educators need to understand that bilinguals develop a unitary language repertoire. They need to understand both translanguaging theory and how a translanguaging pedagogy can advance emergent literacy.

Translanguaging theory offers a robust conceptual framework for understanding how young bilingual children use all the features of their repertoire flexibly and dynamically (García, 2009). Through this lens, language is not simply a bound system. Named languages (i.e., "English" or "Spanish") are recognized as important and valuable social and political constructions. However, named languages do not exist as separate cognitive realities for the bilingual child. That is, languages are not separate in the child's mind. The young bilingual child's unitary repertoire does not reflect dual separate linguistic systems. Consequently, bilingual children do not "switch codes" but rather call upon the linguistic features needed within particular social and cultural contexts (García & Otheguy, 2016; Otheguy, García, & Reid, 2015, 2018). We can then talk about how very young emergent bilingual children *translanguage* or go beyond what we call different languages in the natural course of self-expression and meaning making. For example, in the interaction below, a bilingual prekindergartner employs translanguaging to describe what she knows about birds.

TEACHER: *Tell me about the little birds.*
CHILD: *Mmm… This the casita and they fly (pointing to the opening of the bird house). The babies stay there and la mama brings them un corn.*

Using all her words, this little girl demonstrates an important emergent literacy skill that prekindergartners must develop—the ability to add details to enrich and amplify a narrative. Through careful attention, her teacher can assess this ability recognizing that the child has responded with multiple details: She knows birds use birdhouses to nest and she identifies the opening they fly into. She knows that the mother bird leaves and returns with bits of food for the babies. As this interaction illustrates, very young emergent bilinguals translanguage to communicate and make meaning using a variety of linguistic features and resources, and this should not be seen as a problem to be overcome, but rather as a valuable asset to be drawn upon (Axelrod, 2014; García & Otheguy, 2016; Neu, 2013).

Play, translanguaging, and emergent literacy

Just as children need human interaction to learn language, they need active engagement in rich, meaningful activities they can initiate and control. In what Mraz, Porcelli, and Tyler (2016) term "purposeful play," children hone the critical thinking that is needed for all academic learning. The authors write:

> There is no better place to develop a child's imagination than in play. When children engage in imaginative play, not only do they develop their creativity; they learn to be flexible thinkers, and they develop core social skills, such as negotiation, collaboration, and empathy… We believe that

all the skills children learn during play contribute to and enhance academic rigor in the classroom. (pp. 7–8)

Research in psychology, neuroscience, and early childhood development, has made it clear that young children learn, develop language, and make meaning through play (Ginsburg, 2007; Hassinger-Das, Hirsh-Pasek, & Golinkoff, 2017; Van Hoorn, Nourot, Scales, & Alward, 2010). During play, children exercise power and agency over their own learning as they engage in deeply gratifying activities that naturally fuel their motivation to learn. Thus, play is a crucial tool for social development and interaction and language and literacy learning mediated by sociocultural contexts (Franco, Orellana, & Franke, 2019; López, 2019; Vygotsky, 1978, 1986). We strongly support play-based teaching and learning for young emergent bilinguals whose language skills are often poorly assessed in English, and as a result are often relegated to low-level procedural activities (i.e., worksheets) to teach them the "basics" (Neuman, 2006).

In the prekindergarten classroom, play-based instruction is distributed across centers where children engage in age-appropriate activities that are inviting and enjoyable to them. Children's play often involves imitating adult behavior. Pretend play is an excellent way to introduce literacy activities where children can invent their own writing or imitate the teacher reading (Mraz, Porcelli, & Tyler, 2016). In the case of emergent bilinguals, translanguaging is often the way in which play is performed. Early childhood professionals should encourage children to leverage their translanguaging. A child may narrate a drawing using her own words, which may be in the child's own language (which we might identify as English or Spanish, or with home language practices that go beyond the boundaries of these named languages). While early childhood professionals may have been trained to strictly promote reading and writing in English, research in emergent literacy indicates that there is a recursive relationship between language and literacy development in young children. The acquisition of English emergent literacy skills is enhanced, not threatened, by translanguaging, as literacy is about bringing oneself as a reader into the text, and young bilingual children engage in translanguaging to make meaning (García & Kleifgen, 2019; García, 2009). For emergent bilinguals, English-only instruction typically results in a decline of home language skills and no greater gains in English (Barnett, Yarosz, Thomas, Jung, & Blanco, 2007). In fact, in a meta-nalysis of comparison studies, limiting instruction to English did not represent any advantages to language growth for emergent bilinguals (Barnett et al., 2007; Rolstad, Mahoney, & Glass, 2005).

Relatedly, the ways in which children engage in oral and/or signed language impacts the ways in which they engage in literacy practices and vice versa. For example, the work of Griffin, Hemphill, Camp, and Wolf (2004) suggests "[t]hrough early practice using evaluative strategies in oral storytelling, children may also be acquiring skill at using such techniques in their own narrative and other forms of writing" (p. 126). This reciprocal relationship between oral and written language requires educators to view listening, speaking, reading, and writing as interrelated language skills that children develop in specific contexts (Lave & Wenger, 1991).

In order to understand the nuanced and dynamic ways in which bilingual children make meaning with text, we embrace a translanguaging literacies perspective. According to García and Kleifgen (2019) "Translanguaging privileges the meaning-making process of multilingual people as they leverage their linguistic and multimodal repertoire in 'spontaneous, impromptu, and momentary actions and performances' (Li, 2011, p. 1224) with people, objects, places, and spaces (p. 6)." For early childhood educators, this means that language and literacy learning cannot be adequately captured through quantitative measurements of cognitive "skills" but must be understood as "complex performances and human activities enacted by multilinguals within social space, rather than solely what happens within the minds of individuals or even groups" (García & Kleifgen, 2019, p. 6).

Bringing our ideas together, emergent bilinguals should also be encouraged to *play with language*. Songs, chants, poems, stories, rhymes—all part of the playing that takes place in prekindergarten—develops oral language use and encourages young children to engage with language and texts in dynamic, multimodal, and meaningful ways using their entire linguistic repertoires.

Diverse cultural practices, translanguaging, and emergent literacy

Often, what is highly valued in early childhood literacy instructional programs is the background knowledge built through storytelling and experiences with books. Children living in poverty have fewer resources of print material and consequently, less experience with books and the types of stories told in schools (Brooks-Gunn & Markman, 2005). Additionally, not every cultural group emphasizes parents reading to their children. Rather, children's background knowledge is often built through oral traditions or shared experiences. Background knowledge represents a child's cultural capital, all children come to prekindergarten with sufficient background knowledge, but often there is a mismatch between the knowledge of the home and that of school, and especially between the ways in which that knowledge is expressed through language. It is incumbent on early childhood professionals to recognize and engage with cultural differences in knowledge systems, especially when working with families of bilingual children who are most often immigrants or refugees.

Young bilingual children are able to participate "in multilingual and multicultural social networks that are not accessible to monolinguals" and "can experience a range and variety of literacy practices" using multiple linguistic resources (Bauer & Gort, 2012, p. 2) that may be unfamiliar to their teachers. Zentella (2005) describes varied approaches to language socialization even within just the Latinx community. Viewed monolithically as a homogenous ethnic group, Latinx families actually have many differences in beliefs, practices and knowledge systems emanating from diverse traditions, religions, and experiences both in their countries of origin and in the United States. Latinx families also have diverse approaches to child-rearing. If we envision a family's contribution as simply "read to them every night," we miss the richness of diverse cultural practices and their contribution to varied emergent literacy experiences.

The families of emergent bilinguals do share a common experience as multilingual individuals in the extended prekindergarten environment. Their insights and experiences are an invaluable resource for the teacher and other students, as everyone benefits from learning about the language and cultural practices of diverse families. With a rich multicultural, multilingual, and anti-racist curriculum, for example, young children learn about diverse cultures, histories, traditions, and understand how to interrogate social inequities and work toward a socially just world (Souto-Manning, 2013; Souto-Manning et al., 2019). Rather than emphasize what it means to develop the use of English, children benefit from learning about diverse cultural and language practices. Toward this goal, teachers can organize critical multilingual language awareness (CMLA) activities (García, 2017) where the entire prekindergarten community—children and their families—can experience inclusive, enriching group activities or events that challenge the notion that English is the only language valued for learning. At the prekindergarten level, this may include singing songs in many languages, learning to count in many languages, learning about languages themselves (how they are written, for example), and listening to the experiences or stories of multilingual individuals. Language awareness activities have the added benefit of enabling meaningful parental involvement in the multilingual prekindergarten classroom (see, for example, Chapter 15 and Teacher/Researcher Box 11, this volume). Activities that enhance the children's critical multilingual awareness also challenge the prejudice directed at speakers of what are often perceived as "foreign" languages.

Harnessing the incredible linguistic resources and cultural traditions that emergent bilinguals and their families bring to the prekindergarten classroom enhances learning and enables children to realize their full potential. Scholarship on translanguaging, child development, and emergent literacy makes evident that emergent bilinguals use language in flexible and dynamic ways, learn through play and social interaction, and engage in literacy practices in complex and socially contingent ways rooted in culture and language. If our plan for family involvement is not flexible and open to the broad diversity of child-rearing practices, not only do we fall into the trap of operating from a deficit perspective, but we also miss the opportunity to promote and extend children's learning with the help of their families.

The actual classroom—setting up a multilingual environment

Many early childhood teachers are well aware of the important role of the classroom environment in supporting children's learning. It is not uncommon for the environment to be referred to as the "third teacher"—a concept of the Reggio Emilia approach (Strong-Wilson & Ellis, 2007). For educators working with emergent bilingual children who are committed to using bilingualism as a resource in their classrooms, this becomes an even more important task. It involves creating a multilingual classroom ecology in which home language practices are valued and not simply seen as a scaffold to develop English (Espinosa & López, 2017; see also Chapter 9 and Teacher/Researcher Box 5, this volume). In this kind of environment, bilingualism and multilingualism are honored, celebrated, and reflected in the linguistic landscape of the classroom.

The first step in creating this environment is getting to know students and families, their linguistic resources, cultural backgrounds, and funds of knowledge (Moll, Amanti, Neff, & Gonzalez, 1992). Teachers can draw on students' home languages and cultural knowledge to set up a classroom environment that is welcoming and affirming. According to Magruder, Hayslip, Espinosa, and Matera (2013): "The classroom's physical environment sets the stage for active and engaged learning. It conveys a crucial message to children that they will be safe, nurtured, and valued" (p. 11).

Once teachers know who their students are and what are the language practices of the home and their communities, they must consider how these uses can be reflected in the linguistic landscape of the classroom. It is important to ensure that all environmental and functional print reflects the students' home languages. All children and families should be able to access the information shared on walls and bulletin boards. Welcome signs can be posted in the home languages of children. Teachers can invite children and families to cocreate labels and signs in their home languages, which would provide families with a sense of ownership and belonging in the classroom space. Accompanying labels and signs with photo or illustration visuals can aid comprehension. One common practice of daycare and preschool classrooms is dedicating a space for children to bring in pictures of their families to display. Labeling this space with the word "family" in multiple languages is a small but meaningful way to help build a multilingual ecology. It is important to note that languages should be written side by side to convey the message that all languages are equally as valued and important in the classroom.

After thoughtfully designing a multilingual landscape in the classroom, teachers must think about the kinds of materials, books, and artifacts that support the development of bilingualism and emergent literacy. Bilingual and home language books should be stocked in the classroom libraries and reading corners and made accessible to all children. Again, it is crucial that the teacher think about who the students are and their specific cultural and linguistic assets. When possible, teachers should make available authentic literature in the home languages of students, rather than simply translations of English texts. Teachers should offer a wide variety of books that both resonate with students' lived experiences and introduce multiple perspectives, including fiction, nonfiction, poetry, folk tales, traditional stories, nursery rhymes, etc. (España & Herrera, 2020; Espinosa & López, 2017). It is also important to ensure that there are appropriate books in all areas of the classroom instead of isolating the non-English or bilingual books to one area.

In addition to books, teachers can also include other community texts by asking parents and families (or reach out to local businesses) to bring in newspapers, menus, and brochures in the home languages of the children. Though young children may not be fully literate in their home language, texts may be recognizable if they use a completely different alphabetic system (such as Mandarin or Arabic) or are marked in other culturally significant ways. Other examples of culturally relevant materials are artifacts and items from children's homes that can be used in dramatic play areas (such as authentic clothing and accessories, empty food containers from community restaurants and stores) (Espinosa & López, 2017).

Another idea for teachers to consider is the creation of a multilingual listening center (using computers, ipads, or ipods) that features audiobooks and read-a-long books in multiple languages. Teachers might think of asking family volunteers to audio record themselves reading one of the featured books in their home languages.

These are just some of the ways in which early childhood educators can create a multilingual environment in their classrooms and draw upon the cultural and linguistic assets of their students to support translanguaging literacies (García & Kleifgen, 2019; Pacheco & Miller, 2015).

Bringing it all together

We argue that, taken together, emergent literacy and translanguaging theories discussed here have much to offer early childhood educators who work with culturally and linguistically diverse children and families. We build on the work others have done to apply these concepts to the early childhood classroom and provide specific and practical pedagogical recommendations. Bilingualism can be leveraged in all classrooms, even when the teacher is monolingual herself.

Educators can intentionally draw upon and make space for all home language practices, use texts in languages other than English, and engage in "activities that validate and include bilingual and biliterate perspectives and practices" (Delbridge & Helman, 2016, p. 307). In the following pages, we offer suggestions for putting these ideas into practice.

New York State's *Emergent Multilingual Learners in Prekindergarten: A Protocol for Identification, Instructional Planning, and Programming* (2017b) lists strategies for teachers that are worth highlighting here (pp. 11–12):

Some specific strategies include:

- Coordinate with families to have them read translations of familiar classroom books at home.
- Encourage family members to conduct all home assignments in the home language.
- Invite community members to read books in multiple languages.
- Introduce translations of target vocabulary teaching both the English word alongside the word in the home languages.
- Play songs and narrations in the home languages.
- Label objects in the classroom in both English and the home languages. Learn the translation of these objects from families or from translation software.
- Sing in multiple languages.
- Incorporate familiar objects (i.e., instruments, household items, clothing, toys, etc.) from children's countries and cultures in the classroom and encourage children to name and use them.
- Learn and use key phrases in the home languages of the children.
- Encourage children to speak to classmates who share their language.
- Develop a thorough selection of visual aids labeled in multiple languages.
- Use audio and video resources in multiple languages.
- Create a multilingual library.
- Partner with community members who can aid in translation and interpretation.
- Invite community members to scribe children's narrations on their drawings.
- Record children telling stories in their home language, ask them to interpret their stories in English.
- Display children's work in multiple languages.

Now imagine the typical prekindergarten teacher. A seasoned professional, she has witnessed the growth in cultural and linguistic diversity in recent years. Her classroom is now described as "super diverse," where there is not just one additional language other than English but where there are sometimes five and six languages and multiple cultures represented in her classroom. She knows that one English-based generic approach to instruction alienates many children and weakens her effectiveness as a teacher. She believes in the efficacy of play-based teaching and learning and so she has organized instruction across classroom centers where children can select their preferred activities. They may evidence their emergent literacy as they play across centers, for example:

- Writing recipes in the kitchen corner.
- Singing and chanting at the music center.
- Narrating their drawings to adult scribes.
- Reading favorite books in the library corner.
- Conducting plays in a puppet theatre.

The teacher recognizes that any and all of these activities can occur in the child's own language, which includes what teachers interpret as English, a home language, or beyond the two named languages. That is young bilingual children should be encouraged to use their entire repertoire, that is, their translanguaging. The teacher also knows, that to accurately assess and then to extend learning, she needs to ensure that she is allowing the child to use all the features of their repertoire to show what they know. In her instructional planning, she identifies words, phrases, songs, and stories that reflect the home languages of the children. To do this, she uses technology, including translation software, as well as engages family members and school staff who speak those languages. She uses recordings as she builds her own familiarity with words in multiple languages. She understands that she extends children's learning with intentional interactions and so the class schedule is organized around time for her to enter the centers and engage children individually and in small groups. She dialogues with the children, asking open-ended questions, as she uses key phrases she has learned in the child's home language. In every instance, she encourages her students to express themselves using all features in their repertoire, including gesturing, performing, drawing, and, of course, all their home language practices. Accustomed to seeing multiple languages represented across the classroom environment in labels, posters, books, notices, etc., the children have internalized the value of recognizing and using multiple languages to express their ideas. In this classroom, their bilingualism or multilingualism is a powerful resource for the development of emergent literacy.

Conclusion

Even at three and four years of age, children arrive at prekindergarten with some understanding of the relationship between spoken and written language. ECE moves this understanding toward the development of conventional literacy skills in age-appropriate ways. In order to meet the needs of emergent bilingual children in ECE, the field relies on translanguaging theory to examine the ways in which bilingual children link their unitary linguistic systems to developing reading and writing skills in specific named languages. Translanguaging pedagogy in ECE focuses on the teachers' efforts to incorporate all of children's language practices within multimodal, play-based instruction in order to maximize their learning.

Attending prekindergarten may be a child's first encounter with a formal school setting where he or she will be taught to read and write conventionally. The child's entire history—upbringing, family, culture, home languages, exposure to print, oral traditions, etc.—is tied up in this endeavor. The very first experiences with school should honor and reflect their cultural and linguistic diversity as well affirm their bilingual and multilingual identities. An intentional approach that embraces who they are developmentally, and as multilingual little people, will integrate translanguaging pedagogy within a play-based framework, linking who they are with what we hope to teach them.

Note

1 Universal Prekindergarten (UPK) in New York is a state-funded initiative to provide children as young as 3.9 with a year of preschool instruction prior to attending Kindergarten.

References

Axelrod, Y. (2014). "Todos vamos a jugar, even the teachers" – Everyone playing together. *Young Children, 69*(2), 24–31.

Barnett, W.S., Yarosz, D.J., Thomas, J., Jung, K., & Blanco, D. (2007). Two-way and monolingual English immersion in preschool education: An experimental comparison. *Early Childhood Quarterly, 22*, 277–293.

Bauer, E.B., & Gort, M. (Eds.). (2012). *Early biliteracy development: Exploring young learners' use of their linguistic resources.* New York, NY: Routledge.

Bialystok, E. (2007). Acquisition of literacy in bilingual children: A framework for research. *Language Learning, 57*(s1), 45–77.

Bialystok, E., & Barac, R. (2012). Emerging bilingualism: Dissociating advantages for metalinguistic awareness and executive control. *Cognition, 22*(1), 67–73.

Brooks-Gunn, J., & Markman, L. (2005). The contribution of parenting to ethnic and racial gaps in school readiness. *The Future of Children, 15*(1), 139–168.

Clay, M. (2015). *Becoming literate: The construction of inner control.* New Zealand: Marie Clay Literacy Trust.

DeLoache, J., Chiong, C., Sherman, K., Islam, N., Vanderborght, G.L., Troseth, G., Strouse, G., & O'Doherty, K. (2010). Do babies learn from baby media? *Psychological Science, 21*(11), 1570–1574.

DeLoache, J. (2004). Becoming symbol-minded. *Trends in Cognitive Sciences, 8*(2), 66–70.

Delbridge, A., & Helman, L.A. (2016). Evidence-based strategies for fostering biliteracy in any classroom. *Early Childhood Education Journal, 44*(4), 307–316.

de Houwer, A. (2009). *Bilingual first language acquisition.* Bristol, Buffalo, Toronto: Multilingual Matters.

España, C., & Herrera, L. (2020). *En Comunidad. Lessons for centering the voices and experiences of bilingual Latinx students.* Portsmouth, NH: Heinemann.

Espinosa, C. & López, D. (2017). Using translanguaging to leverage students' bilingualism in 21st century early childhood classrooms. Paper presented at the New York State Association for Bilingual Education (NYSABE), White Plains, NY.

Farver, J., Lonigan, C., & Eppe, S. (2009). Effective early literacy skill development for young Spanish-speaking English language learners: An experimental study of two methods. *Child Development, 80,* 703–719.

Franco, J., Orellana, M.F., & Franke, M.L. (2019). 'Castillo blueprint': How young children in multilingual contexts demonstrate and extend literacy and numeracy practices in play. *Journal of Early Childhood Literacy, 0*(0), 1–27. https://doi.org/10.1177/1468798419841430

Frey, W. (2011). The new metro minority map: Regional shifts in Hispanics, Asians, and Blacks from Census 2010. *State of Metropolitan America Series.* Available from https://www.brookings.edu/research/the-new-metro-minority-map-regional-shifts-in-hispanics-asians-and-blacks-from-census-2010/

García, O. (2009). *Bilingual education in the 21st century: A global perspective.* Malden, MA: Wiley-Blackwell.

García, O. (2017). Critical multilingual language awareness and teacher education, In J. Cenoz, D. Gorter, & S. May (Eds.), *Encyclopedia of language and education, Language awareness and multilingualism* (3rd ed., Vol. 6, pp. 263–280). Dordrecht, Netherlands: Springer, https://doi.org/10.1007/978-0-387-30424-3

García, O., & Kleifgen, J.A. (2019). Translanguaging and literacies. *Reading Research Quarterly, 55*(4). https://doi.org/10.1002/rrq.286

García, O., & Otheguy, R. (2016). Interrogating the language gap of young bilingual and bidialectal students. *International Multilingual Research Journal, 11*(1), 52–65.

Ginsburg, K.R. (2007). The importance of play in promoting healthy child development and maintaining strong parent-child bonds. *Pediatrics,* 119(1), 182–191. http://www.tc.columbia.edu/i/a/document/6468_Ofelia_ELL__Final.pdf

Goodman, Y. (1992). Children coming to know literacy. In W.H. Teale & E. Sulzby (Eds.), *Emergent literacy: Writing and reading* (pp. 1–14). New Jersey: Ablex Publishing.

Griffin, T.M., Hemphill, L., Camp, L., & Wolf, D.P. (2004). Oral discourse in the preschool years and later literacy skills. *First Language, 24,* 123–147.

Hassinger-Das, B., Hirsh-Pasek, K., & Golinkoff, R.M. (2017). The case of brain science and guided play: A developing story. *Young Children, 72*(2), 45–71.

Lave, J., & Wenger, E. (1991). *Situated learning: Legitimate peripheral participation.* Cambridge, MA: Cambridge University Press.

Li, W. (2011). Moment analysis and translanguaging space: Discursive construction of identities by multilingual Chinese youth in Britain. *Journal of Pragmatics, 43,* 1222–1235.

Lindholm-Leary, K. (2014). Bilingual and biliteracy skills in young Spanish-speaking low-SES children: Impact of instructional language and primary language. *International Journal of Bilingual Education and Bilingualism, 17,* 144–159.

López, D. (2019). Jugando y explorando together: Translanguaging and guided play in a bilingual kindergarten classroom in NYC. *Journal of Bilingual Education Research and Instruction, 21*(1), 1-16.

Magruder, E.S., Hayslip, W.W., Espinosa, L.M., & Matera, C. (2013). Many languages, one teacher: Supporting language and literacy development for preschool dual language learners. *Young Children, 68*(1), 8–15.

Méndez, L.I., Crais, E.R., Castro, D.C., Kainz, K. (2015). A culturally and linguistically responsive vocabulary approach for young Latino Dual Language Learners. *Journal of Speech, Language, and Hearing Research*, 1–14.

Moll, L.C., Amanti, C., Neff, D., & Gonzalez, N. (1992) Funds of knowledge for teaching: Using a qualitative approach to connect homes and classrooms. *Theory into Practice*, *31*(2), 132–141

Morell, Z. (2017). Rethinking preschool education through bilingual Universal Pre-kindergarten: Opportunities and challenges. *Journal of Multilingual Education Research*, 7, Article 2. Available at: https://fordham.bepress.com/jmer/vol7/iss1/2

Mraz, K., Porcelli, A., & Tyler, C. (2016). *Purposeful play*. Portsmouth, NH: Heinemann.

NAEYC. (2009). *Developmentally appropriate practice in early childhood programs serving children from birth through age 8*. Washington, DC: Author. https://www.naeyc.org/sites/default/files/globally-shared/downloads/PDFs/resources/position-statements/PSDAP.pdf

National Academies of Sciences, Engineering, and Medicine. (2017). *Promoting the educational success of children and youth learning English: Promising futures*. Washington, DC: The National Academies Press. https://doi.org/10.17226/24677.

Neu, R.A. (2013). An exploration of oral language development in Spanish-speaking preschool students. *Early Childhood Education Journal*, *41*, 211–218.

Neuman, S. (2006). The knowledge gap: Implications for early education. In D.K. Dickinson & Susan B. Neuman (Eds.), *Handbook of early literacy research*, (Vol. 2, pp. 29–40). New York, London: The Guilford Press.

New York State Education Department (2017a). Report of Regents P-12 Education Committee to The Board of Regents. Prekindergarten Emergent Multilingual Learners (EMLLs) Best Practices for Identification. Available from https://www.regents.nysed.gov/common/regents/files/P-12%20-%20Prekindergarten%20Emergent%20Multilingual%20Learners%20%28EMLLs%29%20Best%20Practices%20for%20Identification.pdf

New York State Education Department (2017b). *Emergent multilingual learners in prekindergarten: A protocol for identification, instructional planning, and programming*. By Zoila Morell, created in conjunction with the New York State Education Department. Retrieved from: http://www.nysed.gov/common/nysed/files/programs/bilingual-ed/guidance-document-emlls-in-prek_july_2018.rev-2.pdf-a.pdf. Accessed April 26, 2020.

New York State Education Department (2019). *The New York State Prekindergarten Learning Standards: A Resource for School Success*. Retrieved from http://www.p12.nysed.gov/earlylearning/standards/documents/PKStandards2019accessability.pdf

Otheguy, R., García, O. & Reid, W. (2015). Clarifying translanguaging and deconstructing named languages: A perspective from linguistics. *Applied Linguistics Review*, *6*(3), 281–307.

Otheguy, R., García, O., & Reid, W. (2018). A translanguaging view of the linguistic system of bilinguals. *Applied Linguistics Review*. https://doi.org/10.1515/applirev-2018-0020.

Pacheco, M.B., & Miller, M.E. (2015). Making meaning through translanguaging in the literacy classroom. *The Reading Teacher*, *69*(5), 533–537.

Roberts, T. (2008). Home storybook reading in primary or second language with preschool children: Evidence of equal effectiveness for second-language vocabulary acquisition. *Reading Research Quarterly*, *70*, 475–490.

Rolstad, K., Mahoney, K., & Glass, G.V. (2005). The big picture: A meta-analysis of program effectiveness research on English language learners. *Educational Policy*, *19*(4), 572–594.

Souto-Manning, M. (2013). *Multicultural teaching in the early childhood classroom: Strategies, tools, and approaches, Preschool-2nd grade.* Washington, DC and New York, NY: Association for Childhood Education International and Teachers College Press.

Souto-Manning, M., Falk, B., López, D., Cruz, L., Bradt, N., Cardwell, N., McGowan, N., Perez, A., Rabadi-Raol, A., & Rollins, E. (2019). A transdisciplinary approach to changing inequitable teaching practices in PreK. *Review of Research in Education, 43*, 249–276.

Strong-Wilson, T., & Ellis, J. (2007). Children and place: Reggio Emilia's environment as third teacher. *Theory into Practice, 46*(1), 40–47.

Sulzby, E. (1992). Writing and reading: Signs of oral and written language organization in young children. In W.H. Teale & E. Sulzby (Eds.), *Emergent literacy: Writing and reading.* New Jersey: Ablex Publishing Corporation

Van Hoorn, J., Nourot, P.M., Scales, B., & Alward, K.R. (2010). *Play at the center of the curriculum.* Boston, MA: Pearson Higher Ed.

Vygotsky, L.S. (1978). *Mind in society: The development of higher psychological processes.* Cambridge, MA: Harvard University Press.

Vygotsky, L.S. (1986). *Thought and language.* Cambridge, MA: MIT Press.

Zentella, A.C. (2005). *Building on strength: Language and Literacy in Latino Families and Communities.* New York, NY: Teachers College Press.

BOX 10.1 TEACHER/RESEARCHER

Maeva Lopez-Kaseem

Prekindergarten, dual language bilingual

"Maestra, maestra, ven... ¡Queremos escribir una historia!" This is music to my ears. I look around to see who is calling while trying to guess what my Pre-K students have in mind. I see a group of three emergent bilingual students busy at the block center creating a farm. Oh, I know... They'll tell me a story about our visit to Kelkenberg Farm! Wonderment, that's what I feel toward my students. I'm in awe of their imagination, their ability to recreate their experiences through words and actions. Theirs, I know, will be an amazing story.

My name is Maeva López-Kassem, and until recently I was a Prekindergarten teacher at Bilingual Center School 33 in Buffalo, NY. During my tenure at the Bilingual Center and through the efforts of Principal Miguel Medina (from 2010 to 2018), teachers in grades PK-2 received training in the *Reggio Emilia instructional philosophy*, a social constructivist educational model that places children at the center of learning. Its founding father, Loris Malaguzzi, believed that children constructed learning and communicated their ideas through a hundred languages (Boyd Cadwell, 1997): Speaking, listening, reading, writing, drawing, dancing, sculpting, playing, and others.

Around the same time, a handful of teachers were invited to partake in a series of professional learning opportunities (PLO) on Translanguaging as part of CUNY-NYSIEB. Our mentor, Dr. Kate Mahoney, met with us every 4–6 weeks as we learned about and implemented the use of various translanguaging strategies from *Translanguaging: A CUNY-NYSIEB Guide for Educators* (Celic & Seltzer, 2013). Through this PLO, I realized that the concept of translanguaging far exceeded my conceptualization of bilingualism and cross-language awareness. Translanguaging, I came to understand, is an action that allows students to use their entire language repertoire to make sense of their world and their own learning. I am convinced that the combined paradigms, the Reggio-Emilia philosophy and Translanguaging, serve as a robust foundation for teaching emergent bilinguals in ECE settings. Languaging, after all, is how young children construct learning.

Whenever my emergent bilingual students summoned me as scribe, I answered their call. Most of their stories rose from our shared writing experiences based on the Translanguaging with Language Experience Approach strategy, which I used regularly in the classroom. As CUNY-NYSIEB's Translanguaging Guide explain, the language experience approach is commonly used with emerging writers. Usually a small group of students dictates ideas based on a shared experience while the teacher writes them down word for word, making no corrections. The teacher might elicit ideas through the use of visuals from the experience and/or questions. Following this, the teacher reads the text back to the students, who can make any changes. In Pre-K, I added translanguaging to the approach by allowing students to express their ideas through Spanish and English. I also collaborated with students to translate their original drafts to the target language of instruction. More often, we created bilingual versions of the texts. Through these activities, I supported my students' meta-bilingual development and consequently enhanced their understanding of the relationship between English and Spanish and of how their bilingual practices went beyond two languages. Many of the students' stories were transformed into posters and books, which were proudly displayed around the classroom and used in the classroom library.

Using translanguaging with the Language Experience Approach allows students to share in collaborative learning experiences through the use of their two languages. It also allows them to recreate their understanding of concepts learned in class. The following beginning-of-the-year English narrative illustrates how students interacted using the resources that they presently had in their repertoire.

> Xander—We were painting.
> Jeybian. Paint. Usamos azul y rojo y amarillo.
> Gilbert—We mixed them.
> Xander—They were turning to colors.
> Joriel—Que se volvió mucho a purple.
> Jeybian—Yo lo hice con rojo y con azul.
> Xander— Mixing colors is like cooking! It's like you have to get some food. You have to put some food in there, and you have to put some sprinkles. You have to take a spoon and mix it.

In this particular case, four students were sharing an experience about mixing colors. Two students used more Spanish and two used more English. Had students been denied the right to translanguage, two of them would have likely remained silent, to the detriment of the entire group. This short story was the springboard to robust conversations about colors in nature, teamwork, bilingualism, and language use. It also informed me about the students' language and strengths and needs, which helped shape future instructional decisions.

People often ask me how best to create opportunities for implementing *Translanguaging with the Language Experience Approach* with very young emergent bilinguals. I taught in a two-way dual language 50-50 bilingual program. This means that half of the young 4 year-old children speak Spanish (although they might also speak English) and the other half speak English and not Spanish (although they might also speak a language other than English. Instruction is 50% of the time in English and 50% of the time in Spanish.

Here are some recommendations to make writing with the *Translanguaging with the Language Experience Approach* experience relevant, productive, efficient, and enjoyable.

- **Who:** *This will depend on the make-up of your class. I suggest all students join the activity. Discussion among members tends to be richer when students support, play off others' contributions, and translate for each other. I prefer to work with three to five students so that each emergent bilingual has ample opportunity to speak, especially once they become better acquainted with turn taking and listening to others' ideas.*
- **What**: Once comfortable with the classroom adults, students will eagerly share their life experiences with them. For some students, this will take the form of spoken language. Other students may need to generate ideas through aesthetics or artistic representations. Know your students and allow them time to express themselves through myriad means. Student experiences may take the form of books, posters, and charts. As often as possible, publish their work via your teacher web page to be shared with parents and other students. I have used PowerPoint and Padlet (padlet. com) to publish my students' shared experiences. I simply make color copies of each slide in Power Point, place them in sheet protectors, and put them in a colorful binder. These student-created books become reading magnets that attract eager learners to read and revisit their stories constantly. With the use of Padlet and other similar apps, teachers can almost effortlessly create posters to post in the school and share in their webpages.
- **When**: Young students love to tell stories, so I make every effort to scribe their ideas regularly, preferably within a few days of a shared experience. Some of these ideas are published while others disappear in the ether. I strive to publish one or two children-generated narratives per month, whether via charts, books, or posters.
- **Where**: *Try to work with a small group of students in a quiet area. Make sure to have your writing utensils, whether a laptop, chart, or notebook, at easy reach.*
- **How**: Simply put, follow the writing process. Learners can become familiar with the idea that writing is a complex yet achievable activity from an

early age. I use Engler et al.'s (1988) POWER: Prewrite, organize, write, edit, and rewrite. Be concise and purposeful at each stage, or the students may lose interest or become fatigued. Be willing to *work* on the narrative over various brief writing sessions.

- *Prewrite*: Show students plenty of visuals (pictures, drawings, paintings) about the shared activity to aid their memories and ignite ideas. Ask questions to unearth details and explanations.
- *Organize*: As the prewriting discussion takes place, organize the visuals in order of events. I always emphasize the value of putting the events in the order they occurred for my students because this is an important academic life skill.
- *Write*: The teacher serves as scribe, so make sure to copy the students' ideas word for word. You may ask questions for clarification or to extend the narrative but make no corrections at this time. Allow students to use all their meaning-making repertoire. I have noticed that peers support each other and often make on the spot translations to the target language. It is important to ask the speakers for approval before altering their words.
- *Edit*: Read the narrative back to students and give them space to add or delete ideas. At this point I *usually ask plenty of questions, especially once students have become familiar with the process and become confident narrators, to clarify and expand ideas. This is often the right time to explore cross-language connections: similarities and differences in sentence structure, use and placement of descriptive words, cognates, and others.*
- *Revise*: Thanks to today's technology, editing and revising can occur concurrently if the students' narrative is captured electronically. I make corrections to the narrative and produce a new draft, which is often published in book or poster format.

I have observed how students have become eager participants during class discussions. They feel confident using their language repertoire to express their thoughts, often flaunting new vocabulary in the target language. I also watched my students become keen observers of the connections between their two named languages and with other practices. Above all, I witnessed my students deepen their understanding of the concepts presented in class while expanding their vocabulary across languages. I urge educators to explore the use of an experiment with translanguaging strategies in their classrooms. We owe this to our children.

References

Boyd Cadwell, L. (1997). *Bringing Reggio Emilia home: An innovative approach to early childhood education*. New York, NY: Teachers College.

Celic, C. & Seltzer, K. (2013). *Translanguaging: A CUNY-NYSIEB guide for educators*. Retrieved from https://www.cuny-nysieb.org/wp content/uploads/2016/04/Translanguaging-Guide-March-2013.pdf

Englert, C.S., Raphael, T.E., Anderson, L.M., Anthony, H.M., Fear, K.L., & Gregg, S.L. (1988). A case for writing intervention: Strategies for writing informational text. *Learning Disabilities Focus*, 3(2), 98–113.

11

TRANSLANGUAGING LITERACIES

Latinx children's literature and literacy instruction

Carla España and Luz Yadira Herrera

Introduction

For many of us who are bilingual/multilingual, embracing our identities and the ways we navigate spaces with our language practices is a process that is at times contested, at other times welcomed. Gloria Anzaldúa's (1987) pivotal book, *Borderlands/La frontera: The new mestiza*, names linguistic and cultural identities that do not conform to the static ways of being as defined by colonization. Anzaldúa pushes those of us who find ourselves on the metaphoric and literal borderlands across the world to decolonize our conceptualization of language practices, culture, and identity. Anzaldúa reminds us that we are neither from "here" nor from "there" and that hybridity of identities is a valid way of *being*. In this chapter, we look at fluid language practices as they manifest in children's literature, and specifically consider the ways in which these identities are enacted through translanguaging in literacy spaces.

Translanguaging in Latinx children's literature: An overview

Translanguaging in children's literature affirms fluid ways of being and the role that language plays in our identities (España & Herrera, 2020). Pérez Rosario (2015) argues that translanguaging is often used in Latinx literature for literary effect in order to convey authenticity in the communication between characters in a book. She emphasizes that translanguaging makes it possible for speakers to break free from conforming to monolingual norms. By doing so, they are in fact enacting dynamic bilingualism (Pérez Rosario, 2015, p. iv). In discussing his text on children and young adult literature by and for Latinx readers, Aldama

(2018) notes the impact of authentic and varied language practices as represented in texts: "Movement betwixt and between languages invites readers first to connect with the rich cross-pollination of rhythms, sounds, sights, and smells experienced by Latino protagonists and, second, to experience how polylingual creation is itself a central part of the aesthetic experience" (p. 19).

Alamillo, Mercado-López, and Herrera (2018) examine how language and culture are reflected in Chicanx children's literature and argue that it can raise the consciousness of children because it often reflects their lived experiences. What is more, Chicanx literature also affirms Chicanx children's cultural and linguistic identities since it often reflects the fluid language practices of Chicanx families. Avilés (2018) examines the writing moves of children's book author, Maya Christina González, and argues that the author's choice to include features of English and Spanish in her writing challenges linguistic hierarchies that privilege English above others. Similarly, Alamillo (2018) argues that Chicanx children's literature has traditionally been a space for children to see the "various language practices they engage in with family and community" (p. 152). The author analyzes the language dynamics between grandmothers and their grandchildren depicted in the literature and shows how translanguaging is an important mode of intergenerational communication. Alamillo (2018) further highlights that Chicanx children's book authors use translanguaging "as a means to elevate the use of two languages by speakers of Spanish and English," and describes the use of this literature in classrooms as enacting social justice (p. 154).

Alternatively, a lack of exposure to translanguaging in literature and in classroom instruction negatively impacts children's development of language ideologies that embrace their full identities. In their ethnographic study of 19 Latinx children in a faith-based after school center in South Texas, Bassett-Webb, Masso, and Lewis (2018) found that accountability measures such as high-stakes standardized testing in English impacted the availability of curricula, texts, and experiences in Spanish. They also found that the English-only curricula in children's schools impacted students' experiences and beliefs of their Spanish-language practices. Children "reported that their teachers did not allow translanguaging" (p. 2659). Another child's tutor said: "When trying to write using translanguaging, she felt uncomfortable because she was told at school she could only speak one language at a time" (p. 2659). Children in this study revealed how they were not exposed to children's literature that had translanguaging and were not encouraged to do this in their writing. Yet the teacher candidates and tutors in this third space (Bhabha, 1994; Gutiérrez, Baquedano-López, Alvarez, & Chiu, 1999; Soja, 1996) of the afterschool program provided examples of translanguaging.

Kersten and Ludwig (2018) discuss how Gloria Anzaldúa's (1997) *Friends from the Other Side/Amigos del otro lado*, is in itself an example of going beyond named/separate languages as "the English text is interspersed with Spanish words such as *mojado, gringo,* or *macho*" (p. 22). The authors argue that such a text can help teachers create a translanguaging space as learners interrogate how language practices are used, while being encouraged to "produce their own multilingual texts" (p. 24). For the authors, it is critical to create moments in the classroom for students to grow their metalinguistic awareness; and using multilingual picture books makes this work not only possible but also powerful.

Translanguaging in Latinx children's literature: How authors engage with translanguaging

In this section, we show how several authors enact different forms of translanguaging in their books. We also provide an analysis of these writing moves while making meaning of their use of translanguaging. We begin by discussing books with side-by-side and top-to-bottom translations, and then move on to discuss books that engage a bilingual reader's full linguistic repertoire in a single text. We provide examples from children's picture books that are targeted for use in primary grades, poetry collections that are geared toward middle grades, and further provide examples from the young adult (YA) genre of literature used in secondary grades.

All of the authors that we highlight here integrate language practices as one part of their characters' identity. For some, this means developing a character that is biracial and bilingual (Marisol in Monica Brown's *Marisol McDonald* book series). Monica Brown (2013), Jorge Argueta (2016a,b), David Bowles (2018a,b), and Isabel Quintero (2019a,b) center the experiences of children as these are impacted by immigration policies, some addressing mixed-documented status families, and changes in the community landscape. Other authors and illustrators like Edgardo Miranda-Rodriguez (2016), Carole Boston Weatherford and Eric Velasquez (2017), Elizabeth Acevedo (2018a,b), and Javaka Steptoe (2016) amplify the voices of Afro-Latinx characters and address anti-Blackness across different communities, while authentically representing their language practices. These authors show the complexity and depth of their characters not only by creating spaces on the written page to illustrate their language practices, but also representing the lived experiences and multifaceted identities of bilingual people.

Translating side-by-side and top-to-bottom

Many authors write bilingual children's literature that reflects both languages side-by-side. These books are sometimes written in one language and then translated into another, but still reflect some instances of translanguaging. Below, we illustrate several examples from books that present bilingual literature side-by-side or top-to-bottom, with translanguaging moments within those "separate" sections.

In her book, *Marisol McDonald doesn't Match/Marisol McDonald no combina*, Monica Brown's (2011) writing reflects the interactions of a racially and linguistically mixed family. In this text, the protagonist Marisol is a biracial (Peruvian/Scottish) and bilingual girl who constantly negotiates her languaging during her family conversations, and this is evident in both "sides" of the page. Brown uses translanguaging on both sides of the pages. She uses italics to discern the languages enacted in a particular part of the text. In the "English" side of the text, she italicizes the words in Spanish, and the same is true for the "Spanish" side of the text, in which the English words are italicized. What is more, there is a stylistic difference between each side as the dialogue is indicated through the use of quotations on the English side, whereas in the Spanish side, the dialogue is denoted through the use of the em dash. In capitalizing "Dad" and keeping Mami/mami on both "sides," Brown maintains the authenticity of the way the character narrates their story.

In another book in this series, *Marisol McDonald and the Clash Bash/Marisol McDonald y la fiesta sin igual*, Monica Brown (2013) develops the story of Marisol's birthday party plans. Her mother has to break the news that her beloved abuelita cannot attend. Following is a short excerpt from the "English" side of the page:

> Marisol, "it isn't just the money," Mami explains. "It's hard to get *papeles* to come to the United States. Abuelita needs a special document called a visa to visit us, but sometimes it takes a long time for the visa to arrive." (Brown, 2013, p. 17)

In keeping the word "papeles" in Spanish within the English section, Brown affirms the importance of papers and documents for many Latinx families that live undocumented and separated from other family members. Children experiencing this reality of family separation within Latinx homes are familiar with this terminology, either hearing it in the hushed conversations between family members or when questions arise as to why family members are not present.

At the end of the text, on the day of her birthday party, Marisol is surprised by her family when she gets to "see" her abuelita online (with an internet connection and a computer). In the following excerpt, Brown puts the text in English on the top of a page, followed by the text in Spanish on the bottom:

> 'Feliz cumpleaños, Marisol,' she says, and we both laugh. 'I'm still waiting for my visa, but I used some of the money you sent me to buy my first computer and get an internet connection…'
>
> 'Te quiero mucho,' I tell Abuelita. 'I love you so much.'
>
> —Feliz cumpleaños, Marisol- dice ella, y ambas nos reímos –.

Sigo esperando por mi visa, pero utilicé parte del dinero que me envi-
aste para comprar mi primera computadora y obtener una conexión de
internet ...
–Te quiero mucho – le digo a abuelita–. *I love you so much.*

(Brown, 2013, p. 27)

In *Somos como las nubes/We are like the Clouds* Jorge Argueta (2016a,b) considers
his own experience fleeing El Salvador in the 1980s and the more recent journeys of thousands of youth leaving violence and poverty in Central America.
The poems are always displayed first in Spanish and the English translation follows, an order that reflects the language in which the poems were originally
written. In the opening poem, "Somos como las nubes," Argueta (2016a,b) provides definitions for the words "cuches," "alboroto," and "piscuchas" (p. 2). This
practice continues throughout the rest of the pages with powerful illustrations
by Alfonso Ruano. Argueta's practice of providing the poems in both Spanish
and English, and adding cultural and site-specific definitions below the poems,
honors the journeys and connections to varied representations of home for thousands of migrant youth.

Children's literature that provides translations within texts (side by side, above
and below, page by page) as well as texts that incorporate the translanguaging
of Latinx people provides access to concepts that relate to the varied and unique
Latinx experience. From a Peruvian-Scottish character speaking in Spanish and
in English in Monica Brown's *Marisol McDonald* book series, to Jorge Argueta's
poems on the journeys of migrant children, these texts show the possibilities that
are created when texts show the complexity of bilingual lives.

Translanguaging within a single text

Above, we presented examples from authors who wrote a side-by-side bilingual
text that enacted translanguaging even within that semi-separation of text by
named languages. In this section, we highlight authors who draw from their
entire linguistic repertoire within the writing of a single text.

In a classic anthology of poetry for middle grade and secondary classrooms
on Latinx experiences, *Cool salsa: Bilingual Poems on Growing up Latino in the
United States*, poems are provided in both Spanish and English. But there are
poems like "Race Politics" by Luis J. Rodriguez (1994) where even though the
poem is in English, the author uses some words in Spanish. For example, to refer
to his mom who is always the boss, he uses "jefita." The author addresses the
social issues of food insecurity and injustices around access to food across different neighborhoods. And as he moves in and out of neighborhoods and across
social, racial and language lines, he also does so linguistically. Rodriguez's poem

embodies the complex intermingling of race and class and language not only socially, but also linguistically.

This use of translanguaging is becoming more evident in Latinx children's literature.

Here we look at how four children's authors use translanguaging in their texts—Yuyi Morales in *Dreamers*; Isabel Quintero in *My Papi Has a Motorcycle*, illustrated by Zeke Peña; David Bowles in *They Call Me Güero*; and Edgardo Miranda-Rodriguez in *La Borinqueña*.

In *Dreamers*, Yuyi Morales (2018) beautifully takes us through her own immigration journey to the United States from Mexico with her young son. The book is also available in Spanish and it's called *Soñadores*, but unlike the authors from the section right before, she doesn't provide the Spanish version of her text within one book. In the English version, *Dreamers*, we read "We are stories. We are two languages. We are lucha. We are resilience. We are hope. We are dreamers, soñadores of the world" (Morales, 2018, p. 27). Morales engages with her entire linguistic repertoire in *Dreamers*. In the text itself, there are no italics to alert the reader of a "shift" in the language. To Morales, there are no boundaries in language. Although the book begins with a description of her border-crossing journey, the story develops to show how she navigates a new land where her language practices and reading exist as a borderless world.

In *My Papi has a Motorcycle*, Isabel Quintero (2019a,b) engages with translanguaging in developing themes around family relationships, community bonds, and changes in the community landscape. It begins with "My papi has a motorcycle. From him I've learned words like carburetor and cariño, drill and dedication" (Quintero, 2019a,b, p. 1). Family members say "¡Con cuidado! Be careful!" as Daisy Ramona and her papi leave on his motorcycle for a ride around the neighborhood (Quintero, 2019a,b, p. 5). The signs in the community reveal words and cultural artifacts from Mexico and the United States—"meat, produce, panadería" (Quintero, 2019a,b, p. 6). These appear below the U.S. and Mexican flags on the wall of a neighborhood store adorned with hanging piñatas. We see signs for "Don Rudy's Raspados" where Don Rudy's shop should be—it's closed down now. From family to community conversations and signs, translanguaging is a part of Daisy's life in ways that reveal connections within the community, and how people, places, and experiences hold meaning for the characters.

Edgardo Miranda-Rodriguez's *La Borinqueña* (2016) comic book series also uses translanguaging to develop a character's connection with family and a very special place, Puerto Rico. Marisol, or La Borinqueña, becomes the superhero the island needs to right the wrongs of colonization, a struggle that continues in the present-day. First, we see how Miranda-Rodriguez uses translanguaging to show authentic family communication and connection. For example, in chapter two, when Marisol leaves home to prepare for her senior year research trip to Puerto Rico, she yells "¡Bendición!" and her parents respond "¡Qué Dios te bendiga!" (p. 9). In chapter three, upon her arrival in Puerto Rico, her grandfather greets Marisol with "¡Qué Dios te bendiga y te guarde!" (p. 15).

Second, we see translanguaging used to develop a character's identity. In one powerful scene, Marisol is about to leave her home in Brooklyn, New York to conduct her research in Puerto Rico. Her mother removes a ribbon that was in a frame that read "El Grito de Lares, el 23 de septiembre 1868," proceeds to give it to Marisol, and says "It's been framed since your father and I first met, negrita. Pero sirve mejor ahora contigo" (p. 14). The Grito de Lares was an uprising against colonial rule by Spain. This exchange anchors Marisol's identity in her Afro-Latinidad and in being Puerto Rican. Both exemplify anti-colonial identity and a foreshadowing of her role and impact that is to come in later chapters.

Miranda-Rodriguez also uses translanguaging to show the connection with indigenous roots and how they provide fortitude for Marisol's justice work within the Puerto Rican community. In chapter four, when Marisol embarks on her studies at a cave, the Taíno goddess Atabex appears to her and says: "I am the mother of Boriken. I am the ancient spirit of your deep past. I am the water that flows through your consciousness. I am the love for my people. Mar y sol, my sea and sun. I am Atabex" (Miranda-Rodriguez, 2016, p. 26).

It is as if one can draw a metaphorical thread through the exchange Marisol had with her mother and this exchange with Atabex. At this moment, Miranda-Rodriguez uses "Boriken," the indigenous Taíno name for the island, and not "Puerto Rico," the name given by Spanish colonizers. The translanguaging we see in Atabex's presentation includes features from English, Spanish, and Taíno (part of the Arawak language family). Miranda-Rodriguez also uses translanguaging to show injustice and restoration. Marisol, introduces herself to people as she seeks to help during a flood in Puerto Rico. A mother, holding her child in desperation says: "¿Cómo puede ser si siempre se olvidan de nosotros? ¿Cómo nos vas a poder ayudar?" (p. 36). In the exchanges with people in Puerto Rico whom Marisol helps as la Borinqueña she uses Spanish.

Translanguaging in children's literature: Ways that educators can integrate discussions on translanguaging in children's literature and its impact

It is imperative that classroom discussions across primary and secondary schools not only focus on how language practices are used, but also on how these are embedded in the characters' multifaceted identities and experiences. We want to help teachers create translanguaging spaces where students engage with literature for the purpose of amplifying these authentic stories (see also, Chapter 8 and Teacher/Researcher Boxes 7.1, 8.1, and 11.1, this volume). Below, we show three approaches we use to help teachers create these translanguaging spaces in primary and secondary classrooms—(1) mentor text as chispa, (2) building a classroom library, and (3) the three T's: temas, textos and translanguaging.

Approach #1: Mentor text as chispa

One way that teachers can begin a discussion on dynamic bilingual practices and their connections with our identities is by engaging students in poetry readings. We use the metaphor of a chispa as a way to think about this practice as the spark that affirms the identities of language-minoritized children and encourages them to share their stories.

In the examples that follow, teachers engage students (middle/secondary grades) in reading and discussing poetry. We first look at students reading Elizabeth Acevedo's "Mira Muchacha" poem in *The Poet X* (2018). We then discuss students' reading of Aida Salazar's "A Closet Full" and "Preparations" in *The Moon Within* (2019), Finally, we present students' reading and discussing David Bowles' poem "The Newcomer" in *They Call Me Güero* (2018).

The purpose of the poetry activity is to expose students, in ten-minute intervals, to these texts with multifaceted characters so that they too can write their own. By selecting poems from novels in verse, students can also continue reading and expanding their own language repertoires.

In the award-winning book *The Poet X*, Elizabeth Acevedo's (2018a,b) character, Xiomara, a Dominican teenager, navigates the changes within herself, in relation to her family, friends, and the expectations that society places on her. An audio recording of Acevedo reading the first few poems of *The Poet X* is available in the publisher's website. Sometimes teachers use the clip of Acevedo's reading of "Mira, muchacha" as the starting point for poems students will write. Students can consider these questions: "What are some lines or phrases that come to mind when you think of your parents or family members giving you advice?" "What's something your family is always repeating to you?" As students think and write down some lines, teachers can share their own examples. One teacher added her own family's sayings: "Eso no es de Dios," and "Dime con quién andas y te diré quién eres." Teachers can then ask students to pick their favorite phrase and write down the moment of which they are reminded, just like Acevedo does in her poem.

After students write, students can ask for feedback, specifically asking writing partners which words they would revise. This feedback on word choice considers which features from which named language would be representative of their family's own linguistic practices. After providing feedback, students can then try this with a line from their writing, reading out loud to a classmate. If time permits, students can work with rhythm and notice which words, using features

TABLE 11.1 Mentor text as chispa for poetry writing

1. READ: Select a line from a poem.
2. THINK: Use it to start, finish, structure (repeat at each stanza) your poem.
3. DRAFT: Write, write, write.
4. REVISE: Reread noticing word choice (options: shades of meaning and translanguaging).
5. REVISE: Reread out loud to a classmate noticing places to pause and words to revise to give your writing the rhythm you want.
6. SHARE: Reread out loud again. Ask classmates for feedback.

from their entire language repertoire, can give them different rhythms, as they revise their writing. Table 11.1 provides the steps that students are encouraged to follow when writing poetry based on a mentor text chispa.

For the second round of mentor text as chispa in the poetry immersion, students read excerpts from *The Moon Within* by Aida Salazar (2019a,b,c). It is important that we create the space to look at how language practices are interpreted across different communities (school, home, outside of home) and what connections these have with relationships and cultural practices. In Salazar's middle grade novel in verse, we see how a bicultural Puerto Rican/Mexican protagonist, Celi, connects with indigenous Mexican and Afro-Caribbean practices, including family conversations on her changing body, music in her bomba dance class, and after much resistance, preparing for a moon ceremony to honor the changes in her body.

In the poem "A Closet Full," Celi puts on her new bra in a closet at home and her mom enthusiastically says, "It's amazing, just look at this muchachita, está floreciendo" (Salazar, 2019a,b,c, p. 14). In the poem "Preparations," we learn about statues honoring deities and spirits from Mexico and the Caribbean, such as Tonantzin/Guadalupe, Coatlicue, Yemayá, Oyá, Ochún, Atabey, Xochipilli/Xochiquetzal, and Ometeotl. Celi and Mima build an altar the day before Celi's moon ceremony (Salazar, 2019a,b,c, pp. 195–197). Translanguaging in this text is a way to connect to people, places, and meaning, including self, family, ancestors, and spirits. Students can return to their writing to consider how the characters' language practices reveal something important about themselves and/or how they seek community with others. Students can ask themselves the following when they revisit their writing with this lens: How does this reveal an authentic way of communicating and connecting? Why does this matter to my characters? Is this the best way to express a feeling, idea or move the story along?

For the last iteration of mentor text as chispa for students' poetry writing and analysis of issues of language and identity, we go to David Bowles' poem, "The Newcomer:" "At last I find him,/tucked into a little alcove/near the library,/crying./"¿Qué te pasa?" I ask./His story comes steaming out -/threats against the family,/abandoning Honduras,/risking life/and limb on la Bestia,/the black train that rattles/through Mexico bottom to top" (Bowles, 2018a,b, p. 51). With this mentor text, we share with students how translanguaging can open up spaces for storytelling, amplifying the experiences of minoritized communities. In this case, it is the journey that Andrés takes from Honduras to Mexico and finally arriving in the United States.

Teachers can ask students to create a list of such moments that center children's language practices and minoritized identities. In some instances, students have thought about youth who feel marginalized in schools and their experiences—refugees' journeys, discrimination against youth of color, gender inequality, islamophobia and other religious discrimination, undocumented status, languages other than English, other language practices, disabilities. Then, students are asked to think about what they would say to a student who belongs to one of these groups as well as how they might communicate with them. By engaging in this poetry activity, students get to know the characters' stories, as well as ways to develop their own on the page.

Approach #2: A classroom library that reflects translanguaging practices and identities

Drawing from Paris (2012) and Paris and Alim's (2017) culturally sustaining pedagogy, a children's book library must sustain and celebrate the culture, language practices, and ways of being of children and families. A library must reflect accurate and authentic diversity in race/ethnicity, cultural and linguistic practices, belief systems, gender identities, differently abled bodies, socioeconomic status, and other ways of being and living. Because we believe that a culturally and linguistically sustaining classroom library is most important, we engage teachers in considering how their libraries reflect the multifaceted experiences of children, especially those from minoritized groups. To do so we developed the guide that appears as Table 11.2. Besides taking an inventory of the type of books their classroom libraries already have, we encourage teachers to use this guide to continue to grow their classroom library.

Approach #3: The three Ts—temas, textos, and translanguaging

In España and Herrera (2020), we present ways that teachers can craft meaningful lessons by considering three major aspects of their instruction and shaping powerful learning experience for their students' around what we call temas, textos, and translanguaging (p. 18). Temas refers to the themes or topics that engage students' interests and experiences around language, literacies, and power structures. Powerful textos are those that sustain, affirm, and extend the learning on these topics. Finally translanguaging pedagogical practices extend and amplify

TABLE 11.2 Checklist: culturally and linguistically sustaining children's library

Is your library culturally and linguistically sustaining?★	*Agree/disagree/not sure*
The characters are from different racial/ethnic minoritized groups and are authentically represented (avoiding stereotypes).	
The characters use bilingual/multilingual language practices that accurately reflect the language practices of minoritized groups.	
The stories have a wide range of family structures (single-parent, foster or adoptive parent(s), families with two moms or two dads, families with an incarcerated parent, etc.).	
The characters in the story represent a variety of jobs and careers (farmworkers, artists, professionals, service workers, etc.)	
The stories have a variety of able and differently abled characters from all racial/ethnic groups, genders, and socio-economic classes, and they play an important role in the story.	
The characters represent varied gender identities and expressions (avoiding stereotypical gender roles).	
Stories encourage appreciation and respect for differences between people and their ways of being.	
Stories remind students that they are important, that their voice matters, and that they can make a difference in their family, their community, and their world.	

★ *Adapted from "Creating an Anti-bias Library" by Social Justice Books (2016).*

student learning and expression through the use of their entire linguistic repertoire beyond the use of only English or only Spanish.

In Isabel Quintero's *Mi papi tiene una moto* (2019), readers must confront the ways that a community comes together and how change impacts everyone. Topics such as gentrification, bilingual/multilingual signs and cultural artifacts, father–daughter relationships, intergenerational connections, and working-class life are developed throughout the narrative and illustrations. Translanguaging is one of the ways that these topics are revealed in the text as we see the dialogue between Daisy and her community. Teachers can plan for multiple readings of this text, creating spaces for students to engage with these topics and study Quintero's craft, noticing how these were developed with an understanding of dynamic language practices. This type of instruction that considers temas, textos, and translanguaging together makes room for students to process the content and craft of a culturally and linguistically transformative text and creates a meaningful learning experience.

Conclusion

We began this chapter by reflecting on how Gloria Anzaldúa's legacy has shaped the ways in which we think about our identities and the centrality of our language practices. We examined the ways in which scholars before us have studied translanguaging in children's literature. And we have contributed to a collective understanding of encouraging educators to use and examine children's literature that reflects their own experiences, pedagogy that supports these social and linguistic experiences, and the creation of critical multilingual/multicultural libraries. To us, children's literature includes the middle grade and young adult literature genre, and so we have provided examples from the lower grades, as well as middle school, and high school. We have shown how highly acclaimed authors enact translanguaging in their writing in powerful ways. Children's literature, as we have shown, has the potential to affirm the humanity of language-minoritized children, including their culture, identities, and language practices. It is our responsibility as educators to create these learning spaces that welcome translanguaging literacies, study its use in texts, and support students' creation of their own.

References

Alamillo, L. (2018). Translanguaging *con mi abuela*: Chican@ children's literature as a means to elevate language practices in our homes. In L. Alamillo, L.M. Mercado-López, & C. Herrera (Eds.), *Voices of resistance: Interdisciplinary approaches to Chican@ children's literature* (pp. 151–162). New York, NY: Rowman & Littlefield.

Alamillo, L., Mercado-López, L., & Herrera, C. (Eds.). (2018). *Voices of resistance: Interdisciplinary approaches to Chican@ children's literature.* New York, NY: Rowman & Littlefield.

Aldama. (2018). *Latino/a children's and young adult writers on the art of storytelling.* Pittsburgh, PA: University of Pittsburgh Press.

Anzaldúa, G. (1987). *Borderlands/la frontera: The new Mestiza.* San Francisco, CA: Aunt Lute Books.

Anzaldúa, G. (1997). *Friends from the other side/amigos del otro lado.* New York, NY: Children's Book Press.

Avilés, E. (2018). Chillante pedagogy, "She worlds," and testimonio as text/image: Toward a Chicana feminist pedagogy in the works of Maya Christina González. In L. Alamillo, L.M. Mercado-López, & C. Herrera (Eds.), *Voices of resistance: Interdisciplinary approaches to Chican@ children's literature* (pp. 123–136). New York, NY: Rowman & Littlefield.

Bassett-Webb, K.M., Masso, H.M., & Lewis, K.A. (2018). Latinx children's push and pull of Spanish literacy and translanguaging. *The Qualitative Report, 23*(11:3), 2648–2669.

Bhabha, H.K. (1994). *The location of culture.* New York, NY: Routledge.

España, C. & Herrera, L.Y. (2020). *En comunidad: Lessons for centering the voices and experiences of bilingual Latinx students.* Portsmouth, NH: Heinemann.

Gutiérrez, K.D., Baquedano-López, P., Alvarez, H., & Chiu, M.M. (1999). Building a culture of collaboration through hybrid language practices. *Theory Into Practice, 38*, 87–93.

Kersten, S. & Ludwig, C. (2018). Translanguaging and multilingual picturebooks: Gloria Anzaldúa's friends from the other side/amigos del otro lado. *CLELE Journal, 6*(2), 7–27.

Paris, D. (2012). Culturally sustaining pedagogy: A needed change in stance, terminology, and practice. *Educational Researcher, 41*(3), 93–97.

Paris, D. & Alim, S.H. (2017). *Culturally sustaining pedagogies: Teaching and learning for social justice in a changing world.* New York, NY: Teachers College Press.

Pérez Rosario, V. (2015). *The CUNY-NYSIEB guide to translanguaging in Latino/a literature.* New York: NY: The Graduate Center, City University of New York. Retrieved from https://www.cuny-nysieb.org/wp-content/uploads/2016/05/CUNY-NYSIEB-Latino-Literature-Guide-Final-January-2015.pdf

Social justice books: A teaching for change project. (2016). *Creating an anti-bias library.* Retrieved from https://socialjusticebooks.org/creating-an-anti-bias-library/

Soja, E.W. (1996). *Thirdspace: Journeys to Los Angeles and other real-and-imagined places.* Malden, MA: Blackwell.

Children's authors and texts

Acevedo, E. (2018a). *The poet X.* New York, NY: HarperTeen.

Acevedo, E. (2018b). Mira muchacha. In E. Acevedo (Ed.), *The poet X* (p. 6). New York, NY: HarperTeen.

Anzaldúa, G. (1997). *Friends from the other side/Amigos del otro lado.* New York, NY: Children's Book Press.

Argueta, J. (2016a). *Somos como las nubes/we are like the clouds.* Toronto, Canada: Groundwood Books.

Argueta, J. (2016b). Somos como las nubes. In J. Argueta (Ed.), *Somos como las nubes/we are like the clouds* (pp. 1–2). Toronto, Canada: Groundwood Books.

Bowles, D. (2018a). *They call me güero.* El Paso, TX: Cinco Puntos Press.

Bowles, D. (2018b). The newcomer. In D. Bowles (Ed.), *They call me güero* (pp. 51–52). El Paso, TX: Cinco Puntos Press.

Brown, M. (2011). *Marisol McDonald doesn't match/Marisol McDonald no combina.* New York, NY: Lee & Low Books.

Brown, M. (2013). *Marisol McDonald and the clash bash/Marisol McDonald y la fiesta sin igual.* New York, NY: Lee & Low Books.

Carlson, L.M. (Ed.). (1994). *Cool salsa: Bilingual poems on growing up Latino in the United States.* New York, NY: Square Fish/Henry Holt and Company.

Miranda-Rodriguez, E. (2016). *La Borinqueña.* New York, NY: Somos Arte.

Morales, Y. (2018). *Dreamers.* New York, NY: Neal Porter Books.

Quintero, I. (2019a). *My papi has a motorcycle.* New York, NY: Kokila.

Quintero, I. (2019b). *Mi papi tiene una moto.* New York, NY: Kokila.

Rodriguez, J. (1994). Race politics. In L.M. Carlson (Ed.), *Cool salsa: Bilingual poems on growing up Latino in the United States* (pp. 60–62). New York, NY: Square Fish/Henry Holt and Company.

Salazar, A. (2019a). A closet full. In A. Salazar (Ed.), *The moon within* (pp. 14–16). New York, NY: Arthur A. Levine Books.

Salazar, A. (2019b). Preparations. In A. Salazar (Ed.), *The moon within* (pp. 195–197). New York, NY: Arthur A. Levine Books.

Salazar, A. (2019c). *The moon within.* New York, NY: Arthur A. Levine Books.

Steptoe, J. (2016). *Radiant child: The story of young artist Jean-Michel Basquiat.* New York, NY: Little Brown and Company.

Weatherford, C.B. & Velasquez, E. (2017). *Schomburg: The man who built a library.* Somerville, MA: Candlewick Press.

BOX 11.1 TEACHER/RESEARCHER

Hulda Yau

2nd grade, one-way dual language bilingual

This translanguaging lesson took place in a 2nd grade, One–Way Dual Language classroom where all students are Latinx. It was an Integrated Co-Teaching (ICT) classroom with a fulltime Special Education teacher that supports our differently dis/abled learners. I was the general bilingual education teacher. All my students had a high level of proficiency in Spanish, their home language. I often translanguaged in all subject areas except writing during Spanish Language Arts. This quickly changed when I read Joaquín's narrative about his favorite subjects in school.

As I read Joaquín's paper, I noticed the majority was in Spanish but toward the end he transitioned to English. He wrote, "Me gusta ir a arte porque pegamos papel encima de otros papeles. Cortamos papeles y es muy fun. We decorate them. We even make bracelets with beads. I love art." At this very moment, I realized I needed to follow the path Joaquín was laying out. He was using his authentic voice in writing and I needed to inspire other students to do the same. I decided to take the class on a translanguaging journey that would transform us as bilingual authors.

The following day I gathered everyone on the carpet for Author's Chair. This is a moment when the student author sits on a chair to share his writing, while everyone else sits on the carpet. Before Joaquín began reading, I praised him for doing a beautiful job using his bilingual voice in his writing. I told everyone how natural it was for him to write bilingually because it's how he communicates. I added that we would learn how to use our bilingual voices in writing with intention and purpose.

The following days were very exciting as I introduced three mentor texts I would read as part of our narrative writing unit. A mentor text is a piece of literature you study and then try to imitate. The three books I used to uncover my students, bilingual voice in writing were *Abuela* by Arthur Dorros, *I love Sundays y domingos* by Alma Flor Ada and *The Storyteller's Candle* by Lucía González. As I read the texts, I taught my students how to become creative listeners as they thought about the reasons why the author used English and Spanish at specific times within the text. We began to have incredible dialogues about translanguaging in writing. It was truly magical to see second graders become critical thinkers.

As students began to draft their bilingual pieces, I began to confer with them to ensure there was meaning and intention behind their bilingual choices in writing. The dominant language in their writing piece was up to them because they were at different points in their language continuum. I remember in one of my writing conferences Rosita had written *"Hola awela"* instead of *"Hola abuela."* I told her we needed to correct the spelling, but she disagreed because she didn't call her grandma *abuela*. Again, one of my second graders was teaching me about authentic writing as a bilingual author! I told her she was absolutely right and that it perfectly showcased her voice as an authentic writer.

This unit transformed our writing class in our Spanish Language Arts block to a beautiful bilingual space where students sat on the driver's seat. I released my control and just sat back and learned from them. My writing class became a clear canvas my students painted to create a masterpiece.

As a bilingual educator, I'm committed to teach others how to operationalize translanguaging in the classroom. My hope is that teachers can expand their intellectual capacities and view translanguaging as culturally responsive teaching that serves as a conduit not only for meaning making, but as a practice that validates the amazing contributions students bring to their learning.

12

BUILDING ON STRENGTHS

Translanguaging and writing

Cecilia M. Espinosa, Laura Ascenzi Moreno, and Sara Vogel

Introduction

Emergent bilinguals are a diverse group of students who bring a range of resources and challenges to the classroom. In this chapter, we develop a novel "language as a resource" perspective on the teaching of writing, based on the principles of the City University of New York-New York State Initiative on Emergent Bilinguals (CUNY-NYSIEB) project. From the Spring 2012 to 2019, CUNY-NYSIEB has worked to support school communities around New York State as they improve education for this student population, guided by two non-negotiable principles: (1) Support of a multilingual ecology for the whole school and (2) Bilingualism as a resource in education.

Growing out of the CUNY-NYSIEB work, our goal in this chapter is to consider how a translanguaging lens shifts conceptions of writing instruction, and what it is for, especially in contexts where emergent bilingual students learn. To do so, we merge CUNY-NYSIEB's approach with a rich tradition of thinkers and researchers in the field of writing who posit that writing is a process (Fletcher, 2001; Graves, 2003; Heard, 2014; Murray, 1989). Process writing refers to all of the recursive actions which writers go through in order to produce a text—this includes brainstorming, drafting, rereading of writing, sharing ideas with others, and revising. Language is inextricably intertwined with all of these components of the writing process. Therefore, translanguaging, or the fluid use of a person's whole linguistic repertoire across languages, is a natural fit with this conception of writing (Velasco & García, 2014). In the next sections, we explore a number of questions that have guided our thinking on this topic, weaving an approach that teachers of all grade levels, and across disciplines and programs can use to guide them as they adapt mandated curriculum and find spaces for authentic writing within it.

What is writing?/What is *not* writing?

Samway (2006) argues that writing, good writing, is a "clear and evocative piece that captures the intellect and/or emotions of the reader" (p. 22). Given this holistic definition of writing, Samway (2006) asserts that writing is not filling in the blanks, copying sentences or words, or making sentences from a word list (as an end to the engagement). In writing, writers craft and construct meaning (Perl, 1980). "Making meaning is the work of the active mind and is thus within their [anyone's] natural capacity" (Berthoff, 1981, p. 69). At the heart of writing are communication, dialogue, and enacting one's agency. Everyone can be a writer. It often begins with a scribble and the discovery the power of a mark on a page can have. One becomes a writer by writing. The quality of a given writer's writing may vary depending on the experiences of the writer with the genre, the type of text, knowledge of topic, awareness of audience, purpose, etc.

Central to writing is the development of voice, and writing with power (Elbow, 1998). When a writer writes with intentionality and for an authentic reason, the writer considers purpose, audiences, and context. Often there are large disparities between the kinds of literacy experiences students do at school vs. the engagements they encounter in their daily lives (Street, 2012). In schools, writing is too often reduced to a fixed and narrow view of literacy that ignores the diverse and expansive ways of how writing exists in the world (Dyson, 2016). Writing in school often focuses on grades and disregards the fact that we need writers who can respond critically to the world's circumstances and can imagine more democratic spaces.

Writing, like reading, listening, and speaking is language. Language can never be neutral; it imposes a perspective with regard to how things are viewed, and also a position toward it (Bruner, 1986). Writing can be used as a form of resistance, as poets Adrienne Rich, Pablo Neruda, García Lorca, Nazim Hikmet among many others demonstrated. Eisner (2018) writes that Neruda's writing "has shown us how poetry can be an emotionally potent ingredient in the greater transformative efforts of resistance." Writer Jacqueline Woodson, National Ambassador for Young People's Literature (2018–2019), asserts that, "When we write we can change the narrative. We can change the narrative of the world. We can change our own narrative" (NCTE Chronicle, 2018, p. 21). Author Daniel José Alder argues that writing offers the opportunity to create counter narratives to the official story (Niidas Holm, 2017).

Writing is not a linear process, but a recursive and often spiral process. Writing is much more than what we read on the page or text. When we compose we attend to purpose, ideas, word choices, genre, tone (Wood Ray & Cleaveland,

2018). When composing, the writer also attends to what is on the page and examines if those words—and we add images, form, and genre—encapsulate the intended meanings of the author (Perl, 1980). A question the writer poses is how these will impact the reader (Perl, 1979). When composing the writer asks: Did the words, images, form, genre, I wrote and/or designed capture my intended meanings?

The writing process is also inextricably tied to other language modalities—reading, speaking, viewing, listening, performing, etc. (Lankshear & Knobel, 2011; Medina & Campano, 2006; Whitmore, 2015). As such, it is crucial that students are exposed to a range of authentic reading materials in all varieties of text types, as well as opportunities to speak (dialogue), create, reflect, critique constructively and listen to peers (Fletcher, 2017; Heard, 2014; Horn, 2005; Ebe, 2016). For the emergent bilingual student, meaning-making is only possible if they can participate by capitalizing on their entire linguistic repertoire, what is called translanguaging (Ascenzi-Moreno & Espinosa, 2018; García & Li, 2014; Otheguy, García, & Reid, 2015, 2019). To truly encourage authentic writing and learning, teachers can create spaces for translanguaging in their classrooms (García, Johnson, & Seltzer, 2017). The literacy and linguistic practices students bring with them need to be seen as rich resources to nurture and nudge the writer (NCTE Position Statement Understanding and Teaching Writing: Guiding Principles, 2018)

What do we mean by translanguaging and writing?

Good writing can be "translanguaged," as in the work of Juan Felipe Herrera, Poet Laureate 2015 of the United States. His poem *Borderbus* (2015), written from the perspective of Latinx immigrants, vividly captures those experiences that exist in the space in between named languages, accessible only through his translanguaging practices, which he first unlocked as a writer during the Civil Rights Movement in the 1960s. Herrera's translanguaging capacities confirm what García and Li (2014) argue, that in bilinguals, translanguaging has been and continues to be the norm.

Good writing may also take a multimodal form, making use of 21st century literacies and technologies. According to García, Johnson, and Seltzer (2017), translanguaging refers to "the complex language practices of multilingual individuals and communities, as well as the pedagogical approaches that draw on those complex practices to build those desired in formal school settings" (p. 2). Bilinguals may be taught to operate in monolingual contexts, but bilingual students also translanguage—utilizing their linguistic repertoires flexibly, without suppressing features from a particular language—in order to make sense of their lived experiences and cultural resources of their homes and communities (D'warte, 2014; Moll et al., 1992). At school, educators can leverage emergent bilingual students' translanguaging practices, creating spaces for them to use the linguistic resources they already possess to access rigorous content, and thus to be able to participate fully in all learning events (García, Johnson, & Seltzer, 2017).

Translanguaging can support, expand, and enhance student writing in general. As Hopewell (2011) writes, "the outdated argument that a first language is a bridge to English must be abandoned to make room for a broader conceptualization of all languages contributing to a whole that is greater than the sum of its parts" (p. 616). Translanguaging can assist students along all stages of the writing process and with a variety of purposes. It is often thought of as a powerful scaffold for students when they struggle to write text in one language. However, this is only one purpose of a translanguaging vision for writing, albeit one that is especially beneficial to students who are acquiring a new language. Writers also translanguage to express themselves creatively, to think about a subject, to connect to a given audience, and to promote their own self-development as writers. In this way, translanguaging is essential to the writer's writing process, not only as a scaffold for those at the initial stages of learning a language, but throughout the emergent bilingual students' writing life to truly express their thinking, their inner lives and identities.

Canagarajah (2011) studied the narrative writing of one of his bilingual undergraduate students. He found that while the student was aware of audience and the expertise of her teacher, translanguaging (adding Arabic words, emoticons, italics and even Islamic art to her English text) allowed her to develop her voice, negotiate meaning, and engage with her intended audience in more complex ways. Utilizing her entire linguistic repertoire was transformational for this student as it set in motion her creativity and criticality. Through such acts, Canagarajah (2011) states that multilingual writers create a space to reappropriate and resist traditional, monolingual academic discourses, and through it construct spaces for "rhetorical effectiveness" (p. 23). García and Li (2014), argue that educators need to study the practices multilingual students are constantly adopting. It matters that students' agency is encouraged as they make decisions about their use of translanguaging in their writing (Ascenzi-Moreno & Espinosa, 2018; García & Li, 2014; García, Ibarra, & Seltzer, 2017).

Canagarajah (2011, 2013) coined two related terms to translanguaging in the process of writing—code meshing and translingual practices. These terms refer to the process of fusing a variety of dialects and practices from languages and registers. We prefer the term "translanguaging" as used by García (2009). Translanguaging is multimodal, transdisciplinary, and "it emerges from the contextual affordances in the complex interactions of multilinguals" (García & Li, 2014, p. 40). Works on translanguaging theory in education have tightly linked the term to social justice values (García & Li, 2014; García, Flores, & Woodley, 2012), helping teachers and students imagine a world where people's bottom up language practices are privileged over top-down standards. Translanguaging offers teachers and students powerful and purposeful opportunities "to language new ways of knowing and being" (King & Ridley, 2018, p. 24).

What is writing in the 21st century?

The 21st Century calls for a new paradigm for the teaching of writing. We have named this paradigm the "Translanguaging Pedagogy for Writing." From this perspective, variety, fluidity, and multilingualism are the norm (García & Li, 2014). This pedagogy moves away from an ideology of monolingualism and monoculturalism as the standard (D'warte, 2014; Otheguy, García, & Reid, 2015, 2019). Bilingualism is no longer seen as a problem that needs to be eradicated. Instead, it is a resource that leads to deeper meaning in all areas of language: Writing, listening, talking, reading, viewing, and acting on multimodal ways of conceptualizing writing. It recognizes that inside the bilingual person there is one linguistic repertoire, even though this person lives in a world of multiple named languages (Otheguy, García, & Reid, 2019; Vogel & García, 2017).

A 21st Century perspective on writing challenges the idea that there is a universal standard for writing which is static, discrete and separate. This point of view assumes that language is always changing, that we are all language learners, and are also creators of language (Horner et al., 2011). Language, as García (2015) states, is about using/doing/performing "languages." Language is not something that exists in isolation, outside from our experiences and our being. It exists because we populate it with our own intentions (Bakhtin, 1981). Bilinguals do not simply have two separate languages, but one linguistic repertoire which bilinguals rely on to negotiate situations (García & Li, 2014; García & Klein, 2016). Consequently, the bilingual child needs to come fully into the classroom with their entire linguistic repertoire.

The 21st Century perspective on writing rather than being exclusive, is inclusive of a multiplicity of voices and perspectives (Bakhtin, 1981; Carini, 2010). Teachers need to be aware, understand, and support the many different ways in which students compose through digital media. It matters that emergent bilingual students have access to learning experiences with technology that affords them opportunities to capitalize on their entire linguistic repertoire (España, 2016). Vogel, Ascenzi-Moreno, and García (2018) advocate for, "definitions of translanguaging that integrate all parts of the semiotic repertoire of bilingual learners, including artifacts and technology" (p. 104). Rowe and Miller (2016) describe how touchscreen tablets and digital cameras offered young children experiences to engage in multimodal, multilingual composing that transcended what is possible when composing with paper and pencil alone.

What is the CUNY-NYSIEB vision of writing?

The CUNY-NYSIEB vision of writing embodies a strengths-based perspective (Carini, 2010), and therefore requires that we move away from deficit views and myths, such as: Bilinguals can't write; they have too many writing problems; they don't like to write; they are reluctant writers; they need to be taught the skills of writing before being asked to write originally and independently; and they have to learn to write to pass a test. Emergent bilingual students are invited to utilize their entire linguistic repertoire to construct meaning and fully participate in the life of the classroom, taking a stance of strength (for more on this strength perspective and literacy, see Espinosa & Ascenzi-Moreno, forthcoming).

It is a necessity and a reality for bilinguals to draw on their entire linguistic repertoire on a daily basis. For this, translanguaging lives in the language practices of the writer (García & Li, 2014). CUNY NYSIEB's vision for writing in the 21st century builds on, supports and honors the students' linguistic repertoires. It asks what writers are doing with language, what their intentions and purposes are, and how writing exists in the world. It invites the writer to consider the instance, the reasons, and the purpose of their writing. Therefore, it matters that students have opportunities to write in authentic contexts. Authenticity of writing purpose leads to more opportunities for students to engage their entire linguistic repertoire.

A translanguaging pedagogy for writing builds on the two CUNY NYSIEB nonnegotiable principles (http://www.nysieb.ws.gc.cuny.edu/our-vision/):

- Principle #1: Support of a multilingual ecology for the whole school.
- Principle #2: Bilingualism as a resource in education.

With regard to principle #1: Support of a multilingual ecology and its relationship to writing, the teacher can ask the following questions:

- What opportunities do students and families have to use home language during writing activities that take place in your classroom?
- How are other languages visible, palpable in the writing landscape of the classroom? What does the language landscape of your classroom look like? Does it represent the language practices of the students in your classroom?
- How do different texts support, enhance, nurture and challenge the imagination of the writer's language practices and cultural experiences at the school? How do the texts support multiplicity of voices and deeper thinking?

With regard to *principle #2*: Bilingualism as a resource in education, the writing the teacher can pose the following questions:

- Who are my students? What are their languaging practices? What strengths do they bring? How do I capitalize and build on these?

- In what ways are the writing-language practices of ALL my students not only recognized but also leveraged as a crucial instructional tool? Do I explicitly state in my classroom that students can/should utilize their entire linguistic repertoire in order to fully participate in the writing engagements?
- How do I address these varied language practices in my teaching of writing? What resources do I provide? How do I structure the class so that they can engage their entire linguistic repertoire? What adaptations do I need to provide to the writing tools we use? In what ways do the resources I provide support, nurture and challenge the students' entire linguistic repertoire? How are their home language practices nurtured and developed? (Regardless of type of program: English as a New Language (ENL), transitional bilingual, dual language bilingual, general education.)
- How are the students' entire linguistic repertoires *leveraged* flexibly and strategically in writing instruction, so that they are engaged cognitively, academically, emotionally, and creatively?
- How do I support students in gaining fluency in working across language differences? How do I create an awareness in students that each time they use language, they are gaining new insights?
- How do I create spaces for authentic audiences? How do these offer genuine translanguaging spaces?

The CUNY NYSIEB vision for writing invites teachers to reflect deeply about their pedagogical language knowledge (Espinosa, 2018; Faltis, 2013; García & Kleyn, 2016; Sánchez, Espinet, & Seltzer, 2014) in order to become well informed about how to best capitalize on the language practices students bring with them and must rely on. It challenges teachers to grapple with new ideas about language and the possibilities the pedagogy of translanguaging offers (Espinosa, 2018; García and Li, 2014; Seltzer & García, 2019; Vogel, Ascenzi-Moreno, & García, 2018). These ideological changes often begin with a transformation of the linguistic landscape of the school, so it reflects the communities' and the families' named languages backgrounds (Menken, Pérez Rosario, & Guzmán Valerio, 2016; see also Chapter 9 and Teacher/Researcher Box 9.1, this volume).

How do emergent bilinguals experience writing?

At its core, writing is the creation of meaning (Berthoff, 1981; Hudelson, 2005). Writers learn how writing works and its purposes within their cultural contexts at home, at school and in the classroom, and in their communities and the larger world. While at home, emergent bilingual children may learn that writing has a purpose and an audience and that their bilingualism is part of their lived experience (D'warte, 2014); at school they often learn that their only audience is the teacher, who, for the most part, expects them to write in English solely.

Students view the teacher's job as primarily to correct and grade their work, but rarely to respond to it in a dialogical manner. Too often school offers limited opportunities for emergent bilingual students to seek the support and guidance of an authentic and caring audience (teachers, peers, and others outside of the classroom) as they attempt to clearly convey their ideas. They seldom learn that writing can be a process of discovering what one means (Espinosa, 2006; Hudelson, 2005; Street, 2012). Anne Haas Dyson (2016) states that under these circumstances, instead of learning to write, children learn to negotiate how to be in and how to do school because sadly, writing at school is often only about writing the correct answers.

Teachers' beliefs about the teaching of writing have profound implications for how children understand writing (Ascenzi-Moreno & Espinosa, 2018; Hudelson, 2005). To truly know how the emergent bilinguals in their classes experience writing, teachers should ask themselves: What are the purposes for writing I offer in my class? Do my students have opportunities to write for authentic audiences? In what ways do I support the development of the emergent bilingual writer's ideas? In what ways do I invite emergent bilingual students to bring their entire linguistic repertoire, so that they can fully construct meaning as writers and thinkers? In what ways can translanguaging in writing offer emergent bilingual students at all levels opportunities to express themselves and what they know? In what ways does writing sustain and enhance the child's social worlds within the classroom? (Dyson, 2016). In what ways do the writing experiences in which I invite students to participate create spaces for writing about current social issues? (Herrera, 2017).

When educators view emergent bilingual students' homes, families, communities from a perspective of strength (as having a wealth of socio-cultural writing resources), emergent bilingual children will experience a richer learning writing environment (Fu, 2009; Fu, Hadjioannou, & Zhou, 2019; Genishi, 2016). It matters that the teacher learns what are the contexts, including funds of knowledge for writing in the homes and communities where the children come from (González, Moll, & Amanti, 2005). All children bring resources with them, and these are important to them (Dyson, 2016).

Students need opportunities in the classroom to write for particular purposes and audiences by being able to capitalize on their entire linguistic repertoire (Ascenzi-Moreno & Espinosa, 2018; Velasco & García, 2014). It is only then that they will be able to write for self-expression, to document and present their learning in a content area, to compose in different genres, to respond and examine literature, and to advocate for issues that matter to them in order to create a more just world. While it is evident that emergent bilingual children also need explicit instruction and scaffolding, they also need to learn that conversations, collaborating, receiving feedback, discussing with others their work, examining the work of published authors, including authors who engage in translanguaging, are important recursive components of the writing process. To participate fully in all these aspects of the writing process, writers need their entire linguistic repertoire (García & Kano, 2014; Seltzer & García, 2019; Velasco & García, 2014).

Emergent bilingual students need to know that their voices matter and that they can be developed further—that writing can help them make sense of their worlds, as they use writing to learn and wonder about it. Clearly, the only way to accomplish this is when they are invited to bring in their entire linguistic repertoire as they construct meaning, express their understandings, and have opportunities to consider new ways of using language (Horner et al., 2011; Ebe, 2016).

What is the role of oral language?
What is the role of multimodalities?

Writing for our youngest students begins through talk (Gort, 2012). Students play with language and ideas in order to generate topics and situations in which to write and draw about. This often occurs in the company of other children. For emergent bilingual students, playing with language as a stage in prewriting occurs fluidly within their one linguistic repertoire (Gort, 2012). Therefore, writing instruction for young emergent bilinguals must be supported with ample opportunities—both planned and unplanned—for multilingual talk (Bauer, 2019). This can take shape through turn and talks, writing partners, playing, performing, drawing, and talking while writing.

It is important to emphasize that oral language flows from having strong connections between home and school, feeling a strong sense of belonging, hands-on age appropriate experiences, and access to rich content. Multimodal theory enriches our understanding of how multiple realms of experience "linguistic, visual, auditory, gestural, and spatial"—can enrich language learning and literacy development (Martens et al., 2012). Young children naturally approach the medium of writing in multimodal ways, always mindful of their own purposes and audiences. Sadly, an overemphasis on predetermined skills through a narrowly conceived literacy program only limits children's possibilities for composing, as well as develop voice and agency (Dyson, 2016).

When students focus on the both the text and the illustrations of picture books or explore books through art and drama, they not only develop strong comprehension but are also able to create and write based on those texts (Espinosa & Lehner-Quam, 2019; Martens et al., 2012). Such exploration also helps young students learn about characters, story elements, and text features. For example, in one bilingual kindergarten classroom, before having students work on writing stories for the first time, the teacher engages students in creating puppets of their characters. These characters then became objects used in dramatic play with language and story. After students had ample time to make up stories and scenes with their puppets, they engage in writing, drawing and often performing (officially and unofficially). It is important to note that all of these experiences should occur as students capitalize on their entire linguistic repertoire.

Oral language has a key role to play in older emergent bilingual students' writing. In reference to children in grades 2–6, Swinney and Velasco (2011) note that oral language allows students to talk about what they are learning as well as expand their language. They state that teachers have a crucial role in modeling conversation and dialogue. In her study of adolescent emergent bilingual writers, Kibler (2010) found that students spoke about their ideas for writing assignments, and assessed their writing using their entire language repertoire. Their authorship emerged out of these conversations about writing, underscoring how essential oral home language use was to the writing process.

Siegal (2012) emphasizes that multimodal practices have promise also for older learners. She notes that students bring their multimodal practices to school regardless if they are the focus of instruction. In addition, when a multimodal approach is taken, students who are often viewed as "at risk" are suddenly acknowledged for the resources they bring. As Siegal (2012) writes, "multimodality is in the air in those classrooms where teachers and students read manga, design digital stories, produce podcasts, and perform dramatic tableaux" (p. 678). As her list suggests, adopting a multimodal approach can help ensure writing work is authentic, student centered, and focused on audience.

What is the role of the writing environment?

Sharing one's writing, receiving public feedback, and critiquing the work of others involves taking risks, especially when one is learning to write in a new named language. A strong community can support emergent bilingual students in moments of vulnerability, such as when they make their work visible not only to their teachers, but also to classmates. The goal is to create a community where being a writer who draws from his/her entire linguistic repertoire is valued and nurtured and also the norm in the classroom. How the teacher establishes the classroom community of writers matters (Britton, 1987).

It takes time to establish trust and to get to know students (Graves, 2003). In *Writing: Teachers & Children at Work* (1983), Donald Graves asks teachers to write down everything they know about their students. He posits that it is difficult to teach a student if they do not know them. Often when we have students who present challenges to us, we focus on those barriers to learning, rather than on the possibilities that lay beyond those. Celic (2009) and Cappellini (2005) also emphasize the importance of knowing the emergent bilingual student, their language abilities and histories.

In establishing a multilingual community of writers, it matters that the teacher establishes norms for responding to one another's work inviting students to capitalize on their entire linguistic repertoire. The teacher can do this right at the beginning of the school year by having a dialogue with the students about translanguaging and about translanguaging and writing. In these conversations, students should reflect on what helps create an environment where one feels known, and can safely receive support from others, as well as provide feedback. The classroom needs to be student-centered, which means that even the physical arrangement of the students' seats need to allow for dialogue with one another. It is critical that the students have ample space to enact their own agency as to when and why they deploy their linguistic repertoire in order to engage in deeper and more complex conversations about their writing, as well as to be able to compose in ways that allow them to develop an authentic voice.

The teacher is no longer the sole provider of knowledge (Britton, 1987), neither the one who decides what named language to use. At the same time, the teacher needs to make their own writing process visible to students and provide opportunities for the students to notice their authentic struggles with the writing process. We argue that the teacher should see him/herself also as a writer in the classroom. Katie Wood Ray (2001) argues that we would not take piano lessons from a teacher who does not play the piano. Wood Ray contends that the same stance needs to apply to the teaching of writing. It is critical that the teacher makes explicit how they capitalize on their entire linguistic repertoire as a writer and thinker (Espinosa, Ascenzi-Moreno, & Vogel, 2016).

Students need daily writing routines, ample time to write, opportunities to talk as well as quiet time, high and clear expectations, as well as choice (Wood Ray & Cleaveland, 2018). The students need to write for authentic audiences, including multilingual audiences. While the tone of the writing time is essential, how the teacher organizes the physical classroom environment in order to welcome and fully support the student's entire linguistic repertoire is also of critical importance (Espinosa, Ascenzi-Moreno, & Vogel, 2016).

Conclusion

The 21st century calls for writing that reflects the ways it exists in the world where its users often translanguage (to compose, to think, to share and receive feedback, to communicate, to construct meaning, to publish, etc.). For too long schools have created artificial hierarchies about languages, limiting multilingual learners' potential to build on their own strengths. To write with voice, to develop agency, to become writers who understand its powerful potential, it matters that educators support students' development of identities who translanguage as the norm.

NOTE: To read more about translanguaging and writing we recommend you read: *A Translanguaging Pedagogy for Writing: A CUNY NYSIEB Guide for Educators* written by the authors of this chapter. https://www.cuny-nysieb.org/wp-content/uploads/2016/05/TLG-Pedagogy-Writing-04-15-16.pdf

References

Ascenzi-Moreno, L. &Espinosa, C. (2018). Opening up spaces for their whole selves: A case study group's exploration of translanguaging practices in writing. *NYS TESOL Journal*, 5(1), 10–29.

Bakhtin, M. (1981). *The dialogic imagination: Four essays by M. M. Bakhtin*. In M. Holquist (Ed.), C. Emerson &M. Holquist (Trans.). Austin, TX: The University of Texas Press.

Bauer, E. (2019). Kindergartners writing in a dual language classroom. *Language Arts*, 96(4), 213–223.

Berthoff, A. (1981). *The making of meaning*. Portsmouth, NH: Heinemann.

Britton, J. (1987). *Writing and reading in the classroom*. Technical report N. 8. National Writing Project. http://www.nwp.org/cs/public/download/nwp_file/151/TR08.pdf?x-r=pcfile_dhttp://www.nwp.org/cs/public/download/nwp_file/151/TR08.pdf?x-r=pcfile_d

Bruner, J. (1986). *Actual minds, possible worlds*. Harvard University Press.

Canagarajah, S. (2011). Codemeshing in academic writing: Identifying teachable strategies of translanguaging. *The Modern Language Journal*, 96, 401–417.

Canagarajah, S. (2013). *Translingual practice: Global Englishes and cosmopolitan relations*. London, UK: Taylor and Francis/Routledge.

Cappellini, M. (2005). *Balancing reading and language learning: A resource for teaching English language Learners, K-5*. Portsmouth, NH: Stenhouse.

Carini, C. (2010). Making and doing philosophy in a school. In P. Carini &M. Himley (Eds.), *Jenny's story: Taking the long view of the child, Prospect's philosophy in action*. New York, NY: Teachers' College Press.

Celic, C. (2009). *English language learners day-by-day K-6*. Portsmouth, NH: Heinemann.

Dyson, A. H. (2016). *Child cultures, schooling and literacy: Global perspectives in composing unique lives*. New York, NY: Routledge.

D'warte, J. (2014). Linguistic repertoires: Teachers and students explore their everyday language worlds. *Language Arts*, 91(5), 352–362.

Ebe, A. (2016). Student voices shining through: Exploring translanguaging as a literary device. In O. García and T. Kleyn (Eds.), *Translanguaging with multilingual students: Learning from classroom moments* (pp. 58–82). London, UK: Taylor and Francis/Routledge.

Eisner, M. (2018). What can we learn from Neruda's poetry of resistance. *The Paris Review*, March 26. Retrieved from https://www.theparisreview.org/blog/2018/03/26/pablo-nerudas-poetry-of-resistance/

Elbow, P. (1998). *Writing with power: Techniques for mastering the writing process*. New York, NY: Oxford University Press.

España, C. (2016). Bilingual matters: Using technology to make education more accessible for our emergent bilingual students. *Literacy Today Magazine*. November/December 2016: 26–27.

Espinosa, C. (2006). Finding memorable moments: Images and identities in autobiographical writing. *Language Arts, 84*(2), 136–144.

Espinosa, C., Ascenzi-Moreno, L., and Vogel, S. (2016). A translanguaging pedagogy for writing: A CUNY NYSIEB Guide for Educators. New York, CUNY NYSIEB. http://www.nysieb.ws.gc.cuny.edu/files/2016/04/TLG-Pedagogy-Writing-04-15-16.pdf.

Espinosa, C.M. (2018). PD in developing biliteracy skills in ELT. In J.I. Liontas (Ed.), *The TESOL encyclopedia of English language teaching*. T. International Association and M. DelliCarpini. https://doi.org/10.1002/9781118784235.eelt0881

Espinosa, C. & Ascenzi-Moreno, L. (forthcoming). *Rooted in strength: The power of multilingualism and translanguaging*. NY: Scholastic.

Espinosa, C. & Lehner-Quam, A. (2019). Sustaining bilingualism: Multimodal arts experiences for young readers and writers. *Language Arts, 96*(4), 265–268.

Faltis, C. (2013). Language, language development and teaching English to emergent bilingual users: Challenging the common knowledge theory in teacher education & K-12 school settings. *Association of Mexican American Educators (AMAE), Special Invited Issue, 7*(2), 18–29.

Fletcher, R. (2001). *Writing workshop: The essential guide*. Heinemann.

Fletcher, R. (2017). *The writing teacher's companion: Embracing voice, choice, purpose and play*. New York, NY: Scholastic Teaching Resources.

Fu, D. (2009). *Writing between languages: How English language learners make the transition to fluency, grades 4–12*. Portsmouth, NH: Heinemann.

Fu, D., Hadjioannou, X., Zhou, X. (2019). *Translanguaging for emergent bilinguals: Inclusive teaching in the linguistically diverse classroom*. New York, NY: Teachers College Press.

García, O. (2009). *Bilingual education in the 21st century: A global perspective*. Malden, MA and Oxford, UK: Blackwell/Wiley.

García, O. (2015). *Multilingualism and NYS Schools. Presentation CUNY NYSIEB First Seminar, 2015*. New York: Graduate Center.

García, O., Flores, N., & Woodley, H. (2012). Transgressing monolingualism and bilingual dualities: Translanguaging pedagogies. In Y. Androula (Ed.), *Rethinking education, Volume 5: Harnessing linguistic variation to improve education*. Bern: Peter Lang AG.

García, O. & Kano, N. (2014). Translanguaging as process and pedagogy: Developing the English writing of Japanese students in the US. In J. Conteh & G. Meier (Eds.), *The multilingual turn in languages education: Opportunities and challenges* (pp. 258–277). Multilingual Matters.

García, O., & Kleyn, T. (Eds.). (2016). *Translanguaging with multilingual students: Learning from classroom moments*. New York, NY: Taylor and Francis/Routledge.

García, O., Johnson, S. & Seltzer, K. (2017). *The translanguaging classroom: Leveraging student bilingualism for learning*. Philadelphia, PA: Caslon Publishing.

García, O., & Li W. (2014). *Translanguaging: Language, bilingualism and education*. UK: Palgrave Macmillan.

Graves, D. (2003). *Writing: Teachers & children at work* (20th anniversary edition). Portsmouth, NH: Heinemann.

Genishi, C. (2016). The powers of language: Toward remixing language policy, curricula and child identities. In A. H. Dyson (Ed.), *Child cultures, schooling and literacy: Global perspectives in composing unique lives* (pp. 149–164). New York, NY: Taylor and Francis/Routledge.

González, N., Moll, L. C., & Amanti, C. (Eds.). (2005). *Funds of knowledge: Theorizing practices in households, communities, and classrooms.* Mahwah, NJ: Erlbaum

Gort, M. (2012). Code-switching patterns in the writing-related talk of young emergent bilinguals. *Journal of Literacy Research, 44*(1), 45–75.

Heard, G. (2014). *The revision toolbox* (2nd Edition). New York, NY: Heinemann.

Herrera, J. F. (2015). *Notes on the assemblage.* San Francisco, CA: City Lights Books.

Herrera, L. Y. (2017). Translanguaging practices for educational equity: Moments in a bilingual middle school classroom. *CUNY Academic Works.* https://academicworks.cuny.edu/gc_etds/2125

Hopewell, S. (2011). Leveraging bilingualism to accelerate English reading comprehension, *International Journal of Bilingual Education and Bilingualism, 14*(5), 603–620, DOI: 10.1080/13670050.2011.564274

Horn, M. (2005). Listening to Nysia: Storytelling as a way into writing in kindergarten. *Language Arts, 83*(1), 33–41.

Horner, B., Lu, M-Z, Jones, J. R. & Trimbur, J. (2011). Opinion: Language difference in writing: Toward a translingual approach. *College English, 73*(3), 303–321.

Hudelson, S. (2005). Taking on English writing in a bilingual program: Revisiting, reexamining, reconceptualizing the data. In P. K. Matsuda & T. Silva (Eds.), *Second language writing research: Perspectives on the process of knowledge construction* (pp. 207–220). Mahweh, NJ: Lawrence Erlbaum Associates.

King, N. & Ridley, J. (2018). A Bakhtinian take on language in a dual language classroom. *SYSTEM An International Journal of Educational Technology and Applied Linguistics,* https://doi.org/10.1016/j.system.2018.10.008

Kibler, A. (2010). Writing through two languages: First language expertise in a language minority classroom. *Journal of Second Language Writing, 19*, 121–142.

Lankshear, C. & Knobel, M. (2011). *New literacies: Everyday practices & social learning.* Berkshire, England: Open University Press.

Martens, P., Martens, R., Hassay-Doyle, M., Loomis, J., & Aghalarov, S. (2012). Learning from picture books: Reading and writing multimodally in first grade. *Reading Teacher, 66*(4), 285–294.

Medina, C. & Campano, G. (2006). Performing identities through drama and teatro practices in multilingual classrooms. *Language Arts, 83*(4), 332–341.

Menken, K., Pérez Rosario, V., & Guzmán Valerio, L. (2016). Embracing multilingualism: Linguistic landscape in schoolwide change. Multilingualism and language empowerment: A response to inequality conference. CUNY Graduate Center, New York, NY.

Moll, L. C.; Amanti, C., Neff, D., & González, N. (1992). Funds of knowledge for teaching: Using a qualitative approach to connect homes and classrooms. *Theory into Practice, 31*(2), 132–141.

Murray, D. (1989). *Expecting the unexpected: Teaching myself and others to read and write.* Portsmouth, NH: Heinemann.

NCTE. (2018). Position statement understanding and teaching writing: Guiding principles. http://www2.ncte.org/statement/teachingcomposition/

Niidas Holm, K. (2017). Question and answer with Daniel Jose Older. *Publisher Weekly.* https://www.publishersweekly.com/pw/by-topic/childrens/childrens-authors/article/74760-q-a-with-daniel-jos-older.html

Otheguy, R., García, O., & Reid, W. (2015). Clarifying translanguaging and deconstructing named languages: A perspective from linguistics. *Applied Linguistics Review, 6*(3), 281–307.

Otheguy, R., García, O., & Reid, W. (2019). A translanguaging view of the linguistic system of bilinguals. *Applied Linguistics Review, 10*(4), 625–651. doi.org/10.1515/applirev-2018-0020

Perl, S. (1979). The composing processes of unskilled college writers. *Research in the Teaching of English, 13*(4), 317–336.

Perl, S. (1980). Understanding composing. *College Composition and Communication, 31*(4), 363–369.

Rowe, D. W. & Miller, M. E. (2016). Designing for diverse classrooms: Using iPads and digital cameras to compose eBooks with emergent bilingual/biliterate four-year-olds. *Journal of Early Childhood Literacy, 16*(4), 425–472.

Samway, K.D. (2006). *When English language learners write: Connecting research to practice, K-8* (1st Edition). Portsmouth, NH: Heinemann.

Sánchez, M.T., Espinet, I., & Seltzer, K. (2014). *Supporting emergent bilinguals in New York: Understanding successful school practices.* New York, NY: CUNY-NYSIEB, CUNY Graduate Center. Retrieved from https://www.cuny-nysieb.org/wp-content/uploads/2016/05/CUNY-NYSIEB-Contemporary-Report-Full-Feb-Final.pdf

Seltzer, K. & García, O. (2019). Sustaining Latinx Bilingualism in New York's Schools: The CUNY-NYSIEB Project. Informes del Observatorio/Observatorio Reports. 10.15427/OR048-02/2019EN.

Seltzer, K., & García, O. (2019). Sustaining Latinx Bilingualism in New York's Schools: The CUNY-NYSIEB Project. *Informes del Observatorio / Observatorio Reports.* Observatorio del español, FAS, Harvard University. doi: 10.15427/OR048-02/2019

Street, B. (2012). Society reschooling. *Reading Research Quarterly, 47*(2), 216–227

Siegal, M. (2012). New times for multimodality? Confronting the accountability culture. *Journal of Adolescent & Adult Literacy, 55*(8), 671–680.

Swinney, R. & Velasco, P. (2011). *Connecting content and academic language for English learners and struggling students, grades 2–6.* Thousand Oaks, CA: Corwin.

Velasco, P. & García, O. (2014). Translanguaging and the writing of bilingual learners. *Bilingual Research Journal, 37*, 6–23.

Vogel, S., & García, O. (2017). Translanguaging. In G. Noblit (Ed.), *Oxford research encyclopedia of education.* UK: Oxford University Press.

Vogel, S., Ascenzi-Moreno, L., & García, O. (2018). An expanded view of translanguaging: Leveraging the dynamic interactions between a young multilingual writer and machine translation software. In J. Choi & S. Ollerhead (Eds.), *Plurilingualism in teaching and learning: Complexities across contexts* (pp. 89–106). London, United Kingdom: Taylor & Francis Ltd.

Whitmore, K. (2015). Becoming the story: The joyful world of "Jack and the Beanstalk." *Language Arts, 93*(1), 25–37.

Wood Ray, K. (2001). *The Writing workshop: Working through the hard parts (and they're all hard parts).* National Council of Teachers of English.

Wood Ray, K. & Cleaveland, L. (2018). *A teacher's guide to getting started with beginning writers: The classroom essential series.* Portsmouth, NH: Heinemann.

BOX 12.1 TEACHER/RESEARCHER

Nicole Nichter

H.S. English as a new language/biology

I teach in a High School in upstate New York, in Buffalo. My High School has about 100 students who receive English as a New Language (ENL) services. Depending on their English proficiency level, an ENL teacher will provide instruction in a "Stand-Alone" or "Integrated" setting. "Stand-Alone" ENL settings provide beginning students with more one-on-one time with just an ENL teacher in a smaller context. "Integrated" settings are taught by both an ENL and a content-area teacher and contain emergent bilinguals and general population students together. The school has two ENL teachers; one provides both Stand-Alone and Integrated instruction and I provide Integrated instruction only.

There are approximately 15 linguistically diverse students receiving ENL services in a 9th grade Regents Biology class taught by myself and Sarah Proctor-Bates. These students have tested at various levels on their English proficiency exams. The home languages of students in this class include Bengali, Spanish, Kunama, Arabic, Karen, Malay, Carolinian, Urdu, and Kinyarwanda.

Since most high schools start classes using "bell work," or a task given to students that serves as an anticipatory set for the lesson, our biology class employs specific writing strategies that both build students' background and encourage biliteracy across language domains. The Buffalo Public School District uses the Step Up to Writing curricula. After working with CUNY-NYSIEB and learning about translanguaging, we decided to include writing and translanguaging into our bell work. Over five days (one day a week), students complete three writing strategies that are rooted in biology content and include translanguaging strategies.

On day one, students used the strategy, "2-Column Notes" to define six vocabulary terms in their notebooks. Students used their home language in this strategy to write translated terms and/or definitions alongside their English notes (see T/R Box Figure 12.1).

On days two and three, students use a modified Frayer Model (also known as a Four-Square Organizer) to employ their entire linguistic repertoires. Students translated and expressed their thoughts using all their linguistic resources and, when they needed support, also looked up terms online, worked collaboratively, and referenced several texts and images to produce writing that showed authentic learning via multimodal comprehensible output (see T/R Box Figure 12.2).

T/R BOX 12.1 FIGURE 12.1 Two-column notes of a Karen-speaking Burmese student

In this particular integrated biology class, both emergent bilinguals and general education students are present. The emergent bilingual students are expected to produce translated work using English and their home language. The other students, who are English-speaking monolinguals are not expected to produce translated work, though they are provided with the option to use other modalities such as word art, writing the term backward, or creating a list of synonyms/antonyms. Interestingly, we have found that many English-speaking general education students *will* choose to use the Frayer models that prompt translations and will use their resources, including their classmates, to seek out information.

Finally, on days four and five, students write either a paragraph or a scaffolded essay. Using the six vocabulary words provided on day one, students will write a structured group of sentences explaining what they now know about these terms. They are encouraged to use the knowledge they generated with both their own and their classmates' Frayer Models. Included in their Two-Column Notes and Frayer models from earlier in the week, students record multilingual information from their background knowledge as well as new information from outside their linguistic repertoire (such as a definition in a new word in English). On day 4, this information is summarized in three main bullet points; and on day 5, students rework those points

T/R. BOX 12.1 FIGURE 12.2 Frayer model of Karen-speaking Burmese student

into paragraph form. Translated terms as well as illustrations are used at the students' discretion in their paragraph writing.

The use of translanguaging practices in the classroom has created observable behavioral shifts among students in the class. Friendships and bonds have quickly formed. The students who "buddied up" with those who spoke languages different from theirs are lovingly called "the helpers." They work together with other groups of students using their own translanguaging strategies to answer questions and communicate new content learning.

Another consequence of writing that includes translanguaging strategies have been the complex social relationships and methods of accountability that have formed among students. Those who might otherwise be unfocused or off-task are redirected by their peers to complete the work or help them complete theirs. In general, grades for this class are considerably higher than in other biology classes, despite these students' having many linguistic challenges. The difference in our class is that we leverage students' cultural and linguistic diversity and our instructional delivery includes translanguaging.

13

LEVERAGING THE "LEARNING EDGE"

Translanguaging, teacher agency, and assessing emergent bilinguals' reading[1]

Laura Ascenzi-Moreno

Introduction

There has been a call for literacy educators to build upon students' home language practices to support their literacy development regardless of the type of program they attend (García, Johnson, & Seltzer, 2017). The intentional use of students' entire linguistic and social repertoire to make meaning in school has been referred to as translanguaging (García & Kleyn, 2016). There is an agreement on the part of scholars and educators that a translanguaging approach to supporting emergent bilinguals' learning leads to increased access and engagement in learning experiences. Also, because translanguaging pedagogy repositions emergent bilinguals as capable and full of resources, translanguaging as an approach is intimately tied to educational equity. While teachers recognize the need to incorporate students' home languages into literacy instruction, there is little guidance about how teachers can make this shift within the day to day reading instructional practices in which they engage. In this essay, I hone in on how translanguaging can shift the way we think about how we assess students' reading. I focus on the area of assessment because often teachers feel that they have no agency in impacting the assessment process.

The purpose of this essay is to provide teachers with a practical starting point about how to make adaptations to reading assessments informed by translanguaging. Alongside these practical suggestions, I want to strongly emphasize to all teachers the importance of *your* learning and agency when enacting pedagogical change in literacy teaching. In this chapter, I explore what it means to leverage your "learning edge" when making skilled and knowledgeable decisions about how to best support your students' literacy development. The "learning edge" is the exciting space for teachers in which we feel that we are being challenged in productive ways, excited by our learning and empowered and motivated to make meaningful impact with our students. I begin by providing an overview of translanguaging theory and translanguaging pedagogy and what both mean for literacy instruction. I also offer readers examples of shifts that teachers can make in literacy, specifically in reading assessment, to support emergent bilinguals' reading development.

Translanguaging and translanguaging pedagogy

Translanguaging is both a theory and a framework for pedagogical practices. Translanguaging theory provides teachers with a lens in which to view the varied roles that students' linguistic and social resources play in their interactions with others and in their academic development (García & Kleyn, 2016). Li Wei (2011) defines *translanguaging theory*, in the following way: "people's communication in the 21st century is dynamic, including going between different modalities (speaking, writing, signing, listening, reading, remembering) and going beyond them... the full range of linguistic performances of multilingual language users for purposes that transcend the combination of structures, the alternation between systems, the transmission of information and the representation of values, identities and relationships (p. 1223)." In other words, emergent bilinguals engage in learning through the full use of their language and social repertoire. For example, a child writing a story may call forth a memory of a birthday party (in which party goers used both English and Spanish) and use that authentic experience to compose the piece.

Translanguaging has resulted in much excitement and enthusiasm within the community of educators who teach bilingual students because, for many, it has given teachers and students words for what they already engage in—using their home language practices to remember, process, and move forward with their thinking and work in school. It has also given educators permission to intentionally use students' language and social practices as they make meaning of their academic work. *Translanguaging pedagogy* is the translation of theory into intentional practices and spaces within classrooms to draw upon the linguistic and social resources that students engage in. However, less attention has been given to the transformational power of translanguaging pedagogy. Since translanguaging pedagogy is based on students and their languaging practices, it emphasizes responsiveness to students' realities and therefore elevates the purpose of education to the whole person.

Translanguaging shifts the way we envision literacy teaching. For one, translanguaging pedagogy makes it clear that when students read, write, and speak, they draw upon their varied linguistic and social resources to make meaning of what they are reading or writing (García 2020; García & Kleifgen, 2019). Thus, literacy is re-envisioned as a *unified process* that is comprised of all students' literacy experiences regardless of language. This thinking is different from what is enacted in many bilingual education or English as a Second Language settings. For example, when I was a dual-language bilingual teacher, we planned for reading in Spanish and reading in English. Although we knew that there were some convergences or what we called "transfer" between reading in English and in Spanish, we thought of these skills as basically separate rather than unified. Through a unified lens, bilingual literacy teachers are called to be intimately aware of the language and social resources that their students bring to school and how to draw upon them as they support students' literacy (also see Chapters 8, 11, and 12, this book). Because teachers must inquire to understand the scope of emergent bilinguals' resources, it also means that when teachers take a translanguaging approach, they are at their learning edge. It is from this space that teachers can act upon what they learn about their students in their classrooms to make the assessment process more accurate and equitable.

Leveraging the "learning edge" of biliteracy

The learning edge is what drew us to being teachers in the first place (I hope!). It is the space in which we are learning something new about students, about teaching, and about bringing it all together in the classroom. Rather than sapping our resources, it gives us energy and breathes life into our classroom practices (Graves, 2001). We are so lucky to be in a profession where renewal is part of the job. It's important to emphasize that being on the learning edge does not refer to teachers' acquisition of procedures and routines and the implementation of these in the guise of learning. Rather, the learning I refer to is one that is generative and is premised on teachers being knowledgeable about theory and skilled with regards practice. Teachers who leverage the learning edge are able to wield that "skilled knowledge" in unique ways within the classroom. Leveraging the learning edge is complementary to translanguaging pedagogy because both require that teachers are in tune with students and adapt his/her teaching moves to address students' unique profiles and needs.

Leveraging the learning edge is critical to reshaping how we fashion biliteracy instruction in our classrooms. As literacy teachers in bilingual classrooms, we can fulfill our promise to children to help them in their journey to be readers and writers by making literacy learning meaningful and integrated with their language and social experiences. In the remainder of this essay, I tackle how this process of transforming literacy instruction may look with regard to one aspect of day to day literacy instruction—reading assessment.

Leveraging the learning edge in reading assessment is not easy—more and more frequently the reading assessment process has been wrestled away from teachers' authority. Reading assessments have become a tool to monitor and report students' reading levels. Teachers are told which tools to use to assess their students, when students should be assessed, how the results are to be reported, and how students with certain results should be grouped. This culture around reading assessment has turned the process into one that is more test-based rather than assessment-based. The assessment routines and policy around reading assessment make it even more difficult for bilingual teachers to understand how their emergent bilinguals draw upon their entire linguistic and social repertoire while reading.

For far too long, reading assessments have been tied to performance in one language. Take for instance, the child who reads a book and understands it, but then has to explain and answer questions solely in a language she doesn't yet have enough vocabulary to fully construct her answer. In this situation, a teacher may draw the conclusion that the student didn't understand the text, even though the situation is more complex. Through a translanguaging lens, a pivotal question is, what is the core of what we want to know about students' knowledge and abilities, regardless of the language? In this case, we want to know about the students' reading comprehension and therefore, the language that the child expresses her knowledge in is not the focus of assessing students' reading comprehension.

A translanguaging lens helps us to see that the student can express her knowledge in any named language or a combination of languages to best share her comprehension of a text. It also becomes clear that to have an accurate view of emergent bilinguals' reading, a translanguaging approach can be taken to gather information about how the student enables all his/her language resources while reading. Taking a translanguaging approach to assessments is also a way of practicing equitable literacy practices, ensuring that the assessments capture emergent bilinguals' full range of language practices during assessment. Although the entire reading assessment process can be transformed through responsive adaptations (Ascenzi-Moreno, 2018), I will focus on two key parts of the assessment process in this short essay: (1) listening to and documenting student reading and (2) student translanguaging during retell and comprehension questions.

Listening to and documenting student reading

The heart of reading assessments is when teachers, as Clay (2000) describes, listen to students as they read, noting when students insert cadence, when do they leave it out, when they make errors while they read, and what types of errors they make while they read (miscues). Teachers who support emergent bilinguals to read, must also be aware of how their learning of a named language, such as English or Spanish, affects how they read (Kabuto, 2017). Generally, when teachers listen to students read, they take notes on a documentation sheet (reflecting the text word for word) to capture students' miscues or deviations from the text. These miscues are then studied to understand the students' strategies and cueing systems that they employ while reading. The way that teachers generally annotate students' miscues is standardized to ensure consistency across grades and within a school (Clay, 2000). However, each emergent bilingual reader is different; those students who are at the beginning stages of developing a given named language may have more miscues than those that are further along. All emergent bilinguals may present miscues that are reflective of their knowledge and abilities within a given named language. Emergent bilinguals may read a word in a way that is influenced by conventions in their home language. For example, Spanish speakers are used to pronouncing words that start with an "s" in English as "es." The reason is because words that are cognates such as, "special," in English are similar to words in Spanish, such as "especial."

One English as New Language (ENL) teacher that I worked with started to use a reconfigured documentation sheet which takes into account miscues that are specific to students who are learning to read in a given named language. With a documentation sheet (Figure 13.1, used with permission, *Language Arts Journal*, Ascenzi-Moreno, 2018), the teacher was able to collect detailed information about student reading and differentiate miscues that were related to language acquisition from those that were reading related. In the example featured in Ascenzi-Moreno (2018), the teacher carefully listens to Santiago read and dutifully records him as he reads. Then after he finishes reading, she goes back to him to ask him for clarification. For example, Santiago makes two miscues, "beard" for "bird" and "failen" for "fallen." The teacher marked Santiago's miscues as language-based because she knows that his understanding of what he reads matches the text, although the ways in which he sounds out the words does not yet match conventional English.

Student translanguaging during retell and comprehension questions

During a reading assessment, comprehension questions are meant to determine if students understand the text. The phrasing and language of the questions could change, while keeping true to the gist and the purpose of the question. Additionally, students can respond using any linguistic resource to express their understanding of a given text.

For example, one teacher I worked with, a fifth grade French/English dual language, bilingual teacher explained her view on students' responses in their home language to comprehension questions: "I note that although they [the student] responded in English, it shows that they understood the question. It's fine

Differentiated Miscue Analysis Form

Name: Santiago						
Grade: 5						
Text: A Giant in the Forest Text Level:						
Text/Teacher Documentation of Student Reading:	S/C	M	V	S	L	P
Page 4 _s/c_ Every week the little boy's mother gave _bear_ him a big bar of soap. Then she sent	|					|
him to the lake to take a bath. _You_ "You'll be safe in the lake because the			|	|		
giant can't swim," she always said. "But						
don't forget to be home before dark.						
Page 5						
One day when the little boy was going to _beard_ take his bath, he saw a baby bird on the						|
failen ground. It had fallen out of its nest.						|
the The boy put the bird back in its nest.			|			
Types of Miscues S/C=Self Correction M=Meaning V=Visual S=Syntactical L=Language P=Pronunciation						

FIGURE 13.1 Differentiated miscue analysis form

for me. It means that they are lacking in vocabulary, but they have that comprehension. The problem is in retelling they don't have the language to do that. We must be flexible case by case (Interview, 10/24/2016)."

Sometimes the questions at the end of an assessment may be worded in a way that is confusing to emergent bilinguals. Teachers can ask themselves: What is the purpose of this question? Is it to ask students for their literal understanding, to make inferences, or to make connections? Then the teacher can ask themselves: What language may be difficult for the student to understand? With these two basic questions in mind, the teacher can then keep the heart of the question, while changing some of the language that is difficult for the student to understand. Or alternatively, the teacher may decide to pose the comprehension questions in the language with which the students have most familiarity. These decisions are based on the teachers' unique and expert decisions while weighing who the student is, what literacy and language goals she has for her, and the overarching goals of the program. In this space, the teacher is an active learner and leverages her/his learning edge.

Conclusion

Teachers are active agents in shaping the literacy environments that usher our emergent bilinguals in the reading and writing life. The teacher's engagement, or leveraging the learning edge, is critical for ensuring that their reading assessment practices match their emergent bilinguals' profiles and learning needs. What we learn about our students' language and social practices and how we use our knowledge of these, can transform our literacy instruction. Teachers' knowledge of students' diverse language practices as they assess their students makes the process meaningful and powerful for students and brings us one step closer to ensuring a level playing field in assessment for our emergent bilinguals

Note

1 An earlier version of this article was printed in Fall 2018 *The Bilingual Times Newsletter*, a publication of the New York State Association of Bilingual Educators (NYSABE).

References

Ascenzi-Moreno, L. (2018). Translanguaging and responsive assessment adaptations: Emergent bilingual readers through the lens of possibility. *Language Arts*, 6(95), 355–369.

Clay, M. (2000). *Running records for classroom teachers*. Portsmouth, NH: Heinemann.

García, O. (2020). Translanguaging and Latinx bilingual readers. *The Reading Teacher* 73(5), 557–562. https://doi.org/10.1002/trtr.1883

García, O., Johnson, S.I., & Seltzer, K. (2017). *The translanguaging classroom: Leveraging student bilingualism for learning*. Philadelphia, PA: Caslon.

García, O. & Kleifgen, J.A. (2019). Translanguaging and literacies. *Reading Research Quarterly*, 55(4). https://doi.org/10.1002/rrq.286

García, O. & Kleyn, T. (Eds.). (2016). *Translanguaging with multilingual students: Learning from classroom moments*. London, UK: Routledge.

Graves, D. (2001). *The energy to teach*. Portsmouth, NH: Heinemann.

Kabuto, B. (2017). A socio-psycholinguistic perspective on biliteracy: The use of miscue analysis as a culturally relevant assessment tool. *Reading Horizons*, 56, 25–44.

Li, Wei. (2011). Moment analysis and translanguaging space: Discursive construction of identities by multilingual Chinese youth in Britain. *Journal of Pragmatics*, 43(5), 1222–1235. https://doi.org/10.1016/j.pragma.2010.07.035

BOX 13.1 TEACHER/RESEARCHER

Andy Brown

4th grade, self-contained English as a new language

This is a lesson I did for an English literacy unit with the book *The Tarantula Scientist* by Sy Montgomery, after I started leveraging translanguaging in my pedagogy as a result of my connection to CUNY-NYSIEB. The book is a non-fiction science book about an arachnologist who travels the world looking for and studying new species of spiders, primarily tarantulas. It is a very interesting and informative book, but it can be very challenging to any student learning English. There are plenty of photographs, illustrations, diagrams, captions etc., but there are also many difficult vocabulary words that may not exactly translate very easily into languages other than English. Of course, we only had a few copies of the book, and they are all English versions.

Leveraging my students' translanguaging in my pedagogical practice enabled my emergent bilinguals to understand the text. I asked my students to work in groups according to their home languages and summarize paragraphs in both English and their home language. I also *hung up charts* with important vocabulary words like "spinnerets," "molt," "arachnid," "excavating," and *translated them into the various languages* of my students (with the help of Google Translate and of some of my students). For example, when teaching about how the tarantulas used vibrations on the web to know when prey is close, I displayed the definition of the word "vibrations" in three languages (English, Spanish, and Romanian):

> **Vibrations**: *a continuous slight shaking movement: a series of small, fast*
>   *movements back and forth or from side to side*
> *movimientos pequeños y rápidos de un lado a otro o de lado a lado*
> **mici mişcări rapide înapoi şi înapoi sau dintr-o parte în alta**

I always gave my students the chance to *correct any errors* in the translations and *to explain how they would use words and/or phrases in their own languages*. This translanguaging practice helps to boost confidence and *allows the student to become the teacher*. I often find that students enjoyed how to say a word in another language and in turn, students who only spoke English would often replace English words with words in another language that they had just learned.

Halfway through the unit, I allowed the students to work on collaborative posters. The students often take hints from me that they don't need to only use English and will translanguage on their own, writing in more than one language or writing in both English and their home language within an individual sentence. In the posters, the students take their favorite parts of the text or something interesting that they learned and summarize the facts or information in their own words on chart paper. They can add an illustration when they are done. The posters were displayed around the room and at the end of the lesson, we had a gallery walk where the students give feedback on the posters by writing tips and compliments on post-it notes and attaching them to the chart paper. So many parents and teachers were impressed to see how the kids would write about the habitats of a tarantula and the Chinese characters describing an illustration of a tarantula's head. One of my students, Elena, a Romanian student who had interrupted schooling before coming to the U.S. would use *a* translating app on her phone to write words on her collaborative poster in English, Romanian, and Spanish since her stepfather spoke Spanish. Elena was ecstatic she was able to show him at open school night what she had learned about tarantulas and their diet through translanguaging.

Allowing kids to feel confident in speaking with their home language practices makes them feel at home in any classroom setting. I'm sad to say that in the past few years some of my administrators have asked me to downplay the translanguaging practices during lessons. They feel it takes up too much time, but I feel they don't truly understand the impact it has on students new to the country or students who feel they must "only speak English."

SECTION V
Inquiry en Comunidad

14

INTERROGATING LANGUAGE IDEOLOGIES IN THE PRIMARY GRADES

A community language inquiry unit

Ivana Espinet, Gladys Y. Aponte, Maite T. Sánchez, Diane Cardenas Figueroa, and Ashley Busone-Rodríguez

Introduction

On a busy street in Washington Heights (a New York City neighborhood with a large Dominican population and a long history of Latinx residents), a group of third graders walk, holding notepads and taking photographs. They stop to observe in front of businesses; they take notes and pictures. One group pauses in front of a Chinese restaurant. Many of the signs are in English and there are also some in Chinese. However, one sign called the students' attention: "Buscamos un delivrista" The children begin to discuss the words. "Buscamos" means "wanted", another student adds, but "delivrista"? Is it Spanish? Or is it an English word turned into Spanish? "Delivery is English," one of the kids points out. "The beginning of the word is in English and 'ista' is from Spanish," others say. One of the girls in the group offers: "It's Spanish from Washington Heights." Students agree and that settles the discussion. They take a picture and move on to the next store. Back in the classroom, when they look at the pictures, the children begin to make sense of how language is used fluidly, as it changes and evolves. The discussion shifts into how we value some ways of speaking over others. Students discuss whether new terms that "mix" languages are "incorrect" ways of speaking or creative ways of using language.

The above vignette describes how a group of third graders from a bilingual school who were engaged as bilingual ethnographers in an inquiry project made sense of their observations of language use in their communities. In the context of this work, the children and teachers worked together as they examined their linguistic ideologies. We begin by describing the school, Hudson Elementary School[1] in which Cardenas Figueroa and Busone-Rodríguez teach third grade. We then share some of the work in which they engaged, alongside Espinet, Aponte, and Sánchez. We provide an overview of the inquiry project and describe two of the activities in which the children engaged. During and after the project, there were opportunities for the teachers to reflect on what was happening in their classroom with the CUNY-NYSIEB (City University of New York-New York State Initiative on Emergent Bilinguals) researchers. We documented those moments and end this chapter by sharing the teachers' personal reflections and some of their insights.

Inquiry into language practices and ideologies in bilingual classrooms

Children rarely have the opportunity to reflect on their own linguistic practices, even when bilingual education programs purport to serve them. Language ideologies and how one understands language and language use, permeate how bilingual programs are structured. Teachers, students, and families, come to schools with beliefs about how language should be used and how different language practices are valued.

In New York State, bilingual education programs are an option in public schools. In the past three decades, most bilingual programs in the United States have been "transitional bilingual education programs" (TBE) that use students' home languages in instruction until students learn English. However, in the past two decades, there has been an increase in dual language bilingual education (DLBE) programs, the majority of which are two-way. This means that classrooms are initially composed of a half of students who have been labeled as "English language learners," and another half that has not and is learning the language other than English (LOTE). The goal of the DLBE programs is for students to become bilingual, biliterate, and bicultural. To do that, instruction is carried out in two languages. In the majority of DLBE programs, students receive 50% of their instruction in English, and the other 50% in the LOTE. However, DLBE programs are often set up with a monoglossic expectation that minoritized bilingual students ought to be two monolingual speakers in one (Grosjean, 2010). As a consequence, these programs have often adopted language allocation policies that prescribe an exclusive space for English and another separate one for the LOTE (Sánchez, García & Solorza, 2017).

Within the discrete spaces allocated for each language of instruction (for example, a separate room or time for English, Spanish, or Chinese, depending on the bilingual program), there is also the expectation that students will language using socially constructed "standard" language practices that are said to belong in school. These linguistic expectations perpetuate hierarchies of languages by implicitly and explicitly devaluing the dynamic non-dominant language practices of bilingual students and families (Flores & Rosa, 2015). Normalized language practices, as Flores and Rosa (2015) explain, are tied to dominant white middle-class standards of correctness, or "appropriateness" anchored in "*raciolinguistic ideologies* that conflate certain racialized bodies with linguistic deficiency unrelated to any objective linguistic practices" (p. 150). In order to challenge oppressive ideologies of "language appropriateness" that further marginalize racially and linguistically minoritized communities, bilingual programs must create critical bilingual spaces that call for students and teachers to analyze and interrogate linguistic expectations (Flores & García, 2017; Flores & Rosa, 2015; García & Sung, 2018).

Translanguaging is a political act (Flores, 2014) in which educators disrupt restrictive language practices that are used to minoritize certain bilingual students. Li Wei (2011) reminds us that the act of translanguaging itself can be transformative in nature because:

> It creates a social space for the multilingual language users by bringing together different dimensions of their personal history, experience and environment, their attitude, belief and ideology, and their cognitive and physical capacity into one coordinated and meaningful performance, and making it into a lived experience. (p. 1223)

Sánchez, García and Solorza (2017) call for changes to bilingual education programs that allow for *translanguaging transformation spaces*—spaces in which students draw on *all* their linguistic multimodal resources in ways that challenge existing linguistic hierarchies in school and society overall. A critical translanguaging approach calls for educators to recognize and challenge deficit perspectives of multilingual learners that are informed by raciolinguistic ideologies of language deficiencies (Martin, Aponte & García, 2019). This also entails developing critical multilingual awareness so students and teachers can collaboratively examine the ideologies that underlie the conventions of language in school and society in order to transform them (García, 2017). At Hudson Elementary School, designing a unit in which the students work as bilingual language ethnographers was an attempt to create a translanguaging space to foster students' awareness and criticality of language itself (for another example, see Teacher/Researcher Box 14.1).

School and classroom context

Hudson Elementary School is a public school in NYC that has a school-wide dual language bilingual program (English-Spanish) which serves students from kindergarten to fifth grade. The school's goals are "developing students' bilingualism and biliteracy, providing structures to support analytical thinking and inquiry, ensuring a strong foundation in literacy and math, and working with families to establish positive and trusting relationships that support productive school practices and strengthen student achievement" (Comprehensive Educational Plan, 2018–19). At the time when this project took place, the school had 411 students. More than 75% of the students came from homes in which a LOTE was spoken (mostly Spanish, but a few families speak other languages such as French, German, Hebrew, Italian, Mixteco, Russian, Swedish, Tagalog, Turkish). Of the total population of the school, 29% of the students were classified as what New York State now calls Multilingual Language Learners (previously English Language Learners) (CEP, 2018–19; NYC DOE, 2019). The students in the school learn all academic subjects in both English and Spanish (Math, Language Arts, Science, Social Studies).

The school has two types of bilingual instructional arrangements—a side-by-side arrangement and a self-contained arrangement. In the side-by-side arrangement one teacher teaches exclusively in English and the other teaches exclusively in Spanish. Two groups of students alternate daily between the rooms, and therefore receive instruction in one language on one day, and then in the other language. Diane Cardenas Figueroa teaches the Spanish side of a side-by-side third grade class.

The self-contained arrangement follows what in New York City is called Integrated Co-Teaching (ICT). In these classrooms two teachers provide instruction to the same group of children: Some students (less than 40% of students in the class) have Individualized Education Plans (IEPs) to meet their special learning needs and the others do not. ICT classrooms alternate the language of instruction on a daily basis: One day in Spanish and the next day in English. Ashley Busone-Rodríguez teaches the self-contained ICT class in the third grade.

The teachers at Hudson Elementary School teach their social studies curriculum using an inquiry approach. During the 2018–19 school year, the school collaborated with CUNY-NYSIEB, focusing on designing translanguaging transformational spaces within the Social Studies curriculum. During the planning process, the teachers spoke about ways to ask open-ended questions and approach the inquiry unit as facilitators, rather than teachers. They wanted to center the inquiry in social justice and hoped that conversations about language and the social meanings of language would emerge from students' conversations.

Overview of unit and rationale

In collaboration with CUNY NYSIEB, the third grade teachers designed a mini unit focused on the essential question, "Why does language matter?" The unit was intended to open up a translanguaging space, rather than the separate instructional spaces for Spanish and English. Early on, the teachers introduced the concept of translanguaging. They explained that while school time is generally separated between "English time" and "Spanish time," during Social Studies Inquiry they would use their entire linguistic repertoire to learn and inquire about language. They also described what ethnographers do. They then explained to the children that they would approach the study of language in their community as bilingual ethnographers. After one of the first lessons in the unit, Diane commented during a debriefing session with the CUNY-NYSIEB team:

> A lot of students have different ideas about what that meant as we were learning about translanguaging. I think for a lot of students, they were flexible with that idea and other students were still grappling with it because this is a Spanish classroom and the other classroom is the English classroom.

The notion of using translanguaging to learn challenged students' understanding of the appropriate use of language in school. At the beginning of the unit, the children and teachers brainstormed questions about language that they wanted to investigate. In one of the sessions, they combined the questions and created a concentric graph which started from the center—the student:

- Why does language matter to me in my life?
- Why does language matter in my family?
- Why does language matter to my classroom community?
- Why does language matter in my wider community? (see Figure 14.1)

To answer these questions, the class interacted with members of their communities in and outside of the school.

How do we language?

As one of the first activities in the unit, Diane and Ashley showed the students a video of Julissa, a Dominican-American woman from Buzzfeed's *PeroLike* (Calderón, 2018). As Julissa enters her workspace, she uses language in different ways depending on her interlocutor. After they watched the video, the children analyzed how Julissa used oral language and body language, depending whom she was addressing. They made observations such as:

> "She's excited to see her friend."
> "She's talking street language."

FIGURE 14.1 Why does language matter? Classroom display

"She's screaming at her Dominican friends."
"She spoke differently with the first person she interacted with, which was a Latina, than with someone else. She used a different kind of Spanish that sounded happier."

Students tried to make sense of what they called the "different types of English and Spanish and both together." They discussed that, like them, while Julissa is always the same person, she interacts differently with friends and co-workers. This initial activity unearthed some of the children's initial dispositions about language practices that are part of their daily lives.

After viewing and discussing the video, the teachers modeled how to create a linguistic web to depict their own language practices and experiences (see Figure 14.2). The goal of this activity was to have the students begin to reflect on their own dynamic language practices. The teachers' personal linguistic web reflected languaging across registers. Both Diane and Ashley explained that they were "making sense of all these things together." Diane reflected after the lesson:

> The students started thinking: "What kind of Spanish do I speak and to whom?" I modeled my own language map as well to show them the variations depending on when I'm with my Spanish-speaking relatives from

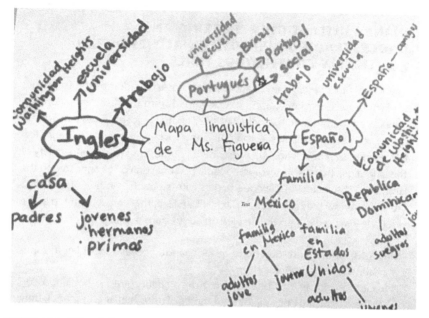

FIGURE 14.2 Diane's linguistic map

Mexico, Spanish-speaking from the Dominican Republic; and even there, when I go to Mexico, to Sinaloa State, my demeanor changes as well. When I'm speaking to my family here, even though it's Mexican Spanish, it is very much California. That's my experience.

As the children created their own linguistic maps, they began to think about their family and themselves. Who do I interact with? How do I communicate? They thought about how they use language in their immediate community in Washington Heights or with family members in other countries and used that information to create the linguistic maps. The children shared their personal linguistic webs and analyzed the data that emerged from them. Then they discussed what they noticed about each other's use of language and began to brainstorm questions that they wanted to ask their parents so they could add a new layer to their research.

In the following reflection, Diane describes a discussion that followed the creation of the linguistic maps. For Diane, listening to her students discuss how their language practices are judged outside of school highlighted how pressing it is for teachers to be prepared to have discussions about those experiences. She also began to unveil her own positioning as a bilingual individual and how it has impacted her language ideology.

DIANE'S REFLECTION: EXPLORING AND UNDERSTANDING OUR POSITIONALITIES DURING POLITICALLY CONTENTIOUS TIMES

In a moment of casual conversation during an exploration of the languages spoken in our classroom community, I learned from my first-generation students born to immigrant parents that their language identities extended outside of school, across family, community, and society and what this might feel like. Students created language webs, identifying the languages and variety of the languages that they used and added a personal drawing connected to the language. The following dialogue began with students commenting at their table about how they also "code switch" like Julissa, the woman featured in the video we watched during the first lesson about translanguaging:

-Nina said: "Hay gente que no le gusta cuando voceas [pausa larga] especialmente en español.
-Monica responds with: "Una vez en el tren cuando estaba hablando con mi mamá y mi tía nos dijeron que no podíamos hablar en español, only English."
-Manuel quickly said: "Pero yo siempre le voy hablar a mi mamá en español."
-Monica then added: "Pero la gente no entiende, tiene miedo."
-Nina stated: "Porque piensan que estás diciendo algo que no entienden."
-Manuel said: "Yo siempre ayudo a mi mamá con el inglés cuando no entiende."
-Monica excitedly responded "Sí es verdad, cuando ella no puede decir algo o no sabe."
-Nina chimed in: "Mi abuelita también necesita ayuda."

First-generation students take on the role of translators, caretakers, students, and teachers within their family unit as they experience the world outside of the school. As an educator, I asked myself: How are students learning to navigate these different language identities in the current political climate? Students at the beginning of the year had expressed how having a president who does not want people from other countries also means not being accepting of their cultures and languages. These conversations with students like Manuel, Monica, and Nina impacted a very important aspect of my teaching. There is a great need for spaces to explore and make sense of how students are growing up bilingually and biculturally in a world of borders and xenophobia.

Preparation of bilingual teachers to plan and facilitate these discussions is crucial, even more so in bilingual education programs. This experience has validated and challenged my view as a teacher, to look beyond the surface and push toward deepening the understanding I have of my students and their everyday experiences with the different language identities they take on: How does privilege and positionality affect how students are perceived in society as they learn about the value of different languages in society?

Students' own exploration of translanguaging and its connection to their everyday lives has disrupted and challenged negative views of multilingualism held in society. As students are raising questions and thinking about why language matters, as an educator I am *becoming comfortable with the idea of being uncomfortable.* My identity and how I enact my own theories on language are based on my experiences. As a Mexican-American first-generation teacher, born and raised in California, my language identities are different from those of my students. Although my Spanish language development stems from growing up in a Mexican community in a bilingual and bicultural environment, I also am aware of my privilege. In the hierarchy of language, Spanish that is viewed as more "standard" or "proper" is also ingrained in the ways we teach. I want students to be able to navigate their **own** language practices, with the ability to use their linguistic repertoire across different spaces, whether it be school, home, community, or society. Language is power, but as a bilingual educator, my responsibility is to create these spaces where students are able to make connections across these different layers of life experience and intersectionalities, working toward preparing students to see themselves as powerful beings.

In her reflection, Diane makes explicit how teachers' identities and linguistic ideologies are intertwined to how they hear their students' voices. As her students began their inquiries by observing and recording their own linguistic practices, the classroom became a space to host discussions about how they are perceived and understood by others. In turn, Diane's students' insights prompted her to reflect on her own stance as a Spanish teacher in a DLBE classroom.

Inquiry goes out of school: a community walk

After children analyzed their personal and family language practices, they also learned about the language practices of the community. For this, Diane and Ashley planned a community walk in which students were to pay attention and ask about the language practices used in their community. First, they listed the shops that they wanted to visit. Some chose places that they had not visited before. As bilingual ethnographers, the children walked around a couple of blocks observing and taking notes. They could hear and see many different languages—there was Arabic being spoken by one of the food vendors, Mixteco conversations held at the fruit stand, Chinese written on one of the nearby restaurants, and when they arrived at a historic Jewish university near the school, one of the children could read some of the Hebrew that was written on the walls.

As students entered different businesses, they interviewed employees and asked questions such as: "Why does language matter to you? Why is it important for you to speak more than one language in this community?" The business owners gave them answers like, "Well, if I want to keep my clientele, I need to learn more languages." Or, "If I want to learn about new things on the tech market, I have to speak more languages." One of the things that they noticed was that in the healthcare facilities, there were more languages represented than in other places. As they tried to figure out why, one of the children said, "Well, everybody needs healthcare, so of course, it wouldn't be fair if the healthcare only spoke one language."

As they continued their walk, the children listened to people speaking in the street, took notes, and photographed signage in the street and on businesses. When they got back to the classroom, students shared their notes and observations about how language is used in their neighborhood. They went back to their essential question: Why does language matter? They began to make initial analyses based on what they had seen and heard. They looked at some of the pictures that they had taken and shared their inquiries and opinions. They also discussed the power hierarchies of languages present in the neighborhood.

Below Ashley discusses how her experience observing and working with one of the students during the community walk made her think about her own journey as an educator and the development of her pedagogical stance. Classroom inquiry, at its core, is an open-ended process in which teachers and students learn alongside each other.

ASHLEY'S REFLECTION: EXAMINING LINGUISTIC IDENTITY DEVELOPMENT AND ATTITUDES IN THE CLASSROOM

Working with Ivan, a white Jewish student, alerted me to some realities of my own positionality and bias that I am still working to address in my own teaching. On our community walk we began by observing signs on the street. I asked Ivan what he noticed, and he pointed out that all the street signs were in English. When I asked him why he thought that might be, Ivan told me, "It's because we're in America and English is the official language here." My initial reaction was to over-correct and emphasize the fact that we do not live in an "English Only" country. I was frustrated by his limited understanding of the prevalence and importance of multilingualism in our community.

Ivan's understandings of the world are evolving. They are derived, in large part, from what he hears and experiences at home and in school. We are responsible for shaping his ideology. In the context of the current political climate in the United States, where the president is attempting to deport immigrants and devalue their worth and importance in our society, it is very likely that Ivan's ideas have been influenced by the "English Only" ideology that is prevalent today.

Carefully, I told Ivan: "Did you know that there are *no* official languages in the United States? Isn't that cool?" Two girls behind him (a new arrival and a first-generation immigrant) chimed in saying "Yeah! ¡Acá se puede hablar lo que quiera!" Ivan looked surprised that the girls were claiming that one could speak whatever in the U.S. My claim was more complex than this. Language officialization is about giving languages power, and in the context of the United States (and the world), English is not lacking in power. Yet, as Ivan observed, most of our street signs are still in English.

I paid close attention to Ivan's observations during the rest of our walk as we passed local businesses with signs in Spanish and Arabic and heard people speaking Chinese on the street. I'd like to say that I could almost see his worldview changing before my own eyes. Of course, language identity development and recognizing the relationship between language and power structures is a much longer process than a walk around the block. But I watched Ivan's curiosity about language grow. When we arrived at the nearby historically Jewish university, Ivan was elated to read aloud the Hebrew that is carved into the stone. Understanding that his community values the power and significance of other languages just as his peers' communities do was a major realization on this trip. Back at the school, we paused to read a construction sign posted by the school district out front. Ivan observed that it stated the information in nine different languages, and he looked proud to tell his peers: "That's because there's no official language in the United States."

Before I could begin discussing the power of translanguaging and addressing metalinguistic awareness with eight-year-old children, it was necessary for me to engage in a process of personal concientización (self-reflection and critical consciousness raising). As a white, US born, formally educated and English-speaking woman, I have been afforded the privilege of choosing to be multilingual. I could have chosen, as many of my peers and family members did, to live my life as a monolingual since my home language is also the language of power. Valdés and Figueroa (1994) outline the differences between elective and circumstantial bilinguals. While I am the former, my students are the latter. Most of my students' families speak Spanish or another language in their homes. They are learning English because it is important to their pursuit of economic and social success.

When I started my path toward becoming a teacher, I fell into the trap of an "English Only" ideology that was presented to me by my teacher education program. It held a dominant ideology and wielded English as a tool of "power" and "empowerment." This prevented me from seeing my students as dynamic linguistic beings, and it stifled the extent to which I truly knew them and their linguistic capabilities. I was fortunate to later be surrounded by pedagogues and thinkers who challenged this notion. During my time learning alongside Mapuche educators in Chile and later in a graduate Bilingual Education Program, I was pushed to recognize the harmful ideologies that my initial teacher education training upheld, and I was given the opportunity to enter a translanguaging space. I came to embrace translanguaging not only as a method but as a mindset.

The former, "English Only Educator" version of myself would have capitalized on my walk with Ivan as an opportunity to teach my students the importance of English. The "Translanguaging Educator" version of myself pushed Ivan to think about why English is so ubiquitous. What structures make it that way? Who benefits, and who is left out by this choice? I encouraged other students to point out their home languages and how they were used as we walked around their blocks. I asked them to listen in on Mixteco conversations at the fruit stands and decipher Hebrew passages written on the walls. The consciousness-building I've done has allowed me to recognize my own privilege as an English language speaker and to wield that for the good of our multilingual community, and ultimately to ask students like Ivan to do the same.

Conclusion and recommendations

As Diane points out in her reflection, one of the most important aspects of the journey that the teachers described is that they "became comfortable with the idea of being uncomfortable." Approaching teaching from an inquiry perspective means understanding that there will be unexpected bumps, detours, and surprises along the way. Becoming bilingual ethnographers prompted both students and teachers to start to examine their own language ideologies. While critical conversations like these can be "uncomfortable," they are necessary (Alim, 2005; Emdin, 2016; Paris & Alim, 2017). When done reflectively and in collaboration, they can set the foundation for the development of a new pedagogical stance.

In the context of a dual language bilingual program, designing a translanguaging transformation space (Sánchez, García & Solorza, 2017) that allowed children and teachers to collaboratively inquire about languaging was a first step in challenging a monoglossic approach to bilingual education. Dismantling the raciolinguistic hierarchies upheld in bilingual classrooms requires educators to include children in resisting the normalization of standardized language practices. While this work requires a long-term shift in how teaching and learning are approached in bilingual programs, engaging children in observing their own language practices, as well as those of their communities, is a first step in questioning those hierarchies.

In order to create more equitable learning environments for bilingual students, educators need to begin to center the rich and complex home language practices that children and families bring into the classroom and validate unique bilingual, bicultural worldviews (Martin, Aponte & García, 2019). We must return to the original purpose of DLBE education—to critically educate students from linguistically and racially marginalized communities in ways that liberate and empower them (Flores & García, 2017; García & Sung, 2018). To do this, we have to encourage explicit, transparent talk about language and a focus on critical metalinguistic awareness (García, 2017). Inquiry is a genuine space for teachers, students, and families to examine and negotiate language ideologies. The teachers and students in this chapter began the process of creating such a space. Their experiences provide an inspiration for others to continue and deepen their work.

Note

1 The name of the school has been modified to maintain confidentiality.

References

Alim, H.S. (2005). Critical language awareness in the United States: Revisiting issues and revising pedagogies in a resegregated society. *Educational Researcher*, 34(7), 24–31.

Calderón, J. (2018). PeroLike on Buzzfeed. *When You Code-Switch at Work*. Retrieved from https://www.buzzfeed.com/perolike

Comprehensive Educational Plan. (2018–19). Retrieved April 9, 2019. https://www.nyce-net.edu/Documents/oaosi/cep/2018-19/CEP_M103.pdf

Emdin, C. (2016). *For white folks who teach in the hood, and the rest of y'all too: Reality pedagogy and urban education*. Boston, MA: Beacon Press.

Flores, N. (2014). Let's not forget that translanguaging is a political act. https://educationa-llinguist.wordpress.com/2014/07/19/lets-not-forget-that-translanguaging-is-a-political-act/

Flores, N. & García, O. (2017). A critical review of bilingual education in the United States: From basements and pride to boutiques and profit. *Annual Review of Applied Linguistics*, 37, 14–29. https://doi.org/10.1017/S0267190517000162

Flores, N., & Rosa, J. (2015). Undoing appropriateness: Raciolinguistic ideologies and language diversity in education. *Harvard Educational Review*, 85(2), 149–171.

García, O. (2017). Critical multilingual awareness and teacher education. In J. Cenoz, D. Gorter & S. May (Eds.), *Language awareness and multilingualism. Encyclopedia of Language and Education*. Springer. https://doi.org/10.1007/978-3-319-02325-0_30-1

García, O. & Sung, K.K-F. (2018). Critically assessing the 1968 Bilingual Education Act at 50 years: Taming tongues and Latinx communities. *The Bilingual Review Journal*, 4(4), 318–333. https://doi.org/10.1080/15235882.2018.1529642

Grosjean, F. (2010). *Bilingual. Life and reality*. Cambridge, MA and London: Harvard University Press.

Li, Wei. (2011). Moment analysis and translanguaging space: Discursive construction of identities by multilingual Chinese youth in Britain. *Journal of Pragmatics*, 43(5), 1222–1235.

Martin, K.M., Aponte, G.Y., & García, O. (2019). Countering raciolinguistic ideologies: The role of translanguaging in educating bilingual children. *Les Cahiers Internationaux de Sociolinguistique*, 2(16), 19–41. www.cairn.info/revue-cahiers-internationaux-de-sociolinguistique-2019-2-page-19.htm.

New York City Department of Education. (2019). *School Register*. Retrieved from https://www.nycenet.edu/PublicApps/register.aspx?s=M103

Paris, D.H., & Alim, S. (Eds.) (2017). *Culturally sustaining pedagogies: Teaching and learning for justice in a changing world*. New York, NY: Teachers College Press.

Sánchez, M.T., García, O., & Solorza, C. (2017). Reframing language allocation policy in dual language bilingual education. *Bilingual Research Journal, Journal*, 41(1), 37–51. https://doi.org/10.1080/15235882.2017.1405098

Valdés, G., & Figueroa, R.A. (1994). *Bilingualism and testing: A special case of bias*. Ablex Publishing.

BOX 14.1 TEACHER/RESEARCHER

Annabelle Maroney & Rebeca Madrigal

1st grade, dual language bilingual

We teach in a dual-language (Spanish/English) elementary school in Washington Heights, New York City. Many of the students in our first-grade classroom have connections to the Dominican Republic, Puerto Rico, and Mexico, and live in households where multiple languages are used.

In first grade, students learn about the community. In previous years, the focus of the community units has been to gather knowledge: Who are the members of the community? What are the public services and businesses? What is infrastructure? This past year, however, with the support of the researchers from CUNY-NYSIEB, we developed a mini-unit focusing on translanguaging in the community. This unit differed from the previous years' units by focusing on the exploration of a key concept, *language use*, instead of the acquisition of knowledge. In this unit, the students worked to answer the essential question: *How do community members use language?*

We designed the unit using an inquiry cycle framework to maximize student agency. In order to answer the central question, the students generated questions and interviewed members of their families, the school staff, and the surrounding community. They interpreted their data through discussion, play, drawing and writing. Finally, they used what they had learned from their research to create projects showing how different people, including themselves, use language in the community.

In our dual-language program, languages are associated with colors.

We use red for Spanish, and English is paired with blue. However, when people translanguage, they are not limited to one language or the other. So, we decided to introduce translanguaging activities in purple, a mixture of blue and red, to show the students that when we translanguage we use of all our linguistic resources.

We knew that in the bilingual community of the school, translanguaging was a common practice. We wanted our students to be able to navigate their community thinking about their language practices. Before we took the walk, we discussed our experiences in our neighborhood. The students shared that the community is predominantly Spanish-speaking, and that some do not speak English. They discussed how they themselves serve as interpreters and translators for their parents or grandparents, and how like them, many in the community were bilingual.

Our students know their community, the people, the stores, and the streets. But they were not fully aware of the power of language and their own power as bilinguals, because sometimes being bilingual is taken for granted, especially if you speak English and Spanish. Our is a thriving community. The music from radios and cars, loud conversations, the products for sale, the street vendors, and the customers are the key elements that give color and life to the neighborhood.

Our first Community Language Walk took place in February, and it coincided with the day celebrating the Dominican Republic Independence, February 27. We decided to carry with us the flag of the Dominican Republic, a country from which many of our students hailed. We walked around the corner saying, "¡Viva la República Dominicana!" Suddenly, we heard cars honking their horns. The students were very surprised and excited by the neighbors' reactions. A student of Salvadoran ancestry commented on how happy people were: "Creo que están contentos porque es su independencia." The positive energy and the ánimo on the streets was evident.

We first approached the street vendors because they really represent the authenticity of the "comunidad." We were able to interview people in the neighborhood like the popular "vendedora de habichuelas dulces." Many Dominicans students were very excited because their families buy their "habichuelas dulces" from this vendor. One Dominican girl said, "mi mamá compra las habichuelas aquí y son muy 'good.'"

We also interviewed an elderly Dominican man selling a very particular and unique product. The students needed to decide who and how to ask the question. Two boys decided to approach the vendor. One child asked, "Excuse me, what do you sell?" The vendor was busy, serving and selling his product to a customer. He replied, "no entiendo." So, the other student told him, "You have to say "Permiso, ¿qué vende usted?" He told him very slowly so he would be able to repeat it to the vendor. The vendor replied, "Yo vendo maíz caquido." Because we did not understand one of us, Rebeca, who is Mexican, asked him: "Permiso, ¿puede repetir lo que dijo? Por favor." The vendor repeated, "maíz caquido." Our paraprofessional, who is Dominican, then approached the vendor and asked him again, "Permiso, ¿qué es lo que vende?" The vendor for the third or fourth time repeated the answer and our paraprofessional said, "He sells "maíz caquiao." We all laughed because we still were not getting what it meant. Even the vendor and other customers were laughing with us.

When we went back to the classroom we looked up maíz caquiao. We learned that it is a cracked corn pudding eaten in the Cibao region of the

Dominican Republic and also known as chacá in the south part of the country. We also learned that were many ways of naming this corn pudding in other Latin American countries. This taught us a lot about language, and how language use reflects also cultures, and how Spanish is not one thing, but many. We encourage our students to appreciate their accents and to use their vernacular vocabulary, so that we can all learn from each other.

The Community Language Walks allowed us to acknowledge our community as a rich resource. We tried to integrate our inquiry unit on Community into "Exploraciones" (Explorations). Explorations is choice-based play time that Kindergarteners and First Graders have every day at the end of the school day. We decided to recreate some of the most popular businesses from the community in our own classroom.

We determined that we would have "el súpermercado," "el salón de belleza y la barbería." These centers would be a great platform for translanguaging and for students to explore their free-play. The first-grade team decided that this would be "purple time," for translanguaging, as opposed to a "red time" for Spanish or a "blue time" for English. During Explorations, the students were encouraged to use all of their linguistic resources to communicate with their peers.

The students' play in the community centers demonstrated how translanguaging is a powerful way to communicate. It also revealed their conceptions of social roles and power dynamics in the community. These are some of the observations that we noticed when the students were playing in the "salón de belleza y la barbería." These have to do with the students' sophisticated understanding of language use and gender roles, language use and power, and language use and situatedness of culture:

For gender

- Only girls volunteered to play in the "salón de belleza."
  - The girls assigned themselves roles and distributed the materials among themselves.
- Only boys chose to play in the barbershop.

For language and power

- Latinx students mostly played the worker/expert role. They were in charge of cutting, combing, washing, and drying the hair.
- Non-Latinx mostly played the role of the customers.

For language and situatedness of culture

- Translanguaging was using constantly during their interactions. But the students' language use in the community centers demonstrate the students' sophistication about how language is used in the community.

Amongst themselves, the Latinx (workers/experts) usually would communicate in Spanish. If they wanted to ask the customer about their hair, however, they would do so in English. Some said things like:

- "How do you want your hair done?" or "Do you like your hair like that?"

Others used Spanish, using a lexicon for "hair" that is highly sophisticated for a first grader, "cabello" for "pelo," but this is what a beautician would say when they invite a customer to wash their hair:

- "Vamos a lavar el cabello."

Others use an English lexicon for the instrument with beauticians blow hair:

- "Tú seca el cabello con el blower. "

This is because the instrument in Spanish is called "la secadora," and the blower is not to dry, but to straighten hair, an important function in Dominican beauty parlors where customers go get their cabello "lacio":

- "Ella dice que lo quiere lacio; you know, straight."

It was evident that many students knew exactly how a beauty salon/barbershop runs in their community.

After our community walk, we also printed pictures of different people we encountered. The students wrote dialogue in speech bubbles to express how people used translanguaging in specific contexts. In one picture, two people sit across from each other in a pastelitos shop. In one speech bubble, the students wrote:"Había muchos niños aquí," and then in another, "We have to make más pastelitos!" The students were beginning to get the idea that to be authentic language users, representing the realities of their communities, translanguaging was needed, for how else could they say "pastelitos?"

As a result of the unit, the students were able to:

- **Explore the ways in which people translanguage within the community.** This unit gave the students an opportunity to observe authentic and fluid language use in a multilingual community, compared to the language separation of a dual-language program.
- **Reflect on their own translanguaging and feel empowered in being multilingual.** Talking about and observing translanguaging in the community helped the students to think flexibly and creatively about their own language use. Many students expressed excitement and pride in their multilingualism.
- **Use creative play and role-playing to express what they had learned about the community.** The Explorations centers encouraged students to use translanguaging freely and make connections to their research.

- **Make connections between the community and the school.** The community walks supported making a close connection with the community. The community (pedestrians, vendors, and consumers) had the opportunity to interact with students using language in ways with which they felt most comfortable. On the other hand, students also had the opportunity to practice translanguaging with vendors and shopkeepers. They reflected on their own language resources and learned that they could use language according to different contexts.
- **To create awareness of the rich resources in the community and at school.** This exploration served to strengthen the student's awareness that every child is a resource in the classroom, at school, in the family, and in the community. It is important for the students to appreciate that each individual is able to contribute something from their culture and language practices.

15

HAND IN HAND: PARENT COLLABORATION IN THE CLASSROOM CONTEXT

Ivana Espinet and Khánh Lê

Introduction

Learning is a social process that is shaped by our languaging. Young people's learning is bound within larger contextual, historical, political, and ideological frameworks. For language-minoritized students, school learning can only be fruitful if they are able to leverage their ways of knowing, use language that they learn from those at home and in their communities, and feel socioemotionally secure in their bilingual identities. However, school and classroom communities do not always see families as partners, and families' and students' language practices have been often stigmatized and devalued.

Whereas teachers and schools invite parents to participate in school and classroom events, parents are rarely seen as collaborators in instructional work within the classroom. Furthermore, collaboration in analyzing and thinking, and leveraging families' language practices is virtually absent. This chapter begins with the examination of some of the critical literature that explores the various facets of parental engagement in children's education. Then, drawing from our CUNY-NYSIEB (City University of New York-New York State Initiative on Emergent Bilinguals) experience with classroom teachers, we focus in family partnerships within the context of instructional work in the classroom. We provide three examples from classrooms in New York City public schools with large populations of emergent bilinguals that challenge the traditional notions of family engagement, validating and leveraging family language practices as resources for learning. We conclude that when teachers center families' language practices and provide a space for parents to co-learn with their children and vice versa, we can shift the narratives vis-à-vis family engagement and language practices.

That is, without the confinement of what the nation-state defines as standard named languages and parental involvement, we can see holistically how parents and students actively engage in classrooms.

Shifting the narratives about families' roles in their children's schools and classrooms

The relationship between schools and families of language minoritized students has often been framed from a deficit perspective (see Chapter 6, this volume). Language-racialized parents are often accused of not being involved enough or not at all in their children's education: That is, they are accused of not attending parent–teacher conferences, school meetings, or taking on leadership positions at schools. Parents are also blamed for what is seen as not caring about academic matters (Olivos, Jiménez-Castellanos, & Ochoa, 2011). As a consequence of such a deficit view, to increase family involvement, schools focus on modifying parental behaviors to be more like those of educators. There is little consideration for the goals the parents have (Olivos, Jiménez-Castellanos, & Ochoa, 2011; Menken, 2017).

There is much research that seeks to disrupt the deficit lens toward language minoritized parents' involvement in their children's education. This research reshapes and redefines the meaning of "involvement" (Poza, Brooks, & Valdés, 2014). It acknowledges that families' relationships with educational institutions and educators are framed in a context of asymmetrical social and political relations (Shannon, 2011). Olivos, Jiménez-Castellanos, and Ochoa (2011) argue that the word "involvement" places the burden on the families for the "success" or "failure" of their children. Instead, they prefer the term "engagement," as the word implies a dynamic and collaborative process between parents and schools.

Families' roles and relationships with schools have multiple facets. Some of these are:

1. Families advocate for changes in school policies (Fabricant, 2010; Mediratta, Shah, & McAlister, 2009),
2. Families advocate and take on leadership roles at school level (Ascenzi-Moreno & Flores, 2012; Menken, 2017), and
3. Families collaborate with teachers within the instructional spaces of the classroom.

In relationship to parent advocacy for policy changes and parental leadership in schools, scholars have explored the role of community-based organizations as a bridge between schools and parents (Mediratta, Shah, & McAlister, 2009). Warren et al. (2009) provide examples of how Community-Based

Organizations (CBOs) act as liaisons between parents and schools. They found three common features that helped parents connect to schools in a meaningful way: An emphasis on relationship building among parents and between parents and educators; a focus on the leadership development of parents; and an effort to bridge the gap in culture and power between parents and educators. Other scholars have explored how, in the context education for bilingual students, distributed leadership in schools sets up the stage for parental leadership in shaping schools as educational communities (Ascenzi-Moreno & Flores, 2012; see also Chapter 5, this volume).

In examining the possibilities of families' partnerships with teachers, González, Moll, and Amanti (2005) conducted a collaborative project with teachers within working class Mexican communities in Tucson, Arizona. The main goal of the project was to develop innovations in teaching that drew from the knowledge of students' households. The project was based on the belief that when teachers draw on household knowledge, student experience is legitimated as valid, and classroom practice can build on familiar knowledge to enhance learning in mathematics, social studies, language arts, and other content areas. In their study, they used the concept of "funds of knowledge" to drive ethnographic work conducted by teachers in their students' households.

> Funds of knowledge are generated through the social and labor history of families and communicated to others through the activities that constitute household life, including through the formation of social networks that are central to any household functioning within its particular environments. From this perspective, the funds of knowledge represent one of the household's most useful cultural resources, an essential tool kit that households need to maintain (mediate) their well-being. (González, Moll, & Amanti, 2005, p. 19)

The teachers in the project established relationships of *confianza* (trust) with families to study what households actually do and how they think about what they do. In this way, they tried to understand how each household draws from multiple cultural systems and uses these systems as strategic resources.

This approach sees families and communities as resources that inform classroom practice. Funds of Knowledge is based on the idea that understanding the social, historical, political, and economic contexts of students' households and communities is of critical importance to understanding teaching and learning. Integrating the experiences of students and the lived practices of households is an important aspect of critical pedagogy. This approach requires flexibility from teachers in planning their curricula and their approaches to teaching.

García, Johnson & Seltzer (2017) describe an educator's stance that fosters collaboration between, children, families, communities, and educators using the term *Juntos* (together). The *Juntos* stance is informed by three beliefs of joint collaboration:

- Students' language practices and cultural understandings encompass those they bring from home and communities, as well as those they take up in schools. These practices and understandings work juntos and enrich each other.
- Students' families and communities are valuable sources of knowledge and must be involved in the education process juntos.
- The classroom is a democratic space where teachers and students juntos cocreate knowledge, challenge traditional hierarchies, and work toward a more just society (p. 50)

Although we believe that family advocacy and leadership in schools is essential to understand the key role that families can play, in this chapter we focus on families' partnerships and collaborations with teachers in *instructional spaces*. In the following sections, we visit three classrooms in which teachers use the *Juntos* stance to design instructional spaces in which family members, children, and teachers learn together, as they examine and build on their linguistic practices.

Learning with families: a social studies kindergarten unit

It is Friday morning and Ms. Flores' Spanish bilingual kindergarten classroom is bustling with energy. Children and family members are sitting around small tables. The children are in charge. They have pens and paper and are interviewing parents, grandparents, and other family members about their language practices at home. The children are full of questions: What language did you speak in school growing up? What languages do you speak now? One child is asking questions in Russian, another one is using Hebrew, many are speaking in Spanish. Most of them move fluidly between Spanish, English, and other languages such as Mixteco, Russian, and Hebrew. The children take notes using invented spelling and drawings. After the parents leave, Ms. Flores reflects: "Niko's mom is from Russia. I had never heard them talking in Russian together." Ms Flores had stopped by his table and suggested that his mom help him write some key words in Russian and that he could add some notes in Spanish or English to share with other children in the class.

This vignette captures an activity with parents in the context of a social studies inquiry unit in a Spanish dual language bilingual kindergarten class. The class started out with an essential question: "Why are families important?" The children worked on different activities related to that question and explored, among other things, "How do families communicate?" In this dual language bilingual program, there is usually a strict separation of languages. One day is in Spanish and the other is in English. However, for this unit, the teacher began by asking the children how their families use language. Most of the children described that in their homes they use both English and Spanish (or English and another language) depending on who they were speaking with. They also said they never had to think first of what language was "correct," since everything they said was valued. Many of the children remarked on the fact that they didn't have set times or ways of using language. Ms. Flores then explained to them that for this inquiry unit, they were going to use language the same way as they did with their families, and she introduced the word "translanguaging."

The family interview was the first activity that the class did together with the parents. The families also came to the classroom later on to share aspects of their family life, family culture, and stories. Ms. Flores welcomed families into her classrooms as "teachers" from whom the classroom community had much to learn. At the end of the unit, Ms. Flores reflected that this work would not have been possible without a full partnership with the families, and that this was a chance not just for the students to learn from the families, but for the families to learn from each other.

In having families participate in interviews, Ms. Flores leveraged the potential of asking questions to help develop oral language. In order for young children to develop their communicative practices and repertoires, it is essential that this development happen in authentic social interactions that welcome children's flexible use of language (Souto-Manning & Martell, 2016). The children used oral language to learn about their families' funds of knowledge. By asking family members questions, children construct meaning, make sense of their worlds, and build their family histories with their families. Throughout the interviews, the children learned not only about language in their families, but also about who they are—and who their classmates are—as historical, social, and cultural beings.

This was just a first step in working with parents to challenge the linguistic hierarchies of the bilingual program as it is set up. It gave children space to use language flexibly, and for those who speak languages other than Spanish and English, to bring in their language practices and share them with their peers.

Thinking about language: Parents analyzing poetry with children

Mr. T invited family members into the classroom to participate in a bilingual poetry analysis activity. When the parents arrived, he distributed poems from the book, *My Name is Jorge from Both Sides of the River* by Jane Medina. The book is a collection of bilingual poems written from the perspective of Jorge, a young boy who recently arrived in the United States from Mexico. In the book, the author uses language flexibly in some of the poems for a range of purposes (see also Chapters 8 and 11, and Teacher/Researcher Box 8.1, this volume).

Each family member was grouped with the children so they could read two poems from the book together and discuss how the author used English and Spanish. Parents and children shared their ideas with the whole class. Martin, a boy from el Salvador, explained, "He uses both languages because some words don't exist in English." One of the parents said, "He is using Spanglish."[1] Ana and her mom shared that "the author wants to show how families speak." Javier, another student, explained that the author is translanguaging.

In Mr. T's fourth grade class, the students had been learning about authors' use of translanguaging as a literary device. While the children were comfortable using the term in their analysis of texts, this was the first time that parents heard it. Mr. T paused and asked the students to help explain the concept of translanguaging. Next, he asked family members and students to think about when they use translanguaging in their daily lives and to collaborate in drawing a scene of one of those situations.

This bilingual poetry analysis activity is an example of how a teacher can partner with parents and students in thinking about their dynamic language practices at home through the collaborative analysis of bilingual poems. Mr. T reflected later that this was the beginning of having families partner with their children and with him in thinking about language practices. As he traveled around the class, listening to family members and children, he heard discussions in which the parents spoke about the author's use of "Spanglish." The children, however, introduced the concept of 'translanguaging' to their families, and they discussed how this was a practice in which they engaged at home. They talked about how the term "Spanglish" is often used to stigmatize their practices because they do not conform to monolingual ideologies of what is seen as grammatical correctness (Bucholtz, Castilla, & Sook Lee, 2017; Flores & Rosa, 2015). And they discussed how their bilingual are actually more complex and "correct" for their interactions than those that strictly conform to what is seen as one language or the other.

Examining an author's use of translanguaging provided an opportunity for families and children to participate in a discussion that disrupted the traditional understandings of language and of their own practices. Spanish speakers make up the bulk of language minoritized students in New York City. Spanish bilingual programs are often tied to the idea that they must teach the so called "standard" or "academic" forms of Spanish and English. Families are not exempt from this notion. Many of the parents come from linguistically racialized communities (Flores & Rosa, 2015) whose language practices have been stigmatized. Therefore, they have internalized the idea that their language practices do not belong in school. The notion of a standard form of language is a social construct that needs to be challenged. In creating a space in which children and families work together analyzing poems, Mr. T began a process of critical inquiry into language.

Whereas the children in Mr. T's fourth grade had participated in class discussions that explicitly addressed authors' languaging in connection to their own languaging, it was essential to Mr. T that parents were also engaged in this work. Using poetry as an entry point into this discussion helped to shift the focus from what are 'correct' forms of language to an embrace of the creativity of language. Teachers, parents, and children together need to be part of critical bilingual spaces in which they analyze and interrogate linguistic expectations in order to challenge oppressive ideologies of "language appropriateness" that further marginalize racially and linguistically minoritized communities (Flores & García, 2017; Flores & Rosa, 2015).

Family assessment in high school: Collaborating and reflection on learning

Michelle, an "English as a New Language" (ENL) teacher in a high school in the Bronx engages parents through assessment using a Family Assessment Tool developed by García, Johnson, & Seltzer (2017). This tool draws from the families' funds of knowledge, validating the resources that families bring.

By the time students reach high school, parents are not often part of the classroom life, either because they are not available, or because as part of the process of developing their independence and identity, high school students do not want their parents visiting their classroom often. Michelle's class is a standalone or self-contained "ENL" class consisting of 10th, 11th, and 12th graders who are emergent bilinguals. Michelle designed a unit in which students wrote their own stories and published them. Since her students' home language is Spanish, Michelle began the unit by introducing them to mentor texts that are relevant to their culture and language practices. The authors of two of the texts used translanguaging in their writing. Using the texts as a foundation, Michelle asked students to look for examples of translanguaging and the reasons why authors translanguage. These mentor texts served as a foundation for students to write their own stories.

Throughout the process, students were encouraged to use their full linguistic repertoire to plan, draft, and revise their stories. The prompt for the stories was to write about a struggle or a change in their lives. In the context of the classroom, Michelle built spaces for peer feedback in which students could move fluidly between different multimodalities—oral and written language, drawings, symbols—as well as what are considered two languages—English and Spanish. For example, the class agreed to use a set of symbols for their feedback: Smiles signified when a student liked a section of the writing, frowns an unhappy reaction, exclamation points signified surprise on behalf of the reader, question marks conveyed an area of confusion. This provided tools for the readers who were doing the peer review, so the writers could better decide how to revise the second draft.

For the final assignment of this project, Michelle had her students share their stories with their parents. Michelle used the "Family Assessment Tool" in the García, Johnson, and Seltzer book as a guide for the parents in assessing their children's assignments. She sent the assessment home in Spanish, since she knew that was the parents' home language.

The "Family Assessment" starts by providing a multimodal platform for parents to share their ideas: "Today your child showed you something he or she learned in school. Can you share what you learned about him/her by drawing, writing, and/or speaking with your son/daughter?" Some of the responses shared the parents' empathy for their children as they understood their struggles as newly arrived immigrants. For example, upon reading her daughter Monica's story about her move from Honduras to the United States, her relationship with her brother, and her struggles with learning English, her mom wrote about understanding her daughter's travails and the pride she feels: "Que mi hija ha pasado por mucho desde que ella llegó y me siento muy orgullosa." José wrote a story about a vacation to the Dominican Republic (the DR) during winter break after he had been living in the United States for about a year. He talked about how he missed being in the DR. He also explained that he feels bullied in the U.S. for not being a fluent English speaker. His mom wrote that from reading the story, she learned "que a mi hijo no le gusta vivir en NY; le gusta viajar a DR." The mom now understood that her son missed the Dominican Republic and had a hard time living in New York. Whereas most of the parents were probably aware of their children's feelings, reading the stories together and having a discussion as they filled out the assessment created a space to open up conversation.

Another question in the assessment asked parents, "In which language did your child speak to you? In English? Spanish? Both? What do you think of the language used by your child?" The parents described their children's fluid language practices: Monica's mom wrote, "En español, pero leyó el texto en English." Monica's mom acknowledges the fact that her daughter read in English, although she spoke to her in Spanish. This is a frequent linguistic interaction in immigrant homes in the U.S., with parents speaking the language of their home countries, and children interacting in English. Furthermore, Monica's mother's language demonstrates that parent-children bilingual interactions do not always follow the one language-one person principle, since she herself says:

"en English." That is, the interactions between mother and child go beyond the classical descriptions of parents speaking a home language and children speaking English, for it turns out that just like the child uses her entire linguistic repertoire, the mother does too.

When asked the same question of the language practices in their interactions, Jacelyn's mom said: "Mi hija me habló en los dos idiomas. Cuando no pudo decir la palabra en español, la tradujo en inglés, y opino que ella está aprendiendo muy bien." To her, her daughter's translanguaging is a sign of learning well [aprendiendo bien]. The fact that her daughter cannot say some words in Spanish and then uses English might be seen by the teacher as a lack, a shortcoming. However, to this mom, her daughter's translanguaging is a virtue, a knowledge of how to use her entire linguistic repertoire to communicate.

The stories that the students brought home to read to their parents were primarily in English with some translanguaging. The questions in the assessment provided a platform for parents not only to reflect on the content and language use of the story, but also to think and share their language practices as they engaged in discussion with their children. Whereas the stories gave parents and young people an opportunity to discuss their work, as well as some of their personal experiences, the parents wanted their children to deepen their learning, to have what Jacelyn's mom called "más aprendizaje." Some of them provided general feedback and others were more specific and detailed in their comments. For example, Amalia's mother wrote, "I think she needs more detail in the third paragraph." Overall, the family assessment provided an opportunity for parents, teachers, and students to be engaged together with the students' writing and languaging, as they all learned and taught.

Like Mr. T and Ms. Flores, Michelle's assessment provided a space for families to use all their language features without adhering to the standard of named languages (Otheguy, García, & Reid, 2015), as well as to leverage families' funds of knowledge to support their learning process. The Family Assessment Tool disrupts deficit ideologies regarding racialized families. It illuminates, acknowledges, and validates the resources that these families bring to the table by capitalizing on "the translanguaging corriente that connects students' homes and communities with the school, and they contribute to a more holistic view of the bilingual child" (García, Ibarra-Johnson, & Seltzer, 2017, p. 94).

Conclusion

In this chapter, we shared how parents, teachers and students generated shared learning spaces that brought to the surface the translanguaging corriente that is present in every classroom. Paris and Alim (2017) call for a *cultural sustaining pedagogy* that focuses on sustaining dynamic communities of practices. This is only possible when parents have an active role within the classroom communities. The relationship between families and schools is a reflection of a larger societal framework in which schools and classrooms have an inherent power imbalance (Olivos, 2006). It is up to leaders and teachers to shift this balance by opening up spaces for family leadership and partnerships. One of the most important, yet most devaluated resources available to racialized young people and their families is language (Bucholtz, Casillas & Sook Lee, 2017). The three teachers in this chapter worked from a *Juntos* stance, partnering with families by designing spaces in which families' languages practices were at the forefront of a joint collaboration. They recognized them as valuable sources of knowledge that can work hand in hand to cocreate knowledge and challenge traditional linguistic hierarchies.

Note

1 The term 'Spanglish' is often used to refer to the speech of Spanish speakers in the USA. However, this term has been used "with the clear implication that it is not Spanish, connecting, sadly, to an old North American tradition of denigrating immigrants from the Spanish-speaking world" (Otheguy & Stern, 2011, p. 97).

References

Ascenzi-Moreno, L., & Flores, N. (2012). A case study of bilingual policy and practices at the Cypress Hills Community School. In García, O., Octu, B., & Zakharia, Z. (Eds.), *Bilingual community education and multilingualism: Beyond heritage languages in a global city* (pp. 219–231). Bristol, UK: Multilingual Matters.

Bucholtz, M. Castilla, D.I. & Sook Lee, J. (2017). Language and culture sustenance. In Paris, D. H., & Alim, S. (Eds.), *Culturally sustaining pedagogies: Teaching and learning for justice in a changing world* (pp. 43-59). New York, NY: Teachers College Press.

Fabricant, M. (2010). *Organizing for educational justice: The campaign for public school reform in the South Bronx*. Minneapolis, MN: University of Minnesota Press.

Flores, N. & García, O. (2017). A Critical review of bilingual education in the United States: From basements and pride to boutiques and profit. *Annual Review of Applied Linguistics 37*, 14–29. https://doi.org/10.1017/S0267190517000162

Flores, N., & Rosa, J. (2015). Undoing appropriateness: Raciolinguistic ideologies and language diversity in education. *Harvard Educational Review, 85*(2), 149–171.

García, O., Johnson, S. I., Seltzer, K., & Valdés, G. (2017). *The translanguaging classroom: Leveraging student bilingualism for learning*. Philadelphia, PA: Caslon.

González, N., Moll, L. M., & Amanti, C. (Eds.) (2005). *Funds of knowledge: Theorizing practices in households, communities and classrooms*. Mahwah, NJ: Erlbaum Press.

Mediratta, K., Shah S., & McAlister, S. (2009) *Community organizing for stronger schools: Strategies and successes* (Vol. 8). Cambridge, MA: Harvard Education Press.

Menken, K (2017) Leadership in Dual Language Bilingual Education. A National Dual Language Forum White paper. Center for Applied Linguistics. Retrieved November 25, 2019 from http://www.cal.org/ndlf/pdfs/publications/NDLF-White-Paper-October-2017.pdf

Olivos, E. M. (2006). *The power of parents: A critical perspective of bicultural parent involvement in public schools.* New York, NY: Peter Lang.

Olivos, E., Jiménez-Castellanos, O., & Ochoa, A. (2011). *Bicultural parent engagement: Advocacy and empowerment.* New York, NY: Teachers College Press.

Otheguy, R., & Stern, N. (2011). On so-called Spanglish. *International Journal of Bilingualism, 15*(1), 85–100.

Otheguy, R., García, O., & Reid, W. (2015). Clarifying translanguaging and deconstructing named languages: A perspective from linguistics. *Applied Linguistics Review, 6*(3), 281–307. doi:10.1515/applirev-2015-0014

Paris, D. H., & Alim, S. (Eds.) (2017). *Culturally sustaining pedagogies: Teaching and learning for justice in a changing world.* New York, NY: Teachers College Press.

Poza, L., Brooks, M., & Valdés, G. (2014). Entre familia: Immigrant parents' strategies for involvement in children's schooling. *The School Community Journal, 24*(1), 119–148.

Shannon, S. (2011). Parents engagement and equity in a dual language program. In Olivos, E. M., Jiménez-Castellanos, O., & Ochoa, A. M. (Eds.), *Bicultural parent engagement: Advocacy and empowerment* (pp. 1–13). New York, NY: Teachers College Press.

Souto-Manning, M., & Martell, J. (2016). *Reading, writing, and talk: Inclusive teaching strategies for diverse learners, K-2.* New York, NY: Teachers College Press.

Warren, M., Hong, S., Rubin, C., & Uy, P. (2009). Beyond the bake sale: A community-based relational approach to parent engagement in schools. *Teachers College Record, 111*(9), 2209–2254.

BOX 15.1 TEACHER/RESEARCHER

Elizabeth Menéndez and Sabrina Poms

Kindergarten, dual language bilingual program

We teach in an Integrated Co-Teaching bilingual (English/Spanish) Kindergarten (ICT). In this classroom some students have Individualized Education Plans (IEPs) because they have been identified as having some disability, mostly "speech and language impairments." Elizabeth is certified as a bilingual elementary school teacher, whereas Sabrina is certified in special education and bilingual education. Together we plan the curriculum, teach the lessons, and support the learning needs of all the children in the classroom.

Most of the children come from Spanish-speaking homes, but all are language learners in some way. Around 40% have been classified as "English learners," whereas the others have different degrees of Spanish language proficiency. In six of our students' homes, languages other than English or Spanish are spoken: Nahúatl, German, Korean, Hindi, Hebrew, and Tagalog. In accordance with the school-wide dual language program, the language of the day in our classroom alternates between English and Spanish. The lessons are not repeated in each language, but instead progress in order each day.

In working with the CUNY-NYSIEB team, we started to think of how to leverage the translanguaging practices of our students. We decided to plan a *Family Unit*, where we could open up an intentional translanguaging space where students could use all of their language resources to investigate and learn about families.

New York City's Social Studies curriculum invites Kindergartners to investigate the essential question, "Why are families important?" Because inquiry and project-based learning are central pillars in our school, we have studied this question in a hands-on, multimodal way in years past. But this year, we made adaptations that incorporated a focus on language as well as opening up a translanguaging space.

We started the unit with a discussion around the many languages spoken by students' families, and how we all use language at home. In order to talk about families throughout the unit, the children needed a space to use all of their language practices to learn, regardless of the language of the day. This translanguaging space was made visual by a purple sign on the daily schedule, indicating that students could use all of their languages, whereas Spanish time is usually written in red and English in blue.

It's the third week of our inquiry unit on families, and we posed this question to our class of kindergartners: "What is something that your grandma or grandpa always says to you?" They chimed in with a variety of responses.

"Let's go to the library!"
"¿Quieres algo?"
"Du schafts das"
"Mi abuela no vive aquí. Mi abuela vive en México."
"Hola mi amor"
"I will buy you whatever you want"
"Estás creciendo"
"Te voy a contar un cuento"
"I love you"
"Do you want some ice cream?"
"Te quiero"
"Let's play songs"

Children had started putting their understanding of a translanguaging space into practice, as they used all their languages to think about and respond to the question.

The children were excited by the newfound choice they had during this "purple time." They could use all of the different resources available to them in the room whether in English or Spanish. For example, usually children use writing resources in accordance with the language of the day, but during inquiry time, they chose which alphabet charts and sight word lists they thought would best help them write about their families.

The translanguaging space gave us as teachers new freedoms as well. We planned learning experiences and chose books without being limited by the language of the day. Conversations around read aloud felt more natural, as we heard from students in either language. We even felt like we could display for our students how we normally communicate with each other, which is in both languages, depending on the context or content of our conversation.

Throughout the unit, children studied various aspects of families while working in centers on different family-related projects. The centers included a dramatic play area, family crests, wooden sculptures, picture collages, family quilt making, house glyphs and book research. We altered the unit to encourage students to use both or all languages and made specific changes to some of these centers to help our students take a closer look at their family's linguistic practices.

For the *Family Quilt Making Center*, we wanted to include student and family voices together with student artwork. In previous years, children painted portraits of a parent or sibling and then put them all together onto a quilt to display in the classroom. The project helped children celebrate different members of their families, while getting to know the families of their classmates, and recognizing that families look differently. This year, in order to focus more closely on how families use language, we paired the portraits with text from their families, and asked the students to focus their portraits specifically on a grandparent so that they would think critically about the language they use with them, which might differ from the language they speak with their parents or siblings. Each portrait was accompanied by a quote of something the grandparent says to the child or vice-versa. Children also labeled their painting with the names they use for their grandparent. Some of their responses were, "Abuelita," "Lola," "Bobo," and "Grandma Candy." Because of the variety of experiences and languages, we found success in working with students one-on-one to learn more about their grandparents. Previously establishing the rules of "purple time" gave students permission to talk and think about their grandparents in the language that they use with that person, not necessarily the language of the day.

In addition to the quotes from grandparents, we wanted to capture how language sounds in students' houses, so we included family messages of encouragement and commonly used phrases into the project. During one of the bi-monthly mornings with families, we asked the adults to talk about and write down some of their family dichos. We took these sayings and displayed them along the outside of the quilt. Conducting one-on-one interviews of students about their grandparents, and surveying families for their commonly used words helped us truly center student and family voices in this project and make students' full linguistic repertoires apparent.

As a part of the culmination of the unit, we facilitated a class share to look at our collective work and voices. Each student shared their quilt square and their grandparent's saying. The children recognized that although families communicate in different languages, many of the sayings had similar messages. When we read aloud the messages and dichos from their parents, some students proudly recognized the sayings and said, "My mom says that!" They noticed that all families show love through their words. The portraits and the accompanying words gave an intimate look into the language use of families in our classroom. An intentional translanguaging space made this reflective conversation possible, as the students and teachers alike used their dynamic bilingualism as a tool to understand how families use language.

Adopting translanguaging pedological practices benefited our students by:

- **Increasing metalinguistic awareness.** Students spoke explicitly about why they use language in certain ways in some contexts, such as with specific family members. All children began to understand themselves as language learners.
- **Acting as bilingual ethnographers.** When sharing completed projects, students practiced analyzing data like ethnographers. They looked across all of the projects to answer questions that addressed class-wide patterns. They used their bilingualism as a tool to investigate.
- **Embracing the similarities and differences of classmates and their families.** When looking at the quilt all together, many students discovered that their classmates spoke languages previously unknown to them. They were interested in learning about languages beyond the daily structured times. During dismissal, a student asked another, "What's the name of the language you speak at home?" She responded, "Tagalog." He said, "Oh, I think I've heard that language."
- **Fostering respect for bilingualism.** Many children were eager to claim their "new" language as a language spoken in their household, even if they don't use that language as a way to communicate at home.
- **Understanding the role of love in language.** Children explored some of the reasons why families use language. They noticed that the most common phrases repeated on the quilt were expressions of love. They also discussed how families can communicate with one another even if they speak different languages.

Transforming Teacher Education

16

TRANSFORMING URBAN TEACHER EDUCATION

The City University of New York

Cecilia M. Espinosa, Laura Ascenzi-Moreno,
Tatyana Kleyn, and Maite T. Sánchez

CUNY schools/programs

The City University of New York (CUNY) is the largest public urban university system in the United States with 24 campuses across the five boroughs of New York City and with approximately 274,000 students enrolled each year. Over 70% of CUNY students are Black, Latinx, or Asian, over one-third come from immigrant backgrounds, and many are the first in their families to attend college (CUNY, 2019). CUNY-NYSIEB (City University of New York-New York State Initiative on Emergent Bilinguals) brought together faculty from five senior colleges (Brooklyn College, City College, Hunter College, Lehman College, and Queens College) to serve as associate investigators in the project to collaboratively support schools, develop the thinking and the instructional material, conduct research, and work alongside doctoral students at The Graduate Center who served as Research Assistants. In so doing, the project also aimed to transform teacher education for emergent bilinguals by engaging faculty in the programs of Bilingual Education and Teaching English to Speakers of Other Languages (TESOL).

In this chapter, we discuss how transformative shifts in our own understanding of bilingualism, as a result of our participation in CUNY-NYSIEB, spurred changes in the teacher education programs at each of our respective institutions. Specifically, we discuss how through our work in CUNY-NYSIEB, we opened up spaces for the voices of emergent bilinguals to emerge. And we infused translanguaging theory and pedagogy across CUNY campuses. Each of the authors of this chapter represents a different senior college—Laura Ascenzi-Moreno (Brooklyn College), Tatyana Kleyn (The City College of New

York in Manhattan), Maite T. Sánchez (Hunter College in Manhattan), and Cecilia M. Espinosa (Lehman College in the Bronx). Prior to participating in CUNY-NYSIEB, there was little communication among the faculty working in Bilingual Education and TESOL at the different campuses. There was also very little interaction among bilingual scholars, doctoral students in bilingual education, teachers preparing to work with bilingual students (pre-service), as well as teachers already working with emergent bilinguals (in-service). Through our association with CUNY-NYSIEB, we had opportunities to develop new understandings about translanguaging, exchange ideas, and learn from each other. Thus, the collaboration that CUNY-NYSIEB established was not one way, flowing from The Graduate Center to the other campuses, but also ran horizontally among the teacher education programs that now had opportunities to dialogue intensively about the ways in which they were working with their teacher candidates.

Translanguaging tensions and touchpoints across fields

Although bilingual education and TESOL are two fields that serve a similar type of student—those who are considered to be developing English and are classified as "English language learners" —they have historically been distinct in their approaches. In most of the campuses, the TESOL and Bilingual Education Programs are administratively separated and housed in different departments and schools within the university. But CUNY-NYSIEB's collaborative structure made it possible for faculty from across both programs to come together (see Chapters 3 and 6, this volume). Juntos/together we started developing understandings of how a translanguaging approach went beyond the English-only approach of traditional TESOL programs and the English-only and Language-other-than English-Only of traditional bilingual education programs. Translanguaging theory focused on the ways in which these emergent bilinguals used language in ways that were similar, and how the traditional pedagogical approaches did not always meet their needs (García, 2011, 2014).

Students' translanguaging in any of these programs had always been evident to all of us, but because these fields were focusing on "models," "programs," "curriculum," and "pedagogy," its presence as a pedagogical resource and asset for learning had been denied. TESOL has traditionally been a field grounded in the English language, as its name implies. The thinking has been that students' home language practices would get in the way of learning English, rather than serve as a support and extension to their linguistic repertoires (García, 2014). And although bilingual education programs have supported bilingualism, the structures and pedagogical practices that have been put into effect are often ways to remediate perceived language deficits and even the bilingual practices of students (García, 2011). As bilingual education lost political ground in the 2000s, dual language bilingual programs, designed to also serve English-speaking mono-lingual students grew in interest. These programs were modeled after Canadian immersion and held a monoglossic view of bilingualism that supported strict separation of languages as one of the core principles of the program (Cloud, Genesee & Hamayan, 2000; Howard et al., 2018; Lindholm-Leary, 2005). This resulted in a move away from the bilingual practices of minoritized communities and toward the commodification of bilingualism for language majority, mostly white, students (Cervantes-Soon, 2014; Valdés, 1997).

In our work, we have found the TESOL profession more open to trans-languaging and to moving in a multilingual direction (García, 2014, Kleyn & García, 2019). Teachers understand that opening up a space for translanguaging assists students in making meaning of the English language lesson. However, teachers and administrators in dual language bilingual programs are finding the concept of translanguaging more challenging. Some feel that opening up a space for translanguaging would work against the bilingualism that they are trying to promote, as English would creep into the space that is reserved for the use of the minoritized language. Therefore, in a somewhat ironic turn, the fields have inverted their position in their openness or closed approaches to translanguaging.

As CUNY faculty in teacher education programs we have taken steps to unpack the political origins of bilingual education and its community grounding against linguistic and racial oppression (Flores & García, 2017; García & Sung, 2018). As we educate our future teachers of emergent bilinguals, we take care not to fall into any form of language policing, while also ensuring that minor-itized students' bilingual practices are acknowledged and viewed as an important resource for learning and teaching.

Transforming faculty ideologies and programming

Our work with CUNY NYSIEB, and in particular the work with translanguag-ing theory and pedagogies, has had a significant impact on our thinking as teacher educators of bilingual students. We have been faced with a paradigm shift toward notions of language. It has challenged us to rethink our understandings about bilingualism, TESOL, and bilingual education, including dual language bilin-gual education. The work in CUNY-NYSIEB has helped us recognize the limi-tations of holding a view of the students' bilingualism/multilingualism as rigid and separate, rather than as dynamic and whole. Our work with translanguaging has challenged us to begin with the practices of the speaker, our students, rather than with a more traditional view of named languages as separate entities. The direct work we have done with teachers as they plan instruction to incorporate translanguaging, the multiple discussions with the CUNY-NYSIEB team, and the publications that resulted from that work have helped us to understand the importance of carefully planning for translanguaging. This work has enabled us

to challenge not only the monoglossic views of monolingual English-only programs, but also of the bilingualism that prevail in dual language bilingual programs and that make invisible the practices of bilingual children from language
minoritized families (see, for example, for dual language bilingual education
programs, Sánchez, García & Solorza, 2017; Solorza et al., 2019).

García and Li Wei (2018) write:

> Bi/multilinguals have a more extended semiotic repertoire (they have
> more linguistic features and more multimodal features) and, metaphori-
> cally speaking, they live their lives in borderlands (Anzaldúa, 1987) that
> do not neatly correspond to two different worlds each with its assigned
> named languages. They are therefore often criticized because their use of
> language is simply different from an imagined and idealized monolingual
> norm. (p. 2)

These theoretical and practical understandings about translanguaging have
helped us see that it matters that as teacher educators we leverage and capitalize
on our students' linguistic repertoires. Our task is then to help all our teacher
candidates and in-service teachers to develop the knowledge to be able to do so
in their classrooms. As García and Kleyn (2016) argue in their edited book highlighting some of the work of CUNY-NYSIEB, translanguaging "legitimizes all
the language features of individual speakers that are important for communication and for identity" (p. 187). Our work with CUNY NYSIEB has forced us
to unsettle 20th century conceptions of languages and has defied us to position
our students' multilingualism as the norm, rather than continue to minoritize
their linguistic practices.

In addition, the work of CUNY-NYSIEB has challenged us to re-envision our
own practices as teacher educators as we implement our always evolving understandings about translanguaging. To fully construct meaning, bilinguals need to
capitalize on their entire linguistic repertoire. In each one of our respective programs we have not only integrated readings about translanguaging and dynamic
bilingualism, but we also include in our framework's readings on raciolinguistic
ideologies (de los Ríos & Seltzer, 2017; Flores & Rosa, 2015; Vigouroux, 2017),
the myth of the language gap (García & Otheguy, 2017; Johnson, 2015), funds of
knowledge (González, Moll & Amanti, 2005; Moll, Amanti, Neff & González,
1992), and culturally sustaining pedagogies (Paris, 2017).

Our commitment is to strive to ensure that through translanguaging we
help transform spaces for our students' bilingualism/multilingualism to be seen
from a perspective of strength at each CUNY college. We understand that to
truly engage in undoing the linguistic oppression (Flores & Rosa, 2015) that a
large number of our teacher candidates experience, the transformative work that
translanguaging proposes cannot be limited to our respective teacher education

programs. In bilingual education and TESOL programs we can ensure some consistency among required readings and experiences/activities that focus on reflections about translanguaging in theory and practice. We have also brought understandings of translanguaging to teacher education programs in early childhood, elementary and secondary education, and special education. Thus, our understandings of language and translanguaging have also impacted the more "mainstream" teacher education programs, as well as our other colleagues.

In our programs to prepare teachers for bilingual education and TESOL, our candidates write and reflect on their own languaging journeys. They also critically engage in studying the language ecologies (García & Menken, 2015) of their campuses, schools, neighborhoods and classrooms. They write lesson plans that include spaces for translanguaging. They are offered opportunities to engage in their own translanguaging practices as college students, not only as readers, writers, speakers, and listeners, but also including other multimodalities such as singing, acting, drawing, etc.

As we reflect on our journeys, we note that the impact of translanguaging is more consistently enacted within our own bilingual and TESOL programs. At each college all of our courses integrate theory and pedagogy about translanguaging. We later give a few specific illustrative examples of how translanguaging is integrated in our programs and beyond our programs. Yet, we understand that the work with translanguaging cannot be relegated solely to candidates pursuing their bilingual or TESOL certification or to those who are going to work with emergent bilingual students. All teachers working with multilingual students today need to be knowledgeable about bilingualism and translanguaging. This new stance toward bilingualism and multilingualism is helping us to radically change how our bilingual and TESOL candidates conceive their languaging practices, as we seek to impact the other teacher preparation programs within our respective campuses.

Transforming student voice

All of our institutions strive to be responsive to the needs of students in multifaceted ways. This goal of being responsive to students corresponds to one of the main tenets of the CUNY-NYSIEB project—to draw upon students' resources and then shape curriculum and programming which honors these resources. Given that translanguaging centers the practices of bilingual individuals, at some of the college students are introduced to the *descriptive review process* (Carini, 2000). Its aim is to help candidates become keen observers of emergent bilingual children and their bilingual lives, while learning to address their needs as a starting point for translanguaging.

In the following examples we show how the principle of capitalizing on students' linguistic and socio-cultural resources unfolds at the higher education level. At each of the colleges, we delve into understanding the linguistic backgrounds of our students, since the population is changing rapidly from one that had been mostly Spanish-English bilingual to one that is much more linguistically heterogeneous. For example, at one of our colleges, students had been mostly Latinx and Spanish-speaking, but other languages are emerging, especially Bengali, Kru, and Albanian. We have started to look for opportunities to capitalize on these by creating spaces for all teacher candidates to critically examine and experience what is possible when their and their students' languaging practices become visible and palpable.

In each of our courses, students are given the opportunity to reflect on their language journeys, as well as that of other multilingual people that they know. Through these reflections, students identify how they live out their bilingualism, as well as how it is viewed by others and/or themselves. These reflections on their personal journey sit alongside new content such as translanguaging theory. These opportunities provide pre-service and in-service teachers with a way of developing a translanguaging stance and of integrating these new understandings into their pedagogical practices. For example, one teacher candidate who was pursuing certification explained:

> I want to continue being a bilingual teacher because it's so powerful. The kids and the families are able to communicate with the teacher in whichever language they feel most comfortable in. The students are able to express themselves fully and not feel restricted. (Collins, Sánchez & España, 2019, p. 13)

These reflections also provide an opportunity for advocacy across bilingual programs in other languages. For example, in one class titled, "Biliteracy and Content Instruction," teachers research and write a paper about literacy instruction in their "home" language and present it to their peers. From this assignment, teachers start to understand the ways in which literacy takes place within particular socio-cultural communities; in other words, they develop a view of literacy as a social practice (Street, 1984, 2017). A translanguaging stance challenges our teacher candidates to add a view of literacies and multilingualism as these exist in the world, as the norm. In so doing, they forge respect and a deep sense of value for the diverse language communities across the city.

Students' voices also provide a means to understand the challenges they encounter in the field and the ways in which they are faced. For example, a student wrote in a mid-semester reflection,

> I learned about the meaning behind the Funds of Knowledge and the theoretical philosophies as to how we, multilingual individuals, acquire language. I learned the importance of nurturing the home language in

order to help students learn in the new language. This contradicts some philosophies that DOE (Department of Education) schools adhere to, but it is important for educators to understand how they can find ways and strategies to bypass such school philosophies so that we are meeting the students where they are, rather than setting them up for failure.

At each of the colleges, students in the program related that they were met with opposition when they brought translanguaging to their schools. Some were met with the message that "we don't do translanguaging here." This was especially the case in dual language bilingual programs, where language separation was "the law of the land." A strategy we used to subvert this directive was by adding "Translanguaging Spaces" to the program's lesson plan format. Candidates were then required to tell their schools this was a program requirement for their certification and thereby were able to at least try out translanguaging in their instruction. In addition, one of the assignments in a course at one of the colleges asks candidates to design a professional development activity on translanguaging that they could implement in their schools (although the presentation is at their college and not their school) and to give specific ideas on how translanguaging can be implemented in dual language bilingual programs. Before they design this activity, they engage in reading Sánchez, García & Solorza (2018). This assignment ensures that teacher candidates have a clear understanding of translanguaging, as well as the language allocation policies that schools follow, so that they are fully informed if they are challenged in their schools. However, all these ideas are only a short-term fix to the larger issue of the language policies followed in schools. The rigid separation of languages in dual language bilingual programs is still an uphill battle and we are keenly aware that we need to continue to look for ways to support our candidates develop strong arguments about the value of translanguaging.

These stories speak to the larger tension felt at all of the CUNY colleges between ensuring teachers can think critically about teaching, and the policies and practices in New York City schools. Our work with CUNY-NYSIEB has supported us as teacher educators in transforming our stance toward translanguaging, as well as developing translanguaging pedagogical practices. We have been able to envision new possibilities to respond to our students' flexible and dynamic languaging practices, as well as help them re-envision their pedagogies with children and adolescents.

Translanguaging as pedagogy and practice across CUNY

Our participation as associate investigators in CUNY-NYSIEB has led to a focus on translanguaging across courses that prepare bilingual, TESOL, and general education teachers at our CUNY colleges. We have developed a strong translanguaging stance, while working with schools to try out and examine the pedagogical possibilities translanguaging offers. Many of our teacher education instructors are either doctoral students who worked in the project or teachers involved in the project. We have taken an approach of not offering translanguaging as a stand-alone course, but of embedding it throughout our programs. This invites our teacher candidates to envision translanguaging as the norm.

We are taking initial steps to work across programs. Many of us have been asked to present at faculty meetings with college-wide faculty about the meaning of translanguaging. Individual colleagues have asked for assistance. For example, a professor of elementary education approached one of us to help her think about working with emergent bilinguals in general education settings. The instructor then took it upon herself to learn about translanguaging and now consistently incorporates it into her courses. While she is one faculty of many, it shows that with dialogue and collaboration, translanguaging does not have to be relegated to specific programs.

Faculty from across the university participate in a year-long seminar on Writing Across the Curriculum (WAC) at one of our colleges. The seminar now has a session that focuses on translanguaging and writing. In this WAC session faculty are asked to read and respond orally and in writing to readings about translanguaging theory and practice. They are also asked to share a recollection of a time when they capitalized on their entire linguistic repertoire in order to construct meaning. At the end of the session, faculty share implications for their own practice with regards to translanguaging. This session generates a fascinating dialogue, not free of tensions, among professors from different fields.

In a general teacher education course, teacher candidates are invited to construct deeper meanings by taking notes in their home language or bilingually as they read about an educational theorist (i.e., Piaget, Vygotsky, Montessori, etc.). As the teacher candidates examine their own language practices, they share on voice thread a song/chant from their background using their home language practices. This experience helps everyone in the class become witness to the rich diversity of languaging practices that are present; it also disrupts official language practices that silence some, while privileging others.

The children's literature section at one of the college libraries has been greatly enhanced by the addition of books that reflect the socio-cultural and linguistic backgrounds of the students. This was the result of a grant written with translanguaging in mind. The new collection of children's literature highlights how bilingual authors translanguage in ways that mirror the candidates' and their students' linguistic communities. This knowledge of children's literature helps teacher candidates and practicing teachers develop a critical eye when selecting children's books for their own classrooms (Espinosa & Lehner-Quam, 2019).

The project "Literacies and Computer Science (PiLaCS)," which emerged from CUNY-NYSIEB work, and is funded by the National Science Foundation, has influenced the content of the class "Mathematics, Science and Technology for Emergent Bilinguals." This class exposes students to ways in which emergent bilingual students can capitalize on their linguistic and semiotic resources as they engage with technology to enhance their learning.

These are examples, among many others, that illustrate what is happening at different CUNY campuses as a result of the faculty participation in CUNY-NYSIEB. As we stated earlier, in spite of a consistent focus on translanguaging, many teacher candidates face opposition when they are asked to take translanguaging into PreK-12 schools. As we described, this is especially true for dual language bilingual programs. This tension has continued to push faculty to consider ways to think through how they can open in more systematic ways small and larger spaces within these schools. Our aim is to continue to advocate for a stance that acknowledges, nurtures and sustains all students' languaging practices (Sánchez, García & Solorza, 2018).

Moving forward

The bringing together of faculty from different CUNY colleges was critical at a time when understandings about bilingualism, TESOL and bilingual education were shifting. Translanguaging challenged long held notions about how languages are learned. CUNY-NYSIEB offered faculty a rare space to come together to think, to reimagine, to develop ideas and to create materials (see Chapter 7, this volume), while also working alongside teachers and principals in schools. The transformation of our bilingual and TESOL teacher education is not only reflected in the addition of new content, but also in our own understanding about bilingualism. Today our teacher education programs focus on students' languaging within schools and society, rather than solely preparing educators to formulate discrete strategies to acquire language. We are educating teachers to create learning environments and instructional practices where emergent bilinguals' authentic languaging is an integral part of their learning and is viewed as the norm, while simultaneously addressing and challenging power relationships which do not allow emergent bilinguals to thrive in educational settings (Ascenzi-Moreno & Espinosa, 2018). As we move forward, we continue to examine the tensions that arise, in particular those that have to do with assessment of emergent bilinguals that truly take into consideration their full linguistic repertoire capacities (Ascenzi-Moreno, 2018; Chapter 13, this volume). We also grapple with how translanguaging pedagogy can be successfully applied in dual language bilingual programs that continue to insist on language separation. The solid foundation that CUNY-NYSIEB has imprinted on each of us continues to move us forward and to center emergent bilingual students' languaging practices.

References

Anzaldúa, G. (1987). *Borderlands/la frontera: The new mestiza*. San Francisco, CA: Aunt Lute Books.

Ascenzi-Moreno, L. (2018). Translanguaging and responsive assessment adaptations: Emergent bilingual readers through the lens of possibility. *Language Arts*, *95*(6), 355–369.

Ascenzi-Moreno, L. & Espinosa, C. (2018). Opening up spaces for their whole selves: A case study group's exploration of translanguaging practices in writing. *NYS TESOL Journal*, *5*(1), 10–29. http://journal.nystesol.org/january2018/3Ascenzi-Moreno.pdf

Carini, P.F. (2000). Prospect's descriptive processes. In M. Himley (with P. Carini) (Ed.), *From another angle: Children's strengths and school standards* (pp. 8–20). New York, NY: Teachers College Press.

Cervantes-Soon, C.G. (2014). A critical look at dual language immersion in the new Latin@ diaspora. *Bilingual Research Journal*, *37*(1), 64–82. https://doi.org/10.1080/15235882.2014.893267

Cloud, N. Genesee, F., & Hamayan, E. (2000). *Dual language instruction. A handbook for enriched education*. Boston, MA: Heinle ELT.

Collins, B.A., Sánchez, M.T., & España, C. (2019). Sustaining and developing teachers' dynamic bilingualism in a re-designed bilingual teacher preparation program. *International Journal of Bilingual Educational and Bilingualism*. https://doi.org/10.1080/13670050.2019.1610354

CUNY. (2019). A profile of undergraduates at CUNY senior and community colleges: Fall 2018. https://www.cuny.edu/wp-content/uploads/sites/4/page-assets/about/administration/offices/oira/institutional/data/current-student-data-book-by-subject/ug_student_profile_f18-1.pdf

de los Ríos, C. & Seltzer, K. (2017). Translanguaging, coloniality, and English classrooms: An exploration of two bicoastal urban classrooms. *Research in the Teaching of English*, (52), 55–76.

Espinosa, C. & Lehner-Quam, A. (2019). Sustaining bilingualism: Multimodal arts experiences for young readers and writers. *Language Arts*, *96*(4), 265–268.

Flores, N. & García, O. (2017). A critical review of bilingual education in the United States: From basements and pride to boutiques and profit. *Annual Review of Applied Linguistics*, *37*, 14–29. https://doi.org/10.1017/S0267190517000162

Flores, J. & Rosa, J. (2015). Undoing appropriateness: Raciolinguistic ideologies and language diversity in education. *Harvard Educational Review*, *85*(2), 149–175. https://pdfs.semanticscholar.org/b22a/80e988ef6f37a22f7b1776368efb4e94792d.pdf

García, O. (2011). From language garden to sustainable languaging: Bilingual education in a global world. *Perspective. A publication of the National Association for Bilingual Education*, Sept/Oct 2011, 5–10. https://ofeliagarciadotorg.files.wordpress.com/2011/02/2012nabenewsletter_34n1_nov2011_dec2011.pdf

García, O. (2014). TESOL translanguaged in NYS: Alternative perspectives. *NYS TESOL Journal*, *1*(1), 2–10. https://ofeliagarciadotorg.files.wordpress.com/2014/01/tesol-translanguaged.pdf.

García, O. & Kleyn, T. (Eds.). (2016). *Translanguaging with multilingual students: Learning from classroom moments*. New York, NY: Wiley-Blackwell/Routledge.

García, O. & Li, W. (2018). *Translanguaging: Language, bilingualism and education*. London, UK: Palgrave Macmillan Pivot.

García, O. & Menken, K. (2015). Cultivating an ecology of multilingualism in schools. In B. Spolsky, O. Inbar-Lourie, & M. Tannenbaum (Eds.), *Challenges for language education and policy: Making space for people* (pp. 95–108). New York, NY: Wiley-Blackwell/Routledge.

García, O. & Otheguy, R. (2017). Interrogating the language gap of young bilingual and bidialectal students. *International Multilingual Research Journal, 11*(1), 52–65. https://doi.org/10.1080/19313152.2016.1258190

García, O. & Sung, K.K-F. (2018). Critically assessing the 1968 Bilingual Education Act at 50 years: Taming tongues and Latinx communities. *The Bilingual Review Journal, 4*(4), 318-333. https://doi.org/10.1080/15235882.2018.1529642

González, N., Moll, L., & Amanti, C. (Eds.). (2005). *Funds of knowledge: Theorizing practices in households, communities and classrooms.* Mahwah, NJ: Erlbaum.

Howard, E.R., Lindholm-Leary, K.J., Rogers, D., Olague, N., Medina, J., Kennedy, B., Sugarman, J., & Christian, D. (2018). *Guiding principles for dual language education* (3rd ed.). Washington, DC: Center for Applied Linguistics. https://www.csuchico.edu/cbms/_assets/documents/guiding-principles-for-dual-language-education-3rd-edition-rev.pdf

Johnson, E. (2015). Debunking the "language gap." *Journal for Multicultural Education, 9*(1), 42–50. https://doi.org/10.1108/JME-12-2014-0044

Kleyn, T. & García, O. (2019). Translanguaging as an act of transformation: Restructuring teaching and learning for emergent bilinguals. In. Luciana de Oliveira (Ed.), *The handbook of TESOL in K-12* (pp. 69–82). New York, NY: Wiley-Blackwell/Routledge.

Lindholm-Leary, K. (2005). *Review of research and best practices on effective features of dual language education programs.* Center for Applied Linguistics and the National Clearinghouse for English Language Acquisition at The George Washington University. https://www.researchgate.net/publication/240623592_Review_of_Research_and_Best_Practices_on_Effective_Features_of_Dual_Language_Education_Programs

Moll, L.C., Amanti, C., Neff, D., & Gonzalez, N. (1992). Funds of knowledge for teaching: Using a qualitative approach to connect homes and classrooms. *Theory into Practice, 31*(2), 132–141. https://doi.org/10.1080/00405849209543534

Paris, D. (2017). *Culturally sustaining pedagogies: Teaching and learning for justice in a changing world.* New York, NY: Teachers College Press.

Sánchez, M., García, O., and Solorza, C. (2018). Reframing language allocation policy in dual language bilingual education. *Bilingual Research Journal.* 41. 1–15. 10.1080/15235882.2017.1405098.

Solorza, C.R., Aponte, G.Y., Leverenz, T., Becker, T., & Frias, B. (2019). *Translanguaging in dual language bilingual education: A blueprint for planning units of study.* New York, NY: The Graduate Center, CUNY & CUNY-NYSIEB. https://www.cuny-nysieb.org/wp-content/uploads/2019/09/Translanguaging-in-Dual-Language-Bilingual-Education-A-Blueprint-for-Planning-Units-of-Study-RSVD.pdf

Street, B. (1984). *Literacy in theory and practice.* Cambridge: Cambridge University Press.

Street, B. (2017). Learning to read from a social practice view: Ethnography, schooling and adult learning. *Prospects, 46,* 335–344. https://doi.org/10.1007/s11125-017-9411-z

Valdés, G. (1997). Dual-language immersion programs: A cautionary note concerning the education of language minority students. *Harvard Educational Review, 67,* 391–429. https://doi.org/10.17763/haer.67.3.n5q175qp86120948

Vigouroux, C. (2017). The discursive pathway of two centuries of raciolinguistic stereotyping: 'Africans as incapable of speaking French.' *Language in Society, 46,* 5–21. https://doi.org/10.1017/S0047404516000804

BOX 16.1 TEACHER/RESEARCHER

Olivia Mulcahy

0000-0001-5702-6859

Education Specialist, Illinois Resource Center, Chicago

Translanguaging became an integral part of my professional development work years ago when a district asked some colleagues and me to help generate bilingual standards-based exemplar units. It seemed the original idea was to create units in English that were deliberately attentive to English learners, and similarly themed, equally thoughtful units for instruction in Spanish. As we clarified the task, I became concerned that in a large district with over 100 languages spoken, this approach would yield units that would be useful only in specific instances in certain bilingual classrooms. I also became very aware that the undertaking we were considering was not really to generate "bilingual units" but rather, pairs of comparable monolingual units in two languages.

The challenge became how to create units that could be used flexibly to serve bilingual *students* in *any* of the programs in which they might find themselves placed. I wanted the work to be useful for teachers of any language background, serving students of any language community, in any variation of the available dual language bilingual education, ESL, or general education programs. I wanted to create tools to help teachers affirm and be responsive to "bilingual*ness*" in their curriculum, and to create exemplars that would help reveal what it looks like when bilingual perspectives are baked into the design decisions of a unit.

At this point, a big part of the challenge became more obvious: How could we create standards-based bilingual units when all of the standards were monolingually oriented? Though we could transadapt content standards intended for instruction in English to languages other than English, and though we had language development standards in both English and Spanish, using these standards side by side to guide the curriculum would still mirror a conceptualization of bilingualism as a set of parallel monolingualisms. We had no standards to work with that were intrinsically *bilingual*.

So we asked teachers: What are the unique skills and understandings that bilingual students can develop that other students do not necessarily have the opportunity, pressure, or need to develop? What are the awarenesses and knowledge that bilingual students have that are typically ignored, undervalued, or misunderstood in the existing curriculum? What are the unique *expectations* we have for bilingual students that do not necessarily apply to other students?

We gathered and sorted the responses together in a huge affinity mapping process. We discussed, clarified, debated, noticed trends, explored perspectives, and eventually identified what we agreed reflected our expectations for bilingual students. Translanguaging, along with multilingual, multicultural and sociolinguistic awareness, and the expansion of the repertoire were identified as expectations. I eventually named these expectations "Learning In-between Languages And Cultures," or LILAC for short, and this is what we used in lieu of any formal bilingual standards (for what are standards, but expectations?) to guide our unit planning, and to keep it grounded in bilingual*ness.*

The LILAC schema reflects a combination of what the teachers thought was uniquely important for bilingual students in the curriculum, acknowledging both the expectation to navigate and study language as a discipline (an externally named system) and protecting space to engage in what I learned to call bilingual ways of knowing and the natural language practices of the students (taking the perspective of the *users* of language). As I have continued to refine the idea of LILAC, I've found it has served as an invitation for teachers to recognize the translanguaging corriente all around them, make connections with their bilingual students, and see the implications for teaching. Naming the expectations and literally making space for these at the standards level on the unit templates helped teachers to claim space in the design process to be deliberately thoughtful about bilingual ways of knowing and to anticipate the kinds of shifts this implied for practice. For many teachers, the shifts were not exactly new—they had been instinctively using translanguaging with their students as part of their practice, for example in the form of an impromptu mini-lesson, or a sidebar conversation, but often feeling that this had to be informal, or even un acto clandestino, because it represented a deviation from the established language allocation. What was new was having these practices and this understanding of bilingual*ness* overtly validated in the written curriculum.

I began to see how translanguaging could be integrated throughout my work. In an ongoing "Biliteracy Saturday" series with a local high school district, we got teachers from the newly formed School for Biliteracy together with colleagues from across the rest of the district to investigate how each and any of them could have a role in creating a multilingual ecology and supporting students' bilingualism. Teachers who identified as monolingual English speakers and those who spoke languages different from those of their students, along with teachers directly involved in the School for Biliteracy, all explored their pivotal encuentros with languages through storytelling and poetry. As we debriefed the work, we realized the deep worth of exploring identity, our own lenses, and our lived experiences (often considered extraneous to the curriculum), and how this, for bilingual people or when exploring bilingual moments, was fairly impossible to do without translanguaging. We later expanded this work through community writing with students, families, and teachers together and further recognized the potential of conversation about and practice of translanguaging to begin to dissolve some of the boundaries that divide our school communities.

Similar reflections emerged in another school where I helped the faculty undertake a study of translanguaging as a way to open up professional dialogue across the several programs in their building. Teachers undertook self-guided exploration of online resources (like the CUNY-NYSIEB website), observed translanguaging in their community, and reflected on the implications for practice. The school's bilingual coordinator facilitated discussion to complement this work with teachers and simultaneously engaged parents from the school's many language communities in reading and analyzing translanguaging in picture books. In this case, investigating translanguaging catalyzed connections across groups, and created fertile ground for a more coherent vision around the school as a multilingual ecology.

I have found that the translanguaging conversation allows us to use language as an entry point to talk about all of these things that are so interconnected and fundamental to teaching and learning and human be*ing* (as a verb, to borrow the idea from Carla Shalaby). The translanguaging stance embraces the same fundamental principles that I value as an educator.

To open up dialogue about translanguaging and help teachers to create spaces for translanguaging in their classrooms I have a growing collection of infographics that can be found on my blog site: https://claimed.blog/infographics/infographics-translanguaging/[claimed.blog]. I also can be followed on my Twitter account @MaestraOlivia

17

DIFFERENT PLACES, DIFFERENT ISSUES

Teacher education reimagined through the CUNY-NYSIEB experience

Heather Woodley, María Cioè-Peña, Sarah Hesson, and Cristian R. Solorza

Introduction

The four authors of this piece started working with CUNY-NYSIEB (City University of New York-New York State Initiative on Emergent Bilinguals) when they were doctoral students at The Graduate Center of The City University of New York. Since then, we have become faculty members in different institutions and in different locations. Solorza and Woodley are faculty in teacher education programs in New York City in two different private universities. Cioè-Peña is in a public university in neighboring New Jersey. Finally, Hesson is faculty at a public college in Rhode Island. In this chapter, we explore four teacher education spaces where the work of CUNY-NYSIEB has uniquely shaped our experiences and that of our students. In each of these contexts, CUNY-NYSIEB and translanguaging pedagogies have been used to reimagine aspects of learning and teaching to serve the needs of specific learners and their teachers.

Because each of the institutions faces different challenges, we describe below how we have built on what we learned about translanguaging in the CUNY-NYSIEB project to address different issues that emerged from different local contexts. Cioè-Peña looks at how she uses the lessons she learned in CUNY-NYSIEB to work with mostly White teacher candidates who will be teaching racialized bilingual students, especially in special education programs. Solorza addresses how he uses translanguaging theory to reimagine language policies and structures of dual language bilingual education (DLBE) programs in the city. In a major private university, Woodley engages translanguaging in the education of many of her international TESOL teacher candidates. Hesson turns her attention to ensuring that teacher education in Rhode Island assumes a social justice vision facilitated through a translanguaging lens. A focus on educational equity through the use of translanguaging pedagogies defines our work across varied contexts and diverse student populations.

Because our work is now produced in different spaces, we write in our own individual voices, echoing and yet going beyond the voices we heard as part of the CUNY-NYSIEB team. These are our individual journeys following, negotiating, and yet expanding the path that we entered when we joined CUNY-NYSIEB.

Reimagining places, spaces, and possibilities: Cioè-Peña and teaching students with disabilities

As an adjunct instructor in the CUNY system while I was studying for my doctorate, I, María Cioè-Peña, worked with racially and linguistically diverse teaching candidates who were preparing to work with, and in, multilingual communities. As such, the opportunities to inject my work with translanguaging were more apparent.

When I started as assistant professor in a public university in Northern New Jersey, Montclair State University, I found myself working with students who in many ways represented the polar opposite of my CUNY students: Mostly White, suburban and monolingual. Additionally, these teaching candidates were primarily preparing to work in special education settings where they would be tasked with responding to needs rooted in disability labels. As a result, the translanguaging stance and the space for translanguaging became less visible and I was left wondering where and how translanguaging would fit now—not just in these students' teaching and learning experiences but also in my own practice and research.

It was not the prospective teachers' identity markers that created this tension but rather the spaces in which they would work and types of learners that they would teach. When White, monolingual teachers in NYC would ask about where and how translanguaging spaces would fit in their practice, my response was centered on the needs of the children: Translanguaging is not just about making space for language, it is about making space for children (Cioè-Peña, 2015). Thus, a translanguaging approach fits alongside our desires for equity and justice for students and their families (Cioè-Peña & Snell, 2015). After some reflection, I realized that geography did not alter the trueness of those ideas and values. It was this understanding of the political nature of translanguaging that allowed me to reimagine how to incorporate it into my practice (Flores, 2014; Kleyn & García, 2019).

While it would have been easier to lean on the fact that emergent multilingual students can be found in almost every school, it is not the perceived pathology, categorization or assumed needs for remediation of a child that should drive the use of translanguaging. Instead, we should call on the understanding that when we allow children to use their full linguistic repertoire, we allow children to present us with their fullest selves. Armed with this belief, I have been able to use the rich resources that CUNY-NYSIEB developed in order to help teachers uncover the place for language in their classrooms. Part of this reimagining has meant working with colleagues in disabilities studies in education to conceive an intersectional framework which looks at translanguaging through the principles of Universal Design for Learning (UDL). The philosophical grounding of UDL is the belief that as educators we are always looking for ways to increase access, to maximize the ways in which our students connect to, develop and reflect learning (Berquist, 2017; Nelson & Ralabate, 2017). These values are very similar to the translanguaging focus on intentionality, on strength-based teaching and learning, and on holistic teaching (García, Johnson, & Seltzer, 2017). It was my time in CUNY-NYSIEB that allowed me to see this inclusivity. It was my time at CUNY-NYSIEB that allowed me to see the need for translanguaging spaces and practices in all classrooms, not just those created with emergent bilinguals in mind.

Although for a brief moment I questioned how I would continue the work of CUNY-NYSIEB outside of NYC, I now realize that the need for the philosophy that CUNY-NYSIEB espoused and the pedagogical practices that it developed is not geographically bound. The work of translanguaging and of CUNY-NYSIEB has not only liberated language in the classroom, it has created a space in which to imagine the possibilities.

Reimaging the learning and teaching of "international" students: Woodley extending translanguaging to teachers beyond the United States

The work of CUNY-NYSIEB is a cornerstone of my syllabi and classes at New York University where I teach. The vast majority of our TESOL and Bilingual Education prospective teachers are students on F1 visas from China. The university refers to these students as "international students," yet this term can be problematic, erasing the transnational and complex realities of so many students with various citizenship and immigration statuses. As a teacher-educator, I, Heather Woodley, strive to support these prospective teachers in unique ways considering many of them are seeking New York state teaching certification and would like to work with learners in NYC public schools.

Translanguaging offers a powerful lens to work with this group of students from China who are at the same time bilingual learners and simultaneously learning about teaching bilingual learners both in China and in the United States. Although prek-12 classrooms are becoming increasingly linguistically diverse and schools are finding ways to disrupt traditional monolingual notions of schooling, international students are facing increased complexities in higher education. Within the 83% White, and predominately middle-class teaching force, our international preservice teachers are unique in their cultural, linguistic and racial positioning (Picower, 2012). Because of their "international" status, these students face a lack of access to financial aid and paid work opportunities, as well as language and cultural bias from professors, classmates, and administrators. We have witnessed professors admonishing these students for using their home languages in learning and social spaces. These attacks on languages are attacks on students' identity and self (Anzaldúa, 1987). Translanguaging and the work of CUNY-NYSIEB seek to counter this narrative. I have explicitly created space for home language use in our own graduate-level TESOL education classrooms. For me, this is a new level of "you belong here" and "this space is for you" so as to include our international students. Whether it be giving them opportunities to turn-and-talk so that they can do so using Chinese or encouraging their use of Chinese in independent research, I implore these graduate students to use all their linguistic repertoire. In this way, they experience learning from a multilingual perspective, and I give them the space to make personal linguistic choices in their learning.

The resources created by the CUNY-NYSIEB team have proved valuable for our international students to reimagine what it means to be educators of emergent bilinguals. Translanguaging allows them to challenge notions of how "best" to learn and to critically consider their own English education growing up in China. Many of these students come to their education classes with the notion that English-only is the ideal path because "that's what I was given in China." We deconstruct this notion intentionally. I push them to think about, "How was your Mandarin used or positioned outside your classroom? Where was the power in languages? What did English mean to you?" After these reflections, students are faced with understanding that everyone experiences language and learning in very different ways.

Prior to coming to the US for their studies, these "international" students from China had never reflected on their own language oppression. They had never felt that Mandarin would be considered "less than" or an academic barrier. Introducing the experiences of bilinguals narrated and seen through a translanguaging lens has meant that they begin to see their own students and their own learning differently. Furthermore, CUNY-NYSIEB publications and videos provide these prospective teachers with concrete ways to not only support their students' academic and linguistic growth, but to address the power structures of language they find in their new context (see Chapter 7, this volume).

Reimagining dual language bilingual education: Solorza negotiates

Translanguaging theory disrupts how bilingual educators conceptualize language and pedagogy in DLBE classrooms (see also Chapters 8 and 14, this volume). Students must be able to access their entire linguistic repertoires as they learn new content and language. I, Cristian R. Solorza, as a teacher-educator, have experienced how taking up translanguaging theory and including trans-languaging pedagogical practices in two monolingually designed spaces create ideological and structural challenges for DLBE educators. First, strict language allocation policies prevent students from using their full linguistic repertoires freely by requiring them to perform monolingually. Second, standards-based curricula restrict language production to content-aligned phrases, vocabulary, and standardized language varieties. Translanguaging theory pushes us to think beyond current models of bilingual education to reimagine DLBE language allocation policies and curricula.

The Dual Language Bilingual Education & TESOL programs at Bank Street College help prepare teachers to enter public and private school bilingual educa-tion settings. The addition of translanguaging in our curricula called for pro-grammatic changes. As program director, I was able to help revise the course sequence and readings, develop multi-model assignments, and establish a trans-languaging stance in our pedagogies. With the support of CUNY-NYSIEB, four Bank Street graduates and I were also able to write a guide that provides a theoretical framework for envisioning translanguaging in DLBE, practical examples to help translate theory into practice, and two sample units of study (see Solorza, Aponte, Leverenz, Becker, & Frias, 2019).

Even with a strong translanguaging focus in the program, teachers still expe-rience difficulty accepting students' use of language features that they consider *informal, social,* and/or *non-standard* as academic resources in classrooms. I believe academia creates this bias and teacher education faculty must make significant pedagogical shifts to model how we embrace students' full linguistic repertoires in academic settings.

In 2015, the entire college engaged in developing their racial literacy through workshops, monthly inquiry groups, reading discussions, and student-led assem-blies. Bank Street's focus on race has helped the faculty explore raciolinguistic issues as they pertain to classroom participation and writing (Drago-Severson & Blum-Destafano, 2017; Flores & Rosa, 2015; Grinberg, 2005; Love, 2019; Oluo, 2018; Paris & Alim, 2017; Pollock, 2008; Rankine, 2014; Shalaby, 2017; Steele, 2010; Zeus & Broderick, 2011). We are now exploring decolonizing pedagogies in hopes of making structural changes that will better align to our educational philosophies.

Translanguaging theory embodies a social justice liberatory project that requires personal and institutional shifts. I have learned that this work goes beyond using translanguaging strategies as instructional scaffolds. It demands that we critically confront our biases as well as question existing hegemonic structures in schools and academia. Translanguaging not only pushes us to think beyond current models of bilingual education and TESOL, but it calls for a reimagining of higher education institutions that must also honor graduate students' full linguistic repertoires.

Reimagining a program and vision: Hesson in small Rhode Island

One of the most rewarding aspects of my work in the TESOL program at Rhode Island College has been the opportunity to collaborate with my colleagues to develop a new vision for the program grounded in educational equity and linguistic justice for emergent bilingual students. As a faculty leader, I, Sarah Hesson, have witnessed the reverberations of this vision in the teaching philosophies and practices of our candidates, as well as in school practices and policy discourse among stakeholders statewide.

In the context of developing a vision for our teacher preparation program, we define linguistic justice around the following four tenets. First, all bilingual children have the right to learn bilingually. Second, all language practices are equally valuable. Third, welcoming students' home language practices into school is critical to disrupting unequal power dynamics. Fourth, using students' entire linguistic repertoires is an essential component to providing an equitable education. Grounded in the tenets outlined above, our vision promotes bilingualism for all bilingual students and communities, encourages active self-reflection and criticality in teacher candidates, and works to recognize, challenge, and reimagine systems of power.

In aligning our teacher preparation program, research, and advocacy work with our vision, we have grappled with the question of how ideological change occurs, both within systems (e.g., TESOL program, local public schools) as well as for individuals (e.g., teacher candidates). How can we engage with teacher candidates, colleagues, administrators, and policymakers to consider and prioritize how bilingual children learn best? How can we discuss broader issues such as racism, discrimination, and poverty with stakeholders in ways that will challenge current pedagogical practices as well as "what 'counts' as educational policy" (Anyon, 2005). The vision of the CUNY-NYSIEB project and the tangible resources it has produced have proven invaluable in creating significant change within and beyond our program.

First, we infused the concepts of dynamic bilingualism and translanguaging throughout our ESL and Bilingual Education certification sequences. Our approach to these concepts aligns to the two principles and practices of the CUNY-NYSIEB project: (1) a multilingual ecology for the whole school, and (2) bilingualism as a resource in education (see Chapter 3, this volume). In our foundational language acquisition course, candidates first explore these concepts theoretically, then use them to analyze their schools' linguistic landscapes. In a sociocultural foundations course, candidates study one of the bilingual communities they serve, including interviewing community members to better understand the community and their language practices. In methods and assessment classes, candidates learn and implement translanguaging pedagogy. Finally, candidates incorporate translanguaging in their field experiences, as well as articulate their own teaching philosophy regarding bilingualism, family and community partnership, and a vision for social justice. Dynamic bilingualism and translanguaging pedagogy are woven throughout the curriculum, giving candidates many opportunities to understand and take ownership of the concepts.

Second, my colleagues and I have had the opportunity to share the core principles of the CUNY-NYSIEB project through professional development, research, and advocacy in the state. In professional development, I have worked with groups of General Education, Special Education, and ESL teachers in districts throughout the state on utilizing students' home language practices in all educational settings. In research, my colleague Rachel Toncelli worked with a practicing ESL teacher to analyze and improve the multilingual ecology of the public high school where she worked. Alongside emergent bilingual high school students, they replaced English-only signage throughout the school with multilingual signs that included culturally significant images of the students' choosing. Students reported feeling an increased sense of belonging, and pride that their families would be able to better navigate the school building as a result.

In advocacy, I had the opportunity to participate in a panel discussion with US Congressman Jim Langevin, in which I used the term "emergent bilingual" to highlight the emerging multilingual proficiency of students learning English. In turn, Congressman Langevin used the term in addressing Congress[1]; many stakeholders in the state have adopted it as well. These examples are not exhaustive but offer a window into the impact of the CUNY-NYSIEB project here in Rhode Island, and the potential for change in a small state context.

The CUNY-NYSIEB project offers many useful resources for schools, districts, and teacher preparation programs, but the most valuable resource is its underlying vision. In such dehumanizing times, particularly for communities of color and immigrant communities, the vision of the CUNY-NYSIEB project offers an entry point into an educational philosophy and pedagogy that is both humanizing and liberatory.

Conclusion

From participants in CUNY-NYSIEB to faculty at universities, we are, and continue to be, uniquely and powerfully shaped by the legacy of CUNY-NYSIEB and translanguaging pedagogies. While our students come from diverse racial, linguistic and cultural backgrounds, the thread of equity ties our realities together as a common goal, particularly as we reimagine what it means to be a teacher-educator through a translanguaging lens. This connection to issues of educational justice runs deeply through all areas of our work, impacting the personal experiences of prospective teachers, the lives of bilingual youth in local schools, and the structures of programs and schooling itself. Disrupting monolingual ideologies, empowering bilingual teachers and communities, and creating new and innovative programmatic structures in teacher education are just some of the legacies of CUNY-NYSIEB that can be seen in vibrant new spaces of teacher education beyond New York (see Teacher Box 16.1 for a US example, and Teacher Boxes 16.1, 17.1, and 18.1 for international examples).

Notes

1 The term "foreign" is used here only with a juridical connotation, since in Italy, as regards the acknowledgement of citizenship, the so-called *jus sanguinis* is still in force.
2 https://www.youtube.com/watch?v=UrIZJBINZOE&feature=youtu.be&fbclid= IwAR0Bope-W0hKlqEzTFa6Ijfc3ZfApP_ZMsiLnXTrf-oDqkc-p-DavRgVpKw

References

Anyon, J. (2005). What "counts" as educational policy? Notes toward a new paradigm. *Harvard Educational Review, 75*(1), 65–88.

Anzaldúa, G. (1987). *Borderlands/la frontera: The new mestiza*. San Francisco, CA: Aunt Lute Books.

Berquist, E. (2017). *UDL: Moving from exploration to integration*. Wakefield, MA: CAST Professional Publishing.

Cioè-Peña, M. (2015). Translanguaging within the monolingual special education classroom. *Theory, Research, and Action in Urban Education, 4*(1). Retrieved from http://traue.commons.gc.cuny.edu/volume-iv-issue-1-fall-2015/translanguaging-within-the-monolingual-special-education-classroom/

Cioè-Peña, M. & Snell, T. (2015). Translanguaging for social justice. *Theory, Research, and Action in Urban Education, 4*(1). Retrieved from http://traue.commons.gc.cuny.edu/volume-iv-issue-1-fall-2015/translanguaging-for-social-justice/

Drago-Severson, E. & Blum-Destafano, J. (2017). The self in social justice: A developmental lens on race, identity, and transformation. *Harvard Educational Review, 87*(4), 457–481.

Flores, N. (2014). Let's Not Forget that Translanguaging is a Political Act. Retrieved from https://educationallinguist.wordpress.com/2014/07/19/lets-not-forget-that-translanguaging-is-a-political-act/

Flores, N. & Rosa, J. (2015). Undoing appropriateness: Raciolinguistic ideologies and language diversity in education. *Harvard Education Review, 85*(2), 149–171.

García, O., Johnson, S.I., & Seltzer, K. (2017). *The translanguaging classroom*. Philadelphia, PA: Caslon Publishing.

Grinberg, J.G.A. (2005). *Teaching like that: The beginnings of teacher education at Bank Street*. New York, NY: Peter Lang.

Kleyn, T. & García, O. (2019). Translanguaging as an act of transformation. In L.C.d. Oliveira (Ed.), *The handbook of TESOL in K-12* (pp. 69–82). Hoboken, NJ: Wiley-Blackwell.

Love, B. (2019). *We want to do more than survive*. Boston, MA: Beacon Press.

Nelson, L.L. & Ralabate, P.K. (2017). *Culturally responsive design for English learners: The UDL approach.* Wakefield, MA: CAST Professional Publishing.

Oluo, I. (2018). *So you want to talk about race.* New York, NY: Seal Press.

Paris, D. & Alim, H.S. (2017). *Cultural sustaining pedagogies: Teaching and learning for justice in a changing world.* New York, NY: Teachers College Press.

Picower, B. (2012). *Practice what you teach: Social justice education in the classroom and the streets.* New York, NY: Routledge.

Pollock, M. (2008). *Everyday anti-racism: Getting real about race in school.* New York, NY: The New Press.

Rankine, C. (2014). *Citizen: An American lyric.* Minneapolis, MN: Graywold Press.

Shalaby, C. (2017). *Troublemakers: Lessons in freedom from young children at school.* New York, NY: The New Press.

Steele, C.M. (2010). *Whistling Vivaldi: How stereotypes affect us and what we can do.* New York, NY: W.W. Norton & Company, Inc.

Solorza, C., Aponte, G., Leverenz, T., Becker, T., & Frias, B. (2019). *Translanguaging in dual language bilingual education: A blueprint for planning units of study.* New York, NY: CUNY-NYSIEB. Retrieved from https://www.cuny-nysieb.org/wp-content/uploads/2019/09/Translanguaging-in-Dual-Language-Bilingual-Education-A-Blueprint-for-Planning-Units-of-Study-RSVD.pdf

Zeus, L. & Broderick, A. (2011). Smartness as property: A critical exploration of intersections between whiteness and disability studies. *Teachers College Record, 113*(10), 2206–2232.

BOX 17.1 TEACHER/RESEARCHER

Valentina Carbonara

and

Andrea Scibetta

Università per Stranieri di Siena, Italy

"L'AltRoparlante" project

Integrating translanguaging practices in Italian schools

The Italian project L'AltRoparlante has drawn inspiration from the CUNY-NYSIEB initiative in theoretical and practical aspects. In 2017/2018, there were 841,719 "foreign"[2] students within the Italian school system, 61% of whom were born and, in most cases, had grown up in Italy. This number accounts for 9.7% of the total number of students, although the number varies by areas. Most "foreign" students are in primary schools.

Italian dominating pedagogy leans toward the whole child approach. That is, priority tends to be given to the need to create learning environments which do not only promote the development of academic skills, but also emphasize the role of social and emotional competences for the individual well-being of students. And yet, Italian schools have not been effective in multilingual repertoires in the schools, despite recent local efforts to promote bi/multilingualism, biliteracy, and language awareness.

Translanguaging as a pedagogical praxis has also gained an increasing attention in Italian research in the past few years. Hence, a few projects inspired by translanguaging pedagogy have been carried out at a local as well as national level. "L'AltRoparlante," conducted since 2016 within an inter-regional network of multilingual schools with percentages of emergent bilinguals between 20% and 70% is one of these. The first two schools involved are the "Martiri della Benedicta" school in Serravalle Scrivia (Piedmont) and the "Collodi" school in Cerreto Guidi (Tuscany). Moreover, since 2017 the "Marco Polo" in Prato (Tuscany) has been integrated in the network, and since 2018 the "Bertolotti" school in Gavardo (Lombardy) has joined. Since 2019, a fifth institute, the "Gasparini" school in Novi di Modena (Emilia Romagna) has taken part in the project. At the moment, the project has involved more than 700 pupils and 70 teachers, mainly belonging to primary schools, but also to kindergartens and middle schools.

The name of the project "L'AltRoparlante" is the result of putting together two Italian words: "altro," which means "the other" (understanding the "otherness" as a resource and as an added value), and "altoparlante," which means "loudspeaker." The main goal of the project, is in fact, to give high voice to all the languages and varieties spoken in Italian schools, besides standard Italian. Through "L'AltRoparlante," we aim to legitimize the multilingual repertoires of the students, trying to activate dynamics of empowerment and to prevent youth marginalization and language hierarchization phenomena. In order to pursue this aim, we try to draw on translanguaging pedagogy, integrating and combining it with the European perspective on plurilingualism.

As regards the phases of articulation of the project, we follow the steps of transformative action-research. First, in each school we established a close contact with the Headmasters and with all the teachers. After that, we delivered seminars and workshops in order to provide professional development about bilingualism and its advantages, multilingual education and translanguaging as a pedagogical praxis. Moreover, before starting the fieldwork, we met the parents of the pupils involved, in order to explain the purposes of the project and to investigate micro-level family language policies. The fieldwork, which is usually carried out during the curricular teaching time, consists of a preliminary phase of ethnolinguistic investigation in the different classes, aimed at collecting detailed information about collective and individual multilingual repertoires, as well as specific percep-tual and emotional patterns toward language plurality. Afterwards, with teachers we design translanguaging-based pedagogical activities. At first, we attempt to transform the schoolscape and we involve parents in moments of bi/multilingual storytelling. At an advanced level of implementation, we plan and conduct more complex activities. We work on oral, written or multimodal translinguistic texts, also content-related ones, in order to let students develop language awareness-related skills, foster biliteracy and fully legitimize their whole linguistic repertoires. Finally, with the help of the teachers, every year we organize final open meetings, addressed to parents, cultural mediators, teachers and headmasters from other schools, and local authorities, with the purpose of disseminating the main results obtained through the application of translanguaging pedagogy.

Besides the educational dimension, we have gathered and analyzed dif-ferent data, including parental sociolinguistic questionnaires, teacher and children interviews, as well as focus groups, video-recordings of classrooms using translanguaging-based activities, and student language portraits.

The project L'AltRoparlante has greatly transformed teaching practices and school-home relations. All the schools now display a much more eco-logical multilingual schoolscape, which is not only symbolic, but a concrete trace of the new educational perspective adopted. Teachers have rediscov-ered the potentiality of their challenging contexts, usually perceived as trou-bling and marginalized, but now considered ways of creating more equal learning opportunities. For instance, teachers are working on peer-coaching professional development. Parents have been invited to participate in trans-languaging-based activities, rediscovering the great contributions they can bring to their children's education, regardless of their linguistic competences. The corpus of video recordings shows examples of dynamic translinguistic interaction during curricular teaching time and of deconstruction of linguistic compartmentalization in favor of more flexible multilingual practices.

The following example shows a teacher from Prato, Sandra Martini, guiding her students in filling in a questionnaire based on multilingual wh-questions concerning a migration story they have read in class:

Docente: Allora, rileggiamo tutta la scheda, pronti? Ognuno lo legge nella lingua...ognuno si senta libero di dirlo, ok? ... "Dove?" S1: Where? S2: Ila ayn? S3: Nǎlǐ S4: Sad? D: Ku? S6: Donde? S7: In una nave in mezzo al mare! S8: Yī sōu zài dà hǎishàng de chuán!	Teacher: [Italian] So, let's read again the sheet, are you ready? Each one reads it in the language...each one feels free to say it, ok? "Where?" S1: [English] Where? S2: [Arabic]: Where? S3: [Chinese] Where? S4: [Georgian] Where? T: [Albanian] Where? S6: [Spanish] Where? S7: [Italian] On a boat in the middle of the sea! S8: [Chinese]: On a boat in the middle of the sea!

The analysis of focus groups conducted with students reveals dynamics of empowerment of immigrant minority pupils, in terms of identity affirmation and competence enhancement. Many students expressed feelings of pride and liberation which contributed to increase their motivation toward school and to develop a deeper awareness regarding their language rights, as the following emergent bilingual child from Ecuador, attending Serravalle School, underlines:

N: Io quando l'ho letta [la poesia] mi sono ricordata prima di tutto del mio paese, quando sono andata in Ecuador e poi mi è piaciuto leggerla perché ho fatto capire agli altri che anche la mia lingua è importante come tutte le altre. Non è che solo l'italiano e l'inglese sono importanti, e tutte le altre non sono importanti. Quindi se io sono nata espanola, lei è nata albanese e lui italiano, un'altra indiana ... non importa perché siamo tutti uguali.	N: When I read it [a poem], I remembered, first of all, my country, when I went to Ecuador and I liked to read it because I made the others understand that also my language is important like all the others. It is not true that only Italian and English are important, and all the other languages are not important. So, even if I was born española, she was born Albanian and he was born Italian, another one Indian...it doesn't matter because we are all the same.

Italian students were able to revalue dialectal varieties and regional languages and to cultivate a sense of appreciation and legitimation of multilingualism in class, overcoming stereotypical cultural and language ideologies. All the children, learning from each other, had and still have the opportunity to reflect on metalinguistic aspects and to learn through their peers' languages, broadening their semiotic boundaries. In 2018 L'AltRoparlante was awarded the European Language Label. Our website can be found at http:// altroparlante.unistrasi.it/

18

REIMAGINING TEACHER EDUCATION FOR EMERGENT BILINGUALS

Going upstate

Erin Kearney and Kate Mahoney

First steps on a path to reimagining teacher education in upstate New York

When the New York State Education Department asked that CUNY-NYSIEB (City University of New York-New York State Initiative on Emergent Bilinguals) extend their work beyond the city, the team needed to expand to include experienced professors in universities upstate. The collaboration was thus extended to include the State University of New York (SUNY), the public institution encompassing campuses beyond New York City. We, Erin Kearney and Kate Mahoney, are professors at different SUNY campuses. Kate Mahoney is faculty at SUNY-Fredonia, whereas Erin Kearney teaches at the University at Buffalo. Both of us play an important role in preparing teachers enrolled mostly in Teaching English as a Second Language and bilingual education programs, but also general education and world languages education.

When we were first appointed associate investigators and became members of the CUNY-NYSIEB team, we traveled to New York City and began our journey of change. We walked away from the first meeting energized, knowing our work ahead would be meaningful and challenging. As researchers, we were well aware of the decades of scholarship documenting the positive effects of including and developing home languages. Voluminous evidence of longitudinal or meta-evaluated designs shows that bilingual education (of all varieties) is as effective or more effective than English-Only Programs on measures of achievement and proficiency (Padilla, Fan, Xu, & Silva, 2013;

Rolstad, Mahoney, & Glass, 2005; Slavin, Madden, Calderón, Chamberlain, & Hennessy, 2011; Umansky & Reardon, 2014; Valentino & Reardon, 2015). We also have evidence documenting the negative or absence of effect on achievement and proficiency when home languages are restricted (Garcia, Lawton, & Diniz De Figueriedo, 2012; Guo & Koretz, 2013; Jiménez-Castellanos, Blanchard, & Atwill, 2014; Mahoney, MacSwan, Haladyna, & García, 2010). Our experiences as scholars and teacher educators actively engaged with our communities also alerted us to the complex social and political realities of advocating for schools to be sites for developing multilingualism and a more plurilingual and pluralist educational experience.

Together we became the support system for schools across approximately 200 miles in the Western New York State region where there were large numbers of emergent bilingual students. Our schools were located in Syracuse, Rochester, Buffalo, and Dunkirk. The first three cities already had established Dual Language Bilingual Education and Transitional Bilingual Education programs. Dunkirk, however, was nestled into a very rural county that had no bilingual education program despite many bilingual learners and a state law mandating provision of such a program.

The two of us did not know each other, although we knew some members of the CUNY-NYSIEB team. Once we started to collaborate with each other, as well as the entire team, it became clear to us that we shared a similar professional goal of promoting the idea of *multilingualism for all*, and like our colleagues, we were as well acquainted with socio-political and historical challenges to such a vision as we were committed to addressing these through our work. In what follows, we describe in more depth the nature of that shared vision of an expansive, inclusive valuing of multilingualism in schools, and we describe shifts in our own and others' practice as we engaged in collaborative, ongoing learning and professional development through CUNY-NYSIEB. We also reflect on our transformation process itself. At various stages of our participation, from working with practicing teachers and school building leaders to engaging with the novice teacher candidates in our respective preservice teacher education programs, we found ourselves returning to the question: What does it mean and what does it take to support teacher change? Especially when it comes to substantial shifts in mindset, professional vocabulary/discourse and approaches to instructional practice, what roles can teacher educators play? These driving questions spurred forward our work with practicing teachers participating in the CUNY-NYSIEB project and prompted program-level culture shift in our university-based teacher preparation programs. This becomes the thesis of this chapter: In the context of translanguaging theory/pedagogy, what does it mean to support teacher change (epistemological and pedagogical) and what is the role of teacher educators in that process?

Teacher change toward translanguaging philosophy and pedagogy

The CUNY-NYSIEB project envisioned transformation of many scales and scopes. A statewide effort and network, supporting development and implementation of individual school change plans while supporting district-level and regional initiatives to flourish as well, the project was arguably grounded in the situated actions of many individuals and collaborative groups who helped bring a translanguaging philosophy to life in everyday practice. This was mostly operationalized through Emergent Bilingual Leadership Teams (EBLT) (see Chapter 5, this volume) and action plans. We met with EBLTs on a regular basis as facilitators of the change that was deemed important at schools. Each school organized an EBLT and articulated proposed changes within the broad CUNY-NYSIEB principles.

Clearly this work is complex and challenging, and it led us to meditate on and engage with pressing matters of theory-action, to ask ourselves how we can support real and continuous change alongside school partners, respond with them to counter-currents, and promote broader transformation through our situated and collaborative actions. As a direct challenge to deeply entrenched monolingual/monoglossic (Blackledge, 2000; García & Torres-Guevara, 2009) and raciolinguistic ideologies (Rosa & Flores, 2017), the project built an infrastructure for practical action undergirded by a particular view of language and education. The nonnegotiables of participation in the project—making home languages and linguistic diversity more visible and audible in schools, through concerted efforts to nurture multilingual ecologies, and treating multilingualism as a resource in education—reflected radical departures from normalized discourses about multilingualism in schools, about emergent bilingual students and about pedagogical practices that support them.

Whereas it is conventional in schools and in society to name languages (e.g., English, Somali, Chinese) and to treat them as existing discretely in minds and in the world, translanguaging adopts a unitary (Otheguy, García, & Reid, 2015) repertoire (Rymes, 2014) view and considers individuals' languaging as a unified whole. Consequently, the project and its participating schools took up a stance valuing all of the features of an individual student's linguistic repertoire and their potential for promoting that student's learning and sense of belonging in school. Beyond the individual speaker, dynamic bilingualism theory highlights and valorizes the natural semiotic abundance and fluidity of multilingualism as a social phenomenon. In the CUNY-NYSIEB project, then, translanguaging pedagogies, both with the purpose of creating a more welcoming environment in classrooms for all students and promoting better access to and more meaningful engagement with curriculum and instruction, were more deeply a means of enacting change toward a more resounding pluralism in schools. Our work in schools, as associate investigators, was to work alongside school leaders (mostly teachers) to shift discourse, shift policies and shift practices along these lines. We learned a great deal about educational change from working with them.

Some teachers we worked with responded to the idea of adopting a translanguaging philosophy and pedagogy with relief; they had for many years invited their students' home language practices into the classroom, following their instincts that such practice translated to more meaningful engagement and learning for students. Yet, many times they did this in secret or in violation of schoolwide policies or conventional practices that pushed for substantial or exclusive use of English as medium of teaching and learning. *The Translanguaging Guide* (Celic & Seltzer, 2012) offered teachers new tools and strategies (as well as a new vision and a name) for expanding their instructional practices. Certain teachers were so empowered by the school's embrace of the translanguaging project and the new tools and advocacy space that came with it that they not only stepped into the school-based leadership team for the project, but they also became ambassadors to other schools in their districts and to the entire state. Hulda Yau, from the Rochester City School District, was one such teacher, effecting a transformation and development of her own teaching while also growing as an advocate and champion of multilingualism as a value in our schools and communities (see Teacher/Researcher Box 11.1). Another teacher in Buffalo, Dr. Maeva López Kasem, also became an ambassador for CUNY-NYSIEB at the state-level and has a short video on the state government website highlighting promising practices for young bilingual children (see Teacher/Researcher Box 10.1). Both of these teacher-leaders emerged through this project and now have district level coaching positions. One has a doctorate and one is currently in a doctoral Educational Leadership program.

Though these two teacher-leaders left the classroom for leadership roles, positioned to advocate on a broader level for translanguaging, a phenomenon was notable to us as we considered the nature of teacher change; while it has been demonstrated that teachers most often leave the profession because of working conditions and climate, feeling little autonomy and decision-making authority (Ingersoll & May, 2016), we saw in the CUNY-NYSIEB project a way for galvanizing school communities around a challenging, complex and worthy change effort. We also witnessed a type of teacher engagement and teacher leadership on issues of pedagogical philosophy and practice that nurtured the teacher who was leading, as well as her students and colleagues, through her transformed and transformational practice.

Participating in and helping to grow CUNY-NYSIEB's shared vision also included a network of support for teachers called *Circle of Care*. During these encuentros, current and previously participating schools and teachers shared practical and teacher-centered materials, resources and insights. The shared vision cultivated in the project made it possible to help teachers resist mono-lingual biases that still tend to permeate the field. We were able together to actively cultivate and normalize a multilingual perspective in the school com-munity. The CUNY-NYSIEB team helped translate vision into a range of concrete actions and spurred a wide variety of teacher change and leadership trajectories.

Translanguaging as a pedagogical philosophy and practice became a power-ful way to reshape conversations within schools about mission and process. In meetings with one Buffalo school and one Rochester school to draft school-level language policies, we found that translanguaging practices raised many ques-tions about the monolingual bias inherent in existing language allocation poli-cies and the actual privileging of English, no matter what language allocation policy looked like on paper. As teachers worked to change and clarify language policies in their schools, they grappled with the question of where translanguag-ing would fit in the old way of allocating time and language use in ESL and bilingual programming or whether the old way of thinking would even work at all. In the end, both schools found a way to establish a language allocation policy assigning a socially named language as medium of *teaching* over the course of the school day, but they also drafted explicit language to acknowledge in written policies that translanguaging was natural and essential to student learning no matter what the language of instruction. For example, despite the district having a 60% (Spanish):40% (English) written language policy for bilingual education programs, one school articulated a 50:50 language allocation (50% English and 50% Spanish) with translanguaging infused across all areas. In effect, this explic-itly sanctioned the use of translanguaging in instruction whenever it made sense to do so. Policies therefore became more flexible, and through policy revision, teachers were able to reshape their discourse around multilingualism, students, teaching and learning in their schools.

For other practicing teachers we worked with, the idea of inviting students' home languages into the classroom was daunting. Based on the assumption that translanguaging pedagogy required knowledge of or proficiency in all of students' home languages, some teachers balked initially. While many came around when we explored possible translanguaging strategies and distinguished translanguaging as conceptually and pedagogically different from translating or code-switching, these interactions prompted us to consider how teacher change looks different for those who do not readily embrace a translanguaging philoso-phy or any adjustment to instructional practice in a broader sense. We also won-dered how we could support teacher change in school environments where not all teachers actually value multilingualism as a resource. Apart from the concerns teachers sometimes voiced at being ill-equipped to design multilingual ecologies in their classrooms, the more implicit devaluing of multilingualism was harder to counter in our work with schools and our teacher-leader partners. These interactions often led us to rethink our approach to supporting change and led us to integrate more immersive and experiential elements to our professional development sessions with teachers. In this way teachers would gain first-hand knowledge of what it is like to understand little during a classroom lesson and to perhaps develop new perspective and empathy for students' experiences in their own classrooms. In other cases, we simply listened as teachers spoke to us of the conflicts they encountered as a result of subtle or more overt linguicism in response to their change efforts.

We were confident that the sustained engagement with schools through CUNY-NYSIEB was more likely to lead to school and teacher change; the research literature supports such long-term, collaborative, content-focused and reflective engagements, supported by experts and rich with feedback (Darling-Hammond, Hyler, & Gardner, 2017). Another benefit to advocating a translanguaging pedagogy, and one that supported greater likelihood of sustaining change, was the accessibility of these strategies across programs (TESL, World Languages, General Education, Language Immersion, etc.) and across teachers (those who know one language, two languages, multiple languages and those who taught different grade levels and content).

Our experiences made clear that while teacher change was slow to happen and complex, teachers who experimented with translanguaging pedagogies often expressed profound realizations. For example, when a veteran teacher from Buffalo, known as one of the best in her school, tried a translanguaging strategy based on the relationship between Arabic and English she was impressed with how much one of her Iraqi students knew, and how engaged he was. Following the lesson she remarked in a surprised way: "I didn't know he [the student] knew so much!" This simple but powerful statement sums up the importance of teacher change with translanguaging strategies. As a result of trying a translanguaging pedagogy, teachers discovered more about their students' languaging, cultural resources and belongings, and importantly, began to express new perspectives and see in new ways when they looked out onto their classrooms and students.

Through our long-term engagements with schools, we found thankful teachers who believed in the power of home language practices and who needed validation, guidance and in some cases a name for the practices they had long invited and employed in the classroom—translanguaging. Our visits and the shared vision of the statewide project endorsed and brought a sense of public legitimacy to what many teachers knew to be right and good pedagogy, but which they had only previously practiced behind closed doors or in less-visible ways because of lack of support for, or in some cases complete interdiction of, using home language practices in instruction.

Despite the positive response we received from many teachers, we found that even among the willing, the eager, the thirsty for new and more pluralistic approaches to teaching, change was still quite hard or not always long-lasting. This is when we turned to our own practice as teacher educators. Our work in CUNY-NYSIEB prompted us to ask: How can we improve teacher education programs and ongoing teacher learning?

University program-level shift

There were ripple effects of the work we did with schools and teachers, into the teacher education programs where we work and where questions of theory-action are equally relevant and pressing. Participating in CUNY-NYSIEB prompted substantial shifts in both of our teacher education pedagogical processes. Our courses and programs were redesigned to reflect a theory of dynamic bilingualism and translanguaging pedagogy. Similar to our work with practicing teachers through the project, which hinged on shifts in mindset, policy and practices in order for teacher change to unfold, shifts to our teacher education work revolve around revisiting and reshaping the values in our programs to actively promote practices through which change becomes more possible. Of course, this involves reevaluation of our own values and practices, redefining our commitments and interrogating our own "normal" practices. In a moment where a focus on "practice" in teacher education is increasingly critiqued as advancing hegemonic Whiteness (Daniels & Varghese, 2019; Philip et al., 2019), we feel strongly that it is not sufficient in our teacher education programs to focus new teachers' attention on translanguaging and how this might be enacted in practice (although we do this work), nor is it adequate to talk about dynamic bilingualism or translanguaging as intellectual or abstract theories. There also must be conscious attention and effort toward designing teacher education spaces that invite critical examination of situated practices and that emphasize the people, the subjectivities, the histories and the power that operate in particular interactions as well as schooling more broadly.

Remodeling program structures, foci, and practices

We have turned increasingly to emphasizing issues of classroom environment and culture and to preparing teachers who are conscious of their classrooms as multilingual ecologies (see Chapter 9, this volume). We also pay more attention to who our teacher candidate students are, as well as how to prepare them to be teacher-leaders. We encourage them to develop practices to more deeply know their own students. Finally, we support new teachers in clarifying and enacting effective, meaningful instructional practices.

The shift in which we have engaged can be seen in the courses we regularly teach at the university in teacher education programs in TESOL, Bilingual

Education, World Languages, and General Education programs. Specifically, we have enriched our courses and programs by including readings about translanguaging theory, the review of the CUNY-NYSIEB *Translanguaging guide*, and other resources. We support our colleagues in learning how to use these materials with preservice and in-service teachers. In our own instruction, we incorporate CUNY-NYSIEB video clips and webinars as a basis for analysis, discussion, and a way to deepen our understandings of translanguaging philosophy and pedagogy (for more on materials, see Chapter 7, this volume).

Emphasis on teacher leader advocates

We emphasize development of teacher-leaders and encourage students to pursue research projects that help them develop the conceptual and practical knowledge to approach these leadership roles, even as new teachers. One recent example is a student named Emily Voegler. Emily carried out a study of the linguistic landscape in the Seneca Nation and how this related to language status, revitalization efforts and community members' perceptions of the Seneca language and English as a majority language (Voegler, 2016). Following her graduation and anchored in this research, Emily went on to establish a heritage language program in Syracuse with the help of an ESL instructional coach. Today Emily has taken her own teacher-leader path toward deepening our field's understanding of translanguaging pedagogies and how teachers adopt such approaches through her doctoral research.

As was the case when we worked with teachers in the CUNY-NYSIEB project schools, we have seen new leaders develop amongst our teacher candidates, and we similarly position ourselves as resources for these burgeoning leaders, offering concepts and terminology that can push dialogue and advocacy in a more pluralistic direction and offering feedback on and support of all kinds for their efforts.

A further example illustrating the ways students in our teacher education program incorporate ideas from the CUNY-NYSIEB project, involves a graduate student, Chelsea Gifford, who after learning about multilingual ecology in her coursework, noticed her middle school had virtually no representation of students' languages. Upon realizing this, her thesis topic became transforming the multilingual ecology at her school. She designed parent events to invite valuable cultural and linguistic resources from families, and she negotiated with school leadership for the products of these efforts to become a permanent installation in the foyer of the school (Gifford, 2016). Despite several obstacles, Chelsea Gifford and bilingual families in the school created a culture quilt and a tapestry of hope. Figure 18.1 shows some of the expressions that the bilingual families wrote for the tapestry of hope, which was then displayed in the school entryway.

There is evidence, in our view, that through the efforts of teachers, the principles of CUNY-NYSIEB are becoming more normalized in schools.

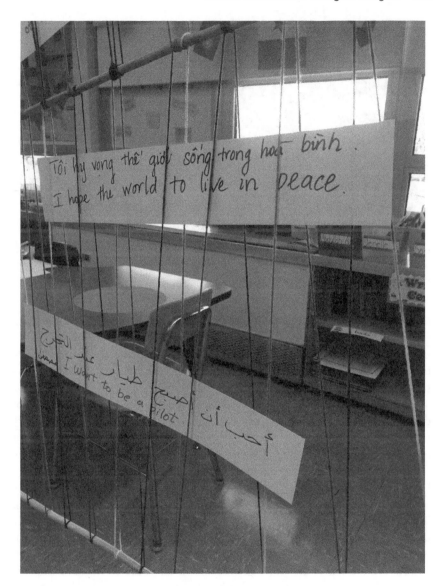

FIGURE 18.1 Bilingual families write their hopes

Clarifying instructional practices and encouraging critical conversations of practice

While deeply knowledgeable about their own setting and content area, teachers' ability to begin seeing specific translanguaging strategies as feasible in their own classrooms was greatly facilitated when video was available. Given this

FIGURE 18.2 Virtual reality immersion in translanguaging-infused high-school classroom

experience, the teacher education program at the University at Buffalo has extended the use of video by engaging preservice teachers in virtual reality immersions featuring segments of translanguaging-infused classroom instruction. Figure 18.2 depicts a classroom in a local high school (here in two dimensions) that teacher candidates in the program experience in 360 degrees. Through the use of virtual reality headsets the teachers can gaze in a variety of directions and notice different elements as they do (see Figure 18.3). The ability to look everywhere in the classroom, to view teaching-learning interactions multiple times and to analyze and reflect as a group following the virtual reality immersion has promoted an understanding of what translanguaging pedagogy looks like in practice. In addition, virtual reality has the additional affordance of bringing the teacher candidate viewers into an actual classroom as teachers. These benefits are especially valuable for preservice teachers who have little or no experience of multilingual classrooms and little or no experience with instructional approaches like translanguaging.

Preservice teachers across all certification areas (childhood education, science, math, English, music, social studies, literacy specialist, world languages, TESOL) have opportunity to do more than read about translanguaging as a philosophy and pedagogical stance. They also can explore the classroom from the point of the view of the teacher. Beyond offering rich material for analyzing pedagogical practice as it plays out in instructional realities, these observations have the benefit of provoking a more visceral and realistic experience of such a pedagogy. It makes space in teacher education for critical conversations of practice that focus on who teachers are, who students are, what they are doing, and

FIGURE 18.3 Teacher candidates immersed in translanguaging instructional segments

importantly, prompting teacher candidates to engage with who they are themselves and what interpretive frames they bring to teaching.

Post-viewing discussion focuses on what the teacher candidates notice about the teacher's moves to support students' language and cultural practices and to draw on the full range of students' resources as assets in learning. They also focus teacher candidates' attention on the students and the classroom itself, again with carefully crafted discussion questions prepared for when the virtual reality headsets come off. Being able to see and carefully unpack instructional practices that depart from the norm was so crucial to the practicing teachers we worked with in CUNY-NYSIEB, it seemed a logical next step to also engage the teacher candidates we work with in similar video analysis.

This dovetails with the professional vision (Goodwin, 1994) concept driving the teacher education program at the University at Buffalo. The virtual reality medium helps to design experiences that productively challenge teacher candidates who may not have thought much yet about the multilingual character of their future classrooms or who may not yet have considered how their own identities and subjectivities are in play in instructional practice.

The cultural shift we have implemented in our university programs by drawing on the CUNY-NYSIEB shared vision clarifies translanguaging practices for novices and encourages them to see multilingualism as a resource in teaching and learning. As we encourage analysis and development of pedagogical practice, we are cautious not to lose sight of the critical dimension that must accompany our efforts to grow teacher candidates' instructional repertoires and overall outlook when it comes to students' language practices. We are routinely pushing ourselves to engage teacher candidates in critical conversation that asks not only to analyze what happened and how in a particular moment of teaching, but why and to whose benefit or detriment does it work in this way.

Moving forward

We have witnessed many moments of teacher change through our work to support the professional development of educators. These experiences have shed light for us as scholars and as teacher educators on the complexity and dynamism of professional transformations. They have especially raised questions about the supportive role that experts and researchers can play in supporting teacher change. As our formal participation in the CUNY-NYSIEB project wound down, our attention shifted to reconsidering the way we work with preservice teachers and how our ongoing engagements with practicing teachers outside the structures of CUNY-NYSIEB could sustain teachers seeking to promote multilingualism and support emergent bilinguals in schools. We have learned that our role is to keep posing challenging questions, to continually interrogate our own positions, stances and practices as teacher educator-researchers, and to help hold spaces in teacher education for critical analysis and discussion of teaching.

We continue to engage with difficult important questions: How can university-based actors support ongoing change? Where and how can perspective shift and adjustments to multilingually conscious professional discourse occur? How can we continue partnering with schools and districts as they seek to establish or revise their policies and approaches? How do we connect teacher candidates to schools throughout their teacher education programs? How can we carry out and supervise graduate students' research that keeps the translanguaging current flowing in our localities? Our work with CUNY-NYSIEB was only the beginning of what must be an ongoing project.

References

Blackledge, A. (2000). Monolingual ideologies in multilingual states: Language, hegemony and social justice in western liberal democracies. *Estudios de sociolinguistica, 1*(2), 25–45. https://doi.org/10.1558/sols.v1i2.25

Celic, C. & Seltzer, K. (2012). *Translanguaging: A CUNY-NYSIEB guide for educators.* New York: CUNY-NYSIEB. https://www.cuny-nysieb.org/wp-content/uploads/2016/04/Translanguaging-Guide-March-2013.pdf

Daniels, J. & Varghese, M. (2019). Troubling practice: Exploring the relationship between whiteness and practice-based teacher education in considering a raciolinguicized teacher subjectivity. *Educational Researcher, 49*(1), 56–63. https://doi.org/10.3102/0013189X19879450

Darling-Hammond, L., Hyler, M.E., & Gardner, M. (2017). *Effective teacher professional development.* Learning Policy Institute. https://learningpolicyinstitute.org/product/effective-teacher-professional-development-report

Garcia, E.E., Lawton, K., & Diniz De Figueriedo, E. H. (2012). The education of English language learners in Arizona: A history of underachievement. *Teachers College Record, 114*(9), 1–18. http://www.tcrecord.org/Content.asp?ContentId=16601

García, O. & Torres-Guevara, R. (2009). Monoglossic ideologies and language policies in the education of U.S. Latinas/os. In E. Murillo, S. Villenas, R. Trinidad Galván, J. Sánchez Muñoz, C. Martínez & M. Machado-Casas (Eds.), *Handbook of Latinos and education: Research, theory and practice* (pp. 182–194). Lawrence Erlbaum.

Gifford, C. (2016). Changing the multilingual ecology in school through the collaboration of English Language Learners (ELLs) and their parents. The culture quilt and tapestry of hopes project. Unpublished Master's thesis. State University of New York, Fredonia.

Goodwin, C. (1994). Professional vision. *American Anthropologist, 96*(3), 606–633.

Guo, Q. & Koretz, D. (2013). Estimating the impact of the Massachusetts English immersion law on limited English proficient students' reading achievement. *Educational Policy, 27*(1), 121–149. https://doi.org/10.1177%2F0895904812462776

Ingersoll, R. & May, H. (2016). Minority teacher recruitment, employment and retention: 1987–2013. Learning Policy Institute. https://learningpolicyinstitute.org/sites/default/files/product-files/Minority_Teacher_Recruitment_REPORT.pdf

Jiménez-Castellanos, O., Blanchard, J., & Atwill, K. (2014). Beginning English literacy development and achievement among Spanish-speaking children in Arizona's English-only classrooms: A four-year two-cohort longitudinal study. *International Multilingual Research Journal, 8*(2), 104–123. http://dx.doi.org/10.1080/19313152.2013.875812

Mahoney, K., MacSwan, J., Haladyna, T., & García, D. (2010). Castañeda's third prong: Evaluating the achievement of Arizona's English learners under restrictive language policy. In P. Gándara & M. Hopkins (Eds.), *Forbidden language: English learners and restrictive language policies* (pp. 50–64). Teachers College.

Otheguy, R., García, O., & Reid, W. (2015). Clarifying translanguaging and deconstructing named languages: A perspective from linguistics. *Applied Linguistics Review, 6*(3), 281–307. https://doi.org/10.1515/applirev-2015-0014

Padilla, A. M., Fan, L., Xu, L., & Silva, D. (2013). A Mandarin/English two-way immersion program: Language proficiency and academic achievement. *Foreign Language Annals, 46,* 661–679.

Philip, T., Souto-Manning, M., Anderson, L., Horn, I., Carter Andrews, D., Stillman, J., & Varghese, M. (2019). Making justice peripheral by constructing practice as "core": How the increasing prominence of core practices challenges teacher education. *Journal of Teacher Education, 70*(3), 251–264. https://doi.org/10.1177/0022487118798324

Rolstad, K., Mahoney, K., & Glass, G.V. (2005). The big picture: A meta-analysis of program effectiveness research on English language learners. *Educational Policy, 19*(4), 572–594. https://doi.org/10.1177/0895904805278067

Rosa, J. & Flores, N. (2017). Unsettling race and languages: Toward a raciolinguistic perspective. *Language in Society, 46*(5), 621–647. https://doi.org/10.1017/S0047404517000562

Rymes, B. (2014). *Communicating beyond language: Everyday encounters with diversity*. New York, NY: Routledge.

Slavin, R., Madden, N., Calderón, M., Chamberlain, A., & Hennessy, A. (2011). Reading and language outcomes of a multiyear randomized evaluation of transitional bilingual education. *Educational Evaluation and Policy Analysis*, *33*(1), 47–58. https://doi. org/10.3102/0162373711398127

Umansky, I. & Reardon, S. (2014). Reclassification patterns among Latino English learner students in bilingual, dual immersion, and English immersion classrooms. *American Educational Research Journal*, *51*(5), 879–912. https://doi.org/10.3102/0002831214545110

Valentino, R.A. & Reardon, S.F. (2015). Effectiveness of four instructional programs designed to serve English language learners: Variation by ethnicity and initial English proficiency. *Educational Evaluation and Policy Analysis*, *37*(4), 612–637. https://doi. org/10.3102/0162373715573310

Voegler, E. (2016). Artifacts and actors: Delving into the context surrounding the linguistic landscape of the Seneca Nation. Unpublished Master's thesis. State University of New York, Fredonia. https://dspace.sunyconnect.suny.edu/bitstream/handle/1951/70438/ Voegler_Emily_MastersThesis_Spring2016.pdf?sequence=1&isAllowed=y

BOX #18.1 TEACHER/RESEARCHER

János Imre Heltai

and

Bernadett Jani-Demetriou

A Romani project in Hungary

Several million people in Europe identify themselves as Roma. A significant proportion of these people are bilingual, speaking Romani and some other language(s), mainly the official language(s) of their home country. However, Romani is not used as the language of instruction: At best, it is offered as a heritage or a foreign language, but it is seldom included in the curriculum even as an optional subject. Due to the transnational character of Romani (i.e., it is present in several European states) and the lack of a nation-state-like power center, Romani standardization has always been problematic. Attempts at standardization (made mostly on the national level) promote the spread of standard ideologies, but do not provide for the spread of standard resources (Abercrombie, 2018). Local Romani ways of speaking continue to have low prestige and are marginalized.

The project *"Translanguaging Classroom Communication and Effective Learning Organisation in Tiszavasvári"* is based on emerging translanguaging research worldwide and on the work of CUNY-NYSIEB. The project is located in Tiszavasvári, North-Eastern Hungary, home of one of the biggest Romani-speaking communities of the country. Based on the findings of our previous linguistic ethnographic fieldwork, it is designed to exploit the pedagogical potential of translanguaging in a school attended by the children of the Roma community. It started in 2016 and uses Romani ways of speaking in everyday learning activities. To reach these goals, experimental lessons and translanguaging workshops have been organized to promote a translanguaging stance among the teachers involved in the project.

The project activities follow many of the CUNY-NYSIEB recommendations and principles. Besides the introduction of Romani ways of speaking into everyday classroom work (Heltai, 2019), the project promotes the use of translanguaging theatre or movie projects.

Although these initiatives have not yet made an impact on national educational policies, in January 2020 project activities were supported by a grant from the European Union (Erasmus+ Strategic Partnership). The participants of the project have committed themselves to developing an e-volume and a video repository to familiarize trainee teachers in Hungary, Slovakia, and other European countries with the possibilities of leveraging translanguaging to teach bilingual Roma students.

See more at: translangedu.hu/en; romanitranslanguaging.eu

References

Abercrombie, A. (2018). Language purism and social hierarchies: Making a Romani standard in Prizren. *Language in Society, 47*, 741–761.

Heltai, J.I. (2019). Translanguaging instead of standardisation. Writing Romani at school. *Applied Linguistics Review*. https://doi.org/10.1515/applirev-2018-0087

THE CUNY-NYSIEB TEAM

(The names of team members appear in alphabetical order. Names are followed by academic credentials at this time, role in CUNY-NYSIEB, and present position, if not a doctoral student)

Gladys Y. Aponte, Doctoral student, The Graduate Center, CUNY. Research Assistant.

Laura Ascenzi-Moreno, Ph.D., The Graduate Center, CUNY. Associate Principal Investigator. Associate Professor, Brooklyn College, CUNY.

Diego Vargas Barona, Ph.D., The Graduate Center, CUNY. Administrative Assistant. Adjunct Associate Professor, Hunter College, CUNY.

Kathryn Carpenter, Ph.D., The Graduate Center, CUNY. Research Assistant. Teacher, I.S. 145, Queens, NYC.

Christina Celic, M.A., Teachers College, Columbia University. Field Associate. Consultant, Switzerland.

María Cioè-Peña, Ph.D., The Graduate Center, CUNY. Research Assistant. Assistant Professor, Montclair State University.

Brian Collins, Ph.D., New York University. Associate Principal Investigator. Associate Professor, Hunter College, CUNY.

Ann E. Ebe, Ph.D., University of Arizona. Associate Principal Investigator. Associate Professor, Hunter College, CUNY.

Carla España, Ph.D., The Graduate Center, CUNY. Advisor. Instructor, Bank Street College of Education.

Ivana Espinet, Ph.D., The Graduate Center, CUNY. Project Director (2018–2019), Formerly Field Associate and Research Assistant. Assistant Professor, Kingsborough Community College, CUNY.

Cecilia M. Espinosa, Ph.D., Arizona State University. Associate Principal Investigator. Associate Professor, Lehman College, CUNY.

Nelson Flores, Ph.D., The Graduate Center, CUNY. First Project Director (2011–2012). Associate Professor, University of Pennsylvania.

Ofelia García, Ph.D., The Graduate Center, CUNY. Co-Principal Investigator. Professor Emerita, The Graduate Center, CUNY.

Luis Guzmán Valerio. Ph.D., The Graduate Center. CUNY. Research Assistant. Adjunct Assistant Professor, The City College of New York, CUNY.

Luz Yadira Herrera, Ph.D., The Graduate Center, CUNY. Research Assistant. Assistant Professor, California State University, Fresno.

Sarah Hesson, Ph.D., The Graduate Center, CUNY. Research Assistant. Associate Professor, Rhode Island College.

Meral Kaya, Ph.D., Ohio State University. Associate Principal Investigator. Assistant Professor, Brooklyn College, CUNY.

Erin Kearney, Ph.D., University of Pennsylvania. Associate Principal Investigator. Associate Professor, SUNY Buffalo.

Tatyana Kleyn, Ed.D., Teachers College, Columbia University. Associate Principal Investigator. Associate Professor, The City College of New York, CUNY.

Khánh Lê, Doctoral student, The Graduate Center, CUNY Research Assistant.

Dina López, Ed.D., Teachers College, Columbia University. Associate Principal Investigator. Associate Professor, The City College of New York, CUNY

Kate Mahoney, Ph.D., Arizona State University. Associate Principal Investigator. Associate Professor, SUNY-Fredonia.

Kahdeidra Martin, Doctoral student, The Graduate Center, CUNY. Research Assistant.

Kate Menken, Ed.D., Teachers College, Columbia University. Co-Principal Investigator. Professor, Queens College, CUNY.

Zoila Morell, Ph.D., The Graduate Center, CUNY. Associate Principal Investigator. Associate Professor, Lehman College, CUNY.

Louis Olander, Ph.D., The Graduate Center, CUNY. Research Assistant. Inclusion Consultant, New York.

Ricardo Otheguy, Ph.D., The Graduate Center, CUNY. Principal Investigator. Professor Emeritus, The Graduate Center, CUNY.

Liza N. Pappas, Ph.D., The Graduate Center, CUNY. Research Assistant. Executive Director, Grow Your Own Illinois.

Vanessa Pérez-Rosario, Ph.D., University of California, Davis. Associate Principal Investigator. Associate Professor, Brooklyn College, CUNY.

Elizabeth Pratt, Ph.D., The Graduate Center, CUNY. Fiscal Administrator. Account Manager, iMerit Technology, New York.

Maite T. Sánchez, Ph.D., Boston College. Project Director (2012–2017) and Lead Advisor (2017–2019). Assistant Professor, Hunter College, CUNY.

Kate Seltzer, Ph.D., The Graduate Center, CUNY. Project Director (2017–2018). Formerly Research Assistant. Assistant Professor, Rowan University, New Jersey.

Tom Snell, Doctoral student, The Graduate Center, CUNY. Research Assistant.

Cristian R. Solorza, Doctoral student, The Graduate Center, CUNY. Field Associate. Instructor, Bank Street College of Education.

Sara Vogel, Ph.D., The Graduate Center, CUNY. Research Assistant. Postdoctoral Fellow, New York University.

Heather Woodley, Ph.D., The Graduate Center, CUNY. Research Assistant. Clinical Assistant Professor, New York University.

Karen Zaino, Doctoral student, The Graduate Center, CUNY. Research Assistant.

INDEX

Page numbers in **bold** refer to tables and those followed by '*n*' refer to endnote.

Acevedo, Elizabeth 173, 178
Anglos 8, 9
Anzaldúa 19
Argueta, Jorge 173, 175
ASPIRA 27
assessment 210-213

Baker, Colin 10, 96
Benjamin-Gómez, Arlen 13
bilingual 3, 4, 5, 8, 11, 18, 41, 82, 117, 119, 120, 122, 127, 153, 234, 268, 299; concept of diglossia 8–9; distributed leadership 68–69; educating teachers 80; education for Latinx community 7–8; education models 42; education, illegality and restrictions 9, 27; emergent 13–14; English Only movement 9; epistemologies of 12, 14; holistic biliteracy 60, 100; immersion programs 8, 10; instructional approach to 10; language categories 6; language policy 30, 31, 41–42; language practices 6–7; language separation 8, 117; metalinguistic awareness 153, 253; and Multilingual Learner 19; orgullo 123–124; parent advocacy for 62, 240; policies for emergent bilinguals 42–43; process approach 11; simultaneous *vs.*

sequential 153; transitional bilingual education 26, 31, 36, 80, 117, 139, 220; and translanguaging 15, 16; *vs.* dual language education 9, 10, 18; and writing 192
Bilingual Education 3, 7, 6, 13, 34, 41, 42, 58, 61, 101, 103, 230, 257, 258, 273, 275, 276, 286
Bilingual Education Act (1968) 8, 41, 42
Bilingual Education in the 21ˢᵗ Century 53
bilingual orgullo 123–124, 130
bilingual pride *see* bilingual orgullo
bilingual reading identities: central principles 116; choice of texts for bilingual reading 119–120, 128; creativity and criticality 121; fostering bilingual orgullo 123–124; going beyond texts 122–123; reading, purpose of 117–118; students' bilingual reading/language practices 118–119; students' metalinguistic and bilingual awareness, importance of 120–122; teaching two languages *vs.* teaching bilingually 117
bilingualism 4, 5, 12, 25, 35, 43, 53, 64, 80, 117, 119, 121, 122, 124, 153, 158, 159, 161, 191, 252, 253, 268; additive 8; commodification of 259; concept of diglossia 8–9; decentering 12; dynamic

14, 30, 43, 44, 45, 53, 63, 100, 117, 171, 252, 276; emergent bilinguals 13–14; English Only movement 9; epistemologies of 12, 14; heteroglossic view of 142; holistic biliteracy 60; illegality and restrictions 9; instructional approach to 10; interferences 6; language acquisition and completeness 7; language categories 6; language knowledge of 4; language policy 30; language practices 6–7; language separation 8, 259; minoritized language and maintenance 6, 9; Spanglish 7, 244, 248n1; and Spanish 5–6, 7, 9, 35, 101, 244; subtractive 8; and translanguaging 15, 16; vs. dual language 9, 10; and writing 192–193
biliteracy 60, 80, 100, 116, 117, 118, 209, 269
book club 118, 127
Bowles, David 173, 176, 178, 179
Brown, Monica 173, 174

Canada 8
capitalism 4, 12
Carini, Patricia 46
Celic, Christina 96, 97
"Circle of Care" 56, 288
City University of New York (CUNY) 3, 4, 257; student advocacy and translanguaging 261–263; translanguaging and teacher transformation 259–261; translanguaging pedagogy and practice 263–265; translanguaging space 263; translanguaging tensions 258–259
Civil Rights movement 27
code-switching 6-7, 153
Collaborative Descriptive Inquiry (CDI) 46, 55, 57, 61, 97
colonialism 4, 11, 12
Common Core State Standards (CCSS) 57, 98
Community Language Walks 234, 235
Community-Based Organization (CBOs) 240-241
critical multilingual language awareness (CMLA) 157
cultural sustaining pedagogy 247
CUNY-NYSIEB (City University of New York-New York State Initiative on Emergent Bilinguals) 4, 12, 41, 95, 96, 101, 116, 192, 222, 239, 257, 258, 259, 265, 273, 277, 287, 295; bilingual

education mandate 27; "Circle of Care" 56, 288; collaborations in 56–59; creative emergence of language practices 43–44; dynamic teaching and learning 44; dynamics of bilingualism 44; guides 106–107; holistic biliteracy 60; implementation issues 27; inception and creation 54–56; interactive web resources 107–108; Language Allocation Policy 26, 30, 80; language separation issues 27, 117; leadership 54-54; level of participation 46–47; literacy instructional elements 116; multimodal topic briefs 103–104, 108; non-negotiable principles 45, 70, 131, 187, 192, 276, 287; online content 101–102; principles of 25, 43, 277; project components 43; reshifting focus of 59–61; resistance to translanguaging 27–28, 33; resource compilation 107; school eligibility criteria 45; school language policies 29–31, 34, 35; school-family relationship 62; scope of work 59–60; structures 28–29; Teacher Ambassador program 103, 108, 288; teacher training materials 107, 165; teacher transformation for translanguaging 287–291; translanguaging guide 14, 17; translanguaging transformation 60, 61, 62; vision 13, 42, 44; vision for writing 192–193; web series 102–103, 108; webinars 108–109; *see also* Emergent Bilingual Leadership Team
A CUNY-NYSIEB Framework for The Education of Emergent Bilinguals with Low Home Literacy: 4–12 Grades 104
A CUNY-NYSIEB Framework for The Education of Long-Term English Learners: 6–12 Grades 104
CUNY-NYSIEB Guides (in chronological order of publicaton)
Translanguaging: A CUNY-NYSIEB Guide for Educators 48, 95, 96, 98, 166, 288
The Languages of New York State: A CUNY-NYSIEB Guide for Educators 99
Translanguaging in Curriculum and Instruction: A CUNY-NYSIEB Guide for Educators 99, 101
Translanguaging in Latino/a Literature Guide: A CUNY-NYSIEB Guide for Educators 100

A Translanguaging Pedagogy for Writing: A CUNY-NYSIEB Guide for Educators 100
Translanguaging and Dual Language Bilingual Education Classrooms 19
Translanguaging in Dual Language Bilingual Education: A Blueprint for Planning Units of Study 273
CUNY-NYSIEB Topic Brief: Translanguaging and Dual Language Bilingual Classrooms 19

dialects 11
diglossia 8
Disinventing and Reconstituting Languages 11
distributed leadership 67; importance of 68–69; leadership structures 69; role of principals 74, 75; role of students 71, 72; role of teachers 74; teachers as language policymakers 69
double immersion 10
dual language 9, 18, 26, 28, 42, 57
dual language bilingual education (DLBE) 27, 28, 30, 31, 34, 57, 62, 80, 117, 220, 230, 259, 274–275; bilingualism as a resource 82–83; central principles 116; fluid language practices 82; goal of 82, 117, 220, 231; language allocation policy in 80, 275; teacher training 81, 82; translanguaging 80, 82; translanguaging documentation 81; translanguaging rings 81

early childhood education (ECE): background knowledge 156; bilingual education, strategies for 160–161; classroom setting 158–159; code-switching 153; family rule in 157; home language in 152–153, 155, 158; language learning and social interaction 152; metalinguistic awareness 153; multilingual practices, changes to 150; multimodal learning 149–150; prekindergarten standards 151–152; pretend play 155; purposeful play 154, 155; simultaneous *vs.* sequential bilinguals 153; symbolic representation 149; translanguaging 154, 155, 156
emergence 13, 19, 43
Emergent Bilingual Leadership Team (EBLT) 29, 35, 47, 67, 81, 100, 287; distributed leadership 67; importance

of distributed leadership 68–69; Leadership Seminars 70; Planning Resource packet 70; responsibilities of 70; role of principal in 74, 75; role of students in 71, 72, 74; role of teachers in 74; structure rationale 69–70; teachers as language policymakers 69; toolkit for 100
emergent bilingual with Individualized Education Plans (EBL-IEPs) 104
emergent bilinguals (EB) 13, 17, 18, 26, 28, 35, 42, 43, 58, 68, 70, 82, 95, 99, 104, 117, 122, 138, 142, 150, 153, 155, 187, 211, 265, 277; and play 154, 155; teaching two languages *vs.* teaching bilingually 117; and writing 192, 193–195
emergent literacy 152, 153, 154, 156, 161
Emergent Multilingual Learner (EMLL) 151
Emergent Multilingual Learners in Prekindergarten: A Protocol for Identification, Instructional Planning, and Programming 160
English as a New Language (ENL) 19, 26, 27, 30, 36, 42, 60, 62, 202
English as a Second Language (ESL) 9, 13, 15, 19, 35; home language strengths 84, 85, 274; linguistic diversity 84; monoglossic English-only ideology 83; teachers, challenges of 83; translanguaging in 83, 84, 85
English language arts (ELA) 35
English Language Learner/Multilingual Learner, 19
English Language Learners (ELLs) 42, 55, 86
English monolinguals 42
English Only movement 9
English Proficient (EP) 42
Espinet, Ivana 14, 53, 61- 63, 64
Expeditionary Learning 99

Family 240; Family Assessment Tool and learning 245–247; family involvement *vs.* engagement 240; family unit 250; family-school relationship 240, 241-238, 239; funds of knowledge 241; juntos stance 242; learning with family 243 (also see parents)
Fishman, A. Joshua 6
Flores, Nelson 13, 14, 53, 54-56, 63

foreign language (FL) 8
Frayer model 202, 203
French 35
funds of knowledge 241, 245

García, Ofelia 3, 9–12, 29, 44, 46, 87, 96, 97 101
general education teacher 116, 127
Graves, Donald 196
Guadalupe-Hidalgo Treaty 5

Haugen, Einar 6
Herrera, Juan Felipe 189
Hesson, Sarah 98, 99
holistic biliteracy 60

immersion programs 8, 10, 259
Individualized Education Plan (IEP) 116, 222, 250
Infante-Greene, Angélica 13
Integrated Co-Teaching (ICT) 116, 127, 184, 222
internationalism 35

juntos 4, 12, 29, 241, 242

Kleyn, Tatyana 256-258

Lambert, Wallace 8
language 3, 4, 6, 8, 9, 11, 15, 16, 35, 55, 62, 122, 124, 128, 131, 152, 153, 156, 158, 171, 187, 195, 209, 220, 223, 227, 250, 252, 253, 270, 274; areas of 191; categories in bilinguals 6; dual language education 9, 10; education policies 25–26, 41–42, 42–43; as an instrument of colonialism and social inequality 11; invention 11; learning and social interaction 152; minoritized and maintenance 6, 9; modalities 223–225; officialization 229; policies 25–26, 29–31; practices in bilinguals 6–7; Spanglish 7, 244, 248n1; vs. translanguaging 15; see also writing
Language Allocation Policy 25, 26
Language Experience Approach 166, 167, 168
language other than English (LOTE) 42, 222
language policies 25
Language Policy Vision Statement 29, 30, 34, 35

Latinx 3, 4, 5, 6, 7, 9, 12, 14, 17, 19, 41, 63, 71, 100, 157; education, focus of 17; dual language education 9, 18
Latinx children's literature: cultural and linguistic library 180, **181**; dynamic bilingualism 171, 252; lack of translanguaging in 172; language and culture influences on 172; mentoring poetry reading/writing 178–180, **179**; three Ts of instruction 180–181; translanguaging in 171; translanguaging side-by-side 174; translanguaging space 173; translanguaging spaces, approaches to creating 178; translanguaging top-to-bottom 175; translanguaging within text 175–177
learning edge 207; definition 208; importance of 209
Learning In-between Languages and Cultures (LILAC) 269
Limited English Proficient (LEP) 43
Lin, Angel 17
linguistic 4, 11, 15, 16, 28, 63, 84, 117, 122, 127, 129, 131, 154, 159, 264, 274; justice 276; landscape, definition 132; purism 28; unitary repertoire 16–17
literacy instructional elements: metalanguage 116; oracy 116; reading 116; writing 116
Li, Wei 12, 208, 221
Long-Term English Language Learners (LTELLs) 103

Makoni, Sinfree 11
Malaguzzi, Loris 166
Menken, Kate 13, 29, 44, 54
metalanguage 116, 120
metalinguistic awareness 89, 253
Mexican American War 5
Mexico 5
Mignolo, Walter 12, 18
Miranda-Rodriguez, Edgardo 173, 176
monolinguals 4, 7, 15, 16, 268
Morales, Yuyi 176
Morell, Zoila 151
multilingual ecology 45, 82, 85, 100, 132, 158, 192, 270, 289; bilingualism, heteroglossic view of 142; definition 131; language education policy shifts 138–140; linguistic landscape 132, 142; multilingual visual landscape 133–137,

140–142; use of home language in
schools 137–138; and writing 192
Multilingual Learner (MLL) 42
multilingualism 4, 11, 25, 30, 35, 44, 45,
53, 96, 127, 130, 135, 153, 161, 227,
228, 236, 253, 260, 286, 295; dynamic
power of 88, 89; language knowledge
of 4; multilingual ecology 45, 82, 85,
100, 131, 158, 270, 289; multilingual
learner 19

native speakers 35
Netter, Yuval 101
New York City Department of Education
(NYCDOE) 133
New York State Education Department
(NYSED) 54, 56, 62, 109, 285; briefs
and other guides 59, 100, 109; resource
guide 109; topic briefs 109
*New York State Prekindergarten Early
Learning Standards* 151
Next Generation Learning Standards 101
No Child Left Behind Act (2002) 42

Otheguy, Ricardo 3, 7, 15–16

Parents and translanguaging 244; parent-
child bilingual poetry analysis 244–245
(Also see family)
Pedraza, Pedro 6
Pennycook, Alistair 11
Pérez Rosario, Vanessa 71, 100
play 154, 155
process writing 187
Professional Learning Community (PLC) 59

Quintero, Isabel 173, 176, 181

Ray, Katie Wood 197
reading assessment 207; bilinguals 210;
key parts in 210; learning edge 207–
208, 209–210; listening/documenting
student reading 210–211; student translanguaging during retell and comprehension questions 211–213
Reagan, Ronald 9
Reggio Emilia 158, 166
Rodríguez, César 101
Rodriguez, J. Luis 175

Salazar, Aida 178, 179
Sánchez, Maite 14, 53, 56–58, 63, 256

Santos, Boaventura de Sousa 4, 12, 14
"Schools in Need of Improvement" 28
Seltzer, Kate 14, 53, 59-61, 64, 96, 97, 99
sequential bilinguals 153
simultaneous bilinguals 153
Spain 5
Spanglish 7, 244, 248n1
Spanish 5, 6, 7, 9, 35, 101, 244
Spanish-American war 5
special education teacher 116, 127, 184
Steptoe, Javaka 173
Students with Interrupted Formal
Education (SIFE) 104
symbolic representation 149

teacher education and translanguaging:
transformations
Bank Street College of Education 272-274
CUNY (Brooklyn College, City College
of New York, Hunter College,
Lehman College) 257-263
Montclair State University, 270-271
New York University 271-272
Rhode Island College 274-275
SUNY (SUNY Fredonia, SUNY-
Buffalo) 284-292
teacher transformation and translanguaging, 259–261, 287–291; teacher-leader
advocacy 292
Teaching Bilinguals (Even if You're Not One!)
102–103
Teaching of English to Speakers of Other
Languages (TESOL) 101, 257
Tenenbaum, Dani 101
translanguaging 3, 4, 10-18, 32, 33, 45,
53, 63, 64, 81, 87, 92, 95, 96, 117, 120,
127, 129, 137, 150, 153, 154, 166, 168,
171, 180, 181, 190, 205, 207, 215, 233,
244, 250, 264, 269, 270, 276, 299;
assessment 210-213; bilingual education mandate 27; bilingual practices
11–12, 16; challenges 18–20; "Circle of
Care" 56–57; corriente, 118; decentering bilingualism 12; definition 15, 16;
design 17; as a disruptor 4; documentation 81; emergent nature of 17; and
English as a Second Language 83, 84,
85; epistemologies of 14; guide 14, 17,
58; holistic biliteracy 60; implementation issues 27; as an instructional
approach 10, 11; international students
273–274; and juntos 4; Language

Experience Approach 166, 167, 168; language separation issues 27, 259; leveraging learning edge 209–210; linguistic justice 276; as a linguistic practice 3, 13, 120, 235; linguistic purism 28; literacy as unified process 209; metalinguistic awareness 89; minoritized bilingual people 4, 9; Multilingual Learner 19; multilingualism, dynamics of 88; pedagogy 208–209, 263–265, 287, 288, 289, 290; pedagogy for writing 191; pedagogy, benefits of 253; pedagogy, components of 17, 30, 33, 57, 63; and play 154, 155; as a political act 14, 272; reading assessment 210; reasons for 89, 121, 128; Reggio-Emilia philosophy 166; resistance to 27–28; rings 81; role of families in 85, 86, 87, 123, 157; shifts 17; space 61, 62, 250, 251, 252, 263; stance 17, 28, 55, 64, 118, 270; student advocacy for 261–263; student with disabilities 272–273; teaching two languages *vs.* teaching bilingually 117; tensions and issues 258–259; theory 10–18, 208–209; transformation 60, 81; transformation spaces 221, 230, 263; transformative, implementation of 88, 95, 221; transforming teachers for 259–261; trans-semiotizing aspects of 17–18; unitary linguistic repertoire 16–17; as a unitary system 10, 287; virtual reality in 294, 295; vision 13; *vs* code-switching 6–7; *vs.* languaging 15, 122; writing, strategies for 168, 169; *see also* translanguaging pedagogy; writing *The Translanguaging Classroom* 88

translanguaging pedagogical material: CCSS standards and emergent bilinguals 99–100; Common Core State Standards 98; first guide 96–98; guides 106–107; holistic frameworks for emergent bilinguals 100, 101; importance of 95–96; interactive web resources 107–108, 292; multimodal topic briefs 103–104, 108; Next Generation Learning Standards 101; online content 101–102; organizing principle 99, 101; practical resources 100; resource compilation 107; second guide 99–100; students' language and origin issues 99; Teacher Ambassador program 103, 108; teacher training materials 107, 292; toolkit for EBLT formation 100; web series 102–103, 108; webinars 108–109, 292

translanguaging theory 4–5, 10–18, 208

translingual practices 190

trawsieithu 10

Two-column notes 202, 203

United States 5, 6, 9, 18, 26, 41, 117, 151, 257

Universal Design of Learning (UDL) 273

Varela, Francisco 13

Velasquez, Eric 173

Vogel, Sara 48, 101

Weatherford, Carole Boston 173

Weinreich, Uriel 6

Weinrich, Max 11

Williams, Cen 10, 96

writing: components in 188; composing 188–189; CUNY-NYSIEB vision 192; definition 188; and emergent bilinguals 193–195; environment for 196–197; inclusive nature of 191; as language 188; language modalities in 189; multimodal forms of 189, 195; and multimodalities 195–196; and oral language 195–196; process writing 187; quality of 188; translanguaging in 189–191, 197, 264; translanguaging pedagogy for 191; voice and power in 188

Yau, Hulda, 98, 103